AMERICAN EDUCATION

Its Men

Ideas

and

Institutions

Advisory Editor

Lawrence A. Cremin
Frederick A. P. Barnard Professor of Education
Teachers College, Columbia University

Curriculum-Making Past and Present

Harold Rugg and Others

ARNO PRESS & THE NEW YORK TIMES
New York * *1969*

Reprint edition 1969 by Arno Press, Inc.

*

Library of Congress Catalog Card No. 71-89228

*

Reprinted from a copy in Teachers College Library

*

Manufactured in the United States of America

Editorial Note

AMERICAN EDUCATION: *Its Men, Institutions and Ideas* presents selected works of thought and scholarship that have long been out of print or otherwise unavailable. Inevitably, such works will include particular ideas and doctrines that have been outmoded or superseded by more recent research. Nevertheless, all retain their place in the literature, having influenced educational thought and practice in their own time and having provided the basis for subsequent scholarship.

Lawrence A. Cremin
Teachers College

Curriculum-Making
Past and Present

THE TWENTY-SIXTH YEARBOOK

OF THE

NATIONAL SOCIETY FOR THE STUDY OF EDUCATION

THE FOUNDATIONS AND TECHNIQUE OF CURRICULUM-CONSTRUCTION

Prepared by the Society's Committee Under the Direction of
HAROLD RUGG

Edited by
GUY MONTROSE WHIPPLE

PART I
CURRICULUM-MAKING: PAST AND PRESENT

By William C. Bagley, Franklin Bobbitt, Frederick G. Bonser, Werrett W. Charters, George S. Counts, Stuart A. Courtis, Ernest Horn, Charles H. Judd, Frederick J. Kelly, William H. Kilpatrick, Harold Rugg (*Chairman*), George A. Works

---

This Yearbook Will Be Discussed at the Dallas Meeting of the National Society, Saturday, February 26, and Tuesday, March 1, 1927, 8:00 P.M.

PUBLIC SCHOOL PUBLISHING COMPANY
BLOOMINGTON, ILLINOIS
1926

Agents
PUBLIC SCHOOL PUBLISHING COMPANY
Bloomington, Illinois
PUBLISHERS OF ALL THE YEARBOOKS OF THE SOCIETY

Published October, 1926
First Printing, 7,000 copies

Printed by the
Public School Publishing Company
Bloomington, Illinois

ERRATA

On page 87, for line five read:—

a needed next step in the improvement of instruction.

On page 103 in the first line under Section 2 read:

1893, instead of 1902.

OFFICERS OF THE SOCIETY

for 1926-7

Board of Directors

(Term of office expires March 1st of the year indicated)

B. R. Buckingham (1929)
Ohio State University, Columbus, Ohio

Werrett W. Charters (1928)
University of Chicago, Chicago, Illinois

Stuart A. Courtis (1927)
University of Michigan, Ann Arbor, Michigan

Charles H. Judd (1928)
University of Chicago, Chicago, Illinois

Leonard V. Koos, *Chairman* (1927)
University of Minnesota, Minneapolis, Minnesota

Harold Rugg (1929)
Teachers College, Columbia University, New York City

Guy Montrose Whipple (*Ex-Officio*)
Danvers, Massachusetts

Secretary-Treasurer

Guy Montrose Whipple (1929)
Danvers, Massachusetts

MEMBERSHIP OF THE SOCIETY'S COMMITTEE ON CURRICULUM-MAKING

William C. Bagley, Professor of Education, Teachers College, Columbia University, New York City

Franklin Bobbitt, Professor of Education, University of Chicago, Chicago, Illinois

Frederick G. Bonser, Professor of Education, Teachers College, Columbia University, New York City

Werrett W. Charters, Professor of Education, University of Chicago, Chicago, Illinois

George S. Counts, Professor of Education, School of Education, University of Chicago, Chicago, Illinois

Stuart A. Courtis, Professor of Education, University of Michigan, Ann Arbor, Michigan

Ernest Horn, Professor of Education, University of Iowa, Iowa City, Iowa

Charles H. Judd, Director of the School of Education, University of Chicago, Chicago, Illinois

Frederick J. Kelly, Professor of Education, University of Minnesota, Minneapolis, Minnesota

William H. Kilpatrick, Professor of Education, Teachers College, Columbia University, New York City

Harold Rugg (*Chairman*), The Lincoln School of Teachers College, Professor of Education, Teachers College, Columbia University, New York City

George A. Works, Professor of Education, Cornell University, Ithaca, New York

ASSOCIATED CONTRIBUTORS TO THE YEARBOOK

Otis W. Caldwell, Director, Lincoln School of Teachers College, Columbia University, New York City

Walter D. Cocking, St. Louis Public Schools, St. Louis, Missouri

Ellsworth Collings, College of Education, University of Oklahoma, Norman, Oklahoma

Flora J. Cooke, Principal of the F. W. Parker School of Chicago, Chicago, Illinois

J. L. Flanders, State Normal School, Oswego, New York

Harry O. Gillet, Principal, University Elementary School, School of Education, University of Chicago, Chicago, Illinois

John A. Hockett, Lincoln School of Teachers College, Columbia University, New York City

Marietta Johnson, School of Organic Education, Fairhope, Alabama

Margaret Naumburg, Walden School, New York City

Jesse H. Newlon, Superintendent of Schools, Denver, Colorado

Raymond W. Osborne, Assistant Principal of the F. W. Parker School of Chicago, Chicago, Illinois

Henry Carr Pearson, Principal, Horace Mann School of Teachers College, Columbia University, New York City

C. A. Phillips, College of Education, University of Missouri, Columbia, Missouri

Caroline Pratt, Director of the City and Country School, New York City

William C. Reavis, Principal, University High School, Chicago, Illinois

Ethel I. Salisbury, Director of Course of Study, Los Angeles City Schools, Los Angeles, California

E. M. Sipple, Headmaster, The Park School, Baltimore, Maryland

Eugene R. Smith, Headmaster, Beaver County Day School, Brookline, Massachusetts

A. L. Threlkeld, Deputy Superintendent of Schools, Denver, Colorado

Carleton Washburne, Superintendent of Schools, Winnetka, Illinois

TABLE OF CONTENTS

PAGE

EDITOR'S PREFACE ix
FOREWORD (Chairman of the Society's Committee) x

SECTION I

A CENTURY OF CURRICULUM-CONSTRUCTION IN AMERICAN SCHOOLS

HAROLD RUGG
Lincoln School of Teachers College, Columbia University, New York City

CHAPTER

I. THE SCHOOL CURRICULUM AND THE DRAMA OF AMERICAN LIFE 3
II. THE SCHOOL CURRICULUM, 1825-1890 17
III. THREE DECADES OF MENTAL DISCIPLINE: CURRICULUM-MAKING *via* NATIONAL COMMITTEES 33
IV. CURRICULUM-MAKING AND THE SCIENTIFIC STUDY OF EDUCATION SINCE 1910 67
V. CURRICULUM-MAKING IN LABORATORY SCHOOLS 83

SECTION II

CURRENT PRACTICES IN CURRICULUM-MAKING IN PUBLIC SCHOOLS

VI. CURRENT PRACTICES IN CURRICULUM-REVISION IN PUBLIC ELEMENTARY SCHOOLS 119
Stuart A. Courtis, University of Michigan, Ann Arbor, Michigan
VII. CURRENT PRACTICES IN CURRICULUM-MAKING IN PUBLIC HIGH SCHOOLS 135
George S. Counts, School of Education, University of Chicago, Chicago, Illinois
VIII. PROGRESSIVE PRACTICES IN MAKING STATE AND RURAL SCHOOL COURSES OF STUDY 163
George A. Works, Cornell University, Ithaca, New York

SECTION III

EXAMPLES OF PROGRESSIVE CURRICULUM-CONSTRUCTION IN PUBLIC SCHOOL SYSTEMS

IX. CURRICULUM-CONSTRUCTION AT DETROIT 189
Stuart A. Courtis, Educational Consultant, Detroit Public Schools, Detroit, Michigan
X. A UNIT-ACTIVITIES CURRICULUM IN THE PUBLIC SCHOOLS OF BURLINGTON, IOWA 207
E. M. Sipple, Headmaster, The Park School, Baltimore, Maryland, and formerly Superintendent of Schools, Burlington, Iowa

CHAPTER PAGE

XI. THE PHILOSOPHY OF THE WINNETKA CURRICULUM 219
Carleton Washburne, Superintendent of Schools, Winnetka, Illinois

XII. THE DENVER CURRICULUM-REVISION PROGRAM 229
Jesse H. Newlon, Superintendent of Schools, and A. L. Threlkeld, Deputy Superintendent of Schools, Denver, Colorado

XIII. THE ST. LOUIS PROGRAM OF CURRICULUM-REVISION 241
Walter D. Cocking, St. Louis Public Schools, St. Louis, Missouri

XIV. THEORETICAL FOUNDATION OF THE LOS ANGELES ELEMENTARY COURSE OF STUDY 249
Ethel I. Salisbury, Director of Course of Study, Los Angeles City Schools, and Associate Professor of Elementary Education, University of California, Los Angeles, California

SECTION IV

CURRICULUM-MAKING IN PRIVATE LABORATORY SCHOOLS

XV. CURRICULUM-MAKING IN THE LABORATORY SCHOOLS OF THE SCHOOL OF EDUCATION, THE UNIVERSITY OF CHICAGO 259
Harry O. Gillet, Principal, University Elementary School, and William C. Reavis, Principal University High School, School of Education, University of Chicago, Chicago, Illinois

XVI. THE LINCOLN EXPERIMENTAL SCHOOL 271
Otis W. Caldwell, Director, Lincoln School of Teachers College, Columbia University, New York City

XVII. CURRICULUM-MAKING IN THE UNIVERSITY ELEMENTARY SCHOOL OF THE STATE UNIVERSITY OF IOWA 291
Ernest Horn, College of Education, and Maude McBroom, University Elementary School, State University of Iowa, Iowa City, Iowa

XVIII. THE MCDONALD COUNTY, MISSOURI, EXPERIMENTAL SCHOOL... 297
Ellsworth Collings, College of Education, University of Oklahoma, Norman, Oklahoma

XIX. FUNDAMENTAL CONSIDERATIONS UNDERLYING THE CURRICULUM OF THE FRANCIS W. PARKER SCHOOL 305
Flora J. Cooke, Principal, and Raymond W. Osborne, Assistant Principal, Francis W. Parker School, Chicago, Illinois

XX. THE TECHNIQUE OF CURRICULUM-CONSTRUCTION IN THE HORACE MANN SCHOOL, TEACHERS COLLEGE, NEW YORK CITY 315
Henry Carr Pearson, Professor of Education and Principal of Horace Mann School, Teachers College, Columbia University, New York City

XXI. THE PRINCIPLES OF CURRICULUM-MAKING IN THE BEAVER COUNTRY DAY SCHOOL 319
Eugene Randolph Smith, Beaver Country Day School, Brookline, Massachusetts

CHAPTER PAGE

XXII. Curriculum-Making in the City and Country School...... 327
Caroline Pratt, Principal, City and Country School, New York City

XXIII. The Walden School.. 333
Margaret Naumburg, Founder of the Walden School, New York City

XXIV. Some Features of Curriculum-Making in the Elementary School of the University of Missouri.................. 341
C. A. Phillips, University of Missouri, Columbia, Missouri

XXV. The Educational Principles of the School of Organic Education, Fairhope, Alabama.............................. 349
Marietta Johnson, Director, School of Organic Education, Fairhope, Alabama

XXVI. Curriculum-Making in Laboratory or Experimental Schools 353
F. G. Bonser, Teachers College, Columbia University, New York City

SECTION V

Miscellaneous Curriculum Studies

XXVII. Review and Critique of Curriculum-Making for the Vocations 365
W. W. Charters, School of Education, University of Chicago, Chicago, Illinois

XXVIII. Curriculum-Reconstruction in the College.............. 381
F. J. Kelly, Dean of Administration, University of Minnesota, Minneapolis, Minnesota.

XXIX. Curriculum-Making by the State Legislatures............ 407
J. K. Flanders, State Normal School, Oswego, New York

XXX. A Critical Appraisal of Current Methods of Curriculum-Making 425
Harold Rugg, Teachers College, Columbia University, and George S. Counts, School of Education, University of Chicago, Chicago, Illinois

XXXI. The Literature of Curriculum-Making: A Selected and Annotated Bibliography 449
John A. Hockett, The Lincoln School of Teachers College, Columbia University, New York City

---

SEE PART II OF THIS YEARBOOK FOR—

Constitution of the Society
Minutes of the Washington Meeting of the Society
List of Honorary and Active Members
Information Concerning the Society

EDITOR'S PREFACE

This Yearbook is in several respects among the most ambitious undertakings of the Society. The idea of attacking the problem of the curriculum in a fundamental way—not trying to determine what the content of the curriculum should be, but trying to determine how that content should be selected and assembled—was broached by Dr. Harold Rugg, the chairman of the Society's Committee responsible for this Twenty-Sixth Yearbook, more than two years ago; indeed, the original intent had been to finish the Yearbook in the fall of 1924. The proposal met with ready reception in view of the current widespread interest in the problem of the curriculum. It was felt that the National Society for the Study of Education could perform a real service to the movement for curriculum-revision by directing its contribution to this preliminary problem of method, and particularly by making a special effort to bring together, and so far as possible to unify or to reconcile, the varying and often seemingly divergent or even antagonistic philosophies of the curriculum that were being espoused by leading authorities or by their adherents in this country.

This ambition could be realized only by means of numerous conferences for the free interchange of views. Accordingly, the Directors voted this Committee the (for us) unusually large appropriation of $2,500. It is hope that this subsidizing of the Twenty-Sixth Yearbook will be amply justified in the minds of the Society's members when they scan the pages that follow, especially the formulation, in Part II, of the General Statement of Principles acceptable to the entire Committee and the frank and interesting individual statements that follow in exposition of the views of the several members of the Committee.

It is also hoped that the members of the Society will approve the plan, on trial this year, of issuing the yearbook in the fall preceding the February meeting at which it is to be discussed.

G. M. W.

FOREWORD

The chief purpose of this Yearbook is the inventory and appraisal of curriculum-making in American schools — past and present. From time to time, in a dynamic society it is imperative that we stand aside from the movement of affairs to review trends, to assay products, to map out new paths. The chief outcome is reorientation, a balanced perspective; especially is this needed in these days of vigorous experimentation. It is most important that those who are constructing our school curriculum shall maintain an overview of the total situation; lacking that, their orientation will be biased, their emphases misplaced. There is grave danger that they will continue to commit themselves uncritically to plans and movements — to take up the current modes only to discard them as unthinkingly as they adopted them. Much of the machinery of American education has indeed developed in the past fifty years by just this method.

Synthesis is needed especially because of the gap between school and society, and between curriculum and child growth. Life on the American continent has moved in two parallel but rarely merging currents. One has been the dynamic rush of land settlement, industry, and politics—exploitive, mercenary, unmeditative. The other — the academic stream of letters, art, and education — has lagged sluggishly behind. The first is thoroughly indigenous and has dominated American life for three centuries; the second, imitative, looking toward Europe and the past, has been unconsciously determined by it, although never in touch with it. No problem confronting the school is more insistent or more difficult than the rechanneling into one broad stream of these isolated currents of practical and cultural life.

To bring this about, the curriculum must be fashioned out of the very materials of child activity and of American life. Curriculum-making must become comprehensive, all-embracing, and continuous, not partial and intermittent, as it has been during a century of national development. The chapters of this volume show that no group responsible for the organization of the materials of instruction has really viewed the whole problem. The chief cause lies in the orientation, personnel, and procedures of those who have directed it.

In fifty years of curriculum-making the greatest need has been for a comprehensive overview of the currents of American life and education, appraisal of all the factors in the educational situation. Rarely — and then only by fast striding pioneers — have the child, American civilization, and the school been considered together.

Each of the three outstanding forces engaging in the organization of the curriculum during the past thirty-five years certainly has lacked a complete overview. Each was biased toward academic formulae, child interests, or the scientific study of society. The successive national committees, for example, have viewed the school from the starting point of fixed boundaries of subject matter and have been thoroughly committed to doctrines of scholarship and discipline. The protagonists of the philosophy of dynamic growth were also limited in their attack, although much closer to the truth than the subject-matter specialists. They focussed their attention so sharply upon the child that they tended to ignore the real end points of growth in our current complex order. Similarly, the newest group of curriculum reformers, students of the more scientific study of education, have been somewhat unduly immersed in their techniques. Hence, they, too, have moved on a tangent, emphasizing the study of social needs and tending to minimize child growth.

No agency in American life, therefore, has been sufficiently concerned with the *total* situation. Although the task is difficult, there is great need for a new synthesis, a comprehensive orientation of the relation between the school curriculum and the content of life on the American continent to-day. With three systematic movements for curriculum-making well under way and with an accumulating capital of experience to build upon, it is now possible to evaluate the current needs and to obtain a new vision of the direction in which the educational machine should be guided.

Now, the scope of American life is staggering. Its content is almost hopelessly complicated. The American scene is a welter of interrelated forces, institutions, ideals, cultures, prejudices, conventions, protests, what not. The school curriculum is the only great organized agency which can muster sufficient potential to prepare the younger generation to understand it.

Because of the complexity of American life, it has become increasingly clear that a sound orientation will be produced only by the coöperative endeavor of many minds. The tasks of curriculum-making are manifold, highly technical, and they demand special professional training and experience.

An ideal conference on the reconstruction of the school, therefore, would assemble a great variety of interests and experience; far wider, indeed, than we have been able to bring together. The group would comprise, in addition to technically trained students of education, disinterested students of contemporary civilization — analysts aloof from the academic formulae of education — the poet, the novelist, the dramatist, the architect, critics of economic, political, and cultural life, students of the development of society, specialists in contemporary industry, business, government, population, community, and international affairs. These would coöperate with students of the scientific study of child capacities, methods of learning, educational experimentation and measurement, school administration, and the documentation of materials. Such a range in personnel would produce, of course, a confusion of vocabularies and would necessitate a more prolonged exchange of views than it is feasible to provide for in the present instance. Lacking the resources to organize the wider company, these two volumes have been prepared, therefore, by a group representing a partial range of specialized equipments, but a pronounced interest in the *general public school situation.* The members of the committee are all professional students of the curriculum and have sought constantly to maintain a broad perspective of American life and of growing childhood.

Recognizing clearly, therefore, the difficulties in the way of a total analysis of the current educational situation, they have joined hands, nevertheless, in the endeavor to compass it. For two years they have been engaged in the development of one phase or another of the work, either in collecting and appraising the contemporary situation, in studying the chief trends of development in the past century or in prolonged round-table conferences over similarities and divergences in educational theory.

This Yearbook presents three results of their efforts: a historical review, a description and evaluation of contemporary practices, and a statement of foundational principles for curriculum reconstruction. There appears first, in Volume I, therefore, an outline of the major movements of curriculum-making, the chief trends, the crucial forces operative in a century of development. Our historical study, although attempting to lay a foundation in earlier movements, concentrates naturally upon the movements of the past forty years. It is out of an understanding of the achievements and deficiencies of recent movements that we shall secure the greatest help in redirecting our current efforts; so this more recent historical study attempts to set in relation the work done by three groups: (1) the national committees composed of 'subject-matter' specialists — mathematicians, scientists, philologists, etc.; (2) experimenters in the laboratory schools; (3) the students of the more 'scientific' study of education. This material is presented in Section I of Volume I.

Second, a description and evaluation of current methods of curriculum-construction is presented in Volume I. Again, the need is for a synthesis of undertakings. In Section II, Mr. Courtis and Mr. Counts describe current methods of curriculum-construction in town and city systems. Mr. Works does the same thing for the state systems. Recent developments in a few conspicuous school systems have produced additions to the administrative techniques of curriculum-making. In Section III, therefore, examples of progressive curriculum-construction in six public school systems are given. The laboratory schools, furthermore (at least a dozen of which stand out for their trial of new materials and methods), are also brought into our review. The techniques and philosophies underlying curriculum-making in ten of these laboratory schools are set forth in Section IV. Appraisal is needed—critical evaluation—hence the chapter by Mr. Bonser.

During the past ten years, marked progress has been made in job analysis of the occupations and professions and in character and trait analysis. Mr. Charters, a prominent leader in this movement, presents in Section V a review and critique of curriculum-making for the vocations.

The reader will note in the General Statement in Part II, *Foundations of Curriculum-Making,* our commitment to the view that the bases and techniques of curriculum-making in the colleges should not be unlike those employed in the elementary and secondary schools. Since the close of the World War a movement for the reconstruction of collegiate curricula has gathered momentum. Mr. Kelly, who has been concerned for some years with the development of research in college administration, presents in Section V of this volume a series of illustrations and evaluations of these beginnings of reconstruction within the college. Finally, we round out our description by setting forth the rôle that state legislatures are playing in our day in curriculum prescriptions. To an astonishing and alarming degree, legislatures are prescribing the content of the materials of instruction. Mr. Flanders, who has made an intensive study of the last quarter century of development, reviews this important matter in Section V.

Description is worth little unless it leads to evaluation—critique. Hence the third task that we have undertaken in preparing these two volumes has been the critical interpretation of both historical developments and contemporary practices. The results of our attempts to appraise the historical movements will be found in Section I, while the evaluation of contemporary practices appear in successive chapters by Mr. Courtis, Mr. Counts, Mr. Bonser, Mr. Charters, Mr. Kelly and in Chapter XXX. In the last chapter Mr. Counts and I undertake to review briefly the chief forces and trends discernible in contemporary public and private school practice.

The third, and really the major interest of the Committee, has been the problem of a more fundamental orientation in curriculum construction. Believing that *divergences* in theory have been overstressed at the expense of *agreements,* we have joined together in the attempt to find a common basis for understanding the problems of curriculum-making. As the "General Statement" says: "We have sought to unite to discover agreements which may serve as a working basis for the next practicable step in curriculum-reconstruction." The methods by which we attack that problem are described in the Foreword to Part II entitled: "An Adventure in Understanding."

Summing up, therefore: Part I of the current Yearbook attempts a description and critical synthesis of curriculum-making, past and present. Part II presents our joint platform for curriculum-construction—a general statement of the foundational principles upon which we desire to see the next steps taken in the reconstruction of the school curriculum.

HAROLD RUGG, *Chairman.*

SECTION I

A CENTURY OF CURRICULUM-CONSTRUCTION IN AMERICAN SCHOOLS

CHAPTER I

THE SCHOOL CURRICULUM AND THE DRAMA OF AMERICAN LIFE

HAROLD RUGG
Lincoln School of Teachers College, Columbia University, New York City

I

Not once in a century and a half of national history has the curriculum of the school caught up with the dynamic content of American life. Whether of colonial reading or reckoning school, Latin grammar school, academy, or modern junior high school, the curriculum has lagged behind the current civilization. Although the gap between the two has been markedly cut down in the last three-quarters of a century, nevertheless the American school has been essentially academic. To-day, much of the gap persists.

Not only has there been a huge gap between the curriculum and American life; a similar one has persisted to the present day between the growing child and the curriculum. There are, indeed, three critical factors in the educative process: the child, contemporary American society, and, standing between them, the school curriculum.[1]

Now, in more than a hundred years of systematization of the national educational scheme, the materials of instruction have not only been largely aloof from, indeed, foreign to, the institutions and culture of the American people; they have failed equally to provide for maximal child growth. If the curriculum of our schools is to serve its true function, however, it must be reconstructed on a two-

[1] Under proper conditions, of course, the true educational intermediary between the immature child and adult society is the teacher. If we had 750,000 teachers, (or even, say, 300,000) who, like William Rainey Harper, "could teach Hebrew as though it were a series of hair-breadth escapes," the *curriculum* itself would stand merely as a subordinate element in the educational scheme. The teacher would occupy the important place of guidance we have given to the materials of instruction. But under the current hampering conditions (better, of course, than in earlier decades and improving slowly) of inadequately trained teachers of large and numerous classes, heavy teaching programs, insufficient facilities and lack of educational perspective—I fear we tend to reverse the process and teach hair-breadth escapes as though they were Hebrew. Hence my allegiance to the curriculum rather than to the teacher as the effective educational intermediary between child and society.

fold basis. Adequate provision must be made for creative personal development, and tolerant understanding of American life must be erected as the great guiding intellectual goal of education. Its reconstruction, therefore, must concentrate upon two foci—child growth and the dynamic content of American civilization.

Now, from the early days of colonization, American life has been dynamic. With each succeeding generation the rhythm has accelerated. The dominant theme is change, movement. The innovation of to-day is relegated to the scrapheap of to-morrow. Even national points of view are altered overnight. The great slogan, "He kept us out of war," is magically transformed in a few months into "Kill the Boche!" The radical proposals of 1895 became the law of the land in 1910.

The American tempo, I say, is *prestissimo*—and its intensity *fortissimo*. The current of American life is torrential. It is personified by the pervading hum of motors and the dynamic syncopation of our new national music. The American mind, like its industry, displays itself in movement, building, exploitation, "bigness and bedamnedness."

In a hundred years, however, the public school has lagged far behind. It has never caught up with the momentum of industry, business, community life, or politics. Only rarely has it succeeded in dealing with contemporary issues and conditions; never has it anticipated social needs. The masters of the American mind have fashioned the public school as a great conserving agency, and the halo of the past has oriented those who have made the content of our school curriculum. Rarely have educational leaders affirmed for the school a preparatory and prophetic function.

II

The current American scene makes it evident, however, that the school, especially through the curriculum, must assume this prophetic leadership. Current conditions in America throw into sharp relief the critical need of teaching our youth to understand contemporary life. We are attempting to produce a unique national culture and to carry on a great experiment in democratic government under the most hampering conditions—a heterogeneous congeries of people of less than eighth-grade education, huddled in towns and cities, sprawled over a huge continent of 70,000 communities, engaged primarily in the quest for food, many totally ignorant of, and indifferent to, their collective affairs.

It is especially important that our youth should develop clear comprehension of life in America because of the cleavages which dominate it. The whole continent resounds with the impact of groups; in this respect it merely reflects the contemporary order in other countries. Suspicion, misunderstanding, friction, pervade the social life of peoples in many parts of the earth. Successive decades of American political and economic history have been characterized by the realignments of countries, sections, and groups. The contemporary order reveals this same division of our people into cliques. They exhibit distressing cleavages; for example, that of proletarian worker and capitalist owner, of Protestant and Catholic; producer and middleman; black and white; industrialist and farmer.

Industrialism has transformed an individualistic order into a social one—and life in America has become compellingly coöperative. Since 1800, the peoples of the great industrial nations have been forced to adjust their modes of living to a most startling social transmutation. Communities and countries that were entirely isolated and self-sufficient have become almost completely interdependent. The peoples of the world are now so linked together that no nation can live to itself; no section lives to itself; no industry lives to itself; no person lives to himself—all are interdependent.

Now the school is the only organized agency at all competent to cope with the problem of developing in our youth tolerant understanding of this complicated order. Neither the home, the church, nor the press can be expected to do it. Certainly, the home, which in an ideal democracy would serve as the most potent educational agency, is not now equipped to attack the problem. In spite of the advances of the past two generations, American home life gives little promise of being able to lift itself above the dead level of humdrum monotony which now characterizes it. It is the product itself of an eighth-grade education; it is still too often supported physically by an income insufficient to maintain even a minimal comfort standard of living; hence its attention is still centered on the struggle for physical existence. Typical American home life, dominated as it is by fatigue, seldom reflects. Conduct in it is fundamentally impulsive and, owing primarily to its eighth-grade education, unintelligent. Hence to it can not now be delegated the task of educating twenty million young Americans.

Neither can we call upon the press to serve an educational function. The press is a great newsgathering agency. Its rôle in American life is informational, reportorial. Its mode of financial maintenance, resting as it does upon the interests of large numbers of people (for without readers no paper or magazine can secure the necessary advertisements) compels it to cater to those interests. Hence the headline, the journalistic style, the lack of historical background, the pervasiveness of scandal and sensation, and the disregard for accuracy. These are all characteristics of the press in the civilization of a people of limited education.

It is even more obvious, we believe, that the church is unequipped and unable to serve the great constructive educational function that is urgently demanded by the present situation. The church can, and will, render assistance; it cannot completely solve the problem.

Upon the school, therefore, devolves the duty of bringing a generation of youth to an understanding of American life. Its task is no less than the creation of a generation of men and women, informed about, and interested in, the American drama, who tend to settle matters of controversy on the basis of reflection rather than prejudice. It is the task of leading millions of growing youth to an understanding of an industrial civilization which is exceedingly difficult to understand. A candid review of the events of the past few years reveals the imperative necessity of attempting to help solve this tremendous problem. So, American life being what it is—complicated, difficult to understand, highly dynamic; the school constituted as it is—large classes, relatively uninformed teachers, early elimination of pupils—only one conclusion can be drawn. This is that the greatest hope for improvement in our generation lies in the construction of a curriculum which shall as fully as possible overcome the handicaps of the present school situation, and which shall lead the great body of pupils to an understanding and appreciation of the conditions and problems of our complex civilization.

III

Is it not clear that we should set our curriculum-makers at the enterprise, first, of understanding American life, and second, of trying to interpret it for children—and, by the same token, for teachers? How, in the present emergency, can we escape the necessity of falling back upon the materials of instruction to pull us through? Imagine how much more probable would be the emergence of a generation of people informed and trained to think if the curriculum of our schools not only prepared adequately for life, but actually anticipated the problems of the generation of youth now growing up.

Lacking a half-million dynamic teachers, are we not forced to put into our schools a dynamic curriculum? A curriculum which deals in a rich vivid manner with the modes of living of people all over the earth; which is full of throbbing anecdotes of human life? A curriculum which will set forth the crucial facts about the community in which the pupils live; one which will interpret for them the chief features of the basic resources and industries upon which their lives depend in a fragile, interdependent civilization; one which will introduce them to the modes of living of other peoples? A curriculum which will enable pupils to visualize the problems set up by human migration; one which will provide them with an opportunity to study and think critically about the form of democratic government under which they are living and to compare it with the forms of government of other peoples? A curriculum which will not only inform, but will constantly have as its ideal the development of an attitude of sympathetic tolerance and of critical open-mindedness? A curriculum which is built around a core of pupils' activities—studies of their home community, special reading and original investigation, a constantly growing stream of opportunities for participation in open-forum discussion, debate, and exchange of ideas? A curriculum which deals courageously and intelligently with the issues of modern life and which utilizes in their study the cultural and industrial as well as the political history of their development? A curriculum which is constructed on a problem-solving organization, providing continuous practice in choosing between alternatives, in making decisions, in drawing generalizations? A curriculum consisting of a carefully graded organization of problems and exercises, one which recognizes the need for providing definite and systematic practice upon socially valuable skills? Finally, a curriculum which so makes use of dramatic episodic materials illustrating great humanitarian themes that by constant contact with it children grow in wise insights and attitudes and, constructively but critically, will be influenced to put their ideas sanely into action?

Such a proposed curriculum may sound visionary to many workers in our schools. Nevertheless, close contact with curriculum-construction convinces one that the characteristics described can be produced. Their attainment will require the deepest vision and the clearest thinking our American educational scheme can bring forth. Hard intellectual work will be demanded of many persons. Most important of all, at the present juncture, will be the necessity for the creation of a more truly experimental attitude than is now common.

Let us consider first, therefore, in this attempt to understand curriculum-making, the startling contrast between life and education on the North American continent from Washington to Coolidge. Because of the hiatus between the two, it is of crucial importance that we study its course. Indeed, no task confronting the curriculum-maker is of greater importance with that of bridging the current gulf between them. He who would undertake the task, however, must have a clear understanding of the development of the curriculum during the past century and of the method of its construction, as well as an appreciation of the ever-increasing momentum of American life during this period. To these historical considerations we shall now address ourselves.

IV. The Conquest of the Continent

A century and a half of American independence have been marked by the development of two parallel but rarely merging currents; one, the overwhelming human torrent which resulted in the physical conquest of a great continent; the other, the sluggish stream of education.

To the present day, the former has struck the dominant tone of the American mind. For three hundred years the 'realtor' has directed the course of action and thought. From Peter Minuit's $24.00 purchase of Manhattan Island in 1626 to the collapse of the boom of Florida real estate in 1926, the land has dominated the American scene. There is no more spectacular human migration in recorded history than that bound up in our great westward movement.

In one hundred years, from 1790 to 1890, the land-hungry immigrants subdued a huge continent. The ground-work had been laid even during the struggle of the American colonial business men and plantation owners to free themselves from their English creditors. But the great trek across the Appalachians was really begun in the moment when the merchants of the North and the landed proprietors of the southern plantations were writing into history the American Constitution of 1787.

The impulse behind the new movement was economic. Always—the trade of the West.

In 1800, New York, Baltimore, and Philadelphia looked with envious eyes upon the trade of Black Rock and Fort Pitt. The fruits of northern New York's orchards, the salt of Syracuse, pelts, other valuable articles of trade were moving down the Susquehanna, the Delaware, and the Appalachian streams. A rich hinterland of resources and trade lay just behind the mountains and the growing cities of the eastern plain launched themselves into a frenzied competition to secure the prize. Fine macadam roads began to crawl out from Albany through the Mohawk Valley; the countrysides of New Jersey, Connecticut, and Pennsylvania were joined to New York by rolled stone highways and the old post roads hummed with coach and Conestoga. By the time Jefferson had argued the New American nation into paying Napoleon $15,000,000 for the great plain between the Mississippi and the Rocky Mountains, Conestogas were creaking by the thousands through the passes of the Allegheny Mountains.

As the frontier rolled westward thirty miles a year and the volume of trade piled up, ever-lengthening treks initiated the period of canal and railroad development. The "poor Irishman with his wheelbarrow," as Emerson called him, was everywhere, digging the great ditches in the Mohawk, laying tracks for the new dumpy engines, unloading ships. Begun in 1817, the Erie Canal joined the waters of the Great Lakes and the Atlantic in 1825. By this time, the Ohio, not long since the paddling ground of red men, was the scene of a picturesque movement of goods. Trading posts carried a variegated array of pioneer products, dramatizing daily the life-flow of the chief arteries of the new civilization. Whole communities moved out and moved in.

In the same year the whites were scattering out over the midland prairies. The young Abe Lincoln, ferryboy at Anderson Creek, saw the downward pageantry of the new flatboat civilization and, shortly after, the novel steamboats chugging upstream their twenty-day passage from New Orleans to Pittsburgh.

The year 1828 saw the first horizontal boiler engine "made in America" puffing along the little Baltimore and Ohio stub line. Railroads spread from town to town; terminals sprang up; Cornelius Vanderbilt standardized gauges and joined New York and Chicago in a continuous system.

V

Not only was the trek westward. A great dynamic New South came to life in this first half of the nineteenth century. Down the Mississippi and across the Tennessee and South Carolina mountains, the youth of the old aristocracy—offspring of six generations of mining the land—moved to the rich soil of Alabama, Mississippi, and Louisiana; and the Cotton Kingdom was established. Superb timber was hacked down and burned to make room for cotton. The wilderness was transformed into an empire of snowy blossoms. As stumpage was cleared and new white acres bloomed each year, the merchant marines of Massachusetts, Great Britain, France, swarmed into the harbors of Charleston, Savannah, and New Orleans. Down the Mississippi, also, the pioneers floated in their queer craft—houses on rafts, flatboats, arks, keelboats, and later the new steamboats—to the Creole Capital of the South. In 1825, New Orleans was a world city of English, Dutch, Norwegians, Spanish, and Italians.

VI

The dynamic movement of peoples in the New America reflected an impetus of European origin. A fuse had been lighted that was to trail round the world. At last—artificial power controlled and harnessed to wheels! Acres of smokestacks reared themselves, and new cities, both in the old and the new world, sprang up full of the strange clack and roar, products of the inventions of Watts, Arkwright, Cartright, Hargreaves and company. The first rumblings of the Industrial Revolution had come. They manifested themselves in a unique scheme of international manufacturing and merchandizing—gigantic, intricate, but fragile and increasingly interdependent.

Merchants, manufacturers, bankers, now regarded the entire earth as their proper sphere of action. Even the sleeping giants of Asia slowly woke before the pounding of industrialism at their gates. The ships and the guns of England and France were exploiting Asia Minor, Algeria, Egypt. The great British merchant marine was substituting steel funnels for sails, and the earth was engirdled with the new transportation. European foreign offices began to speak the jargon of "protectorates," "zones of understanding," "spheres of influence," "balance of power." Community and national isolation broke down and world interdependence was accomplished.

New and frightening human problems confronted the administrators of this industrial regime. The Occidental world was producing goods by the new looms and spindles more quickly than it could be consumed. When factories shut their doors, laborers smashed the looms of Lancashire, threw sewing machines into the streets of Paris, and rioted in Lyons. In Germany, the university students organized in protest against the oligarchial regime of the aristocrats and the new industrialists. Insecurity, unrest, pervaded Europe. Hence, the lure of American land at $1.25 an acre and the lure of the broad religious and political horizon under which the American lived. In the 1830's more than 600,000 immigrants docked in the ports of our Atlantic seaboard.

VII

The unceasing westward movement of America was made possible by the startling multiplication in population from a bewildered Europe. How it mounted! In 1790, four millions; 1810, seven millions; 1830, thirteen millions. Eighteen-forty-eight: revolution in Europe, the Chartist movement, the suspension of habeas corpus in Ireland and the failure of her potato crop, the breakdown of Liberal uprising in Hanover—and 1850 sees America's population at twenty-three million.

1849, Gold in California! The torture of the western barriers. The pioneer has spanned the continent.

Behind the moving frontier, hamlets appear where a year ago only gophers and jackrabbits lived. Hamlets become towns; towns, cities. The nation grows.

Paralleling the multiplying smokestacks of the cities, a new agricultural civilization unfolds on the western prairie. While thieves and crooks govern San Francisco and the Vigilantes conduct a little revolution in the name of "law and order," 459 wagons are counted in ten miles on the Platte River. In the 50's and 60's, the trail "north of 36" was constantly under the trampage of Missourian, Texan, even Mexican herds driven north for sale and slaughter.

In the East, the embryo industrialism slowly forms. The bonds of handicraft which held back mass production, automatic skill, and efficiency are being broken by the inventive genius of Kelly, McCormick, Howe, Goodyear.

The spirit of craftsmanship begins to die in America and the lazy giant—the public school—sleeps peacefully on, unaware of the shaping issues!

The civilization of leather and wood is giving way to one of iron and coal. America produced 54,000 tons of iron in 1810; 347,000 in 1840. In spite of jeering neighbors and jesting iron-makers ("Some crank will be burning ice next!"), Kelly succeeds in blowing air through melted pig iron and the age of steel has arrived. The steel bridge and the ninety-pound rail speed urbanization, and cities of a million and more lose the fine spirit of neighborhood life.

The Civil War! Shirts, socks, belts, shoes by the 10,000 gross. Production must be speeded up! Generals weep for guns and ammunition, and the new railways forestall the division of the Union. While the Civil War stuns industry in the South, it bestows cumulative momentum upon it in the North.

From Reconstruction, in spite of ruthless exploitation and financial debacles, the expansion was terrifying. Witness population multiplying three-fold, city dwellers ten-fold. The multiplication of wage earners, banks, corporations, miners, transportation employees, all far outran the sheer increase in people. "Bigness and bedamnedness!" In a century more we built half as much railway mileage as the rest of the world. Asa Whitney finished "what Columbus had started" and 1867 saw Atlantic and Pacific joined by a steel web.

A wild era of exploitation began. The slogan of the time was "*laissez faire.*" Settlement, land-clearance, homesteading, the development of the corporation—everything was in a state of flux. Everywhere the American people were acting, moving, generally unaware of—at least indifferent to—the momentous problems and issues they were creating.

And the school and its curriculum in complacent aloofness!

The 70's and 80's saw a free-for-all era of competition. Thousands of individuals drained the oil of Pennsylvania. Two hundred companies (75 in New York alone) manufactured harvesting machinery, mowers, and reapers. Fifty different owners controlled the copper mines. One hundred independents were taking the silver out of Nevada. A war of price-cutting nearly ruined the fifty competing manufacturers of salt in the Saginaw Valley. Thousands of lumber men denuded the forests and ruthlessly fought each other by fair means and foul. Not only were the national resources of the country despoiled by greedy competitors; ruinous underselling by the corporations forced thousands of small shopkeepers out of business. Close on its trail came the era of 'wildcatting,' with its concomitant financial disaster for the many and the ever-pyramiding wealth for the few. Out of it came the first colossal American fortunes. Cornelius Vanderbilt worth $10,000,000 in 1865, left in 1877 an estate of $104,000,000.

Unique economic problems for the new nation to grapple with. What of the content of instruction in its growing national school system?

Out of the ever-increasing demand for "more" came the standardization of processes and concentration and integration of business ownership. They made possible such Colossi as the International Harvester Corporation, United States Steel, Standard Oil, the American Woolen Company.

"Big Business" started to abolish the middleman, reduce prices, and increase profits. In 1902, the Harvester Corporation reached an annual output of $75,000,000. One central ownership controlled all the resources and processes necessary for the manufacture and marketing of its products. It bought forests and employed lumbermen, built sawmills near the trees, moved logs to lake-port docks over its own railroads, loaded its Great Lake freight steamers with its own loading machinery, developed woodworking factories and steel mills to produce wooden and metallic parts, research laboratories for the development of new inventions, and marketed its products direct to the consumer. And what the Harvester Corporation did for agricultural machinery, Standard Oil, United States Steel, American Tobacco, American Woolen, *et al.*, did for the other great industrial enterprises of the nation.

Specialization of labor, of machine operation, of assembling, pandered to the shibboleth of "Efficiency."

More problems! Problems of morale, of nervous tensions speeding whole populations.

And the curriculum of the school?

Finally, the problems of control of economic and political life. The Age of Big Business was the period in which the merchant princes evolved the great banking houses of the latter half of the century. For many generations men had accumulated wealth and had drawn interest on invested capital. The rise of the House of Morgan, of Harriman and National City, for example, was coincident with the change in the meaning of the word "capital." In 1850 New York banking houses had greatly concentrated the control of the major industrial operations of the country ("The Northwest and the South were paying their large debts in New York."). They instituted the device of capitalizing earning power, both present and predicted, as well as actual physical investment. Speculation was rife in this era and the chief impulse of financial growth was the 'boom.' From 1890 to 1915 the stock and bond capitalization of public service corporations in the United States grew from $200,000,000 to $20,000,000,000. This gigantic sum represents a valuation of about $100,000,000,000 in a country the entire wealth of which is estimated at only approximately twice that sum.

Concentration extended into financial control. So far and so rapidly did the movement proceed that in 1913 the Pujo Investigating Committee of Congress declared three banking houses, directly and by their officers indirectly, to have under their control resources amount to $2,104,000,000. Their directorship was represented in one hundred twelve corporations having an aggregate resource of capitalization of $22,245,000,000.[2]

---

[2] Figures are from Leon C. Marshall, *Readings in Industrial Society*, pp. 723-725.

VIII. The American Scene

What, then, is this American Scene, product of a century of spectacular "mining and moving?"

A territory as large as that of twenty-five nations of Europe, governed by one political administration, sheer size creating staggering difficulties of understanding, complicated by an unending surge of immigration that made of America's citizenry a patchwork of races, nationalities, cultures, and provincialisms. With the passing of decades, the difficulties of creating an informed thinking citizenship were enormously complicated by the startling momentum of urbanization. The "intolerable city," with its anonymity and impersonalness, its tense rhythm and rapid tempo, its mad search for food and excitement, the erection of complicated political machinery, and the increasing political indifference and bewilderment of its electorate, the extravagant wastage of resources, huge losses of timber, coal, oil, soil, and of human energy in unemployment, labor turnover, misfits in occupational life. The highest physical standard of living of any nation in recorded history. The product of "efficiency"—that is, of mass production, standardization, the automatic worker, enormous concentration of ownership of coal, iron, meat-packing and other basic industries, clever integration of related processes, and pyramiding control of credit.

Engaged in digging ditches, pumping oil, rolling steel, and running trains, America borrowed her architecture, looked to classical Europe for her art norms and disowned Whitman. Passing the *fin de siècle* with the physical basis laid, the faintest outlines of an indigenous culture—literature, art, the stage, architecture—appear.

In the century from 1825 to 1925, therefore, as America developed her institutions, her people were constantly confronted by problems and issues. Problems of conservation of natural and human resources. Problems of immigration, of assimilation, and of heterogeneity of cultures. Problems of wise use of leisure time. Problems of governmental control of great industries and of credit, the economic foundation of industrialism. Problems of proper distribution of the social income, continuous employment. Problems of neighborhood and community living and of family life. Problems of creating an informed thinking citizenship in the midst of city life. World problems of economic imperialism and of war and peace. Problems bound up in an emerging national culture.

And with these staggering issues confronting the American people, what of the school and its curriculum?

CHAPTER II

THE SCHOOL CURRICULUM, 1825-1890

HAROLD RUGG

I

The steps of a century of development in America: industrialism, urbanization, mass education. Machines and rapid transportation produced factories, cities, the graded school. As towns grew, the task of educating youth became complicated, and even by 1800 the mounting hordes of youth swamped the itinerant and intermittent "reading, writing, and reckoning schools." As early as 1805 New York took up enthusiastically Lancaster's "monitorial" plan; hundreds of pupils were herded together and lessons were heard by the youthful corporals of the teacher's regiment. By 1847 the Quincy Grammar School of Boston had set the model of the new type of central community school house. Henceforth, for town and city youth at least, education was to be via "classes." As the frontier rolled westward, in the towns growing up behind it, twenty, forty, sixty children (in metropolitan centres, even hundreds) were to be taught in grade groups by a single teacher. Mass education slowly formed.

So in the decades prior to 1850 America produced the grammar school and the academy, and these cast the structure of the educational system of the eastern half of America for three-quarters of a century. Children were graded horizontally, roughly in accordance with chronological age—Grade I for the six or seven-year-olds; Grade II for the sevens or eights, and so on through the entire range of the school. And thereafter, for three quarters of a century, school reformers were striving to undo the evils of a rigid graded system.

Subject matter was graded, too, to fit the new groupings of young people. First, Second, and Third Readers made their appearance. Arithmetics were numbered accordingly; language books, as well. American schools were becoming reading schools; the curriculum was taking the shape set for it by the new school books. By the middle of the nineteenth century a rapid succession of inventions and improvements in methods of printing made it easier for those of means to obtain books. The printed word usurped the rôle of oral expression in the classroom and the textbook domineered over the curriculum of American schools. Slowly but surely, the curriculum became more wordy. Gradually, the leaders recognized that education consists of enlarging experience and that experience expands hand in hand with vocabulary.

II

Now, paralleling the centralizing and grouping of the younger children in urban "graded" elementary schools, America produced for her "better economic classes" a new kind of secondary education. The years from 1790 to 1900 saw the spectacular rise of the academy and the slow evolution of the free public high school.

During the second quarter of the nineteenth century an astonishing transformation took place in the administrative features of the school system. It represented a revolt against the domination of the college and the supremacy of the Latin grammar school (with its emphasis on the theological and classical). The academy, with its roots in the middle eighteenth century model of Benjamin Franklin, *et al.*, caught the imagination of America's well-to-do. Massachusetts had 17 academies in 1800, 403 in 1850. New England had 1007, the Middle Atlantic States, 1636; while 753 were counted in the adolescent towns of the Mississippi Valley. At the mid-point of the century, the wave of interest reached its crest. A grand total of 6085 institutions with 12,260 teachers and 263,096 pupils enrolled. A truly startling growth, revealed by the fact that as late as 1890 there were only 6000 public high schools.[1]

Until well along toward the middle of the nineteenth century the academies regarded themselves as 'finishing schools.' They supplied the lower schools with the best educated teachers of the time. They aimed to prepare youth 'for life,' and made little attempt to constitute themselves a lesson agency for higher institutions. For a while they kept free from the domination of the colleges. But not for long. Although the academies began life independently, as the

[1] These figures are from Stout, J. E., *The Development of High School Curricula from 1860 to 1918.* Supplementary Educational Monographs, University of Chicago, 1921. What constituted an "academy" was never clearly defined, of course. However, these figures do not unfairly set forth the momentum of the new secondary movement.

years went on their aspirations for scholastic respectability and the desire of the colleges to utilize them as preparatory institutions finally brought them under the sway of higher education. By 1880, owing largely to the free high schools, their independence was destroyed. They declined steadily, thereafter, in numbers and influence.

As that happened, free secondary education gathered momentum. The new midland towns and cities organized high schools. The public high schools had come weakly into being by 1821 via the English High School of Boston, but a national scheme of free secondary education gripped the American imagination slowly. During these early years the European tradition persisted that secular instruction other than the 'three R's' was an unnecessary acquirement for any but the well-to-do. The more prosperous years of the 1870's, however, brought an almost naive faith in the efficacy of education which bestowed public approval and financial support on popular secondary education. Thus, the rise of the publicly financed high schools and the decline of the academy went hand in hand. By 1890 the number of each of the two kinds of institutions was practically the same. From that point on, the academy declined in influence sharply and permanently. Following 1890 the growth of the high school was startling; in less than twenty-five years from that date there were 12,000 high schools in existence. The public high school—"the people's college"—had become the great secondary educational institution of America.

III

Thus, the administrative outline of America's public educational system was evolved prior to 1890.

What about the curriculum? In a half century it had been tinkered into a patchwork of "School Subjects," graded horizontally to fit the chronological grading of boys and girls. The curriculum was always an "assembly of parts," to borrow a figure from the dominant transportation of to-day. For more than a half century some one has always been patching up the weak spots. To 1890, the curriculum ignored almost totally the emerging economic, political, and cultural problems and institutions.

The study of abstract theology and the classical languages which had held unchallenged sway over the Colonial, began to give way before the emphasis on the study of real things. Under the stimulus of Pestalozzianism in the period from 1800 to 1840, educational reformers were pleading that children should be brought to a much better understanding of their physical environment. Their exhortation, however, brought little more than a change in the character of the book-knowledge of the curriculum. A host of new 'subjects' of study was introduced. Those in charge of the schools between 1825-50 conceived of algebra, astronomy, chemistry, surveying, botany, general and United States history, intellectual philosophy, debate, American literature, declamation, as 'subjects' which would lead youth to an understanding of 'real things.'

The sheer statistical aspect of what happened in the early stages of the academy movement is startling. Between 1787 and 1870, no fewer than 149 new titles ('subjects,' or 'courses') found their way into the printed program of study of these new secondary schools. Actually, seventy-five of these were interjected into the scheme of instruction in the three years between 1825 and 1828. This was the organizing-programming period in the rise of the secondary school.

Herbart's leadership was felt in the construction of the newly developing curriculum, in that under the drive of the Herbartians greater emphasis was placed upon preparing youth for social usefulness. New 'subjects' appeared in the curriculum to do that.

IV. Economic and Political Life and the Curriculum

Take, for example, those subjects that could have been expected to introduce youth to an understanding of the new and startling economic, political, and cultural problems—geography, history, *et al.*

Geography had entered the curriculum even before the American Revolution. Jedediah Morse had produced a textbook[2] in 1784—a huge systematic thing, emphasizing the various motions of the heavenly bodies, describing the earth and its great land and water divisions, bounding the Eastern empires, kingdoms, and states, and descriptive of soil production in inhabited regions. It was the encyclopaedic progenitor of the compendiums of reference which young people to-day use to obtain their knowledge of contemporary modes of living. Arnold Guyot[3] came to Massachusetts in 1848,

[2] Morse, Jedediah: *Geography Made Easy,* 1784.

[3] Lectured on geography for the State Board of Education in the Normal Schools of Massachusetts, 1848-1854; Professor of Physical Geography at Princeton, 1854-1884.

and although his "School Geographies" were too advanced for widespread use in the schools, they exerted a very great influence on the curriculum. Between 1820 and 1860 both history and geography became rapidly established as widely prevalent units of the elementary-school curriculum, and geography was finally required by law.

Three hundred sixty different histories had been published in America before 1860. At least a dozen civics textbooks and ten geographies were in existence. Some of these books ran through more than 50 editions, and C. A. Goodrich's *History of the United States* had sold by that time more than a half million copies. Noah Webster,[4] S. G. Goodrich[5] (the famous Peter Parley), and Emma Willard,[6] wrote histories with long subtitles and characterized by heavy, compact style and content.

As was true of the geographies, the content of the histories was primarily an encyclopaedic presentation of militaristic developments of old world history, supplemented by a little of the American chronical. Political history was dominated by the recital of names of rulers, officials, dates of battles, legislative enactments, and constitutional provisions.

Industrial history was never mentioned, nor the economic and social problems shaping on the frontier and in the towns.

The civics books came into the curriculum largely in response to the demand of educational leaders and laymen before 1860 for the development in the minds of the young of an understanding of government. The prevailing conception of that day, however, was that understanding of government would come from the memorization and dissection of the American Constitution.[7] Following the conclusion of the Civil War, history and civics were turned to, to teach patriotism. In the hysteria of the reconstruction era, many states passed laws requiring a study of the Constitution of the United

---

[4] Webster, Noah. *Letters to a Young Gentleman Commencing His Education, to Which Is Subjoined a Brief History of the United States.* New Haven, 1823.

[5] Goodrich, S. G. *Peter Parley's Common School History,* Philadelphia, 1849; *American Child's Pictorial History,* 1881.

In 1853 Goodrich wrote *First Book of History Combined with Geography Containing the History and Geography of the Western Hemisphere.*

[6] Willard, Emma. *Abridged History of the United States.* 1849.

[7] One of these early books on the Constitution was re-edited as late as 1901 and "seems still to be taught in the schools."

States and of the pupil's state constitution. Gradually, under the impetus of Hinsdale and others, this analytical, dissectional, memorizing study of the Constitution was transformed into a study of the national, municipal or state government. However, the emphasis was still on the machinery, upon the form of government—not upon the problems and issues which faced the American people.

It is clear, therefore, that something was gained by the interjection of the new 'subjects' into the course of instruction. 'History' and 'geography,' academic as they were, represented less divergence from the industrial, political, and social life of the pre-Civil War days than the contents of the old theological and classical curriculum. But while the titles of the courses were changed, the contents were very little improved.

From science comes a term which aptly describes the school curriculum prior to 1900. It was essentially "morphological." Its designers were interested in classification, in naming parts and describing forms, rather than in developing an understanding of function and functioning. Although approaching the problems, conditions, and institutions of adult and child life more closely than was true in the earlier periods, the school rarely dealt with them as problems and conditions which confronted Americans under a changing political and economic regime or with the institutions which were being built up by the American people.

And the gap between curriculum and society persisted.

V. American Culture and the Literary Curriculum of the Schools

The same gap which was evidenced between the curriculum and political, industrial, and social life in America, existed between cultural life and the curriculum. Toward the end of the nineteenth century a new culture of industrialism was beginning to take shape. In the high school during this time, however, there appeared only the faintest outline of a corresponding culture curriculum. During the last thirty years, the fine arts and dramatics found their way hesitatingly into the program of studies, being offered timorously in certain progressive quarters as optional, elective courses. Music, practically confined even to the present day to auditorium and assembly singing in the high school and formal class singing in the elementary school, did actually appear upon the scheduled list of courses. But it, too, was a formal thing. 'Standardization' was developing in the social arts of the school. Technique was mastered at the expense of musical appreciation and joy of being. The chief burden of introducing young America to the cultural elements of life fell upon that department which during the middle 1800's came to be known as "English."

From the close of the Civil War to the present time, there was probably no greater achievement in the development of school curricula than that revealed in the larger emphasis upon the vernacular. It must not be thought, however, that this growing emphasis meant a reduction of time devoted to other subjects. So rapidly did the movement spread that, by 1900, English had entrenched itself as the most important unit in the secondary course of study. Two-thirds of our high schools offered courses in "rhetoric," about two-thirds in "English literature" and about one-third gave a course merely called "literature." More than one half offered courses in composition and grammar. Between 1885 and 1900, furthermore, English became of such recognized importance that systematic "year" courses were organized. In 1900 nearly half of the high schools of America offered a course called "First-Year English;" thirty-five percent offered "Second-Year English;" twenty-seven percent "Third-Year English;" and fifteen percent "Fourth-Year English."

In this book-knowledge era of curriculum-making, did the "English" curriculum of the schools train in literary judgment, create the habit of enjoyment of fine writing and develop the tendency toward creative self-expression?

It did not.

The content of the materials of the culture curriculum lagged two and three generations behind the content of American life, and the method of its presentation and the atmosphere of the classroom totally negatived the possibility of producing the desired understanding of American culture or the ability to contribute to the development of it.

"English," for half a century, was a formal, pedantic thing. It was dominated by grammar, English analysis, word analysis, rhetoric, composition, parsing, memorizing of definitions, learning rules for developing skill with oral mechanics.

In 1862, Welch said in the preface of his textbook:[8] "The systematic analysis of the English sentence should hold a prominent rank merely as a means of mental development." There we have it! The analysis of the English sentence dominated over a curriculum which should have been devoted primarily to an understanding of the poetry of the American rhythm. Instead of letting children read and feel deeply, and through literature develop an understanding and appreciation of American life, Welch and Greene[9] in the 1860's, Clark[10] and Swinton[11] in the 1870's, Reed and Kellogg[12] in the 1880's and 1890's, and their colleagues in every decade, drilled children in the mastery of syntax and in the critical study of figures of speech, etymological analysis, explanation of mechanical forms, spelling, paraphrasing, language structure. By their very emphasis upon dissection they effectually prevented true understanding of the reading materials.

The entire school curriculum was under the sway of a mythical faith in mental discipline. The current point of view was that learning, to be effective, must be hard and disagreeable. The faculties of the mind, the powers of logical analysis, critical judgment, were to be trained by observation, collection, and systematization of facts. And this could be done equally well in preparation for life activities by the *Idylls of the King,* the forty-seven irregular French verbs, the binomial theorem, geometrical demonstration, or Latin declension!

The criticisms which have been made about grammar can be duplicated for rhetoric and composition. Rhetoric was closely tied up to logic. Chapter titles and classroom discussion dealt with argument, persuasion, perspicuity, elegance, eloquence, etc. Children were asked to write "in good form" when they had little or nothing in their minds to write about. During the entire half

---

[8] Welch, Adonijah S. *Analysis of the English Sentence, Designed for Advanced Classes in English Grammar.* 1862.

[9] Greene, Samuel Stillman. *A Grammar of the English Language. Adapted to the Use of Schools and Academies.* 1860.

[10] Clark, Stephen W. *The Normal Grammar, Analytic and Synthetic; Illustrated by Diagrams.* 1870.

[11] Swinton, William A. *A General Etymology and Syntax of the English Language: A Progressive Grammar of the English Language.* 1872.

[12] Reed and Kellogg. *Higher Lessons in English—A Work on English Grammar and Composition.* 1877, 1885, 1896.

century there was little or no recognition that creative self-expression develops only when the writer has something on his mind to say.

VI

As for "literature," from our pioneering days we rarely produced or used American writings for our schools. The reading books so commonly used in the schools of the 1850's and 1860's were compendiums of short selections culled from classical writers, mostly British. Even the high schools depended for their content very largely upon such books as these. In their form and emphasis, they defeated the purpose of their inclusion in the curriculum. Their emphasis was upon the mechanics of reading—not upon ideas and feeling. In McGuffy's, which is typical of those in popular use at the time, a very large amount of material is devoted to accent, emphasis, voice inflection, articulation, and gesture.[13] Rules and definitions to control oral reading and speaking pervaded both the books and the exercises. Elaborate rules were developed for controlling the voice in pitch. Pages were given describing how to use the hands and face in making gestures.

In the English curriculum of Civil War and Reconstruction days, mechanics held sway over meaning and emotion.

By 1885 the high school had come under the dominance of higher education, and the English curriculum, as well as that of mathematics, Latin, the languages, and the sciences, came to be dominated by the requirements of college entrance. The eyes of the academicians were focussed upon literary masterpieces (particularly those emanating from Great Britain), not upon youth understanding American life. Less than one in six of our high schools offered a course in American literature. Contemporary American writers were almost never represented in the reading lists of our people. A contempt for the contemporary itself was prevalent in the selections of reading material through which young America was to be given its understanding and emotional view of life. *Silas Marner, The Iliad, The Odyssey, The Vicar of Wakefield, The Lady of the Lake* ("sitting comfortably in the high-school curriculum for 75 years")

[13] McGuffy's *Sixth Reader* gives examples of poetic materials to develop medium pitch, high pitch, low pitch, etc. The familiar "Under the spreading chestnut tree, the village smithy stands," he used as an example of material "which will develop medium pitch." This was typical as well of *The Student's Reader, The Independent Fifth Reader*, etc.

usurped the place which should have been devoted to creating an insight into the stirring movements in the new industrial America. The point can not be made too emphatically that the academicians of our colleges and schools ignored the materials of American self-expression.

A tradition had grown up that culture meant an understanding of European life, both ancient and modern, a mastery of current European languages; of the art, literature, modes of living, institutions of earlier peoples. More than half of the high schools of America offered German throughout this entire period. French was not conceived of as having as high cultural value, but about 15 percent of our schools included French in their program of studies.

VII

It was again in the 1870's and 1880's that the tradition became established in curriculum-making that new subjects should be added in response to the demands of the changing times, but that the old subjects should be retained. And so there came in new types of social studies, various industrial manual arts, home-making studies, occupational guidance, and a great multiplicity of regular grade courses. All sorts of interests, mostly practical, clamored for a place in the curriculum of the high school and slowly but surely pushed their way in. But strongest among these were the sciences. Under the dominance of the scientific philosophy of the middle nineteenth century textbooks, 'science' came to occupy a very strongly entrenched position in the school curriculum.

From the first establishment of high schools, various sciences were included in the program of studies. Botany and chemistry were given in the Boston High School for Girls in 1826. Natural history appeared seven years later. The Northampton High School gave courses in geology and mineralogy in 1837. Edgartown added anatomy the same year. Physiology and agricultural chemistry made their appearance in the Ipswich curriculum in 1839 and 1845 respectively. These dates (all for Massachusetts schools) illustrate typically the interval during which the new sciences entered the schools. Massachusetts' high schools were required by law in 1857 to teach chemistry and botany; astronomy and zoology were required in towns of 4000 inhabitants and over as early as 1841.

Spencer was producing his *First Principles* in 1862. Darwin had long since voyaged on the *Beagle* and launched his revolutionary attack upon the old dogmas. Chairs for the new sciences began to be established in universities in rapidly increasing numbers and under their sway the curriculum of the secondary schools opened to the new materials of instruction. By 1841 natural philosophy was offered in more than half the high schools in the state of Massachusetts, and it became a required subject in 1857.

Science, therefore, at the middle of the century, found itself in a strategic position in the curriculum—a position of leadership which it held until well into the 1890's. Practically every student 'took' one or more of the sciences. Prior to 1890 physiology and physical geography, chemistry and botany had made a place for themselves in the senior high school. Natural history, as a titled subject, disappeared, and geology and astronomy declined in importance in the curriculum. Their places in the sciences were taken by the new zoölogy and physics. The latter was offered in practically all the high schools in 1890.

Viewed in the large, however, in terms of pupil enrollment in the sciences, the period from 1895 to 1922 reveals the steady decline in all the branches of science.[14] The decline of physics was so abrupt that in spite of huge increases in high-school enrollment the demand of 1922 was less than half that of 1890. Physiology and physical geography declined at astonishing rates; geology and astronomy passed almost entirely out of the high-school curriculum. "General Science" entered the curriculum to take their places and by 1922 had attained a greater importance in the catalogued offerings than chemistry, botany, physical geography, or zoölogy.[15]

Did all this effort devoted to the study of science contribute to a dynamic understanding of one's physical environment, of how people live? Certainly in no direct way. Physics and chemistry never gave a real understanding of the bases of mechanical civilization nor did physical geography teach how people live together. "Understanding," in the larger sense of the term, has never been the outcome of the science study.

Mental discipline, even religious aims, still held the academic imagination. Textbooks aimed at the retention of the religious

[14] See Downing, *Teaching Science in the Schools*, pp. 28.
[15] Downing, *Op. cit.*, p. 26.

note were prefaced by such statements as these: "'Consider the lilies of the field, how they grow; they toil not, neither do they spin: and yet I say unto you that Solomon in all his glory was not arrayed like one of these.' (Math. vi, 28-29) Our Lord's direct purpose in his lesson of the lilies was to direct the people's attention to God's care of them."[16] etc. Throughout these books there are frequent references to the Divine Insight which creates plants and animals, rocks and human beings.

Textbooks sponsoring the second aim, phrased their credo as one that would "discipline the senses to habits of quick and accurate observation, and the mind to the habit of forming correct judgments from the facts which the senses reveal."[17]

In consequence, the acme of the morphological was reached in the scientific curriculum. Zoölogy abounded in technical terms and classifications of animals. Concise descriptions of animal life and dry enumeration of physical characteristics took the place of vivid accounts of their habits of life.[18] Botanies dealt with the anatomical structure of plant life. The aim seemed to be an encyclopaedic grasp of the physical constitution of the animal and plant species. Anatomical structure ousted comprehension of the functioning of life. Textbooks were compilations of technical terms and minute texts of classification. Authors in revising them were more concerned to include the latest classification of animals than they were to give a broad understanding of the natural science world. The point of view of textbook construction is admirably illustrated in the statement that the "most important discovery made since this book was first published is that the two lowest mammals, that is the duckbill and the echidna, both lay eggs."![19]

It can be said that only in the most remote manner did zoölogy or botany give youth an understanding of "why we behave like human beings."

Physical geography, like botany and zoölogy, was an encyclo-

---

[16] Asa Gray. *How Plants Grow.* 1858.

[17] From Cooley's *Natural Philosophy.* 1872.

[18] I have before me Professor Downing's graphic analysis of representative zoölogy texts from 1848 to 1915; also his elaborate table portraying minutely the contents of twenty-nine textbooks published during the same interval. Every decade from 1860 is represented by one or more books. The findings established clearly that to 1900 morphology actually comprised the major portion of the zoölogy course.

[19] Packard's *Zoölogy.* 1892.

paedic compendium of the features of the earth, rivers, oceans, plains, mountains, valleys, etc.

Ethnological materials consisted of the classification of races, descriptions of anatomical structures and other physical features.

Enough has been said, therefore, to illustrate vividly the prevalence of the dominant aims of science throughout the entire period, and their manifestations through the textbooks.

VIII

The burden of the foregoing comments, therefore, is that the curriculum throughout the past three generations in nowise spanned the gap revealed between the earlier school and society. To the present day the hiatus has persisted. It is only during the past three decades—especially because of the concentrated attacks of students of the new biological conceptions of growth, of the dynamic psychology (James, Dewey, Thorndike, Woodworth, Judd, and their colleagues), and of the scientific and experimental study of the curriculum itself—that the gap is being partially obliterated. Before considering the course of this change, however, an orientation is needed concerning the cause for the lagging of school behind society.

There are several good reasons why the curriculum has been static in the midst of a febrile world, the tempo and rhythm of which have been far more dynamic than those of any preceding age.

Perhaps the most far-reaching cause has been the tendency of the American mind to divorce education from practical life. The preceding pages have developed the thesis that American life has moved in two quite separate streams: one, the practical economic stream; the other, the academic, intellectual, other-worldly stream of education and letters. Dominated constantly by the fear of economic insecurity, your typical American—the urban artisan, the clerical worker and the farmer of to-day as well as his frontier ancestor of a century ago—is driven by an unceasing current of energy. The American has been throughout his history a doer, a maker, an exploiter, an accumulator of things and dollars, a hard metallic man in whom meditation and reflection rarely had an opportunity to develop. Life on the American continent has been governed primarily by the quest for food; generalization has played little part in the mind of man.

Having its beginnings in the aura of religion and often financially supported through its agency, education became a thing apart from the "catchpenny current of business." As the religious aim gave place to the gospel of social efficiency, the curriculum and American life spanned a part of the chasm that separated them, but the American people still wanted their schools and their churches to give voice to a spiritual idealism for which they vaguely sensed a need but which they lacked—or had lost.

The second cause of the lag in the curriculum is found in the academic orientation of the professors who have written the textbooks. From the days of the early grading of schools in the 1830's and 1840's until the close of the nineteenth century, the selection of the detailed content and the arrangement of the materials of our school courses were left practically altogether to the individual judgment of the textbook writer. Until the work of the Committee of Ten[20] there was little or no coöperation among teachers and specialists in committees or other organized groups for the careful discussion of the content and arrangement of the curriculum. During more than a half century from the days of Noah Webster and S. G. Goodrich, Emma Willard, McGuffy, and Steele to the regime of George Wentworth, school books were made by two groups of writers. One group was made up of lay citizens and professional textbook writers like the foregoing. The other was composed of the professors of the various school subjects—mathematics, history, English, and the like.

Until very recent time, therefore, school textbooks have been written by university professors or by public-school administrators who have reflected the point of view of the professors with whom they studied. I have commented more in detail in another source upon the manner in which the school subjects entered the curriculum from the college and from the senior high school and dropped, decade by decade, as experience accumulated from trial and error use, to grades lower in the academic ladder. Suffice it to say here that as school populations grew from the middle 1800's and pupils and materials of instruction were graded to satisfy the increased demands for more universal education, the college professors of mathematics, the sciences, English, history, the modern languages,

[20] See Chapter III.

etc., constituted the only group equipped to prepare the textbooks. They did this, therefore, first for the college and later, with the aid of their assistants and students, for the secondary and elementary schools.[21] Now they, being primarily interested in the discovery of new truth, organized the textbooks which they prepared for college classes on the lines laid down by the limits of the academic research in which they were engaged. Hence, the curriculum came to consist of a program of narrow school subjects, for each of which a specific textbook determined the content of instruction. Gradually, therefore, the curriculum became oriented about the research materials which the professors were developing in their laboratories and their libraries—not about the conditions of youth and adults in American society. Furthermore, the professors, because of their prolonged intellectual training and grounding in cautious research methods, their prudence in generalization from their data, tended to concentrate their attention upon the past and upon those materials which, because of prolonged use, had come to have scientific prestige. Having a fear of unsound generalization, hence a fear of the contemporary in history, the new, the unauthenticated in science, they more and more neglected the vital affairs of current life.

And there is a third reason for the lag: the entrenchment of authors and publishing houses in the curriculum. We must not forget that the publication of the materials of the school curriculum is founded upon profit; it has a thoroughly commercial basis. The control of the publication of textbooks has practically never been in the hands of the state. As school populations have pyramided, the business of publishing textbooks has become one of first commercial magnitude. Under the leadership of a few large publishing houses, the quality, workmanship, and content of our school books have put the American textbook in the world lead. But the costs have mounted correspondingly.

The task of publishing and distributing schoolbooks for twenty-three million children is one of such huge magnitude that it seems

[21] The practice developed of making secondary-school and elementary-school books on the lines of the content of the more mature texts but, peculiarly enough, of making them briefer, more compact, and more encyclopaedic than the books used with collegiate youth. In this manner, for example, Day's *Algebra* (1824, 1848, etc.) was revised and rewritten for high schools by Day's assistant, Thompson. The order of topics and treatment in the *Algebra* of Thompson and Day was closely patterned after those of the original college book.

very clear that the important services of the publishing houses must be recognized and continued. In my comments, therefore, there is no suggestion that curricular materials should be made available to schools except through the agency of the established commercial houses. Nevertheless, the careful study of the development of the school curriculum makes very clear that one of the outstanding reasons for the conservatism of the curriculum is the entrenchment of private interests of both publishers and authors. The curriculum can advance not much more rapidly than the great publishing houses of America and *a small group of authors who dictate its major outlines can be persuaded to permit it.*

The forward-looking curriculum-maker is compelled at the outset, therefore, to undertake the education of these agencies—both publishers and authors. Naturally, both agencies tend toward the perpetuation of the major outlines of the curriculum as they have made it. It is but natural that having invested hundreds of thousands of dollars in large editions of books organized on a rigid grade basis, publishers tend to make changes in schoolbook materials slowly. However, during the past two decades, under the impetus of scientific research and laboratory schools, the publishing houses have supported marked modifications in both the content and arrangement of the materials of instruction.

It is one of the tasks, both of the professional curriculum-maker and of the school administrator and teacher, to bring constantly before the authors and publishers of schoolbooks the need for continuous reconstruction of their materials and especially for the inclusion of up-to-date materials.

CHAPTER III

THREE DECADES OF MENTAL DISCIPLINE: CURRICULUM-MAKING VIA NATIONAL COMMITTEES

HAROLD RUGG

I

1890! The frontier obliterated, a continent conquered! The crude physical pattern of the new nationality sketched in. The world's greatest experiment in democracy under way, based on the premise of universal education at public expense.

The American *Zeitgeist* already reflected, at the end of the century, a trusting faith in the efficacy of education. The public school was to provide the panaceas for all political, economic, and social ills.

What, then, had a century of curriculum-making produced?

A twelve-grade scheme of housing children from the ages of six to eighteen divided into eight elementary and four secondary grades. Public secondary instruction, an accepted American doctrine, organized about a dozen or more school 'subjects,' and based essentially on the reading and memorizing of textbooks. The textbook in each subject, a morphological and encyclopedic compendium of facts. Mental discipline and knowledge for knowledge's sake, the dominant purposes of the school. Growth—physical, mental, and cultural development—although already the center of the new evolutionary faith and the basis of the reform ideas of Francis Parker,[1] William James, and John Dewey—was totally missing from the educational philosophy of the collegiate and administrative rulers of our schools.

In 1890, mass-education, like its compatriot, economic mass-production, was ready for standardization, crystallization. The next two decades witnessed its consummation.

II

Two forces opposed each other in these formative years. One group, the collegiate and private secondary-school people, advo-

[1] See Chapter V.

cates of the *status quo,* desired standardization, uniformity, organized methods of teaching; the other, protagonists of change, was led at first by Charles W. Eliot, William T. Harris,[2] and Francis W. Parker; later by Harper, Greenwood, Burk, and Dewey. These sought flexibility, individualized instruction, more rapid entrance into the professions, an enriched course of study based on child activity.

The Agitation for Administrative Reform of the Graded School

It was natural that the first point of attack should have been the reform of the administrative outlines of the graded school. A few far-seeing educational leaders waged war against the rigidifying effects which they saw to be inevitable in this strong trend toward standardization.

Among superintendents of schools, a liberal leadership had developed in the person of William T. Harris. For nearly forty years, (as superintendent of the St. Louis Schools from 1867-1880, and United States Commissioner of Education from 1889 to 1906,) Harris, on the platform and in the educational press, waged a vigorous propaganda for the breaking up of the ''procrustean bed of grades'' into which pupils and subject matter had been organized. Reform was to come via more frequent promotions, and for fifty years under the impetus of Harris's early work, St. Louis has reclassified pupils every ten weeks during the school year—instead of annually as was done in most school systems prior to 1910.

As the result of the work of Harris and his colleagues, a widespread movement was initiated during the 1880's and 1890's aimed at the development of more flexible promotion plans and arrangement of materials of instruction. There resulted, in addition to the St. Louis plan of promotion, the ''double track'' plan of Cambridge, the Santa Barbara ''concentric circle plan,'' the attempts of Preston Search, and two decades later of Frederick Burk, to indi-

[2] Harris, William T. (1835-1908), principal of grammar school in St. Louis, 1866-67, Ass't Supt. of Schools; 1867-1880, Supt. of Schools. One of the founders of the Concord School of Philosophy and Literature and engaged in philosophic study and travel from 1888. From 1889-1906 U. S. Commissioner of Education. Last work in connection with editorship of Webster's *New International Dictionary.*

vidualize the materials of instruction,[3] various schemes for supervised study and credit for quality, standardized methods of marking the work of pupils and finally, the nation-wide movement for the creation of the junior high school.[4]

The movement for a seven-year elementary school represented another aspect of this administrative attempt to reform the school program. It was initiated about 1900 in the Middlewest[5] and led by college men like President William Rainey Harper and Professor John Dewey[6] of the University of Chicago, and by superintendents of schools under the leadership of Superintendent James Greenwood of Kansas City. The University of Chicago, under the personal vigor and initiative of Harper and through affiliated academies, led an agitation for the seven-year elementary school, to be followed by a secondary school of four grades. The topic was discussed animatedly for years by various associations and a widespread literature grew up.[7]

It is clear, however, that these movements for reorganization were primarily administrative in character. They dealt only casually with the nub of the educational situation—the vitalizing of the activities and materials of the curriculum.

III. The Reign of College Entrance Requirements

For nearly a century, as we have seen, professional textmakers and professors of 'subjects' prepared textbooks and the textbook

[3] And to-day, of Carleton Washburne.

[4] An excellent review of this movement for administrative reform is given in Bunker, F. F.: *Reorganization of the Public School System.* U. S. Bureau of Education Bulletin, No. 7, 1916.

[5] We must not overlook the fact that the Cook County Normal School (Chicago) under Colonel F. W. Parker was from 1883 to 1899 a storm center of reform for the elementary school. See Chapter V of this volume, "Curriculum-Making in Laboratory Schools."

[6] See Dewey. *The Educational Situation.* University of Chicago Press, 1902.

[7] In spite of it, the schools of the country remained essentially on a twelve-grade basis. In 1911 the United States Commissioner of Education made a canvass of the organization of 550 city systems, each having a population of 8000 or over. Four hundred eighty-nine of these had an eight-year elementary course and four-year secondary course; 48 were organized on a 7-4 plan; 86 on a 9-4, with 46 utilizing some other modification of grade organization. In other words, a century of school administration had produced in American cities a nearly standardized system of twelve school grades. The seven-year elementary school had been defeated, in my judgment, not on the merits of the case at all, but by sheer administrative inertia.

dominated the curriculum. The content of instruction was determined by the point of view, knowledge, and interest of the individual writer, who frequently had no direct connection with the schools. Curriculum-making was an 'armchair' procedure.

During the 1870's and 1880's, with the rapid expansion and systematization of city and town schools, the introduction of a host of new 'subjects' and the necessity for quick preparation of materials of instruction, great diversity developed. The economic doctrine of *laissez faire* operated also in education in the construction of school courses. 'Local option' in school practice; each state and each chartered city was left free to make its own course of study. This was done generally by the adoption of textbooks for the various school subjects. By 1890 diversity was becoming a characteristic of the American public school system.

To students of politics and culture, freedom from standardization is a positive indication of the worth of democracy, but to college presidents and principals of private preparatory schools, it was anathema. Diversity in school curricula produced difficulty of administration; hence it was not to be tolerated.

The administrative literature of the 1880's abounds with evidences of the anxiety of the administrators of higher education over the "chaotic condition" of the secondary school. Although giving lip service to the creed that the high school is the "people's college," both college presidents and headmasters of the private school (and it must also be said of a considerable body of high-school principals) wanted the high-school curriculum standardized on the basis of preparation for the higher institutions. And they had their way. For twenty years college presidents and preparatory-school people took charge, determining the form and spirit of the materials of instruction throughout the entire range of the school.

Even before 1880, the entrance requirements of the individual colleges—Harvard, Yale and other New England institutions especially—had played an important rôle in determining the content, sequence, and arrangement of high-school courses. In "English," from 1865 to 1880, for example, prescription became more and more rigid. The accumulating control of "the masterpieces of English literature" can be seen in the successive entrance requirements from 1865 to 1874. Even in such liberal institutions as Harvard was in those days of Eliot's early administration,[8] the catalogues made more rigid year by year the stipulation that the subjects for English composition should be "taken from such works of standard authors as shall be announced from time to time. The subject for 1874 will be taken from one of the following works: Shakespeare's *Tempest, Julius Caesar, The Merchant of Venice,* Goldsmith's *Vicar of Wakefield,* Scott's *Ivanhoe* and *The Lay of the Last Minstrel.*" By 1890, lists from the standard authors had steadily been augmented and examinations were always to be set upon the readings of "certain masterpieces of English literature."

New textbooks appeared, meeting the standard prescriptions of the college. The "scissors and paste" method of constructing them began to attain usage. New books were cut to the pattern of those already most widely adopted; standardization of order of topics and treatment ensued.

Against the rigidity and wastefulness of the twelve-grade system and the control of college entrance vigorous protests were heard, even within the college field itself. In 1888, Charles W. Eliot read an epoch-making address before the Washington meeting of the National Education Association.[9] In it, he advocated many administrative reforms, such as the reduction of the twelve-grade public-school curriculum by two years, and greater flexibility in promotion and in organization of instruction. To secure these he urged the colleges to permit more latitude in entrance requirements. Eliot not only advocated reforms; he practiced them. He led the way by developing a liberal spirit and practice in Harvard University during four decades. From 1872, under his leadership, Harvard had slowly opened the gates for reform in entrance requirements by permitting greater variety in the lists of Latin, Greek, and English composition on which examinations should be based.

In spite of the increasing dictatorship of the individual colleges and the growing standardization of the new textbooks, however, most administrators of universities and preparatory schools feared the non-uniformity that still prevailed. They wanted continuity in the educational system. Smooth mobility of the scholastic popu-

[8] Charles W. Eliot was elected president of Harvard in 1869.

[9] Charles W. Eliot: "Can School Programs be Shortened and Enriched?" a chapter in his *Educational Reform,* p. 169. Also U. S. Bur. of Education, Circular of Information, 1888, No. 8, pp. 101-118.

lation was their desideratum of efficient school administration: such as would allow a graduate of Philips-Andover or Newark Academy,[10] for example, to enter Harvard, Princeton, Yale, Michigan, or Colorado with equal facility. On school administration, indeed, and not on growth and learning their minds were focussed.

President Eliot's 1888 address initiated a vigorous discussion of the need for the reorganization of the high-school curriculum. His attack on the public-school program, although aimed at increased flexibility and effectiveness, actually served as the impetus to bring about a prolonged movement for standardization and uniformity.

In the two years immediately following his address, 1889-1891, Eliot and President James H. Baker of the University of Colorado led the agitation for a national conference on secondary education. The National Council of Education, an important subsidiary of the National Education Association, discussed the matter vigorously and finally appointed the first National Committee. This was the famous "Committee on Secondary School Studies," generally called "The Committee of Ten."

IV. The Rôle of the Committees of the National Education Association in Standardizing the American School Curriculum, 1892—

Curriculum-making, from the day of the Committee of Ten, has been predominantly via National Committees, and most of the important ones have been sponsored by the National Education Association. This organization, through its important subsidiaries —the National Council of Education, the Secondary Department, and the Department of Superintendence—has been one of the few great formative influences in the development of the school curriculum. Specifically, it sponsored such important reports as that of the Committee of Ten (on secondary education, 1893), the Committee of Fifteen (on elementary education, 1893), the reports of its two Committees on Economy of Time (elementary education, 1908 and 1914-19), the reports of its Commission on the Reorgani-

[10] See Wilson Farrand's address, "English in the Preparatory School," before the Association of Colleges and Preparatory Schools of the Middle States and Maryland, at Columbia College, December, 1893.

zation of Secondary Education (1920) and the more recent year-books of the Department of Superintendence (1924-25-26).

Curriculum-making by national committees was so vigorous that by 1900 the prestige of these committees, made up of subject-matter specialists, was unquestioned. Our review of curriculum-making since 1890 begins therefore, with the work of the first important national committee—namely, the Committee of Ten.

V. The Curriculum Work of the Committee on Secondary School Studies: The Committee of Ten, 1892-93

Under the Committee of Ten, nine separate conferences[11] were organized on a subject basis: (1) Latin, (2) Greek, (3) English, (4) other modern languages, (5) mathematics, (6) physics, astronomy, and chemistry, (7) natural history (biology, including botany, and zoölogy), (8) history, civil government, and political science, (9) geography (physical geography, geology, and meteorology). It is significant that the committee conceived of the curriculum as a mosaic of school subjects. Accordingly, the reorganization of the secondary school meant to them the revamping of the separate subjects of study, mathematics, classics, history, English, etc., as well as the better articulation of elementary, secondary, and collegiate instruction. From that day to this, curriculum-making by committees has been piecemeal—subject by subject—no committee has ever brought itself to view in close juxtaposition the total American scene and the whole school curriculum.

The Committee of Ten started a generation of curriculum-making by national committees of subject-matter specialists. The personnel was composed of persons of a classical and subject-matter interest. This is revealed by the composition of their personnel, their methods of procedure, and their published reports.

The personnel of the Committee of Ten itself consisted of five college presidents, one college professor, two head masters of private schools, one principal of a public high school, and the United States Commissioner of Education—eight of the ten men representing colleges and private preparatory school interests.

[11] The directors of the National Education Association appropriated $2,500 to meet the expenses of these nine conferences; seven of the meetings, organized in 1892-3, were held in colleges.

The ninety members of the nine conferences were divided as follows:

47 were college professors and administrators
21 were head masters of private schools
14 were principals of public high schools
1 was a government bureau head formerly in university service
2 were superintendents of schools
4 were representatives of normal schools
1 was a director of a public school department

Thus, 84 members of the conferences were either college professors or college preparatory administrators. The discussions and the reports of the committees reflect the interest of this personnel.

An instructive contrast can be gotten by reading the reports of the Committee of Ten (1893) and of the Committee of Fifteen (1895) in parallel with the First and Second *Yearbooks of the National Herbart Society,* 1895 and 1896. The latter were filled with vigorous debates on the selection and organization of the materials of instruction, the interests and development of children, the correlation of studies, the principles of learning and growth. The Committee reports, however, dealt with "time-allotment," entrance requirements, articulation of high school and college, the optimal length of courses—in short, with administration.

Each subject conference made a plea for uniformity in entrance requirements. They all wanted their subjects taught earlier in the high-school curriculum. Six of them—all but classics, mathematics, and geography—asked specifically for more time in the school program. They discussed the question of differentiation of curricula between college preparation and life, but they unanimously declared that "every subject that is taught at all in the secondary school should be taught in the same way and to the same extent to each pupil so long as he pursues it, no matter what the probable destination of the pupil may be or at what point his education is to cease." On the criterion of the need for "simplification of the programs," they urged that the curriculum of the high school should be based primarily upon college preparation. They condemned the general custom in American high schools of preparing "separate courses of study for pupils of supposed different destinations," and said that "the principles laid down by the conferences will make for a great simplification in secondary-school programs." A very large proportion of the material of the report is devoted to a discussion of the time-allotment.

According to this first national committee, therefore, the curriculum was to be determined by the need of flexibility in school administration, not by the peculiar learning and growth needs of young people. A large proportion of the space of the report is devoted to the need for uniformity and standardization of requirements in English, mathematics, history, Latin, the sciences, and the languages, to the end that young people could be prepared systematically for entrance to college.

Thus was launched the era of *curriculum-making by college entrance.*

During the 1890's, schoolbooks reflected specifically the recommendations of this report, and public-school systems were profoundly influenced in organizing their "courses of study" by its recommendations. For thirty years public-school reformers have been trying to remedy the difficulties into which the curriculum fell under the standardizing and academic influences of the reports of these committees.

VI. The Reorganization of Elementary Education Was Also Affected by the Report of the Committee of Ten: the Committee of Fifteen, 1893

The widespread discussion of the report of the Committee of Ten led the Department of Superintendence to appoint the Committee of Fifteen in 1893 for the purpose of considering the reconstruction of the eight-year elementary school. This Committee was divided into three subcommittees, one of which, under the chairmanship of William T. Harris, dealt with the correlation of studies in elementary education. This Committee, however, like the Committee of Ten, devoted itself chiefly to administrative problems. It was concerned with the length of the elementary course (Should it be eight years or six?), with the earlier introduction of such high-school studies, like Latin and the modern languages, into the elementary school; only slightly with the differentiation of the school materials to fit individual differences in scholastic ability. The discussion revealed great conservatism among school administrators and little desire to reduce the length of elementary education. They did recommend the earlier introduction of such academic studies as Latin and algebra.[12]

[12] *Report of the Committee of Fifteen on Elementary Education.* Published for the National Education Association by the American Book Co. 1895.

It can be seen, therefore, that the interest of the elementary-school administrators, like that of the Committee on Secondary School Studies, was focussed chiefly upon administrative organization.[13]

VII. The Work of the Early Committees Led to the Establishment of National Committees in the Various School Subjects

The Development of Formal Standardization of High-School English

The agitation for uniformity in college entrance requirements is revealed conspicuously in the field of English.

Immediately after the report of the Committee of Ten was published a new committee of professors and head masters was appointed by the Association of College and Preparatory Schools of the Middle States and Maryland. This committee agreed emphatically with the findings of the Committee of Ten and proposed a joint conference with other associations that dealt with the problem of entrance requirements in English. Their proposal resulted in the creation of the "National Conference on Uniform Entrance Requirements in English," an organization that locked rigid the reading materials of the high-school curriculum for nearly two decades. The regulations of the conference confirmed the earlier dictum of the colleges that examinations should be based upon the

[13] This interest in administrative organization is illustrated again in the appointment of a new committee in 1895 by the Department of Secondary Education; namely, the Committee on College Entrance Requirements. It spent four years upon its work and made its final report at the Los Angeles meeting of the National Education Association in 1899. This Committee worked with four committees representing the outstanding associations of schools and colleges, namely, the New England Association of Colleges and Secondary Schools, the Association of the Middle States and Maryland, the Southern Association of Colleges and Secondary Schools, and the North Central Association of Colleges and Secondary Schools. Furthermore, the Committee on College Entrance Requirements of the National Education Association asked the Philological Association for a report on Latin and Greek, the American Historical Association for a report on the scope and place of history in the secondary schools, the Modern Language Association of America for a report on German and French and the American Mathematical Association for a discussion of mathematics.

These committees, likewise, were concerned with the length of the course, the age at which studies should be introduced, the articulation of the various levels of the school. There was practically no proposal to modify the academic nature of the subjects of study. Its chief influence was to solidify the domination of "college entrance," so that under its sway the control became almost complete.

reading of "masterpieces of English literature." It confirmed the practice of minute dissection of "classical" literary works. It went far toward making the reading of American high-school youth, British.[14] It laid great stress upon the writings produced prior to 1800 and gave almost no attention to American writings produced after the Civil War.

The reports of the National Conference and of the College Entrance Examination Board, organized in 1900, were copied into most college catalogues. They influenced directly the organization of the English curriculum of every private preparatory school and of the great preponderance of public high schools.

The extent to which the curriculum had been standardized by that time is clearly revealed in the report in 1899 of the National Education Association's Committee on College Entrance Requirements in English. "Narration, both in literature and composition" was to occupy the first half of the first year; description, the second. The successive years were prescribed in a similar manner; exposition in the second year correlated with the novel; the drama was emphasized in the third year; the history of English literature and of the English language and the writing of compositions governed the fourth-year work.

Formal discipline, memorization, literary dissection, held sway over vivid understanding.

The Revolt of High-School Teachers of English

At no time had uniform requirements given general satisfaction. It was the judgment of progressive English teachers that "the Committee on College Entrance Requirements made a report which tended to foster a type of English study that practically ignored oral composition and subjects of expression drawn from the pupil's own experience and that consequently applied in the study of literary masterpieces formal rhetorical categories.[15]

Under the dominance of the various requirements and examinations public-school teachers of English began to protest. The discontent was voiced most animatedly in the New York State and New York City Associations of English Teachers at their annual

[14] A recent survey of 225 high-school courses in literature shows the current dictatorship of 28 college entrance books, 24 of which are of British authorship.

[15] See Report of the Hosic Committee of Thirty, *Reorganization of English in Secondary Schools,* U. S. Bureau of Education, Bulletin No. 2, 1917.

meetings in 1907, 1908, 1909. As a result, a national movement for reform was launched by public-school people themselves at the Boston meeting of the National Education Association in July, 1910.

The agitation for curricular freedom from the control of the college resulted in the appointment of a committee to make formal protest to the National Conference on Uniform Entrance Requirements in English and to the College Entrance Examination Board.

This committee, conspicuous because of the fact that it was made up entirely of public-school workers and also because of the factual methods of its procedure, laid before the National Education Association in July, 1911, the results of a survey of the work of several hundred schools. These demonstrated the strangle hold which the National Conference on Entrance Requirements in English, the College Entrance Examination Board, and various college examinations had attained over the English curriculum and methods of teaching.[16]

The report emphasized the fact that the colleges refused to include "any but books out of copyright;" furthermore, that they failed to "recognize the value and increase the practice of oral expression both in composition and in literature." The English work as a whole, they averred, tended to formality, scholasticism, and overmaturity and needed to be vitalized throughout and definitely related to the life of the present."

The rebellion in English received its most effective leadership, however, in 1911 from the National Council of Teachers of English. Under the leadership of Professor James F. Hosic, for many years the Secretary of the National Council and Editor of the *English Journal,* this organization of public-school teachers worked unceasingly for the liberalizing of the English curriculum.[17] The studies of this group revealed clearly the dominance of a short list of 'classics' over the work of the English classrooms.

The Secondary Departments of the National Education Association also took up the cudgels against the rigid prescriptions of the higher institutions. In none of their departments was there more vigorous protest than in that of English.

In 1911 the Committee on Articulation of High Schools and

---

[16] Final report printed in *English Journal,* February, 1912; also in the *Proceedings of the National Education Association* for 1912, pp. 707-761.

[17] One of its early investigations was published in the *English Journal,* for 1913—"Types of Organization of High-School English."

Colleges had reported its new plan for the organization of high-school courses and for college accrediting. The discussions laid before the National Education Association by this committee resulted in the organization of "*The Commission on the Reorganization of Secondary Education.*" The English Department of this commission was joined with the new committee on College Entrance Requirements in English to form the "National Joint Committee on English," representing the Commission on the Reorganization of Secondary Education. This joint "Committee of Thirty," under the chairmanship of Professor James F. Hosic, held several meetings in 1912, 1914. It was composed practically altogether of public-school workers—thirteen of them were English high-school teachers. There were only three professors of English from colleges and universities on the committee. It based its discussions and recommendations upon the facts of actual classroom practice and upon historical trends in curriculum-making.

The report of this committee, the most influential national committee in English, is of a quite different character from those of the earlier committees. It was written from the standpoint of the needs of high-school pupils, not from that of college entrance. The report consisted of a series of recommendations on composition and literature, oral expression, business English, general reading, libraries, and administrative problems. Although recognizing the need for preparing those high-school pupils who went to college, the report emphasized the development of the ability to read and write English, the appreciation of literature, and the enjoyment of good reading for the rank and file of our young people. Young people were to be given practice in writing out of their own lives and experiences, rather than from their analytical studies of "masterpieces of literature." The work in English was to be tied up definitely to geography and history. Excellent reading lists were given which would suggest to teachers desirable materials to use in the correlation of English with civics, history, geography, and science.

The report is by far the most forward looking report of any national subject committee up to 1920. Although this was curriculum-making by subjective committee procedure, it was an improvement on current forms of that procedure in one respect: the work was oriented distinctly by a public-school attitude.

VIII. The Curriculum in History and Related Studies Also Determined by National Committees

While the Victorian professors were fastening British literature upon American youth, a succession of national committees was determining the content of history and related studies by a similar procedure.

In the course of the development of the school curriculum the materials that deal with the economic, political, and cultural life, in so far as they were brought into the curriculum at all, were scattered through several departments, especially history and geography. For three quarters of a century, because of the dominance of political interests in the organization of history, the study of civic matters was organized in fairly close relationship to the history of government. Indeed, historical study was largely the study of the development of organized government. After 1890, with the expansion of research in the fields of economics and sociology, those matters that related in any distinctive way to government came under the influence of the historians. Not until after 1900, with the leadership of Charles A. Beard and his associates, were the economic threads running through history regarded as basal.[18]

Now, for nearly a century, guided by the classical geographers, the materials of "geography" included two fairly unrelated types of subject matter. There were first the facts and principles of the physical environment, known as geology, physical geography, etc. There grew up, in the second place, an increasing body of material which dealt with the influence of the physical environment on where and how people live together. It is only in our own generation that curriculum-makers have seen clearly that this latter material overlaps in large part upon the facts and principles organized in the new subjects of "economics," "industrial and business organization," and "industrial history,"—hence the current demand that the whole field of economic, political, and cultural life be reflected in a broad department of the school to be known as the social studies.[19]

---

[18] Beard, C. A. *The Economic Interpretation of the Constitution of the United States,* Macmillan, 1921; *Contemporary American History,* Macmillan, 1921.

[19] The current quarrel among geographers over the dichotomy of geography, goes far to explain the inability of historians, economists, and political scientists to coöperate with the geographers in the development of a unified social science curriculum.

Thirty years of committee procedure in history and related studies led therefore to the fashioning of a curriculum which until recent years has been predominantly political in character. In all of this time, although conspicuous advances have been made in the direction of introducing discussions of contemporary life into the school (community civics, for example, as a description of community life; "current events," "problems of democracy," elementary courses in sociology, etc.), curriculum-making has been organized about the limited scope of these separate school subjects and not upon the total task of "how people live together."

Since 1890, the curriculum of history and related studies has been determined by a series of national committees of great prestige. Their personnel and procedure have reflected the influence of the subject-matter specialists to almost exactly the same extent as have those of the English committees. In the same interval, on the other hand, the content of geography has developed through the work of textbook writers and almost entirely independent of national committees. The work of the Herbartians, conspicuously Charles A. and Frank M. McMurry in the field of geography, in collaboration with university professors and professional textbook writers, has played the most important rôle in constructing the course in geography. The early discussions of the Herbart society (1895 to 1900) abound with references to the inclusive character of geography. These people gave to it (as the nucleus of the school curriculum) much the place that Herbart gave to history and literature.

Including the Committee of Ten and excluding the Social Studies Committee of the Commission on Reorganization of Secondary Education, seven national committees have made recommendations for the content of the elementary and secondary curriculum in history. Facts concerning all of the nine committees are presented in a condensed form in Table I.[20] The table shows very clearly that these committees, like those of other subjects, were dominated by an interest in historical research. The total personnel

[20] Table I is based upon an original tabulation of the personnel, procedures, and conclusions of national committees which I made in 1920. This work has never been published. It has been checked and brought up to date by comparison with a table of Earle U. Rugg (*Twenty-Second Yearbook* of this Society, Part II, pp. 62-63), and Edgar Dawson, "The History Inquiry," *The Historical Outlook*, June, 1924.

TABLE I

Name of Committee	Date	Membership of Committee	Third Grade	Fourth Grade	Fifth Grade	Sixth Grade
Committee of Ten N. E. A.[1] A. H. A.[2]	1892 1894	7 Professors 3 Principals			Biography and Mythology	Biography and Mythology
Committee of Seven A. H. A.	1896 1899	6 Professors 1 Principal	Stories from the Illiad, etc.	Biography	Greek and Roman History	Medieval and Modern History
						Course suggested by one
Committee of Eight A. H. A	1905 1909	4 Professors 2 Supt's 2 Teachers	Heroes of Other times Pictures of Historical Scenes and Persons of Various Ages.	American History: Exploration to the Revolution. Historical Scenes and Persons in Early American History.	American History: Revolution of the Civil War. Historical Scenes and Persons in Later American History.	European Background
			(——	3 Year Cycle	——)	(——
						Chiefly Biography; Civics to be
Committee of Five	1907 1912	4 Professors 1 Principal				
Social Studies Committee N. E. A.	1914 1916	5 Professors 2 Supt's 10 Teachers 4 Unclassified				
Committee of Seven A. P. A[3]	1911 1916	6 Professors 1 Supt.	Civic Virtues	A study of simple community activities Little textbook work		
Committee on History and Education for Citizenship A. H. A. N. E. A.	1918 1921	6 Professors of History 1 Professor of Education 1 Supt. 1 Teacher		The Making of the United States		
			Discovery and Exploration	How Englishmen became Americans 1607-1783	The United States 1783-1877	The United States 1877 to date ½ year; civics, ½ year.

[1] National Education Association.
[2] American Historical Association.
[3] American Political Science Association.

of the committees includes thirty-two professors of history and government, nine superintendents or principals of high schools, three teachers in public schools and two professors of education. It is interesting, furthermore, to find that twenty-five of the thirty-two professors of history and government served on two different committees. The same person served as chairman of the Committee

TABLE I—*Continued*

SEVENTH GRADE	EIGHTH GRADE	NINTH GRADE	TENTH GRADE	ELEVENTH GRADE	TWELFTH GRADE
American History and Civil Government	Greek and Roman History with Oriental Connections	French History with background of Medieval and Modern History	English History with background of Medieval and Modern History	American History	One Special Period and Civil Government
English History	American History	Ancient History to 800	Medieval and Modern History	English History	American History and Civil Government
member of the committee Grades 3-8					
Early American History 1500-1789 Still more Civics	Later American History 1789-1909 Civics (Also some emphasis on Modern European History)				
3-Year Cycle	————————)				
taught throughout Grades 1-8					
		Ancient History to 800 (Econ. Pol. & Soc.)	English History with Continental Connections to 1760	Modern Europe with English Connections since 1760 (Econ. Pol. & Soc.)	American History and Government, (separately or Ratio of 3:2)
Geography, European History, and Community Civics	American History Community Civics and Geography Incidentally	Political, Economic and Vocational Civics with History Incidentally	Ancient and Medieval History to 1700 (1 yr.) Modern European History (½ or 1 yr.) American History since the 17th Century (1 or ½ yr.) Problems of American Democracy (1 or ½ year)		
Community Civics (emphasis upon functions but some treatment of the machinery of government.)			An advanced course in civics (Report does not state in which year it is to be offered, nor whether it is a 1 yr. or ½ yr. course).		
American History in its World Setting			The Modern World		
The World before 1607 (including Spain in America)	The World since 1607 with emphasis on Economic and Social History of the United States	Community and Nat'l Activities including (commercial geography) civics, social and economic history	Modern European History since 1650	American History during the Nat'l period	Social, Economic and Political Problems and Principles

of Five and of the Committee of Seven and three other men were on both committees.

Table I merits careful study by the student of curriculum-making as an interesting exhibit of the outcome of the conventional type of committee procedure. This procedure has throughout its history been 'armchair,' *a priori*. Practically no objective investigations have been made by these committeees upon which to base recommendations for the reconstruction of the curriculum. The almost universal practice has been to hold a number of roundtable conferences of the committee, to delegate to the individuals the task of writing sections of a 'report,' to have those sections read and revised by members of the committee and to discuss them in further roundtable meetings. Aims and purposes of historical instruction in the schools have generally been included as one unit of the report; also the scope and outline of the content to be taught in the various grades of the school, and suggestions concerning methods of instruction. These have not been based upon investigation, measurement of results attained in current instruction, objective determination of desirable content, or upon experimentation.

As the result of thirty years of this sort of work, the gap between curriculum and the concrete discussion of industrial, political, and cultural forces and institutions in America has been perpetuated. As a further result of the work of these subject-matter committees, we have to-day almost no objectively ascertained facts and principles for the determination of the content or for its grade-placement and organization. Witness, for example, the recommendations of the successive history committees (see Table I) concerning what should be taught in the various grades of the schools. Glance down the column headed "Ninth Grade." The Committee of Ten wanted French history; the Committee of Seven, Ancient History; the Committee of Five, Ancient (the Chairman of this committee and three others were members of the Committee of Seven); the National Education Association Social Studies Committee wanted political, economic, and vocational civics; the Committee of Education for Citizenship recommended American history, community civics, and geography.

XIX. Who Shall Make the Curriculum and by What Method?

To evaluate the work of all of these national committees we need criteria against which to measure their procedure—a list of jobs of curriculum-making and of the abilities needed for the carrying on of those jobs. Let us digress, long enough, therefore, to summarize the various kinds of work involved in curriculum-construction.

The Jobs of Curriculum-Making and Their Scope

There are three definite jobs involved in the task.[21]

First: The determination of fundamental objectives, the great purposes of the curriculum as a whole and of its several departments.

Second: The selection of activities and other materials of instruction, choice of content, readings, exercises, excursions, topics for open-forum discussions, manual activities, health and recreational programs.

Third: The discovery of the most effective organizations of materials and their experimental placement in the grades of the public schools.

All three tasks are of vital importance to the proper construction of the curriculum. Consciously or implicitly, the curriculum-maker is always guided by his objectives in the selection of activities or other materials of instruction, and in their organization and grade-placement.

Because of the orientation of the subject-matter specialists who have dominated its reconstruction, the curriculum has been developed piecemeal, subject by subject, grade by grade, one unit in isolation from another. Curriculum-making has been by the process of elimination and accretion. As Charters put it, the curriculum has become "the amorphous product of generations of tinkering."

The need for the abandonment of this method is obvious. It is becoming increasingly apparent that educational leaders must reconstruct the public-school curriculum from a consideration of American life as a whole, from a synthetic view of it which shall embody its cultural aspects, politics, industry, and business, city and country life, impact of groups upon each other, the American rhythm expressing itself in active accomplishments—everything.

Abilities Needed for the Task

Now the capacity to see 'wholes' is found in its highest development in the creative artist. The poet who sings of America (be his rhythm set in verse or prose), the dramatist, the novelist, the lay critic of American life, prose essayist, the student of society—

[21] The National Society's Curriculum Committee discusses this problem in its *Foundations of Curriculum-Making*, Vol. II of this Yearbook. The present section expresses only my own views on the problem.

all must be brought into this task of setting the great objectives of the school. Deep-seeing analysts must coöperate with the man of science and his fact-founded laws. For the last analysis it is the creative artist and the student of society who will set the far-off, deep-guiding, *ultimate* objectives. To do this, however, there must be an assembly of the facts and trends of society arrived at from the soundest application of scientific methods that can be discovered.

It is the educational man of science, furthermore, testing carefully his specific hypotheses of learning, who will set the *immediate* objectives for a given school. Both—artist and scientist, critics of vision and law—must coöperate with the school administrator in evolving a practical, working scheme of education.

The tendency has been too marked for our philosophers of education to ignore the fundamental principles already emerging from this study. We have divorced science from philosophy in curriculum-making. To secure a wise school practice, they must be united. In the past quarter century the application of more scientific methods to the analysis of social life has already made possible a synthesis of the trends and relationhips between the various parts of our functioning society. Such syntheses of the industrial, political, and cultural order are revealing themselves in America, in occidental industrialism, and in the impact of oriental cultures on western civilization.

The determination of objectives and the selection and organization of material, therefore, is a task for many minds and many kinds of experience and training, perspectives and interests—certainly more varied than those which can be obtained from intensive study of the material of any one of the separate subjects, physics, history, mathematics, etc.

It is clear, then, that the day has passed in which a single individual professor, teacher or administrator, psychologist, educational law-giver or research specialist, can hope to master the manifold, highly professional tasks of curriculum-making. They are far too difficult and complex for any one person to hope to compass them all singlehanded. In this connection no generalization is of more far-reaching importance than that *the proper construction of the curriculum demands the coöperation of several specialists equipped in various fields.* Curriculum-making is a coöperative enterprise.

At least five special fields of work are represented in the total enterprise of constructing a curriculum for a public-school system: (1) the study of contemporary American life—the physical and natural world, economic, political, and social institutions, culture—every aspect; (2) the study of child capacities, interests, rates of learning, etc.: (3) educational administration—child accounting, organization of classes, curriculum materials, library facilities, the daily program, and the like; (4) educational measurement, statistical methods, and controlled experimentation; (5) the professional study of specific fields of subject matter, including specialized documentation and authentication.

The argument to this point shows very clearly that American education can be reconstructed out of the materials of American life only by the coöperation of many well-equipped agencies. One effective mode of attacking the problem is through the organization of national committees. The foregoing critical comments have not been aimed at the abolition of committees—rather they have been focussed upon the enlargement of their personnel, on their proper financing, and on the improvement of their procedure. It is imperative that their personnel comprise individuals equipped to render the services which have been sketched in the foregoing sections and that their procedure be as thorough and as scientific as possible. To further critical consideration of the matter, I reprint next an earlier proposal concerning a program for national committees.

X. A Program for National Committees

A committee should act in three capacities if it wishes to improve school practice generally. First, it should act as a deliberative body, stating ultimate and immediate aims and criteria; second, it should organize important investigations of social and psychological needs which underlie the curriculum; third, it should act as a national clearing-house and forum for controversial discussion.

A. The Committee As a Deliberative Body of Specialists Stating Aims and Criteria

The most important task of the committees is to draw up a scientific program for curriculum-making. This will necessitate frequent and prolonged roundtable conferences.

The program should include: first, a definite statement of aims and outcomes of instruction; second, criteria for the inclusion of material in the courses, for assigning materials to school grades, and for presenting materials within grades. Such statements can be made only by getting the best composite judgment of trained specialists—a judgment which is the result of mature deliberation and roundtable discussion. Two types of specialists should contribute to this discussion: (1) those trained in the study of the validity of materials; (2) those trained in the science of curriculum-making, in the study of society and educational psychology. It is inconceivable that a curriculum can be made properly by either group working alone.

B. The Committee As an Organizer of Investigations of Social and Psychological Needs

The program of a national committee, in the second place, should be investigational. Once the fundamental principles are established, detailed studies of human needs and results must be made. Five types of work appear to be important.

1. Determine the exact status of the present teaching in our public schools. This means an accurate compilation and interpretation of current courses of study from an adequate number of communities—certainly several hundred—selected so as to make a perfectly representative sample of the whole country on such matters as: (a) aims, objectives, and specified outcomes of instruction; (b) scope of the course which is covered in each grade; (c) time devoted to the subjects of each grade; (d) the precise materials used by the pupils—textbooks, activities employed, miscellaneous materials. Also, by the use of trained specialists, adequately financed, analyze by careful quantitative methods and interpret thoroughly the content of school textbooks and other materials and also class activities actually in operation in public schools. The purpose of this is to determine precisely the content and arrangement of our present curriculum. We must know definitely what present practice is in order constructively to evaluate it and scientifically to reconstruct it.

2. Evaluate critically and constructively the scientific investigations of curriculum-making in the subject under consideration that have already been published. In like fashion, borrow and make

similar use of unpublished curriculum studies in our universities and schools of education. The findings of many such investigations are deposited in the libraries of universities like the University of Iowa, University of Chicago, Teachers College, Leland Stanford Junior University, and others.

3. Make and publish an exhaustive evaluation of representative examples of experimental courses. A score or more of important innovations can always be found among the thousands of schools and school systems. Scrutiny and careful weighing of the purposes, programs, and accomplishments of these new types of courses, some of which are truly experimental, are the most important functions of national committees.

4. Test objectively the results obtained from present instruction in a sampling of typical public schools by the employment of standard measures of attainment. This would reveal to what extent pupils have mastered great relationships, principles, and laws; to what extent they have developed a command of technique and have learned how to use it.

5. Make scientific investigations of social and psychological needs for the purpose of discovering what should be included in the courses, to what grades different materials should be assigned, and in what order and arrangement they should be presented. Such investigations should be delegated to expert collaborators—specialists trained in educational research. Similarly, the committee should endeavor to stimulate constructive research by others for the discovery of what ought to be taught and in what grades the material should be given.

C. The Committee As a Clearing-House and a Forum

It should stimulate controversial discussion by publishing and debating with school people generally its own programs, various other programs of work, different hypotheses concerning the selection and arrangement of subject matter, theories of teaching, principles of organization, and the like. It should direct this discussion to the consideration of big and important questions, so that after some years both clear thinking and experimentation will make possible a widespread agreement on fundamental matters. It should get official sanction for, and give widespread publicity to, the findings obtained from the committee's careful investigations, deliberations, and decisions.

D. The Continuing Committee

As a continuing, or standing, body, once its recommendations are put into practice, it should study their application in public schools, collect reactions of school people to the proposed program, test results obtained by different organizations of material found by the committees to be socially valuable, and finally, report these findings periodically to the school public.

XI. Curriculum-Making by National Committees Since 1920

1. The National Committee on Mathematical Requirements (1920-1923)
2. The Classical Investigation (1921-1925)
3. The Modern Language Study (1924, in process)
4. The Preliminary Study of History and related subjects in the schools (1925, in process)

The foregoing statement shows very clearly that money is needed to carry out a modern program of curriculum-making. Until 1920 it was not available. A national committee rarely had more than two or three thousand dollars with which to produce its report. Tens of thousands were really needed for each one to do its work properly.

Curriculum-making was carried on in part through the willingness of universities to subsidize the committee work of its individual officers, and in part by small grants from the National Education Association and other teaching organizations; but money was lacking with which to employ trained executives to conduct nationwide surveys of practices, to set up experiments, and to measure results.

For the last six years there has been no such handicap. Since 1920 several of the great educational foundations have granted large sums of money[22] for the survey of school practice in four of the school subjects and for recommendations for reorganization. The General Education Board, the Commonwealth Fund, the Carnegie Corporation, and the Laura Spelman Rockefeller Foundation have helped to finance enterprises of this kind. Two investigations, dealing with mathematics and the classics, respectively, have been

[22] The grants have ranged from about $60,000 to $100,000.

completed. One (that in the field of modern languages) has been under way for nearly two years. Another (a new inquiry into the organization of history and related subjects) is just now being launched.

During the past few years, therefore, sufficient money has been available to inventory present practices and to set up sound experimentation.

In concluding our discussion of committee procedure let us consider the results of six years of well-financed "investigation."

In doing so, let us keep in mind three questions: (1) Have the committees been staffed so as to represent the manifold difficult professional tasks involved in the construction of the curriculum? Or have they continued to be made up merely of 'specialists' in subject matter? (2) Have the committees viewed the construction of the school curriculum as a whole, or by subjects? That is, has curriculum-making been broad and systematic from the standpoint of American life as a whole, or has it been piecemeal, subject by subject, academic? (3) Have the committees employed objective procedures? Have they based their recommendations upon (a) careful survey of existing practices, (b) the results of scientific studies of learning and of social analysis, (c) the most forward-looking current psychological and educational thought?

The published reports of the first two of these well-financed committees, those which dealt with mathematics[23] and Latin[24] supply data from which we can definitely consider these basic questions.

First: Has the personnel of these committees been constituted of persons specifically trained to carry out the difficult and manifold tasks of curriculum-making?

It has not.

The staffs of the Mathematics Committee, the Classical Committee, and the Modern Language Committee, contained not a single professional student of curriculum-making, not an educational psychologist, not a sociologist, not a critical student of society. The National Committee on Mathematical Requirements was constituted of six university professors of mathematics, five high-school teachers,

[23] *The Reorganization of Mathematics in Secondary Education*; the Mathematical Association of America. J. W. Young, Hanover, N. H.

[24] *The Classical Investigation, Part I, General Report.* Princeton University Press, Princeton, N. J.

one State Commissioner of Education, and one director of mathematics in a state department of public instruction. The Classical Committee consisted of eight university professors of the classical studies and seven high-school teachers. The Modern Language Committee now carrying on its work, consists of 13 professors and 6 high-school teachers and administrators.[25]

Their personnel determined, of course, their point of view and their procedure.

Now, they carried out certain phases of their avowed purpose very well. The large financial support which the committees have enjoyed made it possible to set up effective machinery for inventorying present practices, for sensing the temper of American classrooms. The Mathematics Committee and the Classics Committee adopted the same sort of executive machinery: a central office headed by two full-time, well-paid, experienced persons, one a high-school teacher and the other a college professor.[26] They established most effective machinery for collecting the facts concerning the organization and the teaching of mathematics and classics in the classrooms of the country.

The executives of the committees carried out one aspect of their work in a remarkably thorough-going way. They coördinated the efforts of scores of sectional organizations of teachers. They travelled widely. They question-blanked the entire national school system. They collected the most recent and valid statistics. They were good fact *finders.* They felt the pulse of classrooms all over the country. They studied carefully the educational literature of the reorganization of mathematics and the classics. For the first time in the history of committees, the analysis of school practice was oriented about the current dynamic and inductive point of view in educational psychology. They evaluated the proposals of innovators, and organized the results of *their inventory of what the country could be brought to do* in a program of grade and classroom instruction that advanced materially the organization and teaching of their subjects. The report of the Mathematics Committee, for

[25] The new committee organizing the preliminary investigation of history and related studies in the schools includes one professional student of the curriculum, Ernest Horn.

[26] The three Classics Committee investigators were really all experienced classroom teachers; distinctive progress in committee procedure is, of course, revealed in the composition of this personnel.

example, was the most conspicuous and forward-looking report that had come from the work of any national committee. The work of the investigators can be summed up by saying that it resulted in a clear-cut statement of the extent to which teachers of mathematics could be expected in 1921 (and for the classics, 1925) to put into practice a reorganized scheme of instruction.

Second: Have the 'subject' committees viewed the curriculum as a whole, trying to determine the organization of their departments in relation, first to the institutions, problems, and issues of contemporary life and of their historical development, and second, to the other departments of the school?

Recent national 'subject' committees (like their predecessors) have not viewed the curriculum as a whole. Never have they taken a position aloof and tried to determine the vital social needs of children and adults. Instead, they have been defenders of their particular faiths. They have been special pleaders for their subjects. They have maintained that their function was to inventory present practices. The Classics Report put it: to investigate the "revelant facts of classics teaching" and to formulate programs for improving the teaching of their subject. They never really questioned the wisdom of teaching the existing content. *They assumed that it should be taught.* They stood, like their predecessors of 1890-1920, for the *status quo.*

Never once did these committees open their minds to the really fundamental curriculum questions: Should mathematics and Latin be taught *at all* to all pupils? If so, on what grounds? To whom? With what materials? How chosen? On a broad analysis of the social needs of contemporary America or on the basis of disciplinary values?

Instead of answering these questions the reports (the Classics Report especially, the Mathematics Report much less conspicuously) used their vast arrays of facts to defend the position of mathematics and classics in the curriculum. As one reads the Classics Report especially, he receives the constant impression that the Latinists are on the defense; that they were less concerned to find the truth about desirable content and organization of the curriculum than they were to keep Latin in the high school.

Third: Did these well-financed committees base their recommendations on careful surveys of existing practices, on the results of scientific studies of learning, of societal analysis and upon contemporary psychological thought?

The mathematics committee employed a much more objective procedure than other committees had used, but went almost no further than mere description of present conditions. Meager studies of pupils' interests and of "correlation of grades" were made which contributed almost nothing of value to the problem of determining the content and organization of the mathematics course of study. The personnel of the committee was destitute of professionally trained students of curriculum-making, hence the lack of objectivity and comprehensiveness in its procedure.

The Classics investigators, Messrs. M. D. Gray and W. L. Carr, however, set up an excellent program of investigation and got under way a large number of objective studies. These included, to take only a few typical examples, such studies in vocabulary as the determination of the 25,000 English words most important for reading purposes and the etymological analysis of these words; studies of the reading content of second, third, and fourth-year Latin courses in 100 schools; widespread testing programs in five states to determine the results obtained from current instruction; controlled 'transfer' experiments for the purpose of measuring the influence of Latin instruction on increased ability in English, in French, and other languages. Over 750,000 tests were given to 150,000 pupils in 1313 schools.[27] The facts were collated concerning enrollments in Latin, Greek, and the modern languages in the various years of the high school, the educational qualifications of teachers, and the attitude of state departments with respect to the classics. Measurements were set up, such as that of the ability to read new Latin after the study of Latin had ceased, to understand Latin words, phrases, etc., occurring in English and to understand the exact meaning of English words derived from Latin and increased accuracy in their use, and to speak, read, and write English. The judgments of Latin teachers also were collected concerning desirable changes in the classics curriculum.

The foregoing illustrates the manner in which this committee tried conscientiously to make use of the new techniques of measure-

[27] The schools paid for the test material and the teachers scored the tests and tabulated the results. This indicates the fine spirit with which teachers and administrators coöperated in the work of these national committees.

ment, experimentation, and evaluation that are being developed by the professional students of education.

In view of the investigational program of Messrs. Gray and Carr, therefore, the 'special pleading' character of the Report[28] of the Committee is astonishing. The investigators had collected a vast quantity of data from which to consider the "case of the classics" objectively. Instead of using it objectively, the writer of the report rests his case conspicuously on "disciplinary" values. Let us review the treatment of that problem.

Both committees, mathematics and classics, made much of the problem of "transfer of training." Each collected very carefully the judgment of a considerable number of psychologists as to "whether training transfers." The mathematics committee reprinted and brought up to date my summary of the scientific studies of mental discipline.[29]

To evaluate the work of the committees (we have space for only one illustration) let us consider how they studied one of the major curriculum questions of mental discipline: Does the study of high-school Latin (or mathematics) as now constituted increase one's ability to 'think?' There is only one way by which this question can be answered definitely—by the careful measurement of the ability of a very large group of high-school pupils to 'think' before and after they have had instruction in the subject in question. Did either of the committees undertake to do this? They did not. Professor E. L. Thorndike did, however. He showed by measuring carefully the ability of 9000 tenth-grade pupils before and after taking a year of Latin that one year's study of Latin as now organized does increase one's ability to reason—by a small amount[30]—but that the gain is no larger than that due to the study of other school subjects as now organized. It is of great importance to find, for example, that book-keeping, cooking, and sewing increase one's ability to generalize even more in some instances than does the study of the classics!

---

[28] The authorship of the *General Report* is not stated. It is signed by "*The Advisory* Committee of the Classical League," the chairman of which is Mr. Andrew West of Princeton University.

[29] *The Experimental Determination of Mental Discipline in School Studies.* Warwick and York, 1916.

[30] E. L. Thorndike, "Mental discipline in school studies," *Journal of Educational Psychology,* January and February, 1924.

Did the classics committee discuss the Thorndike investigation? It did—in two sentences. After referring to the fact that the study was made, it says that "the study shows that the amount of growth produced by certain school subjects in the ability measured by this test varies so slightly that no definite conclusions can be drawn therefrom."

Here is a conspicuous instance of the refusal of the committee to consider impartially the facts of objective investigations. Is not the very fact that Latin made no greater contribution in a year to the thinking power of pupils than did commercial or social studies, a "definite conclusion" of importance to the curriculum-maker? Can there be any doubt? Instead of utilizing the Thorndike investigation, the committee collected the judgments of 70 psychologists, following out the program of the National Committee on Mathematical Requirements, as to whether, in their judgment, training transfers.

The General Report of the Classical Investigation is, therefore, a conspicuous illustration of the use of facts to substantiate one's point of view. There never has been another committee report in which statements concerning aims and objectives, the content of the course, and methods of teaching, have been based so completely, page by page, upon quantitative data. The classical investigators carried out their investigational procedure in a way that left little to be desired. The writers of the General Report used their facts excellently to try to secure a better teaching of Latin in the schools. But instead of using the facts to consider whether and to what extent Latin should be taught, they resorted to special pleading for the retention of Latin in the schools.

XII. Summary Discussion

The Personnel and Procedure of National Committees (1892-1926)

We are now in a position to evaluate contemporary American practice in curriculum-making via national committees. From the Committee of Ten to date, national committees have been dominated by specialists in subject matter and by a faith in mental discipline. Their personnel, even to the present time, has only rarely included professional students of the curriculum, that is of child abilities, interests, and capacities, rates of learning, grade-placement, experimentation, and social analysis.

Lacking interest and training in the professional field of curriculum-making, the members of these national committees have used subjective and *a priori* methods in arriving at their recommendations and, with the two recent exceptions, have ignored the results of curricular research. The basis of recommendations throughout has been individual judgment. In the early days there was a great need through roundtable conferences for exchange of views among those who were organizing the curricula of our schools —there is still great need—and because the college men constituted the only group trained to do the job, it fell to their lot to undertake it. Great praise should be given to the hundreds of university men and school administrators who gave freely of their time and energy in those formative years of the national school curriculum.

However, the conclusion can not be escaped that, as the years went on, the technique was not modified to take advantage of progress in the technique of curriculum-making. Once in print, the pronouncements of national committees were quite generally followed, both in major outline and much in detail, by town and city schools throughout the United States. Special academic points of view became entrenched. The curriculum crystallized, became difficult to change. One committee supported another and acquiesced in the elimination of particularly obnoxious elements from the curriculum only after prolonged and reiterated demand from curriculum reformers.[31]

It was curriculum-making by accretion and elimination. New topics were added slowly within the school 'subjects,' but the total reconstruction of the curriculum scheme was never considered by these subject committees.

Until after 1919 there was almost no utilization of objective methods of investigation by these national committees. Careful search of their reports (prior to the report of the National Com-

[31] I recall, for example, the years of argument which were necessary from 1910 to 1917, in the *Central Association of Science and Mathematics Teachers* to secure the elimination from the high-school algebra course of such useless topics as the "factoring of the cubes"! Although we were striving for a complete reconstruction of mathematics to fit the needs of contemporary life, we made progress only by concentrating upon the elimination of particular processes and reorganization around specific themes.

mittee on Mathematical Requirements, 1923) fails to reveal a single instance in which the committee set up experimental and scientific studies to aid them in their choice of recommended content, grade-placement, and organization of the materials of the curriculum.

The case is worse than that, however, for the indictment of the armchair methods of these 'subject-matter' committees. The search reveals practically no use of the conclusions of *available* scientific studies. Not until 1920, with the financing on a large scale of national committees in mathematics, classics, modern languages, and history, did the committee set aside executive investigators actually to make use of quantitative studies of curriculum-making.

The Influence of the Committees Through Courses of Study and Textbooks

In spite of the opinionated basis of the recommendations of the national committees, they have exerted a tremendous influence in shaping the school curriculum. The prestige of their reports was so great that, once published, their recommendations were copied into entrance requirements of universities and they constituted the outline to which textbooks had to correspond if the authors and publishers expected widespread adoption. Both state and local, town and city systems came to base their syllabi definitely upon the recommendations of the committee.[32]

Authors and publishers of entrenched textbooks played an important rôle in this *a priori* committee work. Frequently, they served on the committees and wrote the recommendations. I have before me as I write the report of one national committee representing a great association, in which the outline of topics recommended by the member who wrote the report follows almost exactly—indeed almost verbatim—the order and treatment in his own textbook. According to the statements of members of another committee (one of the most influential of recent national committees), its procedure and recommendations were dominated by the author of the most widely used series of textbooks in that subject.

---

[32] Many examples abound. Professor R. M. Tryon, for example, in reporting a survey (1911) of the content of history instruction in the town and city systems of Indiana proved that the report of the Committee of Eight published in 1909 had influenced directly and systematically the detailed organization of the curriculum in history in those cities. (R. M. Tryon. *Materials, Methods, and Administration of History Study in the Elementary Schools of the United States.* Indiana University Studies, No. 17.)

Naturally, progress in curriculum-making was slow, and will continue to be slow, if such influences are permitted to play an important rôle. It is clear that the curriculum of American schools will be based upon reading materials. It appears to be evident, furthermore, that in carrying on the huge task of preparing and distributing textbooks to 23,000,000 young people, we should make use of the machinery which the great publishing houses have built up.

As matters have stood during the past three decades, however, the 'scissors and paste method' has been used by new authors and publishers desiring to secure widespread adoption of their books and who fear to deviate widely from current practice. New books are made, therefore, from old ones. Since 1895, textbook companies, with an eye to sales, have tended more to form partnerships of 'professors' and public-school workers—superintendents, principals, or teachers. Few schoolbooks get wide adoption that are not prepared by such a partnership of subject-matter authority and practical school administration. The maintenance of the *status quo* is the *desideratum;* innovation is not favored—accepted only grudgingly when new proposals gradually secure a widespread hearing from progressive school people, themselves trained in the new educational teachings.

There is a great need that the publishers of textbooks support programs of more thorough and scientific curriculum-making. Indeed, in their own defense they can well afford to do so. A well-grounded program will make eventually for more stability in the curriculum.

CHAPTER IV

CURRICULUM-MAKING AND THE SCIENTIFIC STUDY OF EDUCATION SINCE 1910

HAROLD RUGG

I

Approximately to 1910 the leadership in curriculum-making was in the hands of college and private-school administrators and of subject-matter specialists, and curriculum-making was dominated by an interest in scholarship, mind training, and knowledge for knowledge's sake. With the close of the first decade of the twentieth century, however, a new and vigorous leadership was offered—that of the students of more objective procedures in education.

Under the leadership of Thorndike,[1] Judd, Cubberley, Strayer, Terman, Whipple, Freeman, Gray, and others, the quantitative method began to be applied to the solution of educational problems. The fact-finding era was launched; it was the day of the question-blank and the school survey. Learning was being experimentally investigated in the laboratory; "tests" had entered the classroom. Thorndike had made available the statistical procedure of the British biometricians (1903); standard deviations and coefficients of correlation were in the air. Promotion plans, the elimination and retardation of children, school buildings, the relation of efficiency of instruction to size of class, the measurement of educational products, and the objective investigation of educational processes—all these and other matters of administrative importance were being studied by the new quantitative technique. It was "administration" that in 1910 to 1915 lured the vigorous minds, and it was dur-

[1] Thorndike, E. L. (1874-). The outstanding leader and initiator of the 'measuring movement' in education. Instructor in Education and Teaching, Western Reserve University, 1898-9; Instructor Genetic Psychology, 1899-01; Adjunct Professor Educational Psychology, 1901-4; Professor since 1904, Teachers College (Columbia University); Director of the Institute of Educational Research; Author of *Mental and Social Measurements, Educational Psychology, Elements of Psychology, Principles of Teaching, Animal Intelligence, The Original Nature of Man, The Psychology of Learning, The Psychology of Arithmetic, The Psychology of Algebra*, etc.

ing this time that a new type of committee personnel and procedure came into existence to further and apply the new methods of educational research.

II

The new movement began with the work of the National Education Association's Committee on Economy of Time, a committee of educationists. The personnel of this committee marked it out sharply from all of the preceding ones. Three of the seven members were professors of education or of educational psychology; three were superintendents of schools; one was a college president. It was organized in 1911 under the leadership of Superintendent H. B. Wilson,[2] was in existence eight years, and made four conspicuous reports.

The antecedents of the committee lay in the work of the Baker[3] Committee on Culture Element and Economy of Time. Economy of time to the Baker committee meant the elimination of a grade or more from the public-school scheme or the rearrangement and recombination of school and professional courses. Beginning with the Wilson Committee, however, economy of time was to be secured through the employment of more 'scientific' methods in the determination of socially worth while materials, their grade-placement, and their organization to fit the *life needs* of pupils. Research began slowly to supplant armchair pronouncement.

In procedure, therefore, as well as in personnel, a turning point was marked. The new committee devoted itself nearly altogether to the utilization of quantitative methods of curriculum-investigation. Indeed, its real aim was to illustrate how these methods could be employed.

The early meetings of the committee revealed the influence of the new measuring movement which was just getting under way. Thorndike's handwriting monograph had appeared in 1910; the Courtis tests in the years following 1909. The reports of the first school surveys of Baltimore, Portland, Cleveland, Salt Lake City, appeared during the years from 1912 to 1915. Programs of annual meetings of the Department of Superintendence included vigorous

[2] Superintendent of Schools in Berkeley, Cal.

[3] James H. Baker, President of the University of Colorado, and primarily instrumental in the organization of the Committee of Ten.

discussions of the new quantitative movement. In these, the four reports of the Committee on Economy of Time played an important rôle. The reports appeared in the Fourteenth (1915), Sixteenth (1917), Seventeenth (1918), and Eighteenth (1919) Yearbooks of this Society[4] and formed the basis of our annual program for four years.

III

The steps by which the new educational measurers began to apply methods of research to the study of the curriculum were: first, the construction and use of tests in arithmetic, spelling, language, algebra, etc.; second, the inventory of the current curriculum by the tabular analysis of 'courses' of study and textbooks; third, the determination of socially worth while skills and knowledge by the tabulation of actual human activities; fourth, and much later, the careful determination of trends in societal development, the chief institutions and problems of contemporary life, standards of appreciation, etc.

A growth in the movement from an initial interest in the mere tabulation of the contents of the existing courses and textbooks towards the difficult analysis of learning and of contemporary society is revealed in the successive reports of the committee. The first report was devoted largely to investigations of standards of attainment in the school subjects, description of experiments under way for economizing time in elementary education and analysis of time-allotments by subjects and grades in representative cities. It is significant, however, that the first report included the result of objective analysis of some dozen investigations of the course of spelling—studies which had been made to determine the words actually used by adults and children in writing. In the main, however, the first report, and to a lesser degree the second, was concerned with the description of existing practices. The second report of the committee, however, illustrates the fact that the quan-

[4] In this connection it is interesting to note that the *National Herbart Society* originally included in its title the words *"for the Scientific Study of Teaching."* In 1902, its name was changed to the *National Society for the Scientific Study of Education.* Not until 1910 was the word "scientific" omitted from the name of the Society, at approximately the very time when scientific methods were beginning to be employed. (For details see the special quarter-century booklet prepared by the Secretary in February, 1926.—*Editor.*)

titative study of the school curriculum was slowly but surely concentrating more attention upon what *should* be taught and was devoting less energy to the analysis of what *was* taught. By the time the second report was issued, a number of objective curriculum-investigations had been completed.

The Bagley[5] investigation of the *Content of American History in the Seventh and Eighth Grades*[6] presented the results of an accurate account of the contents of twenty-three American histories issued under dates of publication ranging from 1865 to 1911. In the field of spelling, from 1910 on, more than a score of investigations were reported of the words actually used in adult and child writing, among which were those of L. P. Ayres,[7] W. N. Anderson,[8] and various studies under the direction of Ernest Horn[9] dealing with the writing vocabulary of bankers and other occupational groups.[10]

From 1913 to 1918, the Illinois Committee on Standardization of Ninth-Grade Mathematics set in motion various investigations of existing content of algebra in the ninth grade. At the University of Chicago from 1915 to 1918, the present writer, chairman of that committee, conducted in collaboration with John R. Clark, investigations of the socially worth while material of algebra, geometry,

[5] Bagley, William Chandler, (1874—). Teacher of Public and Normal Schools, 1895-7, 1901-8; Director of School of Education, University of Illinois, 1908-17; Professor of Education, Teachers College, Columbia University, 1917. Author: *The Educative Process, Educational Values, Human Behavior* (with S. S. Colvin, 1913), *History of the American People* (with C. A. Beard, 1918), *Classroom Management, Craftsmanship in Teaching, Determinism in Education,* 1925, etc.

[6] Bagley, W. C., and Rugg, H. O.: *The Content of American History in the Seventh and Eighth Grades.* Bulletin No. 16, University of Illinois, School of Education, Urbana, Illinois, 1916.

[7] Ayres, L. P. *A Measuring Scale for Ability in Spelling.* The Russell Sage Foundation, 1912-1915.

[8] Anderson, W. N. *Determination of Spelling Vocabulary Based upon Written Correspondence.* University of Iowa Studies in Education, 1917.

[9] Horn, Ernest (1882—). Teacher, 1900-5; Principal University Elementary School, University of Missouri, 1906-8; Assistant in Education, University of Missouri, 1908-9; Professor of Seminary Work and Director of Playground, Colorado State Teachers' College, 1909-12; Scholar in Education, Columbia University, 1912-13; Lecturer, Brooklyn Institute of Arts and Sciences, 1913-15; Professor of Education, State University of Iowa since 1913, and Director of University Elementary School; Director Scarborough School, 1917-18.

[10] Horn, Ernest. *A Basic Writing Vocabulary.* State University of Iowa Studies in Education. In press.

and arithmetic courses, of measured experiments in learning and of results of utilizing standardized tests.[11]

The Third Report[12] of the committee dealt even more largely with the discovery of what skills and factual content *should* be taught. The theory of the quantitative analysis of the curriculum was being rapidly developed. Under Horn's stimulation, discussions were appearing of the utilization of the principles of "frequency," "universality," and "cruciality" of social use. In the Third Report, Mitchell published an outline of his analysis of cook books, factory payrolls, marked-down sales, advertisements, and trade catalogues, which had been made to find out which fundamental arithmetical operations should be taught to all pupils. Camerer tabulated what bankers thought citizens should know about banking. Branom and Reavis tabulated the statistical data of land areas, populations, and trade to determine map location facts in geography. The Third Report continued attempts to determine the content of primary readers by analysis of existing books. Bassett tabulated the content of state and national political platforms from 1860 to 1916 to discover the fundamental recurring problems for the course in civics, and Swisher analyzed the important social science reference books.[13] In the Third Report was continued the practice of discussing the setting of norms and standards.

It was an orgy of "tabulation."

With the Fourth Report,[14] the committee entered upon a new phase of curriculum analysis. That yearbook contained the first synthesis of scientific investigations of learning. In it, school people found definite recommendations as to methods to be employed in the teaching of handwriting, reading, arithmetic, drawing, and music.

IV. The Spreading Influence of the Scientific Movement on Curriculum-Making

After 1920 the studies were characterized by much greater completeness. In 1921, Thorndike published in *The Teacher's Word*

[11] *Scientific Method in the Reconstruction of Ninth Grade Mathematics.* University of Chicago Press, 1918.

[12] *Seventeenth Yearbook* of this Society, Part I.

[13] Until the work of this committee, there was no systematic proposal to ignore the existing "subjects;" that movement was developing independently in laboratory schools. See Chapter V.

[14] *Eighteenth Yearbook* of this Society, Part II.

Book[15] his investigation of the basic 10,000 words needed in the elementary school. Thorndike suggested several practical uses for the list: for example, in determining emphasis in teaching, in establishing grade and age standards, in evaluating textbook vocabularies, in grading and selecting the content of readers, in determining the frequency of phonic elements, etc.

Home Economics Courses were inventoried[16] and studies of home-making were initiated.[17]

By 1923 it was possible to assemble a score and a half of objective studies[18] on which to base the content of the junior-high-school course in mathematics. Important advances were made in the crucial field of the social studies. The Lincoln School Social Science Research Group reported, from 1923 on, a series of systematic analyses of the concepts, meanings, generalizations, map-location facts, and problems and movements underlying the development of contemporary life which should form the foundation of the curriculum in history, geography, civics, and related studies.[19] Ernest Horn synthesized investigations in spelling content made under his direction, carried on new ones, and at the present writing is about to publish a fundamental list of 10,000 words from which the spelling curriculum should be constructed. Since the first report of the Committee on Economy of Time, data have accumulated of the vocabulary of primary readers, second readers, third readers.[20] More recently, elaborate investigations[21] of the vocabularies of cur-

---

[15] Bureau of Publications, Teachers College, Columbia University.

[16] *Home Economics in American Schools.* University of Chicago Press.

[17] See the work of the new Bureau of Home Economics Research at Teachers College, Columbia University.

[18] Schorling, Raleigh. *A Tentative List of Objectives in the Teaching of Junior-High-School Mathematics.* George Wahr, publisher, Ann Arbor, Michigan, 1923.

[19] See, for example, Rugg and Hockett. *Objective Studies in Map Location.* Teachers College Bureau of Publications, 1925. H. Meltzer, *The Social Concepts of Children.* Teachers College Bureau of Publications, 1925. John A. Hockett. *A Determination of the Major Problems of Contemporary American Life* (investigation completed; report in preparation).

[20] See *Sixteenth* and *Seventeenth Yearbooks* of this Society.

[21] Lively, B. A. and Pressey, S. L. "A method for measuring the vocabulary burden of textbooks," *Educational Administration and Supervision,* October, 1923; Powers, S. R. "The vocabulary of high-school science textbooks," *Teachers College Record,* January, 1925; Pressey, L. C. "The determination of the technical vocabulary of the school subjects," *School and Society,* July 19, 1924. Technical vocabularies of the school subjects published in fifteen pamphlets by the Public School Publishing Company.

rently used school textbooks have established that they are extremely technical in character, and that they lack decidedly appropriate recurrence of fundamental meanings. These studies, like those of other aspects of existing curricula, are helpful to determine the direction in which the reconstruction of the school curriculum should move. Studies are under way in a number of educational laboratories to determine the desirable content of the various school subjects. As these investigations accumulate, it will be increasingly possible to fit the content of school textbooks to the mental abilities and attainments of pupils.

By 1920 the scientific movement was directly influencing the public-school curriculum through the new types of school textbooks in the skill subjects. As early, indeed, as 1915, new spelling books appeared in which the content had been selected from the words shown to be actually included in the writing vocabularies of children and adults. General mathematics books and arithmetics were offered to the schools on the argument that the 'skill' operations included in them had been shown by investigation to represent the practical everyday needs of grown-ups and children. Practice exercises in the various elementary-school subjects, and for example, in high-school algebra, were designed on carefully evolved criteria and secured widespread commercial distribution.

The influence of the scientific movement is just now being revealed in the attempt to grade the materials of the school on the basis of proved trial and measured experimentation.[22] There is also emerging a tendency for textbook makers to attempt to apply accepted principles of learning, and conclusions from controlled experiments in the organization of subject matter.[23]

From 1910 the "school survey" has also grown in popularity as an agency for the reconstruction of the school curriculum. More than 150 school surveys of local and state systems have been made and reports published. Included in most of these is an analysis of the course of study. As the investigations have accumulated, school people are slowly becoming more critical in their evaluation of the materials of instruction in their schools.

[22] See unpublished study by Mathews, C. O., *The Grade Placement of Curriculum Materials in the Social Studies.* Teachers College Bureau of Publications, 1926, Columbia University.

[23] See Thorndike, E. L.: *Psychology of Arithmetic,* and *Psychology of Algebra.* Macmillan Co.

In the Lincoln School of Teachers College a number of curriculum-research enterprises have developed since 1920. Several studies have already appeared reporting attempts to validate the materials of the school curriculum.[24] Two systematic reconstructed schemes of curriculum materials have already been developed by the past six years of experimentation in the work of Schorling and Clark in junior-high-school mathematics, and of the Social Science Research Group.

Finally, we have witnessed in the past two or three years the administrative culmination of the various movements in the development of laboratories and bureaus for curricular research. Conspicuous among these has been the development of the Bureau of Research of the National Education Association at Washington, D. C., under the directorship of Dr. John K. Norton and Dr. Margaret Alltucker. A coöperative plan has been organized among a large number of school systems for the revision of the school curriculum. The central bureau at Washington has already published in three yearbooks[25] of the Department of Superintendence and in their various bulletins[26] excellent descriptions of the content of existing curricula, of available research studies, and of discussion of the techniques of curriculum-making. This bureau is a permanent 'going' concern and gives great promise of operating as an effective clearing-house for discussion and improvement of the public-school curriculum.

In Teachers College, Columbia University, there has recently been organized under the direction of Dean James E. Russell, Dr. Herbert B. Bruner, and Miss F. B. Stratemeyer, a bureau of curriculum-research. The first two years' work of this bureau have consisted of a comprehensive analysis of existing school programs as revealed in city and state courses of study.[27]

---

[24] For example, Finley, C. W., and Caldwell, O. W.: *Biology in the Public Press,* Bureau of Publications, Teachers College, 1923. Rugg, Harold, and Hockett, John A.: *Objective Studies in Map Location,* Bureau of Publications, Teachers College, 1925.

[25] Department of Superintendence, *Second Yearbook—The Elementary School Curriculum,* 1924. Department of Superintendence, *Third Yearbook—Research in Constructing the Elementary School Curriculum,* 1925. Department of Superintendence, *Fourth Yearbook—The Nation at Work on the Public School Curriculum,* 1926.

[26] For example, *Keeping Pace with the Advancing Curriculum.* Research Bulletin, Nos. 4 and 5, September and November, 1925.

[27] Bruner, H. B., and Stratemeyer, F. B.: *Rating Elementary Courses of Study,* Bureau of Publications, Teachers College, Columbia University, 1926.

V. New Types of Curriculum-Construction in City School Systems

Young as the movement is, it has already begun to affect the procedure of city school systems, and in a few instances, the technique of state departments of public instruction.[28]

Probably the most conspicuous example of the use of research methods in curriculum-construction in city systems is the work of Dr. Carleton Washburne and his associates in Winnetka, Illinois. During the eight years of his superintendency of schools, Dr. Washburne has not only reorganized the classroom procedure of his school upon a radically individualistic basis but, in addition, has already made several contributions to the objective discovery of needed materials in the school curriculum. Organized as the Winnetka Research Seminar, he and a group of his classroom teachers and principals have produced investigations dealing with the basic facts of the history and geography curriculum for the elementary grades, the grading of elaborate book lists for reading classes, comparative analyses of vocabulary studies to determine the words children are most likely to need to spell, statistical studies of primary reading books to determine the most useful phonograms, analysis of 10,000 commonest words to discover syllables of the greatest frequency of recurrence, measurements of the speed and accuracy possessed by successful and intelligent adults in arithmetical processes, and grade-placement investigations of children's reading books.[29]

As Washburne's Winnetka organization is conspicuous for its scientific and practical curriculum-research, the Denver schools, under the administration of Superintendent Jesse H. Newlon and Deputy Superintendent A. L. Threlkeld, have led the way in experimentation with new types of curricular materials in the elementary and secondary schools, and in the creation of a new type of administrative organization and procedure for curriculum-revision in a large city.[30] The Denver program has been outstanding because of the adequate financial support for curriculum-revision,

[28] See, for example, the recent bulletins of the state department of Connecticut, under the leadership of Commissioner Albert B. Meredith, Hartford.

[29] See Chapter XI of this volume.

[30] See Chapter XII in this book, "The Denver Curriculum-Revision Program," by Jesse H. Newlon and A. L. Threlkeld.

the release of skilful and experienced teachers from active classroom work to enable them to concentrate their efforts upon curriculum-studies and preparation of syllabi, the creation of a separate curriculum division of the central administration in charge of a trained student of the school curriculum, the utilization of outside specialists on curriculum-making who have worked for prolonged intervals with those in active charge of a curriculum-revision, and finally because of the attempt to see the problem of curriculum-revision as a whole. Although the Denver program was carried on by 'subject' committees, already advances have been made by the merging of a number of the traditional subjects.

In a number of the larger cities, programs somewhat similar to that of Denver are in operation or under way. For example, Detroit, Los Angeles, and St. Louis.[31]

In Burlington, Iowa, under the leadership of the former superintendent of schools, Mr. E. M. Sipple,[32] the teachers of the system coöperated for several years in an attempt to break down the lines between the established school subjects and to reconstruct the elementary and junior-high-school curriculum on a basis of five large departments.[33]

Sioux City, Iowa, under the leadership of Superintendent M. G. Clark, is working out a curriculum which at present directs much of the instruction under the two aims which on one side seek growth in power for language expression, and on the other call out ability to understand and take part in the progress of society. For both aims the building of education proceeds by nurturing the personal and fellowship life of each pupil. Both aims seek a means of directing progress in the growth of ever wider relations with human life.

Not only the teachers and the administration but also the pupils in each grade have coöperated step by step to accomplish these ends in Sioux City. The discovery and organization of the required school situations and of the necessary lesson materials is a matter of concern to all if the full nurture of social growth is to be secured by actual as well as by vicarious participation.

---

[31] See Chapters IX, XIII, XIV of this volume.

[32] Now principal of the Park School, Baltimore.

[33] See Chapter X, by Mr. E. M. Sipple, entitled "A Unit-Activities Curriculum in the Public Schools of Burlington, Iowa."

This nurture of the children through active participation requires that they be brought consciously into the entire plan and purpose of the school. Every child seeks information from many sources and through various experiences—even by experiment. Merely to understand a possible meaning in what is presented is but the beginning of knowledge and growth. By checking and testing facts the child exercises judgments which reach toward meanings common to all, and include the dramatic feeling natural to an active participation in the educational process. Gradually a transformed textbook is being worked out which takes the form of a school-developed manual of suggestions and of guidance of study situations as well as that of being one of the sources of information. The recitation, also, is transformed and becomes a conference as well.

For both of these aims of school work a distinct type of literary material is found necessary. Even the best dramatic presentation of the progress of mankind and of personal life in situations stimulating to the thought and imagination of children is not sufficient. In Sioux City success is being reached only as literary material and expressional opportunities are found which keep step year by year with the natural growth of power to understand and feel the full dramatic meaning of the human situations that are involved with instruction. This requires a psychological selection of materials and situations which are found to nurture the natural growth of individual character.

VII. Summary of the Application of Research Methods to Curriculum-Making

The foregoing analysis reveals, therefore, several different types of investigations which have been made as the basis for a more scientific procedure in curriculum-making.

There are two active schools of thought among curriculum-makers. One group emphasizes the preservation of the contribution of the past; the other stresses the more thorough-going discovery of needed next steps. The protagonists of the former view believe in the gradual reorganization of the school curriculum by addition to, or elimination from, the current courses.

Studies of existing curricula. The leaders in this movement are the various bureaus of curriculum-research and such clearing houses for report and discussion as the Bureau of Research of the National Education Association in Washington. For fifteen years they have been tabulating the contents of city and state courses of study, the syllabi of national committees, and the detailed contents of school textbooks.

Studies of social needs. The other school of thought devotes its energy to discovering social needs and basing proposed curricula upon the findings of such research. They stress the premise that curriculum-making consists essentially in the analysis of American life.

This represents one aspect of what this school recognizes as the two-fold problem of curriculum-making. The other is the child—his abilities, interests, and needs as a growing personality. The adherents of this belief are of the opinion that the school curriculum needs to be largely made over, but that that cannot be adequately done by the addition to, or elimination from, the *existing* curriculum. This school of thought, therefore, would make studies of needed materials and in doing so would not be unduly swayed by the existing content. These studies would include the discovery of the skills and facts, the problems, institutions, generalizations, and concepts needed to understand contemporary life; optimal grade-placements; the chief learning difficulties as shown by pupils' traits, abilities as shown by errors; and job analysis in the vocations and professions. Specifically, five other types of studies are needed.

1. Studies of skills and facts of proved social worth. *For economy of time* it is desirable to know which map-location facts, which words, which arithmetical operations and processes, which grammatical forms should be learned by all elementary-school children in order to live together well in modern, interdependent social life. This is especially important because of the need to leave the great preponderance of the pupil's time free to engage in enriching his understanding of himself and of how he and his fellows live together in a complicated world, in bringing over his potential capacity for creative self-expression and for enjoyment of the fine and the beautiful. There are already available many investigational data: lists of words, arithmetical operations, map-location facts, etc., the social worth of which has been proved by objective analysis of human activities.

2. Studies of basic concepts, generalizations, institutions, and problems which are needed for an understanding of contemporary life. Data of these types are coming to be recognized as providing the fundamental skeleton for the entire school course in the social sciences, in the behavior studies, in the literary and artistic fields. On the intellectual side, critical analyses are being launched of vocabulary and of methods by which meanings are developed. In the next few years we shall see the publication of a large number of studies of the psychology of meaning applied to curriculum-making.

3. Studies dealing with grade-placement of material. Already experimentalists are conducting scientific studies to determine the most appropriate ages and grades at which certain types of curricular material can be utilized. I am using the word "scientific" to imply careful organization of controlled experiments, trial of the same materials in a large number of school grades ranging over many ages, and the careful measurement of abilities.

4. Studies of pupil difficulties, errors, and other problems of learning. The movement has already produced tentative studies of pupil difficulties as shown by grammatical errors, the performances of pupils in arithmetic, spelling, algebra, map location, and the like. In the years from 1909 to 1915 scores of learning investigations were carried on. Since 1915, however, with a tremendous swing of interest among educational psychologists and technologists to the investigation of intelligence, educational attainments, and character traits, there has been a great slump in the experimental interest in 'learning.' Because the sound organization of curricular materials will wait for the carrying on of a great many learning studies,[34] it is to be hoped that educationists will secure large financial support for the conduct of such studies. It should be clear, therefore, that national committees with money to spend on educational investigations should by all means endow definite measured investigations of alternative methods of organizing curricular materials.

---

[34] Obviously, one of the key problems of educational psychology is that of "the possibilities and the limitations of training." A committee of this Society, under the chairmanship of Dr. L. M. Terman, will in the near future present a yearbook on this important topic.—*Editor.*

5. Studies of job analysis in the vocations and professions. A large number of analytical studies, many under the direction of Professor W. W. Charters,[35] have already been reported in the field of the vocations and professions. Indeed, these studies have developed techniques of analysis which later on have been utilized in curriculum-research for elementary and secondary schools. Investigations have been made, for example, of traits desirable for the secretarial and pharmaceutical occupations; analyses of the jobs (specifying knowledge and skills needed) in the trades of machinists, bricklayers, paperhangers, the railway boiler-makers, auto mechanics and plasterers, tile setters, the printing vocations, the garment cleaning occupations.[36] Paralleling these, investigations have been made of homemakers' responsibilities, and outlines prepared of short courses of instruction. In these job analyses, trade difficulties have been studied; for example, the difficulties encountered by salespeople or by business executives in handling people. Expert methods which have been found helpful have been assembled in various enterprises.

VIII. To What Extent Can the Selection of Subject Matter Be Made Objective?

With two decades of careful curriculum-study behind us, therefore, we can begin to get a perspective of the efficacy of our various procedures. The story of armchair *vs.* educational laboratory sets out boldly one fundamental question: To what extent can the selection of curricular materials be made objective?

From time out of mind, laymen and school people have discussed the question "What knowledge is of most worth?" Only in our own generation have we systematically attempted to find

[35] Charters, Werrett Wallace (1875-), Teacher Rural School Rockford, Ontario, 1894-5; Principal Model School, Hamilton, Ontario, 1899-1901; Principal of Elementary School, Supervisor of Practice Teaching, etc., State Normal School of Winona, Minnesota, 1904-7; Professor of the Theory of Teaching, 1907-17; Dean of School of Education, University of Missouri, 1910-17; Professor of Education, University of Illinois, 1917-19; Professor of Education and Director of Research Bureau for Retail Training, Carnegie Institute of Technology, 1919-1925; Research Director, Stevens College, 1920; Professor of Education, University of Chicago, 1925. Author: *Methods of Teaching, Teaching the Common Branches, Curriculum Construction,* etc. Editor of *Beverley Educational Series.*

[36] See Chapter XXVII, by W. W. Charters, in this volume.

bases other than that of the personal opinion of the text writer, theorist, professors of collegiate subjects, committee members, what not. In the past it has been very difficult, if not impossible, for even the greater minds[37] to maintain clear perspectives.

It is exactly that tendency of individual human judgment to lose its bearings and fail to "see the woods for the trees" that has led the more scientifically-minded students of education to take the basis of curriculum-making out of the realm of individual judgment. They have been experimenting of late with the criterion of social utility and especially with objective bases of selection. It was natural in the first rush of the movement, with the initial impulse to play with the new idea, that its disciples should have been carried to extremes. It cannot be doubted that many of our workers to-day are dominated by the belief that only those facts, principles, and motives shall be taught in the school which can be utilized immediately and generally by a considerable proportion of our people. If perpetuated, this attitude will result in a mechanistic curriculum of the rankest sort. This view is already serving to make uncritical workers over-emphasize the skills and the factual knowledge of the curriculum.

The Great Goals of Education Are Matters of Human Thought and Feeling, But Even Their Determination Is Profoundly Influenced by the Scientific Study of Society

We can orient our discussion by pointing out a partial distinction between the determination of the purposes of education and the subject matter. The purposes of education, the great guiding outcomes, are ultimates of life. They are discovered by thought and feeling. They are personal, subjective, and individual. Society has evolved a system of creative thought and (on a less advanced plane) one of creative feeling. One of the chief contributions must be a clear orientation as to the outcome of education. The setting up of goals, therefore, is a matter of judgments—of the best judgments we can find. It is a matter of judgment, however, framed by minds confronted by a particular social order. The judgment of the great minds of the meditative East, for example, will be very unlike that of the intellectual leaders of the industrial Occident.

[37] For example, Herbert Spencer's emphasis on "Science" in his famous essay.

Now, it is of great importance for the curriculum-maker to see that the determination of goals for a given social order will be most soundly made only when he has at hand adequate knowledge and a deep and broad perspective of that social order. *The task of stating the goals of education, therefore, is not to be consummated by an analysis of social activities alone. It will be aided by the latter, but must not be dominated by it.* It will be achieved only by hard thinking and by the most prolonged consideration of facts by the deepest seers of human life. For the great bulk of our curriculum, therefore, the analysis of social activities will influence the judgments of frontier thinkers; but it is the judgment of the seer based upon the scientific study of society—not the mere factual results of social analysis—that will determine the more intangible, but directing materials of our curriculum.

Social analysis merely gives us the techniques and knowledges we should have on tap. For the basic insights and attitudes we must rely, as we do for the statements of the goals of education, upon human judgment. It is imperative, however, that we make use of only the most valid judgments. The forecasting of trends of social movement, the perception of the focal problems and issues, and the connections underlying them, demand erudition and maturity of reflection that eventuates only from prolonged and scientific study of society. To the frontier of creative thought and of deepest feeling we go for guidance as to what to teach.

CHAPTER V

CURRICULUM-MAKING IN LABORATORY SCHOOLS

HAROLD RUGG

I

In the rise of mass education in America, following the middle of the century, two opposing theories contended for supremacy: the doctrine of discipline and the doctrine of growth and initiative. Corresponding to those doctrines, two sects arose among laymen and professional school people. These groups, avoiding the more difficult task of thinking to the bottom of the apparent issue, ranged themselves at the two extreme ends of a scale of scholastic theory and practice. Occasionally, others appeared at points somewhere between, seeking a truer educational theory in the integration of the elements of both extremes.

Now, for centuries educational 'reformers'—Comenius, Rousseau, Pestalozzi, Herbart, Froebel, to name a few conspicuous leaders of earlier epochs—have pointed out that educational systems have always tended to set up a conflict between adulthood and child life, between the logical and the psychological, control and freedom, iron rule and spontaneity. But never until our own generation has there been such a vivid picturing of thought concerning the age-long conflict. Industrialism, with its vast machinery for the dissemination of ideas, its cheap and voluminous print, its mass education, and its elaborate training of teachers, has greatly facilitated the discussion and probably expedited the conciliation of certain parties to the issue.

Nevertheless, the conflict rages in our own day, made especially vivid by the expansion of our pedagogical vocabulary. Witness the prevalence in our contemporary educational literature of 'interest *vs.* effort,' 'order *vs.* chaos,' 'subject matter *vs.* child's experience,' 'habit-forming *vs.* self-expression.' The two extremes are represented by schools and school systems which are 'going concerns' in our educational order. There are those, on the one hand, who would have a curriculum made up of formal, carefully organized subjects of study, systematized lessons, rigorous examinations, set practice exercises, and recitations. And there are others who visualize the curriculum as a stream of child activities not broken up in any systematic manner into 'subjects' and growing out of the spontaneous interests and the personally felt needs of children.

The advocates of the most rigorous point of view are concerned lest children grow to adulthood without an adequate grasp of what the human race has accumulated; hence, their emphasis is upon thorough training in logical thinking, upon law, upon systematization of thought. The advocates of freer education, on the other hand, wish to guarantee the continuous personal growth of the child; hence their concentration upon freedom, upon initiative, upon spontaneity, upon vivid self-expression. The apparent conflict, therefore, is between the preservation of race experience and progressive change, between 'subject-matter-set-out-to-be-learned' and the 'unity of child life.' Thus, each decade for half a century has had its 'new' education, sponsoring in an increasingly more vigorous way the guidance of the child's natural impulses or urges, and decrying routine, over-systematization, the repression of native activity.

In brief, therefore, the two extreme schools of thought are to be distinguished in the degree to which one concentrates the effort of the school in exclusive preparation for adult life, the other on the dynamic active growth of the child himself.

II

It should be clear from the earlier chapters of this section that those who have determined the content and organization of the curriculum in the past century—text writers, and school and college administrators—have belonged predominantly to the former of these schools. Their criteria of education have been based upon the growth of discipline, logical thinking, power of sustained effort, classified knowledge. They have coveted better scholarship, exact knowledge, continuity of racial development. They have almost never had clearly in the forefront of their thought, the active growth of the pupil through dynamic whole-hearted self-expression. Hence, the strangle hold of algebra, Latin, ancient history, physics, chemistry, biology, etc.—all of them 'subjects' represented by carefully 'systematized' bodies of printed materials and logically organized methods of teaching. The automatic perfection of the machinery which has been set up for instruction in these subjects has blinded teachers and administrators to the dynamic value of the less easily systematized child activities.

The regimentation of the public-school system set up by the formalists is being broken down in our generation by the efforts of two groups: These two (the "free" educationists and the students of the scientific study of education), although representing very different backgrounds, strive for the same end. I think the leaders of both groups recognize two factors in the educative process—on the one hand the child, a bundle of undeveloped capacities, of dynamic tendencies toward activity, dependent upon his environment for the proper stimulation for growth; on the other, American civilization, a body of economic, political, and cultural institutions, towards which, so far as an individual is a social being, growth must proceed. They see these institutions as an intricate array of ideals, purposes, guiding concepts, principles, expressions of the artistic impulse, standards of beauty. They recognize the task of curriculum-making as that, first, of organizing activities and materials for the development of a fine understanding of this civilization of ours, and second, of bringing the child into contact with them in such a manner that he will gradually grow in maturity of understanding of the contemporary institutions, in tolerance for current issues and problems, and in effectiveness of self-expression.

But the fundamental criterion of success in curriculum-making, according to these two groups of students of the school, is *the growth of the child.* This standard has been sponsored almost not at all by the subject-matter specialists; indeed, only to a slight extent by the 'scientific educationists' (whose minds have been much concentrated of late on their techniques.)

Now, for fifty years this point of view has been adopted in America by a mounting number of educational leaders and teachers. For three decades it has been the central criterion of an increasing number of the 'free,' 'laboratory,' or 'progressive' schools[1] of the

[1] Typified by the F. W. Parker School of Chicago, the Laboratory Schools of the University of Chicago, The Lincoln, and Horace Mann Schools of Teachers College, The City and Country School, The Experimental School of the University of Iowa, the Winnetka Public Schools (since 1920); The Walden School, The Children's University School, New York; The Park School, Baltimore; The Beaver Country Day School, Boston; and others. See the following chapters of this volume.

country. To a brief historical sketch of their theories and practices we shall now address ourselves.

III. Three Chief Factors in the Development of Laboratory Schools (1875—)

The development since 1875 of a freer type of education in America rests, of course, upon the gradual accumulation of the influence of earlier educational reformers, especially of the Europeans —Pestalozzi, Herbart, and Froebel—and, indigenous to our soil, Horace Mann. A more complete history of 'free education,' or 'education for growth,' (whatever caption is preferred) would trace the manifestations of these century-old influences. However, because this chapter is intended merely as a brief introduction to the consideration of contemporary matters, we shall trace out only the direct steps leading to the current activity in the 'free schools.'

It is common practice among educationalists to refer to the work of Dr. John Dewey in establishing the Laboratory School at Chicago as the starting point of the movement for the development of experimental schools in America. In reality, two important influences were in active operation for some years; one prior to the beginning of Mr. Dewey's work and the other concurrent with it: first, the work of Colonel F. W. Parker,[2] and second, the work of Teachers College, and its Horace Mann School from 1887, and its Speyer School from 1899. Mr. Dewey's influence therefore, constitutes one of the three fundamental factors in the breaking up of the lock step of the graded school.

A truly complete account of the impetus behind the movement would give a prominent place to the work of William James.

Such an account would also discuss the Oswego Movement, which had its beginnings in a philanthropic enterprise called "The Orphan and Free School Association." It was organized by Edward A. Sheldon in 1848. The institution, conceived to provide free education for Oswego's poor, received great attention in the early years of its history and Sheldon and his associates used the interest so stimulated to bring into being in 1853 a free city public-school system. Sheldon was appointed secretary and worked out definite courses of study for each grade from the primary classes through the high school.

---

[2] As Superintendent of Schools of Quincy, Massachusetts (1875-80), Principal of the Cook County, Chicago, Normal School (1883-1899), Principal of the Chicago Institute (1899-1901), and first Director of the School of Education at the University of Chicago (1901-02).

The curriculum of the Oswego schools was oriented about the religious aim of education in which Sheldon believed implicitly. He recognized a lack in the school practice, however; and a trip to Toronto convinced him that vivification through pictures, "charts of colors," reading charts, and books was controlled through "The Home and Colonial Infant and Juvenile Society." The following year saw the reconstruction of the curriculum at Oswego which finally emerged as one having five subdivisions, each included because of its contribution to the understanding of God, His Works, and His Words.

Sheldon trained his own teachers, grade by grade. Finding this impractical, in 1861 the Oswego Primary Teachers Training School was established. Sheldon claimed that his training school was the first on the continent. A Model School for observation purposes followed shortly after. In 1881 a kindergarten was established and in 1885 a curriculum was made for the preparation of teachers in industrial work.

The acquisition of knowledge chiefly through object teaching was the most striking innovation upon which the movement grew.

IV. The Pioneer Work in Curriculum-Making of Colonel Francis W. Parker

In 1875, Colonel Francis W. Parker, for 20 years a district teacher, principal, and superintendent of schools in New England and a distinguished officer of the Federal Army in the Civil War, was invited to become Superintendent of Schools of Quincy. Following the close of the Civil War Colonel Parker had spent three years in the University of Berlin, Germany, in graduate study. At that time Charles Francis Adams, by a careful study of the curriculum of the local high school, convinced his associates on the Quincy School Board that the curriculum of the elementary and secondary schools should be radically modified to give less dominance to the doctrine of mental discipline and to emphasize contemporary life more than the "philological and archeological study of the dead days!"

In Quincy, Parker served under the trusteeship of Adams for five spectacular years. At that time, in the midst of reactionary New England, the conventional and artificial school curriculum was markedly vitalized. There was less emphasis upon the memorization of the facts of textbooks and more upon the study of real things. Lessons in science and geography were based upon firsthand observation out of doors. Reading became an exercise in the acquiring of meanings, rather than in the learning of the techniques of oral pronunciation. The schoolroom became a pleasant place of activity. Teachers were brought into the reorganization of the materials and methods of instruction. A central place in the whole curriculum was given to geography and nature study "and the sand table in the schoolroom and the sand piles in the school yards were extensively used in the development of concepts of structure." The skills were taught in connection with other subjects, and language usage took the place of formal grammatical analysis.

Great enthusiasm for the methods of Colonel Parker and his associates developed among the educational liberals of the country, but suspicion grew among the conservative New England school men in whose midst they worked. Under the criticism of the latter, a survey[3] was made of the schools of Norfolk County in 1880 to find out whether the children in addition to being "amused and happy" really learned the "three R's." The State Board of Education conducted an examination in reading, writing, and spelling, written and mental arithmetic, geography, and history. The Quincy pupils excelled the pupils of the other systems tested in all the subjects except mental arithmetic.

Colonel Parker served as one of the assistant superintendents of the schools of Boston from 1880 until 1883, at which latter date he was elected principal of the Cook County Normal School (now the Chicago Normal College). For eighteen years, under his leadership, that institution was a great storm center of educational reform.

During the five years at Quincy, summer schools and institute classes had developed for the training of teachers in the use of new content and organization of materials and in the new methods. The same result eventuated on a larger and more organized scale in Chicago where a kindergarten and an elementary school for practice teaching was maintained from the outset as an essential element in it.

From the beginning, Colonel Parker was compelled to fight both the enmity of partisan politicians who hampered him at every stage of his work and the conservatism of school principals and teachers. By the most unfair and unreasonable examination of his Practice School they tried to injure him and his reputation.

---

[3] Walton, G. A.: *Report of the Schools of Norfolk County, Mass.* Boston, 1880. (The letter "C" in the report refers to the Quincy Schools.)

Nevertheless, he built up in the Cook County Normal School a faculty of experimentalists, of fearless innovators, real students of childhood, and a practice school which proved an influential object lesson for both teachers and the general public. From beginning to end, his mind was upon the production of a higher quality of teacher, and hundreds of young men and women were attracted to the Chicago Normal School by the new regime. The school became a national pedagogical center. The entire work of the practice school was concentrated through experiments and investigation on the work of teaching. It was a great innovation and antedated the schools of observation and practice in all other institutions.

Perhaps the central doctrine in the curriculum-making of Parker's group was that of the Herbartian principle of *correlation and concentration.* He and his Herbartian colleagues saw the growth of the child, especially character building and intelligent citizenship, as the aim of education. In the early discussions of the National Herbart Society[4] Parker constantly reiterated that *the child* was the correlating center of education, not 'history,' not 'nature study,' not 'geography,' or any other subject.[5] He persuaded his entire faculty to unite in the attempt to construct a "course of study" in which the elements of subject matter would be correlated around one great theme, namely, that of effective citizenship and community life. The one question which he asked in selecting subject matter was: "What knowledge does this class need for its present life?" Their selection of subjects of study was not hedged in by the formal classification of knowledge.

Specifically, by concentrating upon effective living as the goal, Parker and his staff made fundamental changes in the organization of the school subjects. They tried to correlate them around the central studies of nature study, history, geography. The work of these studies, for example, and the demand for scientific apparatus and arithmetic suggested the things which children could make in the manual training classes of the practice school. "Thus manual training became interwoven for all classes of study." Instead of formal oral reproduction of the printed symbols of arithmetic, an

---

[4] Now the National Society for the Study of Education.

[5] See especially *First* and *Second Yearbooks of the National Herbart Society,* 1895, 1896.

understanding of number was to be acquired through the close correlation of practical and other types of number work actually needed in the study of various subjects. Skill in expression was to be developed by practice in "the immediate manifestation of thought."

All the school subjects were to be organized in terms of their intrinsic correlation—history and geography were useless without one another. So with geology as the history of geography and their relationships with mineralogy. Sociology was visualized as the study of the environment and home of man.

For geography, in place of the "memorization of a conglomeration of unrelated statements," the Parker group applied the work of Ritter and Guyot in the humanizing of an understanding of the physical world. Parker saw that for a child to understand man he must have more than a mere knowledge of one subject called "history;" facts culled from "anthropology, ethnology, philology, and a long series of sciences united in philosophy" must be used in building up an interpretation. He "wanted history to grow out of a study of contemporary institutions." "Two hours in a great rolling mill means a genuine profitable study of history. Such a study prepares children for the history of the great industrial developments."

Thus, it can be seen that Parker was aiming at the same goal as those who to-day are trying to build up a new synthesis of knowledge. He and the Herbartians were one in their aim of unification of the compartmentalized organization of the subject matter of the curriculum, and in carrying out their aims, they both attempted to reach this goal by correlating existing subjects of study.[6]

Through Stanley Hall, Parker came under the influence of Wilhelm Wundt.[7] His faculty turned eagerly to the new literature of laboratory investigations and experiments which Parker described

---

[6] The facts of this statement are from an Account of the Work of the Cook County and Chicago Normal School from 1883 to 1889, written by Colonel Parker in the summer of 1899 after he had left the Normal School and become president of the Chicago Normal Institute, and published in the *Elementary School Teacher and Course of Study,* Vol. 2, 1902, p. 752. See also the first five *Yearbooks of the National Herbart Society,* 1895-1899.

[7] Organizer of the first psychological laboratory in Europe, at the University of Leipzig. Hall and Cattell were among the first students to go to Leipzig to learn the new methods of precise mental measurements.

as a "more or less scientific child study." The Practice School included "a certain number of defective and backward children." Experimental methods developed with these children brought forth helpful suggestions for methods to be used with normal pupils.

As a result of the first twelve years of innovating work in this remarkable school, ahead of its times, the Cook County Normal School published in 1895, what appears to have been the first *course of study* on the "basis of correlation and under the ideal of community life." Descriptions of new types of materials were studied by tens of thousands of public-school teachers, and new devices and methods were practiced.

V. Parker and the Laboratory Schools of the University of Chicago

In 1899 Mrs. Emmons Blaine gave Colonel Parker one million dollars to endow the Chicago Institute,[8] a private training school for teachers. It was her aim that he should have an opportunity to develop his work free from political turmoil and unhampered by the conventional and financial limitations of a public normal school.

There was delay in the erection of the new building and meanwhile, President William Rainey Harper, of the University of Chicago, suggested the inclusion of the Institute within the University campus and the fusing of it and three other institutions into a School of Education under Colonel Parker's directorship. This plan included beside the Chicago Institute; the Dewey Laboratory School, (founded by John Dewey in 1896, with Mrs. Dewey as principal, as the laboratory and experimental school for the University Department of Education and Philosophy of which he was head) the South Side Academy (a private preparatory school for the University established in 1892 and managed by Dr. W. B. Owen) and the Chicago Manual Training School (fostered by the Commercial Club of Chicago) with Dr. Henry Holmes Belfield as its head.

---

[8] The facts concerning the Chicago Institute and the development of the School of Education at the University of Chicago have been supplied in part by Miss Katherine Stillwell, a teacher in the School of Education from its beginning.

VI. The Doctrine of Growth and the Development of the Free Education Movement

In 1892 William James gave a series of lectures which resulted later in his published *Talks to Teachers.*[9] In that book and in his earlier *Psychology* (1890), the thesis was developed that "education is for behavior and habits are the stuff of which behavior consists." From that time to this, the movements for the reconstruction of education have been oriented on the need for child activity more than upon any other one central doctrine. John Dewey's various writings and the philosophy of many of the laboratory schools which have developed since 1900 were organized fundamentally around that principle.

The theory of the organization of the school curriculum on the principle of continuous child growth rests upon half a century of development following the evolutionary pronouncements of Charles Darwin and his successors. These gave the psychologists their cue for the reconstruction of their ideas of child learning and of the development of curriculum materials. Education was seen in terms of growth—physical, intellectual, emotional, and moral. The criterion of excellence of an educational system was: *Does it produce the constant tendency toward growth? Creative self-expression, rather than the learning of subject matter, was to be the desideratum.* Education was to become dynamic, not static; psychological, not logical. Child activities were to be the core of the curriculum—not studies and lessons. Life experience would orient teaching, not subject matter, ready made.

In the development of educational philosophy on this principle of dynamic child life John Dewey has played the leading rôle during the first quarter of the twentieth century.

VII. The Development of the School of Education from Dewey to Judd

The Impetus to the "Free" School Movement of the Work of John Dewey

Dr. John Dewey succeeded Colonel Parker as Director of the School of Education in 1902. Dewey for years had been active in

[9] James, William. *Talks to Teachers.* Henry Holt, New York City, 1899.

university departments of philosophy.[10] Upon his connection with the University of Chicago, however, he became head of the Department of Education and Philosophy from the founding of the University of Chicago in 1894. His Laboratory School of the University of Chicago, it will be remembered, had become part of the School of Education.

The years which he spent from 1884 in the philosophical field gave him a broad perspective from which to view the rôle of the national educational system on the American scene of 1895 to 1905. His theories developed around the same nucleus of life activities that had served as the orienting center of Parker's work. Indeed, Parker's first syllabus of his training course for the New School of Education[11] credits Dewey with being one of the half-dozen forces operating in the educational situation of the time.

Dewey displayed a catholicity of interest. In 1894 he published his "Interest as Related to Will" in the *First Yearbook of the National Herbart Society*.[12] In 1896 the supplements of the National Herbart Society discussed the fundamental principles of the reorganization of American education. His essay which developed from that presentation, entitled "Ethical Principles Underlying Education," appeared in the *Third Yearbook* of the Society (1897). In this essay he developed the theses which have served more widely than any other previously stated theory as the orienting basis for the reconstruction of the work of education.[13]

---

[10] John Dewey (1859—), Instructor and Assistant Professor of Philosophy, University of Michigan, 1884-8; Professor of Philosophy at University of Minnesota, 1888-9, and University of Michigan 1889-94; Professor and head of Department of Philosophy and Education, University of Chicago, 1894-1904; Director School of Education, University of Chicago, 1902-4; Professor of Philosophy, Columbia University, 1904.

[11] *Elementary School Record*, 1902.

[12] In this, after discussing the current opposition of the theories of interest and effort, he sets forth the psychological foundation of the vital dependence and inter-relationship upon each other of interest and effort and their utilization in the educative activities of the school.

[13] *The Educational Situation*. Contributions to Education, No. 3, University of Chicago Press, 1902.

In 1895 Dewey collaborated with James A. McLellan in the publication of a psychological analysis of arithmetic. In that book (James A. McLellan and John Dewey. *The Psychology of Number*. 1895. Appleton) the thesis was maintained, for example, that the idea of number develops best through practical measurement and around the ratio meaning of number. The authors illustrated their theories by outlining a course of study in arithmetic. Five years

In the years following 1896 Dewey developed his theory in connection with the University Elementary School and contributed papers on the practical reconstruction of the elementary and secondary school. His breadth of interest ranged all the way from the minutiae of administration to the social and ethical foundations of curriculum and method.

In 1899 appeared the first three essays of his *The School and Society*.[14] These represented papers which had been read at meetings of the parent-teacher association of the Laboratory School. They expanded the theory which had already appeared in *Ethical Principles Underlying Education,* in 1902.

It is probably safe to say that Dewey's *The School and Society* and his later *The Child and the Curriculum*[15] have influenced the thought of teachers in service and teachers in training in educational institutions as profoundly as any other educational writings of the past generation. His little monograph, *Interest and Effort in Education,*[16] published some ten years later, has also played an important part in inspiring teachers with the newer point of view. In 1895 the original monograph, (called *Interest as Related to Will*) had appeared in the *First Yearbook of the National Herbart Society.*

In 1904, Dewey said of the Laboratory School (which was by that time a part of the University of Chicago) that it was operated "especially for the purpose of scientific investigation and research into the problems connected with the psychology and sociology of

---

later this was systematically developed by McLellan and Ames (McLellan, J. A., and Ames, A. F. *Public School Arithmetic based on Dewey's 'Psychology of Number,'* Macmillan, 1897) in a practical arithmetic textbook. The ratio meaning of number was made the unifying basis of instruction and practical measuring activities were introduced. That *The Psychology of Number* received close attention from students of arithmetic teaching is illustrated by the fact that it appears in practically every important bibliography on the subject during the past twenty years.

---

[14] Dewey, John, *The School and Society,* first edition 1899; second edition 1915; 18th impression, May, 1925. The second edition and the current impression included in addition to the original three essays (*The School and Social Progress, The School and Life of the Child, Waste in Education*) five others, parts of which had appeared from time to time in his articles in *The Elementary School Record.*

[15] Dewey, John, *The Child and the Curriculum.* University of Chicago Press, 1902; 18th impression, December, 1923.

[16] Dewey, John, *Interest and Effort in Education.* Riverside Educational Monographs, Houghton Mifflin, 1913. Pp. 102.

education. Its aim was to further the application of scientific concepts and methods to the conduct of school work.'' This statement is interesting because of its emphasis upon ''scientific research.'' The literature of experimental education of twenty-five years ago abounds with references to the need of using the techniques which were being developed in the older and well established sciences. Both Dewey and Parker in Chicago and the Teachers College, Horace Mann, and Speyer School groups under Russell made frequent reference to the need of using scientific method in the reconstruction of education. This was some years prior to the real beginnings of the work of Thorndike or Judd in the development of scientific and experimental work in educational research.

In his writing about the school, Mr. Dewey distinguished the experimental nature of his Laboratory School from the work done in the earlier ones, but the records which the *Elementary School Teacher* presents of the work of the Laboratory School, do not reveal clearly a substantial difference in its scientific and experimental work from that of the Quincy Schools, the Practice School in the Cook County Normal School, the Horace Mann Practice School, and the Speyer School. Their purposes were certainly very similar. They were striving to illustrate the reconstruction of education on the basis of maximal child growth and a richer understanding of community and national life. These leaders of the 'protest' schools were oriented by children's ''full spontaneous interests and intentions,'' and urged that school subjects, like reading, writing, and arithmetic, should develop out of children's 'life activities' and methods of living and learning—not out of 'distinct studies.'[17]

The life of the school was to be active, not passive; the children were to work, not merely to listen. The curriculum was to be organized around four chief impulses: ''the social instinct of the children,'' ''the instinct of making—the constructive impulse,'' ''the expressive instinct—the art instinct,'' and in the ''impulse toward inquiry, or finding out things.''

In the years following 1904, Dewey developed his psychological and educational theories and published these in two systematic books.[18]

---

[17] Dewey, John, *The School and Society*, p. 11.

[18] Dewey, John, *How We Think*, D. C. Heath, 1909; and *Democracy and Education*, Macmillan, 1916.

VIII. The Laboratory Schools and the School of Education at the University of Chicago Since 1904

In 1904 Professor Dewey left the University of Chicago to become professor of philosophy at Columbia University, a position which he holds to the present time. From 1904 to 1906, President Harper directed the School of Education and was succeeded from 1906 to 1909 by President H. P. Judson. Until 1904, Professor W. S. Jackman was Dean of the College of Education. This position Dr. Nathaniel Butler held from 1905 to 1909 and William B. Owen[19] and Professor H. H. Belfield were joint principals of the University High School. Mrs. John Dewey was principal of the Laboratory School from 1896 to 1904. In 1902 the name was changed to the University Elementary School.

In 1909 the School of Education was reorganized and the Department of Education was separated from the Department of Philosophy. Dr. Charles H. Judd[20] was made Director of the four-fold organization, including the two laboratory schools, the undergraduate college of education, and the graduate department of education.

The School of Education of the University of Chicago assumed a new leadership in the reorganization of education. Under Mr. Judd's direction the interest of the School became primarily the development of the scientific study of education. Parker and Dewey had earlier advocated the use of scientific method. However, lacking the techniques of science and being, in one case, interested essentially in practical school administration and, in the other, in educational theory, they had done little more than lay the groundwork for a scientific analysis of child learning, the reorganization of the curriculum and school administration.

By 1909, however, scientific methods were coming into their own in both Columbia and Chicago. Under the leadership of Thorndike

[19] Principal, since 1909, of the Chicago Normal College.

[20] Judd, Charles H. (1873-) studied with Wilhelm Wundt, University of Leipzig, 1894-96; Instructor of Philosophy, Wesleyan University, 1896-8; Professor of Psychology, New York University, 1898-1901; Professor of Psychology and Pedagogy, University of Cincinnati, 1901-2; Instructor, Assistant Professor and Associate Professor of Psychology, Yale, 1902-7; Professor of Psychology and Director of Psychological Laboratory, Yale, 1907-9; Professor and Head of Department of Education and Director of School of Education since 1909, also Chairman of Department of Psychology since 1920, University of Chicago.

in New York and Judd in Chicago, the new scientific movement got definitely under way. The Laboratory Schools, while continuing a vigorous interest in child activities and child growth combined, began slowly to attempt to analyze the learning process under laboratory conditions. Under Judd's stimulation a decade and a half of active laboratory analysis of learning in reading, handwriting, and arithmetic was inaugurated. In the same time the School of Education, through its *Elementary School Journal* and *School Review*, lent great impetus to the movement for the reorganization of the grades of the public school. It would not be counted an exaggeration to say that the work of Judd and his associates in those formative years was one of the two or three chief influences which brought about the junior high school, the expediting of the scientific study of the learning process, and the measurement of school practice.[21]

IX. Two Decades of Practical Application of Colonel Parker's Theories: The Francis W. Parker Laboratory School of Chicago, 1901—

"The Francis W. Parker Laboratory School was organized in 1901.[22] Two years before this, Mrs. Emmons Blaine, a public-spirited Chicago woman, deeply interested in education, succeeded in persuading Colonel Francis W. Parker to leave the Chicago Normal School where he had been principal for sixteen years, for a wider and freer field of work.

"Colonel Parker left the Normal School only after he had thoroughly convinced himself that because of the political situation controlling the Chicago School Board, he could work more effectively for public school education outside the system.

"An initial gift of a million dollars was made to establish Colonel Parker's Normal Practice School work on the north side of Chicago. Members of Colonel Parker's old faculty, about eighteen in number, who were selected to go with him to the new school, were given a year's leave of absence for study on full salary, while the building plans were being prepared. In the fall of this

[21] See Chapter IV for further references to this movement.

[22] This quotation is from a statement written by Miss Flora J. Cooke, Principal of the school, in the summer of 1926.

year, 1900, only the plans were completed and the school, called at this stage, the 'Chicago Institute,' went into temporary quarters.

"The intention was to build immediately, but Dr. Harper and the trustees of the University of Chicago approached Colonel Parker, offering a very advantageous proposition to him for moving his school to the south side, where it would become part of 'The School of Education,' of the University of Chicago. After some weeks of serious consideration, Colonel Parker and his faculty, with the full approval of Mrs. Blaine, decided that the University of Chicago offered a much wider field for the work. Therefore, the university's invitation was accepted.

"At this juncture, Mrs. Blaine offered to build an elementary school for the benefit of those children who were already registered for the new north side school, and she guaranteed any deficit in the running expenses for such a school which might occur during the period of ten years.

"In the fall of 1901 the Francis W. Parker Laboratory School on the north side was opened, with Flora J. Cooke as Principal and Ira M. Carley as Associate Principal. The first faculty consisted of sixteen members, eleven women and five men, made up largely of teachers who had had their training in the Cook County and Chicago Normal School under Colonel Parker. In 1926, after twenty-five years, four of these teachers are still members of the faculty, and many others have had the inspiration of Colonel Parker's training through the teaching of members of his old faculty."

It is of interest to the student, therefore, to note the close connection between the Cook County Normal School group, the School of Education of the University of Chicago, the F. W. Parker School (all immediately under Colonel Parker's influence), and the initial staff of The Lincoln School of Teachers College. The similarity in points of view and in method of approach in the early years of these schools is illustrated by the fact that the staffs of these institutions included a number of the same individuals.

From the beginning, the outline of the school curriculum was framed in accordance with the conventional school departments: history, geography, mathematics, English, etc. The instruction of the high school (which for many years was merely a vitalized college preparatory school) has, throughout its twenty-five years been organized definitely in accordance with the school subjects. In the elementary school, however, concrete activities chosen in terms of pupils' needs and to cultivate their personal development have served as unifying themes, or 'projects,' through which materials from a number of school subjects were brought together in broader departments. Conspicuous examples of the use of this principle are found in the physical and natural sciences, and in history, geography, and civics.

In other words, the essential basis of the so-called 'educational project' was in effective operation in the F. W. Parker School, as it was in the University of Chicago Laboratory Schools, for years before the development of the systematic philosophy of the project method. Teachers in the F. W. Parker School believe that "self-actuated work causes the greatest gain in the pupil; that training in initiative is a child's great need, that in his own interests they often find the educative spirit; that freedom, with a balancing responsibility, is the best condition of moral and intellectual growth; that real experience with actual material is an essential of learning; that opportunity for varied expression is necessary for right education; that for purposes of development children must be treated as individuals and not as a group; that one of the most effective and wholesome motives of work is the social motive."[23]

This quotation from the First *Yearbook* of the school is a compact statement of the theory upon which the school developed. The various yearbooks illustrate well the way in which the school tried to evolve a curriculum about the creative activities of children.[24]

These seven volumes not only provide detailed illustrations of the way of which the school has organized its curriculum; they also illustrate the way in which it has tried to influence school practice. Throughout its quarter-century of growth the F. W. Parker School

[23] Francis W. Parker Yearbook, *The Social Motive in School Work,* Volume I, 1912.

[24] The titles of the other six published yearbooks are: *The Morning Exercise as a Socializing Influence,* Volume II, 1913; *Expression as a Means of Training Motive,* Volume III, 1914; *Education Through Concrete Experience: A Series of Illustrations,* Volume IV, 1915; *The Course in Science,* Volume V, 1918. (No yearbooks were issued in 1916, 1917, 1918, 1919, 1921 and 1922.) *The Individual and the Curriculum, An Experiment in Adaptation,* Volume VI, 1920 (with this volume the title of the *Francis Parker Yearbook* was changed to *Studies in Education*). *The Social Science Series: A Course in History,* Volume VII, 1923.

has had no affiliation with teacher training institutions. In this regard the practical exploitation of Colonel Parker's theories has been handicapped. On the other hand, the Laboratory Schools of the School of Education at the University of Chicago and the schools of Teachers College have had effective means of disseminating their methods and findings through the training classes of the two institutions and through their respective educational magazines. Hence, the *Yearbooks* and *Studies in Education* of the F. W. Parker School comprise the sources to which the student of laboratory schools should turn for an understanding of the work of this particular group.

These workers, like those of nearly all the other laboratory schools, have made little or no use of the scientific techniques which have been developed during the past fifteen years. During the past few years standardized tests have been employed in the school with which to check up the results of instruction and to discover for the skills and knowledges of the curriculum specific weaknesses which individual pupils reveal. Scientifically controlled experiments have not been set up in the Parker School any more than in the University of Chicago Laboratory Schools, or the Horace Mann, City and Country, Walden, Children's University School, University of Missouri Experimental School, or in the others.

X. Teachers College and Its Laboratory Schools

1. The Horace Mann School (1887)

The third force most active in the reconstruction of the school curriculum during the past forty years was the work of Teachers College in New York City.

The college was opened for the first reception of students on September 12, 1887. On the same day a school of observation and practice was opened, known until 1891 as the "Model School." This was a school in which "professors of education might experiment with the curriculum and methods of teaching as professors of science experiment in the laboratory."[25] In the same vicinity, but at that time unrelated to it, Columbia University, under the leadership of President F. A. P. Barnard, was endeavoring to establish courses in the professional education of teachers. These early pro-

[25] Russell, J. E. *Teachers College Record,* January, 1902.

posals of President Barnard led eventually to the establishment of courses in the philosophy of education which were later merged in Teachers College. In opening Teachers College, however, it was regarded as "important to have a school in which it was possible to illustrate improved educational principles and to demonstrate the worth of certain new theories in the training of children. In its advocacy of manual training, domestic economy, and the natural sciences as worthy of rank with the other subjects of the curriculum, the school was in advance of its times."[26]

From the beginning, the Horace Mann group of Teachers College aimed at the improvement of education through the *existing subjects of study*—history, geography, arithmetic, reading, etc. They did not propose to abolish them and organize new types of activities, as did other reformers. In this procedure its work is to be contrasted with that of the Laboratory School at Chicago under Dewey, the work of Professor Junius L. Meriam[27] in establishing the University Elementary School at the University of Missouri in 1904 and of the work of Mrs. Marietta Johnson, at Fairhope, Alabama. The Horace Mann School, on the other hand, and the Speyer School and the Lincoln School,[28] from their establishment, and the Laboratory School of the University of Chicago under Mr. Judd's direction, sought to improve the school curriculum by assuming a middle position between chaotic freedom and the rigid formality of the public schools. This they tried to achieve by vitalizing the content of the school subjects and at the same time by organizing a large amount of spontaneous activity on the part of the children.

The staff of the Horace Mann School was permitted large latitude in the developments of its curriculum. Those who were responsible for its development following 1900 (for example, Professor Frank M. McMurry,[29] Principal Henry C. Pearson, working

---

[26] Russell, *Loc. cit.*

[27] Professor Meriam's direction to his new staff in 1904 was that there should be no school subjects and no school furniture.

[28] Also a large number of the other laboratory or progressive schools established since 1910.

[29] McMurry, Frank M., (1862-), Principal, 1883-90; Professor of Pedagogics, State Normal School, Normal, Illinois, 1891-2; Professor of Pedagogy, University of Illinois, 1893-4; Principal Franklin School, Buffalo, 1894-5; Professor of Pedagogics and Dean of Teachers College, University of Buffalo, 1895-8; Professor of Elementary Education, Teachers College, Columbia University, since 1898. Author of textbooks, etc.

under the direction of Dean James E. Russell[30]) recognized the startling advances in modern civilization and the necessity for the school to train children in quick response to new social demands. The school was regarded as a laboratory in which methods could be tested. It was the day of object teaching; textbook memorization was subordinated to the careful observation of real things and to the securing of an all-round development in which hand work was given a central position.

One of the central ideas in the theory of the Horace Mann and Speyer School groups was greatly similar to the nub of Colonel Parker's theory, and coincided with one of Professor Dewey's main contentions. Unity in the school curriculum was to be sought by careful correlation of the work of the school subjects around central organizing themes. Parker's dictum that "the organization of community life should be the end and aim of education" was reflected also in the theory of the New York group. Various phases of social life, especially the occupations, were to be the correlating themes through which unity and continuity would be secured. Under the stimulus of 'recapitulation' many schools were in those days organizing curricula on the basis of the analogy between the development of the race and the development of the individual.

The development of curriculum-making in the Horace Mann School was influenced directly by the necessity for using the school in the training of teachers. It was more of a demonstration than an experimental school, in the sense of the Lincoln School or of the Laboratory Schools of the University of Chicago. Nevertheless, the Horace Mann School has exerted a large influence upon thousands of graduate students and educational visitors who studied its practice and tried to make use of its materials and methods. Indeed, one of the most influential factors in the redirection of public-school classrooms during the years since 1905 was the utilization of the Horace Mann School and of the Speyer School in the training of graduate students. This influence is illustrated by the widespread reading of the *Teachers College Record,* whose pages from 1902 on

---

[30] Russell, James Earl, (1864-), Teacher in Secondary Schools, 1887-90; Principal, Cascadilla School, Ithaca, New York, 1890-3; European Commissioner of Regents of the University of the State of New York, 1893-5; European Agent Bureau of Education of Washington, 1893-5; Professor of Philosophy and Pedagogy, University of Colorado, 1895-7; Professor of Education, Teachers College, since 1897; Dean of Teachers College, since 1898.

frequently included the contributions of Thorndike, Strayer, McMurry, Suzzalo, Pearson, and from 1910, Bonser, Briggs, Kilpatrick, Snedden, and their associates.

It is appropriate to pause here to point out that during the past ten years a new and rigorous impetus has been given to the dissemination of the doctrine of educational growth in the work of William H. Kilpatrick.[31] During that time, through several publications and through conspicuous success with thousands of students in Teachers College, Professor Kilpatrick has exerted a widespread influence on the vitalizing of elementary-school instruction. Kilpatrick has assembled and presented to teachers more concretely than any other worker the essential principles underlying the philosophy of growth through creative experience. He has integrated into a systematic philosophy of educational method the essential ideas of biological evolution and of dynamic psychology as developed by James, Thorndike, Woodworth, and others. In Part II of this Yearbook Kilpatrick presents a systematic statement of the foundation of his curriculum.

2. The Speyer School of Teachers College (1899-1915)

As early as 1902, Dean James E. Russell recognized the need for a school which could be devoted more completely to experimentation than was the Horace Mann School. Such a school was established in 1899 through the gift of Mr. and Mrs. James Speyer. In the list of experimental schools which were established in various parts of the country, the Speyer School was unique in two respects.

It was, in the first place, a school in which no tuition was charged. All of the others—the Chicago Schools, the F. W. Parker, the Horace Mann, the Lincoln School, the University of Missouri, the University of Iowa Experimental School, etc., were private fee schools. This characteristic of the Speyer School guaranteed to its staff a pupil body relatively typical of the rank and file of the urban public schools. This, in turn, made possible a more direct applica-

---

[31] Kilpatrick, William Heard, (1871-), Teacher and Principal of Public Schools of Georgia until 1907; Professor of Mathematics, 1897-1906, Acting President 1903-5 at Mercer University; Lecturer in Education, 1909-11, Assistant Professor, 1911-1915, Associate Professor, 1915-1918, Professor Philosophy of Education, from 1918, at Teachers College, Columbia University. Author: *The Dutch Schools of New Netherland and Colonial New York; The Montessori System Examined,* 1914; *Froebel's Kindergarten Principles Critically Examined,* 1916; *The Project Method; Foundations of Method,* etc.

tion of conclusions, materials, and methods to public-school classrooms.[32]

The school was conspicuous in the second place because it was one of the first, if not the very first, combination experimental school and social settlement. Beside its kindergarten and eight elementary-school grades, a variety of additional adult educational activities was conducted. Classes were formed to meet afternoons and evenings in cooking, sewing, music, freehand drawing, woodworking, and the other industrial arts. In brief, the Speyer School was to serve the local community throughout the day and night and throughout all the seasons of the year. Mother's groups, a girl's social group, and instruction in library work were organized. Practice in experimental teaching was developed and an experimental curriculum adapted closely to the requirements of the local neighborhood was projected, from 1899, under the direction of Professor Frank M. McMurry. A free library was opened for the use of the residents of the neighborhood, with a very large circulation of books. It is significant that there was no other public library in that part of the city.

Perhaps the most conspicuous outcome of the curriculum-reconstruction work of the Speyer School group was that produced under the supervision of the school by Dr. F. G. Bonser[33] from 1910 to 1913. In 1913, the staff of the Speyer School, under the direction of Dr. Bonser, published *The Speyer School Curriculum.*[34] This was one of the most elaborate presentations of the reorganized curricula of laboratory schools which had made its appearance. It will be recalled that the leadership in this sort of publication had been taken by Colonel Parker in 1895. Following that time his own

[32] The average I.Q. of the pupil body in the University of Chicago Laboratory Schools (information orally from Professor F. N. Freeman), in the Horace Mann School, and in the Lincoln School is within two or three points of the same amount—approximately 116. There is good reason for believing that the pupil bodies of all of the private laboratory schools have been selected in terms of economic, social, and linguistic status to approximately the same extent.

[33] Bonser, Frederick G. (1875-), Director Training School of State Normal School, Cheney, Washington, 1902-5; State Normal School Macomb, Illinois, 1906-1910; Professor of Education, Teachers College, Columbia University, since 1910. Author: *The Reasoning Ability of Children, Industrial Education, Educational Use of Recreative Activities of Children, The Elementary School Curriculum.* Editor of *The Speyer School Curriculum.* Co-Author of *Industrial Arts in the Elementary Schools.*

[34] Distributed now by the Bureau of Publication, Teachers College, Columbia University.

Practice School and the Laboratory School of the University of Chicago had published in *The Elementary School Record* (later the *Elementary School Teacher*) a long series of syllabi outlining the instruction of the elementary and secondary-school grades. That is what Dr. Bonser and his associates did in the *Speyer School Curriculum.* The material was classified in accordance with the kindergarten and the eight elementary-school grades. It was presented in outline form, subject by subject, and arranged by seasons.

This curriculum revealed two unique characteristics: First, the attempt, in part at least, to combine the narrow departments of the school into broader units illustrated by history, civics, and social life, and by industrial and fine arts; second, the very large amount of time devoted to the industrial and fine arts. In the allotment of time program, 1600 minutes per week, or 15 percent, were given to that department. This is a larger amount of time than is given to any other department, excepting English, which receives 26 percent of the time. History, civics, and social life was given 13 percent. If one combines history, civics, and social life and industrial and fine arts, one notes the pronounced interest of Dr. Bonser and the Speyer school group in organizing a curriculum which represents "the needs and interests of present-day life in our immediate neighborhood and the world at large." The fundamental aim of the school, namely social efficiency, emphasized the social factor in the life of the school and the psychological adaptation of materials to the needs and capacities of individual children.

In other words, the Speyer School continued the tradition which had been set by the leadership of the Horace Mann group, and of the other experimentalists who were trying to reconstruct education in terms of the next practicable stop. Child growth through self-activity was emphasized, but combined in the organization of the curriculum with an eye to social discipline and control. In 1913 the field to be covered by the Speyer School was changed from that of the elementary school to the junior high school. Professor Thomas H. Briggs,[35] in charge of secondary education in Teachers

[35] Briggs, Thomas Henry, (1877-), Teacher High School, Elizabeth City, North Carolina, 1896-8; Princeton-Yale Academy, Chicago, 1899-01; Professor of English, John B. Stetson University, DeLand, Florida, 1899-1900; Teacher of English, Eastern Illinois State Normal School, 1901-11; Teachers College (Columbia), since 1912; Professor of Education, 1920; Educational Advisor, New York City Experimental Intermediate School, since 1915. Author: *Reading in Public Schools* (with Lotus Coffman), *A First Book in Composition, Formal Grammar as Discipline, The Junior High School,* etc.

College, was made supervisor of experimentation in junior-high-school work. Under his direction a series of experiments were organized and carried on.

3. The Lincoln School of Teachers College
(Founded 1917)

In the autumn of 1917, under the direction of Teachers College, and financed in large part by the General Education Board, the Lincoln School was established under the directorship of Dr. Otis W. Caldwell,[36] "for the purpose of endeavoring by experimental methods to assist in the reorganization of subjects and methods of study which is already under way in the fields of elementary and secondary education. Widespread discontent prevails as to many of the subjects included in the ordinary curriculum; some subjects or parts of subjects, are unsatisfactory, while satisfactory substitutes have not as yet been worked out. Many teachers are already engaged in the task of reorganizing materials in mathematics, science, and language so as to make these subjects more effectively fit the needs of pupils and obligations of modern democratic life. The Lincoln School proposes to address itself to assisting in this important work."[37]

From a staff of twenty-five in 1917, with a pupil body of 116 in the first five grades, the Lincoln School has grown in eight years to a staff of sixty-seven and a pupil body of four hundred eighty, about equally divided between boys and girls and between the elementary and high-school grades. From the beginning the school has been kept as a laboratory institution. No practice teaching is permitted and class and group observation is restricted. The teachers in the school, in addition to attempting to operate an effective and ordered school, are trying to discover new and better materials of instruction and improved methods of organization and teaching. Some of these "are enthusiasts. Others are skeptics;

[36] Caldwell, Otis William, (1869-), Professor of botany, Eastern Illinois State Normal School, 1899-1907; Associate Professor of Botany, 1907-17, Dean University College, University of Chicago, 1913-1917; Professor of Education in Teachers College, Columbia University; Director of Lincoln School since 1917. Author: *Laboratory and Field Manual of Botany, Plant Morphology, Elements of General Science, Laboratory Manual of General Science, Then and Now in Education,* co-author. Editor of *Science Remaking the World.*

[37] Otis W. Caldwell, the Director, stating the purposes of the Lincoln School in the first descriptive booklet (1918) following the establishment of the school.

some *live* with children; others *investigate* children; still others drill them—when they can." "With all their individual differences, the members of the staff are highly sensitive to this much of a common purpose, namely, to find out something about education that will be sound and usable.[38]

"Many members of the staff have been studying the curriculum problem from the point of view of society—its present nature and its needs. Many others have been attacking it from the point of view of the child—his nature and his needs. In the end, each of these points of view should comprehend the other, and will in the Lincoln School, where abundant opportunity is offered for their association. . . . . We have one set of people who try, for example, to get partial clues for biology courses from the references in daily newspapers[39] or to determine the relative importance of geographic location facts from references and articles in magazines, critical journals, and current books, plus many such criteria as are furnished by statistics of trade, area, population, resources, and financial transactions; or to find out from analysis of the writings of frontier thinkers the real predicament of this befuddled world and the matters, principles, concepts, generalizations, terms, and habits of thought that children should master now if they are to do anything about it later.

"On the other hand, there may be observed at the Lincoln School teachers who initiate curriculum study by starting children on fascinating, richly promising activities—for example, the making of play villages[40] out of packing boxes, the construction of boats and bridges, the building and equipping of a Chinese house, the making and use of hand looms, the modelling of medieval castles, the assembling of block floor maps of Manhattan Island, the care and raising of white rats, canaries and baby alligators, the managing of school banks, the productions of newspapers, magazines and plays, the making of drums, marimbas, reed flutes, tubaphones, and primitive looking fiddles; and the composing of music to go with them;[41] the creating of verse, study and essay for personal expression, the pleasure of classmates and for publication in the pupils' magazines.

"Here curriculum study, when once the children are at work, consists in watching them, noting and recording questions, effects, enthusiasms, personal revelations, increase in knowledge, adventures in creativeness, use of and advances in the more traditional arts and skills of the schoolroom; and finally, in

---

[38] Willing, M. H. "The value of an experimental school," *School and Society*, May 15, 1926. (Dr. Willing, now Associate Professor of Education at the University of Wisconsin, was a research investigator in the Lincoln School for four years. The quotations are taken from his current paper, read and discussed and approved by the school staff in April, 1926.)

[39] Finley, C. W., and Caldwell, O. W.: *Biology in the Public Press*, Teachers College Bureau of Publications, Teachers College, Columbia University.

[40] Keelor, Katherine M. *Curriculum Studies in the Second Grade.* Teachers College Bureau of Publications, Teachers College, Columbia University.

[41] Coleman, Sadie E. *Creative Music for Children.* Teachers College Bureau of Publications, Teachers College, Columbia University.

rendering judgment on the whole work-unit as a desirable part of a modern curriculum.

"Among those studies in which children do not directly or initially figure, may be listed questionnaires sent out for news of present practices in history and science sequences; work with national committees in mathematics, science, and history; collecting bibliographies and reading lists; searching for, revising, or creating freshly the actual materials of instruction in every subject and organizing the same; in short, all attempts to get information about objectives, present trends, current opinion, sources of material, and relative importances, and all attempts to put materials together before actual trial with the pupils. A very impressive number of these kinds of studies have been made in the last eight or nine years, and the schedule for the future is crowded.

"The social studies investigation, by far the most comprehensive and striking of all the curriculum studies, has resulted in twelve thick pamphlets of material now in the third experimental edition. Four of these pamphlets are assigned to each grade of the junior high school. They have such titles as these: "Industries and Trade which Bind Nations Together," "America's March Toward Democracy," "America and Her Immigrants." At least two hundred schools are coöperating in the trial of these materials.

"Emphatically, however, the school is not a method school. It commits itself to no one way of doing things. It is not a Dalton plan school nor a Winnetka plan, nor a project method school, nor a visualization school, nor a play school. At various times and in various spots it may partake of all these, but if it does so, it is always with experimental, not devotional, intent."

From the foregoing quotations it can be seen that the staff of the school and its experimentation during the past eight years illustrate both of the most conspicuous aspects of educational experimentation which have been set up through the laboratory schools in the last quarter century. The curriculum of the school, like that of the Horace Mann and Speyer School, is organized (in part in the elementary school and altogether in the high school) around subjects of study. There is a distinct movement, however, to enlarge the scope of the subjects of study, as is illustrated by the work in the social studies, general science, and general mathematics. On the other hand, the teachers of the elementary school are motivated more by the desire to provide a continuous opportunity for dynamic growth through creative activity of all sorts than they are by the desire to have children master specified habits, kinds of knowledge, and principles.

XI. Looking Back at the Three Chief Factors of Educational Reform

The fundamental ideas of these three reform forces, the initial work of Parker, the School of Education, and Teachers College, therefore, playing on the conventional school curriculum between 1890 and 1905 appear to be much the same. The chief distinction seems to me to lie in the method of procedure. Throughout his quarter century of dynamic work, Parker was always running a school and operating a training institution for teachers. He was immersed in the practical details of administration. He wrote little, but spoke much. He rarely took the time to stand aloof from the current and whirl of practical affairs to think through the tangle of educational threads and conditions. John Dewey did hold himself aloof, however, and more than any other worker, he has phrased the philosophy of democratic and social education under which the current educational situation is rapidly becoming oriented. As a writer of basic educational and psychological theory, Dewey's influence upon modern educational practice has been fundamental.

Parker and his colleagues and the Teachers College group made their great contributions in the attempt to improve the conditions of education through practical school experimentation and the training of teachers. Dewey made his by synthesizing and developing in written form the growing body of fundamental educational and psychological theory.[42]

XII. The Spread of the Laboratory-School Movement

Under the impetus of the leadership of the three groups whose activity we have traced in the foregoing pages, 'protest,' 'progressive,' 'laboratory,' 'free,' schools were established in a number of centers after 1910. The state universities were developing professional schools of education, although in the main their practice schools were confined to the secondary level. Nevertheless, occasional elementary experimental schools were established.

---

[42] Lack of space prevents a thorough critical evaluation of the domineering role of ideas in Dewey's educational philosophy and of "social efficiency" as the guiding aim of American education. This I have attempted in my forthcoming *American Life and the Reconstruction of the School*. In press. Harcourt Brace, N. Y.

1. The Meriam Laboratory School in the University of Missouri (1904-)

In 1904 Professor J. L. Meriam attempted to work out in an eight-grade elementary school at the University of Missouri, a school curriculum organized on a non-subject basis. He had recently returned from graduate study at Teachers College. For nearly twenty years this elementary school was operated under his direction. It represented an attempt to organize a curriculum of activities for children on a new departmental basis. The school day was divided into four ninety-minute exercises. This was in sharp contrast to the large number of ten to thirty-minute exercises operating in the public schools. This lengthening of the class period represents an interesting and somewhat novel contribution to the creation of a more leisurely and thoughtful atmosphere in elementary classrooms. Corresponding to this four-fold division, the curriculum was divided into four types of activities: observation, play, stories, handwork.[43]

A general outline of the curriculum can be presented in brief space by the following quotation from Professor Meriam's book.

GENERAL OUTLINE OF THE CURRICULUM. Four "subjects" are used throughout the school: (1) Observation: In Grades I and II, plant life, animal life, people, earth, and sky. In Grades III and IV, local industries and activities. In Grades V and VI, world-wide activities and industries. In Grades VII and VIII, occupations—vocational intelligence.

(2) Play: In Grades I, II, and III, a great variety of games. In Grades IV, V, VI, VII, and VIII, play with nature, electricity, machinery, water, air, etc. All grades: Physical exercises, folk dancing, and free play.

(3) Stories: Reading, telling, dramatizing; singing songs; studying pictures and drawings; assembly exercises; foreign language.

(4) Handwork: A great variety of useful and ornamental articles are made. Only a very few projects are suggested in these outlines. Materials: Paper, cord, yard, textiles, reed, raffia, wood, metal.

2. Other Laboratory Schools

In 1915, the State University of Iowa established its six-grade university elementary school under the direction of Professor

[43] Complete exposition of Professor Meriam's theories will be found in his *Child Life and the Curriculum*. World Book Co., 1920.

Ernest Horn.[44] In 1916 the University high school was organized on a 3-3 plan. In 1922 the junior primary grade or kindergarten was added. The school has grown to a membership of about 400 pupils, with a teaching staff in the elementary school of eight full-time teachers, five assistants, and one school nurse. The school is somewhat novel in that the classroom teachers are students in the university and are training primarily to become supervisors.

In 1914 in connection with the Bureau of Educational Experiments, a laboratory school was established under the direction of Miss Caroline Pratt called the "Play School." The name was afterwards changed to the "City and Country School," under which it now operates. The curriculum of the school has developed with the school itself. Beginning in 1914 with small groups of children classified in accordance with chronological age (instead of Grade I, II or III, the school speaks of "the sixes," "the sevens," "the eights," meaning six-year-olds, seven-year-olds, eight-year-olds). The school has grown year by year until now there are ten groups running from the pre-school group of three, four, and five years, through the twelve-year-olds. These last correspond roughly to seventh-grade children.[45]

In 1915 the Walden School was established by Miss Margaret Naumburg in New York City. The school began "with a group of children between the ages of three and five and grew consciously from this foundation until now it includes the beginning of a high-school department."[46]

In 1920 Miss Helen Parkhurst,[47] following the brief trial of her ideas in the Dalton (Massachusetts) schools and their widespread reception in England, established a private laboratory school in New York City under the name of "The Children's University Elementary School." The theory upon which this school is organized is described in Miss Parkhurst's *Education on the Dalton Plan.*[48]

---

[44] Professor Horn had been the first principal of the University of Missouri Elementary School, established by Professor J. L. Meriam in 1904. The program of curriculum-making in the Iowa school is described by Professor Horn in Chapter XVII of this volume.

[45] The theoretical program of this school is described by Miss Caroline Pratt in Chapter XXII of this book.

[46] See Chapter XXIII by Miss Naumburg in this issue.

[47] Formerly a colleague of Dr. Carleton W. Washburne, working in the staff of Dr. Frederic Burk in the San Francisco Normal School.

[48] E. P. Dutton & Co., 1922.

Relatively little experimentation comparable to the work which has been done in towns and cities has been carried on for rural schools. A striking exception is the work done by Collings in the McDonald County (Missouri) Experimental School. This is described by excerpts from his book[49] which have been assembled as Chapter XVIII of this volume.

The essential theoretical basis of the school is also pointed out in Professor Bonser's chapter.

The laboratory schools have influenced public school practice, by encouraging personal visitation and observation of their work. Thousands of teachers observed and practiced in either the Parker Practice School, the Horace Mann School, or later in the Laboratory School of the University of Chicago. This influence has operated for nearly three decades, gathering momentum year by year; it is now very great; the laboratory schools of the country are visited annually by tens of thousands of teachers or laymen interested in the improvement of education.[50]

---

[49] Collings, Ellsworth. *An Experiment with a Project Curriculum.* Macmillan, 1925.

[50] A critique of these laboratory schools has been included in Chapter XXX of this volume.

XIII. In Retrospect: A Century of Curriculum-Making

This sketch of the past century of curriculum-making constitutes our background for the study of the contemporary situation.

Our historical survey began with the statement that "Not once in a century and a half of national history has the curriculum of the school caught up with the dynamic content of American life. . . . . Decade by decade the curriculum has lagged behind the current civilization. Although the gap between the two has been markedly cut down in the last three quarters of a century, nevertheless, the American school has been essentially static and academic. To-day much of the gap persists."

Nevertheless, our survey has revealed conspicuous changes in the curriculum and in the techniques by which it was constructed.

1. Change in Purpose

In the first place, there is the change in purpose. The theological orientation of the colonial Latin grammar school and of the early academies gave way to a half century of "knowledge for knowledge's sake" and rigorous mental discipline. The disciplinary purpose of education, so all-pervasive in the latter half of the nineteenth century, was slowly displaced under the attacks of the dynamic psychologists by the fundamental principle of maximal child growth at minimal expense.

So to-day in America we find advocates of both the disciplinary and the growth functions of the school. College and secondary instruction is still organized much more largely on the former basis than on the latter. It is in a small, but increasing number of progressive public and private centers of educational reform, especially in elementary schools, that the curriculum is controlled more by child activity, spontaneity, creative self-expression than it is by conformity, regimentation, and unquestioning acquiescence. The desideratum in the work of the more eclectic reformers seems to be that of *disciplined initiative,* rather than chaotic freedom on the one hand or regimental conformity on the other.

Correspondingly, the great aim of tolerant understanding of contemporary life is slowly taking its place beside the fundamental creative one of growth through self-expression. Recently, the dynamic psychologist has modified our thinking concerning the disciplinary functions of instruction. A generation of research has taught that training in tolerance, in generalization, must be given through the direct study of contemporary issues and problems and their historical development. The formerly prevailing conception of general mind training through content remote from American life is being discarded.

2. Change in Leadership

This change in goals, in orientation, has been brought about primarily because of the change in leadership in curriculum-making. The end of the century is revealing the emergence of a new type of professional curriculum-maker. The past decade has shown the manifold nature of the tasks involved in the preparation of the activities and materials of instruction for the great public school system. The setting of ultimate and immediate objectives, the wise selection of content, the discovery of child interests and abilities, the adaptation of materials to levels of growth and to individual differences and the organization of activities and other materials—all of these jobs are difficult and can be managed only by those of definite training and experience. Curriculum-making has become a coöperative enterprise. Frontier thinkers, poets, and other singers of American life, students of child learning and educational administration and specialists in measurement and experimentation must join hands with the students of subject-matter values if the staggering problems of curriculum-construction are to be solved. Already the foundations are being laid for the coöperation which will produce the new curriculum of tolerant understanding and creative self-expression.

3. Change in Method

Personnel determines procedure. The new point of view which is setting up child growth and intelligent understanding in place of academic scholarship and mind training is also beginning to utilize more scientific and unprejudiced methods. Educational classrooms are responding slowly to the demands of the laboratory spirit. In many centers the armchair is being scrapped. The critical eye-witness recorder of school activities is beginning to replace the armchair writer of scholastic textbooks. There is a growing willingness to try new types of materials in public schools, to experiment with new groupings of school subjects, to compare alternative procedures, and to depend more and more upon objective measurement of results. Advances *are* being made, even though but slowly.

4. Change in Content

The new procedures and the new vision are steadily cutting down the lag between American society and the school curriculum. The subservience to morphology, to the very ancient past, to the classical, to the academic, is beginning to be replaced by a dynamic interest in contemporary life. Hundreds of schools do give courses in "problems of democracy," even though the instruction is reserved only for those few who remain in school until the last year of the high school. An increasing number of schools do discuss how people live together and how they are affected by their physical and natural environment. Every year sees a larger area of the nation throwing off the worship of British Victorian literature and utilizing in its place the indigenous writings produced by a growing American culture. Nevertheless, even when viewed in the perspective of a hundred years of development, progress toward the development of a dynamic school curriculum is slow. We need, if for no other reason than to speed up the process, to master a vivid historical perspective of the movements of which we are now an active part.

5. Change in Organization

Although progressive change is clearly discernible in the purposes, personnel, procedure, and to some extent in content, the 'subject,' or 'compartmental,' *organization* of the materials of the school curriculum responds least easily to the demands of the times. Teaching is still badly hampered by the barriers between the school subjects. Learning is still inhibited even more than it is promoted by the network of pigeon holes into which the materials are classified. Although slight beginnings have been made in the direction of merging school subjects into broader and more integrated courses, not more than a mere handful of educational workers now are persuaded to ignore conventional subject divisions in the creation of a new and effective departmentalization of materials.

The *direction* in which we are moving, however, is clearly toward a new synthesis of knowledge and a departmentalization of the curriculum which will consist of a few broad integrations of child activities, readings, pupil research, what not. Under the necessities of mass education and to guarantee smooth administration of class instruction, we shall continue to break up curricular materials into departments of knowledge. The tendency, however, is markedly in the direction of cutting down the number and expanding the area covered by each. To discover the most effective boundaries of the new departments, we shall increasingly tend to experiment with unique schemes of integration, ignoring in this process the unproved academic subject divisions of the past. In this way, by actually sweeping away the barriers between related materials and activities, we may compass at last that unified curriculum for which the reform movements of thirty years ago strove so valiantly.

SECTION II

CURRENT PRACTICES IN CURRICULUM-MAKING IN PUBLIC SCHOOLS

CHAPTER VI

CURRENT PRACTICES IN CURRICULUM-REVISION IN PUBLIC ELEMENTARY SCHOOLS

Stuart A. Courtis
University of Michigan, Ann Arbor, Michigan

No study of curriculum-revision would be complete which did not include a description of the agents who are charged with the responsibility for such revision, the range of their activities, and the methods used. Accordingly, a questionnaire covering these points was prepared and sent to selected cities throughout the United States. One hundred thirty-two replies were received from cities varying widely in size and locality (Table I).

Table I.—Geographical Position and Size of Cities from which Replies to Questionnaires Were Received[1]

Geographical Location	Population of City						
	0 to 10,000	10,000 to 25,000	25,000 to 50,000	50,000 to 100,000	100,000 to 500,000	500,000 or Over	Total
Eastern States							
Northern.........	5	4	1	1	0	1	12
Central...........	7	8	4	3	5	2	29
Southern..........	2	2	4	4	3	0	15
Central States.......	9	12	7	7	3	2	40
Western States......	4	5	3	2	1	0	15
RockyMountainStates	1	4	3	0	2	0	10
Pacific Coast States .	1	1	3	1	4	1	11
Total............	29	36	25	18	18	6	132

[1] A list of the cities contributing will be found at the end of this chapter.

The reports that follow here are based on the returns from these questionnaires; in other chapters of this Yearbook will be found more detailed statements from various of the larger cities and special schools which have attracted national attention in recent years by their curriculum-revision activities.

The American school system is an illustration of organic social evolution. The basic element is the one-room, one-teacher, private school organized to meet a definite need. The final product is the large city public school system, composed of thousand of teachers and rooms, but forming as a whole a great unitary institution with complex inter-relations among its parts and with many other types of agents besides teachers, all of whom in the last analysis exist solely to facilitate the basic function of teaching.

A study of this evolution shows that the final product in the main is the result of the play of chance forces, not of conscious design. First there is growth in size, next division of labor, then creation of special departments. As there is no central control of education in the United States, a given need is met by different localities in many different ways. In time the less successful die out, while efficient methods are quite universally adopted. Standardization thus takes place by natural selection.

The problems of curriculum-construction and the related problems of supervision are just coming to the consciousness of schoolmen as in need of standardization. Each school system has met these problems, and solved them more or less effectively, in its own way. None of the solutions has proved wholly satisfactory. The attempt to gather current practices by a single questionnaire and to present a single picture of the returns is foredoomed to failure. The outstanding characteristic to be presented by this report is *diversity;* diversity in the interpretations placed on the queries in the questionnaire; diversity of practice; diversity in the conclusions drawn from the results by different readers. In the account which follows due allowance should be made for these characteristics of the situation. The writer will attempt to present his judgment of the trends of practice as well as the bare facts themselves.

Responsible Agents

From 117 school systems replies were obtained in answer to the question: "Do you have in your regular administrative organization agents, other than the superintendent, to whom responsibility for the elementary course of study and for its revision is delegated as a distinctive function?" Of these replies, 71, or 60 percent, were "no;" 46, or 40 percent, "yes." Analysis by size of city (Table II) reveals the trend which is not apparent in the gross returns. For, even in the smallest towns there are progressive superintendents who have made curriculum-revision a distinctive function, and there are large cities in which, at present as in the past, differentiation of function and specialization of agents have not yet taken place.

The tendency, however, is clearly toward differentiation as the size of the city increases, and as far as the small number of cases is adequate for such a generalization, the critical point is approximately a total population of 60,000. In other words, if a city has a population of 60,000, the chances are even that there will be a special agent in the administrative organization charged with responsibility for the course of study and its revision. As the size of the city increases, the chances of there being such an agent increase also, until, for cities of 100,000 population or more, the

TABLE II.—RELATION OF SIZE OF CITY TO DIFFERENTIATION AND SPECIALIZATION
(Number and percent of cities answering 'yes' and 'no' to question about delegation of responsibility for course of study as a distinctive function.)

Size of City	0 to 20,000	20,000 to 40,000	40,000 to 60,000	60,000 to 80,000	80,000 to 100,000	100,000 or Over	Total
Number "No"......	36	18	5	5	2	5	71
Number "Yes".....	7	12	5	5	3	14	46
Total............	43	30	10	10	5	19	117
Percent "No"......	84	60	50	50	40	26	61
Percent "Yes"......	16	40	50	50	60	74	39
Total............	100	100	100	100	100	100	100

probabilities are 3 to 1. On the other hand, in the cities of 20,000 or less the chances are 5 to 1 that no special agent will be found.

Where differentiation has not taken place, curriculum-revision is carried on under the direction of the superintendent or principal. In very many cities the ultimate responsibility rests specifically in the board of education itself, and all revision is carried on under temporary assignments. In this connection this statement from one of the very large cities accurately describes the general situation.

"The usual procedure is to have a committee of representative teachers of the subject meet with one or more of the assistant superintendents and with the director of the subject, if there is a director. The course thus prepared is submitted to the board of superintendents for approval and this goes to the school committee for authority to print as a school document."

The attempt was made to find out how many distinctive agents in charge of curriculum-revision there are in cities where differentiation has taken place and what they are called, but some cities included all the teachers serving on committees and the returns probably have little meaning. Cities under 100,000 report one such agent more often than any other number, while no city under 25,000 reports more than 8. On the other hand, the figures for the cities above 100,000 range from 1 through 91.

Titles of Agents

The titles given agents who are in charge of curriculum-revision are extremely varied. Of 194 titles reported, 1 is deputy superintendent, 1 is associate superintendent, and 9 are assistant superintendents. None of these is reported from cities under 10,000, and half of such reports are from cities of 100,000 or more.

In 32 cases the title is "director." In only one city is the agent called "director of curriculum." In 17 cases the title is director of a special subject, as music, health education, etc.; 6 times the title is "director of research" or its equivalent; the remaining 8 titles are miscellaneous, as "director of supervision," "director of platoon schools," "director of boys and girls vocational department," etc.

By far the largest series of titles (71) contains the word "supervisor." Of these, half (36) are designated as supervisors of special subjects—art, music, health, etc. The remainder have more general titles—supervisor of primary grades, elementary grades, upper grades, etc. The person responsible for curriculum-revision is most often called "supervisor" in cities of from 25,000 to 50,000 population, although the range is from the largest to the smallest cities.

In 24 cases the agent was said to be the principal of the school, in 7 cases heads of departments, and in 13 cases the teacher of the subject. In 7 cities, ranging in size from 10,000 to 500,000, the bureau or department of research (statistics, measurements, etc.) is given as the responsible agency. In addition, committees of various kinds, some permanent and some temporary, are mentioned 20 times. In one instance the teachers of the normal school are specifically included.

As a whole, therefore, current practice may be called completely unstandardized. Differentiation begins by temporary assignment of responsibility to committees of teachers under principals, heads of departments, or special agents. As the system grows, the assignment is made permanent and the specialized agent is called a supervisor. With further evolution, the supervisor becomes a director of a bureau. Eventually, the director wins recognition as an assistant or associate superintendent. With such full recognition of instruction as a function of school work coördinate with administration, finance, building, etc., the differentiation is complete. So far, however, most American cities are still in the throes of differentiation, and conditions with respect to degree of specialization, number of agents, and the titles used, are extremely varied.

Date of Last Revision

The amount of attention paid to curriculum-revision is clearly shown by the replies to questions as to the date of last general or partial revision. Only 5 cities out of 106 report no revision, while 19 reply that curriculum-revision is continuous. Fourteen cities report curriculum-revision being carried on this year (1925), 14 other give "last year," and 18 more "1923." That is, 60 percent of the school systems replying, both large and small, have made a general revision of the curriculum during the last three years, 75 percent within the last five years. The replies also indicate that, on the average, but from 5 to 6 years have elapsed since the last general revision.

In addition to the general revision, some schools report partial revision. Other schools have had partial revision only. Of the 47 school systems reporting, 34 (72 percent) have made such partial revision during the last two years, and two-thirds of them report similar partial revisions during the previous four years.

Subjects Revised

Of 34 schools listing the several subjects in which the course of study has been revised, 16 mention mathematics, 15 English, 14 social studies, 13 reading, and 9 all subjects. The remaining subjects mentioned at least once include ten others.

In 93 cases the date of the last revision was given. These show some differences in subject and emphasis according to the size of city (Table III).

TABLE III.—MAJOR COURSES OF STUDY MENTIONED AS HAVING BEEN REVISED DURING THE LAST FIVE YEARS (1921-1925)
(Frequency given as percentage of total of subjects mentioned for each size of city.)

Population: 0 to 10,000		10,000 to 25,000		25,000 to 50,000		50,000 to 100,000		100,000 or Over		Total	
Total Items Reported: 93		138		74		52		158		515	
Subject	Per-cent	Subject	Per-cent	Subject	Per-cent	Subject	Per-cent	Subject	Per-cent	Subject	Per-cent
Social Studies	14	English......	12	All subjects..	12	Social Studies	15	Social Studies	16	Social Studies	13
Mathematics.	12	Mathematics.	11	Mathematics.	12	Mathematics.	13	English......	10	Mathematics.	11
English......	12	Social Studies	11	English......	11	Geography...	12	Mathematics.	9	English......	11
Reading......	10	Reading......	9	Geography...	11	Reading......	10	Geography...	7	Geography...	9
Geography...	10	Geography...	9	Reading......	9	Writing......	10	Nineteen others Total......	58	Reading......	8
Spelling......	9	Spelling......	9	Social Studies	9	English......	10			Spelling......	7
Ten others Total......	33	Seventeen others Total........	39	Nine others Total......	36	Ten others Total......	30			Writing......	6
Total......	100		100		100		100		100		

In general, the most frequently revised subjects are the familiar three, reading, writing, and arithmetic, with their relatives, English, spelling, and geography. However, one exception occurs, the social studies. The movement for the socialization of school work has been making rapid progress the last few years, and revision of the courses for the social studies leads all the others.

Unorganized Revisions

In an attempt to find out what happens in schools where no specially organized revisions, either in whole or in part, have been made since 1915, the question was asked: "How does the course of study to-day differ from that of 1915, and how have the changes been introduced?" Eighty-five answers were received from 43 schools, chiefly from the smaller cities (25,000 or less). Thirty-one (36 percent) gave changes in textbooks as the method of making changes; 27 (32 percent) said that there was a definite program of revision, in spite of the fact that it was not formally organized; while nineteen schools (22 percent) mentioned changes in the teaching staff as the cause of changes. No schools attempted to describe the differences.

As a whole, therefore, curriculum-revision is fairly continuous in American schools. Each year some portion of the curriculum is up for study and change, and once in five or six years, on the average, there is a general revision. Even in the smallest cities where there is no formal program, there is nevertheless constant change. Textbooks are changed; new teachers are constantly being hired; superintendents shift from city to city. Yet throughout all the many and varied activities, convention rules. The old-line subjects receive the major part of the attention, except that from time to time new movements, new points of view, bring new subjects to the fore. During the last four years, the special emphasis has been placed upon the social studies.

Source of Movement for Revision

In view of the range and scope of curriculum-revision activities that are taking place, it becomes important to know from what source the criticism comes which leads to revision. Three hundred and twenty-four answers were given by 99 schools. Except in cities of 100,000 or more, the superintendent is mentioned more often (87 times, or 27 percent) than any other source, particularly as the cause of the general revisions. School principals rank second (72 times, or 22 percent); teachers, third (67 times, or 20 percent); while the general supervisory staff ranks fourth (52 times, or 16 percent). The other replies are scattering; the largest other single item is the state legislature (12 times, or 4 percent). School boards are mentioned approximately 3 times per hundred, parents twice, children once. Parents, book companies, the press, and secondary schools are given approximately equal representation (2 percent each).

To make certain that this information would be obtained, a specific question was asked in slightly different form: "Describe briefly the influence of agencies of a lay or non-professional character" (Question 8). Forty-nine schools replied. Of these 22 (45 percent) answered specifically "no influence" or only "indirect influence." In fact, the only answers given by more than one school were "the legislature" (16 percent) and "the press" (4 percent). From the point of view of those who answered the questionnaire, therefore, curriculum-revision is carried on almost wholly because of the criticisms of schoolmen themselves.

Nature of Criticisms

A more important question is that which pertains to the nature of the criticism. One hundred and six schools furnished 321 answers. "Old course unadjusted to pupil needs" was given first place (81, or 25 percent), although the emphasis here shifts from 30 percent in the smallest cities to 22 percent in the larger cities. "Poor organization" was second (67, or 21 percent), and "uninteresting to pupils" third (42, or 13 percent). Approximately 12 percent of the replies frankly say: "Old course out of style," and approximately an equal number report: "Old course taught by wrong methods." Course "too difficult" or "too long" together account for 13 percent of the answers. None of the remaining answers was given by more than two schools. These replies support the previous conclusions and show that in the judgment of those who answered the questionnaire the driving force behind curriculum-revision is in the main the conscious recognition of defects in existing courses by school agents themselves.

Type of Evidence

A question concerning the type of evidence upon which the criticism was based elicited 200 replies from 101 schools. "General knowledge of facts" leads all other answers (74, or 37 percent); "results of organized but subjective study" came second (61, or 30 percent), while "results of objective study by persons within the system" is given in 54 cases (27 percent). "Surveys by outsiders" is credited with but 3 percent of the answers. It appears, therefore, that in nearly two-thirds of the cases revision is still made on the basis of subjective judgment, rather than upon scientific determination of the defects to be remedied.

Machinery

The machinery of revision employed depends somewhat upon the size of the city. In the smaller towns the agency is frequently one person, the superintendent usually, but principal, teacher, or member of the supervisory staff are mentioned in the order named. In place of single individuals there are frequently small groups, composed usually of members of the administrative staff, principals, and teachers. In all types of schools a committee of teachers under the direction of administrative or supervisory officers constitutes the conventional machinery of revision. The returns make evident the large extent to which the rank and file participate in educational planning. The outside expert is not a factor in more than 4 cities per hundred at present.

Method of Revision

The method of revision used is found to differ in cities of different size. In the smaller cities there is more emphasis upon general revision, and in the larger cities upon partial revision. The two chief factors in all cities, however, are "progressive practice elsewhere" and "the results of committee discussion" (each, 30 percent of total answers). "Results of previous research measurement or experimentation" is given in 16 percent of the instances, while "research undertaken for the purpose" drops to 11 percent. The only other reason given at all frequently is "orders from the superintendent."

These figures support the conclusion previously reached that scientific curriculum-revision has not yet made much headway, even in the larger cities. "Progressive practice" and subjective opinion are still the chief determining factors.

Limitations

To get some idea of the degree to which school systems are free to make their curriculum ideal, a question was asked in regard to the factors which restrict or limit the construction of an ideal curriculum. Ninety-one schools supplied 282 answers. Five answers are given with approximately equal frequency and account for 81 percent of the replies. In order of frequency these are:

(1) training and present abilities of teaching force,
(2) cost of ideal content or method,
(3) character of existing textbooks,
(4) limitations of our present knowledge about the curriculum,
(5) character of existing buildings or equipment.

There is little variation from city to city. In general, the limitations of existing buildings and equipment are more often a restricting factor in the small than in the large city. The conservatism of the public makes up but 6 percent of the total answers, while the conservatism of the school board or of administrative officers each has a frequency of but 3 percent. There seems no escape from the conclusion that desirable changes might be brought about freely, if only their desirability could be objectively proved. The answers given in these questionnaires seem to the writer to indicate that "lack of knowledge" is the basic and perhaps the only major factor operating to restrict progress.

Subjects Added

To make more clearly evident the nature of the changes which have taken place in the content of the curriculum, schools were asked to list the subjects added and dropped. Ninety-six schools reported a total of 227 answers and listed 58 subjects added. The ten subjects most frequently mentioned are:

Physical or Health Education	48 times
Civics	14 times
General Science	14 times
Nature Study	11 times
Safety Education	11 times
Music	9 times
Manual Training	8 times
Fire Prevention	6 times
Home Economics	6 times
Thrift	5 times

Morals and manners are given four times, ethics twice, and service work once. Ten cities replied that no subjects had been added.

Subjects Dropped

But 56 schools responded by supplying lists of subjects dropped and the total answers on this point were but 66. Thirty-eight schools reported no subjects dropped and the remaining 28 answers must be credited to 18 schools. Seventeen different subjects are mentioned, none more than 3 times. These are: old-time physiology, manual training, domestic science, nature study, history and geography replaced by social science.

In general, the larger school systems have added fewer subjects and dropped more. The general tendency of American schools seems to be to add new subjects freely and to drop subjects seldom. It seems to be easier to modify by adaptation than to drop outright.

Modern Tendencies

To get some indication of the extent to which certain modern philosophies of education are affecting school practice, the schools were asked specifically whether or not they provided for certain types of work. From 117 schools there were furnished 221 answers. The results are as follows:

			Percent of Total
1. Teach certain subjects with acquisition of knowledge and skill as an important aim	Yes	103	
	Qualified Yes	6	49
2. Organize subject matter around large topics based on the social activities of the day	Yes	44	
	Qualified Yes	14	27
3. Divide curriculum into socialized group work and individualized study and drill work in tool subjects	Yes	37	
	Qualified Yes	14	23
4. Provide an activities curriculum with no division into subjects and no provision for other than incidental learning	Yes	3	1

These figures tell an interesting story of curriculum evolution from the old conception of learning as memorization toward the new conception of education as life. Approximately one-half of the schools have been markedly influenced by the movements for the socialization and individualization of instruction, but have been influenced scarcely at all by the more radical ideals. To-day the conventional curriculum is a subject-matter curriculum, less rigidly organized in terms of logical sequence and textbook than formerly. The tendency of change is toward socialization of school work and organization in terms of units of content or activity. Those who contend that the logical outcome of such a tendency is the complete abolition of subject-matter divisions and the organization of courses of study in terms of functional activity, must count themselves on the extreme radical wing of American practice.

Use of Standards

Obviously, one of the most important educational movements of our times has been the development and use of tests and measurements, particularly from the point of view of definition of aim. To the question: "In what subjects does the present elementary course of study set up standards by age and grade?" 79 schools furnished a total of 469 answers. Thirty-six subjects are mentioned at least once. The more important, arranged in order of frequency of mention, are:

Standards Objectively Measurable by Standard Tests		Standards Objectively Measurable by Examinations and Informal Tests		Standards not Objectively Measurable	
Total Replies	226	Total Replies	165	Total Replies	82
Arithmetic	53	English	24	Drawing	14
Reading	47	Geography	18	Music	8
Spelling	40	Arithmetic	16	Physical Training	6
Writing	31	Reading	16	General Science	5
English	19	History	15	Social Studies	4
Geography	10	Spelling	14	Household Arts	4
None	6	Writing	11	None	5
All other replies	20	All subjects	10	All other replies	36
		Music	6		
		Social Studies	6		
		None	5		
		All other replies	24		

These figures seem to the writer to prove that anything useful that is made available for schoolmen will be put to use. The simpler, more objective tests have already become a part of routine classroom work. The larger cities apparently make a little more use of these newer tools than the smaller cities.

Amount of Adaptation Permitted

An important and much debated subject is the freedom allowed teachers and pupils in adapting their work to their needs. From 119 schools were obtained 396 answers to the questions asked on this point. The data have been summarized as follows:

	Yes	No
1. Specify precise ground covered, no option	5	72
2. Specify general ground to be covered and give some measure of option	88	2
3. Specify minimal essentials and provide for teacher's choice beyond	61	15
4. Specify requirements for bright, average, and dull; teachers choice beyond	41	29
5. Provide rich suggestions and complete freedom	30	18
6. Provide general directions only	6	26

The different sized cities show small differences. The smaller cities as a rule are more liberal and have fewer exact specifications. All the schools exhibit tendencies away from the old autocratic administrative control toward a more democratic spirit. This is shown also by the returns from the question in regard to control of methods.

	Yes	No
1. Exact method and devices prescribed	2	74
2. General methods prescribed	80	15
3. Leave choice entirely to teacher	46	25

Teacher Training

An important phase of curriculum-revision is provision for the training of teachers in service to understand and use the new opportunities provided by the revised course of study. The 271 answers supplied by 118 schools are:

1. No formal provision	53
2. Visits of special supervisors	81
3. Demonstration and instruction meetings	78
4. Formal teacher training classes	43

Here, also, the larger the city, the greater the problem and the more formal the provisions that are made. The need is clearly recognized and the tendency is to provide specific and formal training when that is possible.

Appraisal

The final question in our series dealt with appraisal. The problem of appraisal is not often recognized, yet it is one upon which intelligent control of progress depends. From 116 schools 187 answers were obtained.

	Yes	No
1. No appraisal made	11	3
2. Informal appraisal by administrative and supervisory offices	87	0
3. Appraisal by research department	54	0
4. Formal, organized appraisal	24	0
5. Miscellaneous replies	8	0

Here, as previously, the returns show that the informal subjective appraisal is the order of the day and that it is chiefly the larger cities that have appreciated this problem and attempted its solution.

Summary

So far as the replies to the questionnaire are representative of current practice, curriculum-revision in the average American school takes place about as follows:

1. The problem is consciously recognized by all. The precise steps taken to solve it are determined in part by the size of the city.

2. In approximately half the cities of about 60,000 population or more, specific agents are set apart charged with responsibility for curriculum-revision. The title and dignity of the office increase roughly in proportion to the size of the city. The number of such agents vary with size of city.

3. Practice is so variable it may be said to be almost completely unstandardized.

4. Some form of curriculum-revision is continuously under way. There are general revisions at five-year or six-year intervals, and partial revisions at all times. In general, there has been a marked increase in curriculum-construction during the last three years.

5. The subjects receiving the major attention are the old-line subjects, but the tendency to revise the social science subjects is quite general.

6. Many changes are brought about informally through change of teachers, textbooks, etc.

7. The source of the criticism that leads to change is pretty largely the school staff itself.

8. Its criticism is mainly subjective and the motive for change is the improvement of instruction.

9. In general, the machinery of revision is a committee composed of teachers, principals, and supervisory officers.

10. The method is revision on the basis of progressive practice and subjective opinion.

11. There are no powerful influences restricting progress except lack of knowledge about the facts and laws of curriculum-construction.

12. Subjects are constantly being added to the curriculum, but few are dropped.

13. The general level of evolution reached in curriculum-construction is that which organizes materials in terms of subjects and topics, but increasing use is made of illustrations from the social life of the day.

14. In the case of the simpler skills, standards are quite generally set in terms of the simpler standardized tests.

15. Teachers are allowed considerable latitude of choice as to items taught and methods by which they are taught. The course of study provides rather definite general directions and standards, but after conforming to these, the teacher has freedom to adjust her work to meet the needs of individual classes and pupils (freedom under law).

16. Most school systems provide in some degree for the training of teachers in putting a new course of study into effect. The problem is clearly recognized, but the exact form of solution adopted depends upon the size, wealth, and situation of the city.

17. Only a few cities have formal scientific appraisal of the effect of new courses of study.

18. In general, the returns indicate healthy activity and growth with progressive tendencies all along the line. It is probable that the next few years will see very large and effective changes in the direction of progress. In general, the returns show that we are in a transition period of vigorous experimentation and change.

APPENDIX

Cities Contributing to the Study Reported in This Chapter

Adrian, Mich.
Alexandria, Va.
Alhambra, Calif.
Alluvir, N. Y.
Alton, Ill.
Anaconda, Mont.
Anacortes, Wash.
Ann Arbor, Mich.
Athens, Pa.
Atlantic City, N. J.
Baltimore, Md.
Beaumont, Texas
Beaver Dam, Wis.
Bellingham, Wash.
Berkeley, Calif.
Beverly, Mass.
Birmingham, Ala.
Birmingham, Mich.
Bloomfield, N. J.
Bloomington, Ill.
Bluffton, Ind.
Boston, Mass.
Branford, Conn.
Bridgewater, Mass.
Burkburnett, Texas
Charleston, S. C.
Charleston, W. Va.
Chester, Pa.
Cheyenne, Wyo.
Chicago Heights, Ill.
Chicopee, Mass.
Cicero, Ill.
Coatesville, Pa.
Cleveland, Ohio.
Colorado Springs, Colo.
Columbus, Ga.
Columbus, Ohio
Concord, Mass.
Corsicana, Texas
Dayton, Ohio
Denver, Colo.
Detroit, Mich.
East Chicago, Ind.
East St. Louis, Ill.
Eldon, Mo.

El Paso, Texas.
Erie, Pa.
Eugene, Ore.
Fairmont, W. Va.
Fairview, N. J.
Faribault, Minn.
Fargo, N. Dak.
Flint, Mich.
Franklin, Mass.
Freeport, Pa.
Galesburg, Ill.
Galva, Ill.
Glasgow, Ky.
Grand Junction, Colo.
Grand Rapids, Minn.
Greeley, Colo.
Hackensack, N. J.
Haverhill, Mass.
Hazleton, Pa.
Homestead, Pa.
Huntington, Ind.
Hutchinson, Minn.
Jackson, Mich.
Jacksonville, Texas.
Jefferson City, Mo.
Joliet, Ill.
Jonesboro, Ark.
Lancaster, Ohio
LaSalle, Ill.
Lenoir, N. C.
Litchfield, Conn.
Long Branch, Calif.
Lorain, Ohio
Lyons, Kan.
Middleton, Conn.
Millville, N. J.
Missoula, Mont.
Mounds, Ill.
Munhall, Pa.
Muskegon Heights, Mich.
Nephi, Utah
Newark, N. J.
Newburg, N. Y.
New London, Conn.
North Bergen, N. J.
Norwood, Mass.
Oakland, Calif.
Oak Park, Ill.
Olean, N. Y.
Omaha, Neb.
Ottawa, Ill.
Paducah, Ky.
Palestine, Texas
Paterson, N. J.
Petersburg, Va.
Philadelphia, Pa.
Phoenix, Ariz.
Piqua, Ohio
Port Arthur, Texas
Port Jarvis, N. Y.
Richmond, Ind.
Richmond, Va.
River Rouge, Mich.
Roanoke, Va.
Rock Island, Ill.
Sacramento, Calif.
St. Joseph, Mo.
St. Charles, Mo.
Salem, Ohio
Salt Lake City, Utah
San Francisco, Calif.
Santa Monica, Calif.
Sault St. Marie, Mich.
Schenectady, N. Y.
Sioux City, Iowa
South Orange and Maplewood, N. J.
Savannah, Ga.
Spokane, Wash.
Streator, Ill.
Sykesville, Pa.
Trenton, N. J.
Washington, D. C.
Washington, Pa.
West Allis, Wis.
Wilmington, Del.
West Newton, Pa.
Winston-Salem, N. C.

CHAPTER VII

CURRENT PRACTICES IN CURRICULUM-MAKING IN PUBLIC HIGH SCHOOLS

George S. Counts
School of Education, University of Chicago, Chicago, Illinois

Owing to the very rapid growth of secondary education during the past generation, the problem of curriculum-making assumes a more urgent form in the public high school than in any other division of the educational system. As the conditions of life change, as knowledge grows, and as the technique of curriculum-making improves, every educational institution should modify its procedures. These factors affect the high school as they must affect every educational agency. But the unprecedented increase in the high-school enrollment has introduced into the situation an additional factor of great significance. Largely as a consequence of this expansion, the very purposes of secondary education are undergoing fundamental change and secondary education itself is passing through a period of reorganization. However perfectly the conventional curriculum may have been adjusted to the realization of the aim of the narrowly selective secondary education of the nineteenth and preceding centuries, it is hardly suited to the needs of the vastly increased high-school population of to-day.

In order to secure data on current practices in curriculum-making in public high schools, a form similar to that used in the study of the elementary schools was sent to some nine hundred cities in the United States. These cities ranged from villages with but 2500 inhabitants to the largest cities in the nation. Owing to the detail asked for in the questionnaire and the shortness of the time allowed for its return, usable reports were received from but a small proportion of the cities. The facts are presented in Table I. According to this table, data for the senior, or conventional four-year high schools were secured from but 111 cities and for the junior high school from but 73 cities. This incompleteness in the returns suggests a rather high degree of selection. In all probability those cities tended to respond which were particularly interested in the problems of the curriculum and active in their solution. The data to be set forth in the subsequent pages, therefore, may be assumed to create a somewhat fairer picture of the practices of curriculum-making than the general situation in secondary schools would warrant. However, if the cities represented in this study are on the average the more progressive cities in the country, they are of special interest because they reveal the direction in which the schools are moving and occupy a position which the more conservative cities will reach in due season.

TABLE I.—NUMBER OF CITIES REPORTING CURRICULUM PRACTICES FOR JUNIOR AND SENIOR HIGH SCHOOLS

(Cities classified according to enrolment in each type of high school.)

Type of high school	Enrollment			Total
	1–499	500–1499	1500–	
Junior high school	20	28	25	73
Senior high school*	38	42	31	111
Total	58	70	56	184

*All four-year high schools of the conventional type are classified as senior high schools.

CHANGES IN THE CURRICULUM

One significant gauge of the importance of the problem of curriculum-making is found in the extent of the changes which are taking place in the secondary-school curriculum to-day. Each city was asked to report the date of the last *general* revision of its high-school course of study. The nature of the responses to this question, for both the junior and the senior high school, is shown in Table II. This table presents unequivocal evidence regarding the enormous amount of time and energy which is being devoted in these cities to the improvement of the materials of instruction. In each of 72 of the 111 cities reporting for the senior high school there has been at least one general revision of the curriculum since 1913. The corresponding figure for the 73 cities reporting for the junior high school is 58. Thus, the reconstruction of the curriculum is proceeding with approximately equal strength in both divisions of the secondary school. Moreover, interest in the problem is by no means confined to the larger cities. Nineteen of the 38 cities having high-school enrolments under 500 reported general revisions during the past dozen years. This report on the last general revision is, of course, but a partial measure of the extent of activity in curriculum-making in these cities. In the first place, previous general revisions are not included. Forty-three cities each reported at least one additional general revision of the senior-high-school curriculum since 1910, and 31 cities made similar reports regarding the junior-high-school program. In the second place, partial, but specially

TABLE II.—DATE OF THE LAST GENERAL REVISION OF THE HIGH-SCHOOL COURSE OF STUDY

Year	Senior High School				Junior High School	Grand Total
	1–499	500–1499	1500–	Total		
1925	3	9	8	20	20	40
1924	5	4	4	13	13	26
1923	2	5	1	8	11	19
1922	1	4	3	8	3	11
1921	0	2	2	4	5	9
1920	5	2	3	10	1	11
1919	1	1	0	2	2	4
1918	1	1	0	2	2	4
1917	0	0	0	0	0	0
1916	0	0	1	1	0	1
1915	0	1	1	2	0	2
1914	1	0	0	1	1	2
1913	0	0	1	1	0	1
Total...	19	29	24	72	58	130

organized, revision of the course of study is known to occur with considerable frequency. For the senior high school thirty-nine such revisions, and for the junior high school nineteen such revisions, were reported for the last five years. In the third place, a city may dispense with periodic organized revisions and may adopt the policy of conscious, but gradual and continuous revision of its high-school program. For the senior high school such a policy was reported from 24 cities, and for the junior high school from 23 cities. In the fourth place, the curriculum is always and necessarily being modified through changes in textbooks and in the teaching staff. These facts all indicate very clearly that the problem of curriculum-making is a problem of great practical importance in the public high school.

Another measure of the frequency and nature of changes in the curriculum is found in the addition and abandonment of individual subjects. Those reporting the practices from the different cities were asked to list the subjects which had been either added to, or dropped from, the high-school course of study during the last five years. The responses to this request for the senior high school are summarized in Table III. According to this table, those subjects which may be grouped under the general heading of social science were reported as added to the program in 71 and as dropped from the program in 19 instances. This gives a net gain for this group of studies of 52. The remainder of the table may be understood if read in similar fashion.

TABLE III.—SUBJECTS ADDED TO, AND DROPPED FROM, THE PROGRAM OF STUDIES OF THE SENIOR HIGH SCHOOL DURING THE LAST FIVE YEARS

(Subjects grouped into fourteen great divisions. Data from 90 cities. The net changes are positive save where minus signs are prefixed.)

Division of Subject Matter	Times Added	Times Dropped	Net Change
Social Science	71	19	52
Commercial Subjects	64	15	49
Industrial Arts	47	9	38
Home Economics	23	1	22
English	21	0	21
Music	14	1	13
Physical Education	12	0	12
Art	8	0	8
Natural Sciences	37	29	8
Mathematics	11	4	7
Agriculture	6	3	3
Normal	4	1	3
Ancient Languages	1	11	−10
Modern Languages	22	37	−15
Total	341	130	+211

Perhaps the most significant feature of this table is the general impression which it conveys. The public-high-school curriculum is obviously in a state of flux. Within the short space of five years there were, according to the reports, 471 changes in the subjects taught in the high schools of these 90 cities. Moreover, the number of changes was probably considerably larger than the table indicates. Frequently, the modification of the curriculum was reported in general terms, such as, commercial subjects, home economics, industrial arts, Spanish, or agriculture. In each of these cases the presumption is that several units of work were involved, but in tabulating the returns their generic character was disregarded. Each change reported was given a weight of one and only one. Another factor which probably worked in the direction of an understatement of the subject changes was the incorrect or incomplete report. The tendency to forget changes that actually had occurred was certainly much stronger than the tendency to set down changes that had not taken place. Quite probably for some of the cities only the more important or impressive changes were reported. That the curriculum is therefore changing as rapidly as the table suggests can hardly be doubted. As few educational institutions have changed in the past, the public high school is changing to-day. And if changes should proceed at the present rate for a single generation, the curriculum might easily assume a form which would make it almost unrecognizable.

There is one problem in curriculum-making revealed by Table III which merits the most earnest consideration. The reader has perhaps observed that, whereas 341 subjects were added to the program in these cities, but 130 were abandoned. Thus, for every subject dropped, almost three were added. That this condition has characterized the evolution of the high school for a half-century is suggested by the rapid expansion of its curriculum during this period. While this practice has resulted in a much needed enrichment of the narrow program of language and mathematics, it cannot be pursued indefinitely. Already the secondary-school curriculum exhibits weaknesses which may be traced to this constant addition of new materials of instruction. It is too often a mere aggregation of subjects, an unintegrated program of unrelated activities. This situation may be traced to a fundamental defect in the traditional technique of curriculum-making. A policy of *laissez faire* has customarily been followed. The responsibility for the state of the program of studies has been neither delegated to, nor assumed by, any effective central agency. The nature of the curriculum has rather been determined by the specialists in subject matter and has been left to the mercy of the conflicts among the vested interests. Under these conditions, while a new subject may be added without great opposition, the clear-cut and complete abandonment of an established subject is extremely difficult. Once it has become firmly rooted in the curriculum, unless it is the victim of violent popular passion, as in the case of German, or unless it dies of old age, as in the case of Greek, a subject is apparently able to maintain itself indefinitely. So long as a subject has friends on the high-school staff, it is relatively safe from outside attack; and, so long as a subject is taught by numerous teachers, it will not lack friends.

An examination of the relative positions of the several divisions of subject matter in Table III shows the direction in which the public-high-school curriculum is moving. Social science leads, with a net gain during the five years of 52 additions. Then follow in order the commercial subjects, industrial arts, home economics, and English. In view of the fact that in the case of the vocational subjects a single reference, such as "commercial subjects," undoubtedly included more than a single subject, it is quite possible that one of these groups, rather than social science, should occupy first place. But however that may be, the evidence shows emphatically that the subjects mentioned, with perhaps music and physical education added, represent the new tradition in secondary education.

At the foot of the table are the subjects which have been most closely associated with secondary education in the past—the foreign languages. The two divisions of these languages, alone among the fourteen groups of subjects, show a net loss in representation during the five-year period. For the ancient languages but one addition was reported, while there were eleven subtractions. This division therefore exhibits a net loss of ten. The position of the modern languages reveals even less strength. Although representatives of this group were added in 22 instances, this show of power was much more than cancelled by 37 subtractions. These facts indicate that in the future the languages will be less intimately identified with the high-school curriculum than they have been in the past.

The fortunes of one other division of subject matter, as revealed in the table, should be considered. In the number of times added, the natural sciences occupy fourth place with a score of 37, while in changes of the reverse order they almost rival the modern languages with 29 subtractions. Thus, the changes which are taking place in this group of subjects would appear to be of a very unusual character. A spirit of unrest seems to permeate the natural science program in the high school. That this program is being reorganized is indicated by the facts presented in Table IV.

TABLE IV.—SUBJECTS ADDED TO, OR DROPPED FROM, THE PROGRAM OF STUDIES OF THE SENIOR HIGH SCHOOL DURING THE LAST FIVE YEARS IN 90 CITIES
(Net changes are positive save where minus sign is prefixed.)

Subject	Times Added	Times Dropped	Net Change	Subject	Times Added	Times Dropped	Net Change
Home Economics	19	0	19	Applied Mathematics	1	0	1
Economics	16	2	14	Architectural Drawing	1	0	1
Problems of Democracy	14	1	13	Astronomy	2	1	1
Public Speaking	13	0	13	Bacteriology	1	0	1
Industrial Arts	12	0	12	Band	1	0	1
Music	13	1	12	Bible	1	0	1
Physical Education	12	0	12	Business Forms	1	0	1
Office Practice	11	0	11	Character Education	1	0	1
Commercial Subjects	10	1	9	Commercial Law	4	3	1
Salesmanship	9	0	9	Dietetics	1	0	1
Sociology	9	0	9	Dramatic Art	1	0	1
Art	8	0	8	Government	1	0	1
Spanish	12	4	8	Industrial Geography	1	0	1
Biology	7	1	6	Marketing	1	0	1
General Mathematics	6	0	6	Mediæval and Mod. Hist.	2	1	1
Printing	6	0	6	Millinery	1	0	1
World History	6	0	6	Pacific Coast History	1	0	1
Chemistry	6	1	5	Photography	1	0	1
Civics	6	1	5	Short Story Writing	1	0	1
Electricity	5	0	5	Textiles	1	0	1
General Science	6	1	5	Thrift	1	0	1
Mechanical Drawing	5	0	5	Business English	2	2	0
Commercial Arithmetic	6	2	4	Psychology	1	1	0
Occupations	4	0	4	Camp Cooking	0	1	−1
Stenography	4	0	4	College Algebra	1	2	−1
Agriculture	6	3	3	Com. Math. (Adv.)	0	1	−1
Auto Mechanics	5	2	3	Forging	1	2	−1
French	5	2	3	Industrial History	1	2	−1
Journalism	3	0	3	Manual Training	2	3	−1
Machine Shop	3	0	3	Pattern Making	0	1	−1
Normal	4	1	3	Philosophy	0	1	−1
Physics	4	1	3	Physiology	3	4	−1
Radio	3	0	3	Retail Selling	0	1	−1
Sheet Metal	3	0	3	Sanitation	0	1	−1
Trigonometry	3	0	3	Strength of Materials	0	1	−1
Typewriting	3	0	3	Zoology	2	3	−1
Bookkeeping	3	1	2	Ancient History	3	5	−2
Business Organization	2	0	2	Geology	0	2	−2
Carpentry	2	0	2	Surveying	0	2	−2
Commercial Geography	6	4	2	Latin	1	4	−3
English	2	0	2	Botany	2	7	−5
Geography	2	0	2	English History	0	5	−5
History of South America	2	0	2	Greek	0	7	−7
Home Nursing	2	0	2	Physiography	0	7	−7
Italian	2	0	2	German	3	31	−28
Library Training	2	0	2				
Acetylene Welding	1	0	1	Total	341	130	211

In Table IV the data regarding subject matter changes are given in detail. The frequency with which each subject was either added or abandoned is indicated. A glance over this table shows at least four important groups of subjects. In the first group would be included certain relatively new subjects, such as home economics, economics, problems of democracy, public speaking, and many others, which are consistently strong. In nearly all cases these subjects are reported as being added and not abandoned. In a second group would be included certain of the older subjects, such as German, physiography, Greek, English history, botany, and Latin, which are consistently weak. Usually, when these subjects are reported, they are reported as being dropped. In a third group would be placed certain subjects, such as Spanish, agriculture, commercial geography, commercial law, manual training, physiology, zoölogy, and ancient history, which seem to show no consistent tendency. In some schools they are being added to the program, while in others they are being dropped from it. In a fourth group would be placed a large group of subjects, such as history of South America, home nursing, Italian, library training, acetylene welding, bacteriology, Bible, character education, photography, and many others, with which particular high schools seem to be experimenting.

The earlier references in Table III to the position of the foreign languages and the natural sciences should be illuminated by the detail of the present table. The weakness exhibited by the ancient languages is seen to be due chiefly to the abandonment of Greek in seven cities, but also to the reduction of the Latin program in four schools. The passing of Greek is particularly worthy of note, because few would have suspected that this time-honored subject had survived in these seven cities to such recent times. The weakness of the modern languages may be traced chiefly to the dropping of German because of the popular revulsion of feeling against German culture following the war. But with the passing of the war psychology this subject will undoubtedly return to a position of some strength in the curriculum. The uncertain behavior of the natural sciences is to be accounted for in terms of the shift of emphasis to a new group of subjects. Physiography, botany, zoölogy, geology, and physiology are apparently being displaced by a program composed of general science, biology, chemistry, and physics.

Thus far, the discussion of subject changes has been confined to the senior high school. Moreover, little will be said here regarding the junior high school. The justification of this relative neglect of the lower institution lies in the fact that it is engaged in the task of establishing itself. As a consequence, changes in its curriculum are somewhat less significant than changes in the program of the older school. Nevertheless, the general facts concerning curriculum changes in the junior high school should be briefly examined. These facts may be found in Table V. If this table be compared with

TABLE V.—SUBJECTS ADDED TO, OR DROPPED FROM, THE PROGRAM OF STUDIES OF THE JUNIOR HIGH SCHOOL DURING THE LAST FIVE YEARS

(Subjects grouped into thirteen great divisions. Data from 57 cities.)

Division of Subject Matter	Times Added	Times Dropped	Net Change
Industrial Arts	21	1	20
Social Science	29	10	19
Natural Science	15	3	12
Home Economics	12	1	11
Physical Education	10	0	10
Commercial Subjects	10	4	6
Art	5	0	5
Ancient Language	5	1	4
Mathematics	5	1	4
Modern Language	5	1	4
Music	2	0	2
Agriculture	1	0	1
English	4	5	−1
Total	124	27	97

Table III, the corresponding table for the senior high school, certain similarities and differences may be observed. Although their order is slightly altered, the industrial arts, social science, and home economics rank near the top in both tables. The foreign languages and mathematics likewise receive relatively equal treatment in the two institutions by being placed near the other extreme in the distribution. But in the case of English and natural science a marked divergence of tendencies may be discerned. In the senior high school English occupies fifth place, while in the junior high school this subject is at the foot of the list, with more subtractions than additions. This is due to the dropping of certain of the traditional grammar-grade subjects, such as reading, grammar, and spelling.

On the other hand, the favored position of the natural sciences is accounted for almost solely through the wide introduction of general science.

From the foregoing analysis of the extent of curriculum-revision and of the frequency of the subject changes in the high schools of these cities, it is clear that the problem of curriculum-making in the public high school is a most urgent one. This is by no means an academic question. The secondary-school curriculum to-day is the scene of extraordinary activity. At frequent intervals the course of study is undergoing either general or partial revision, and subjects are being constantly added to, or dropped from, the program. At a time when the traditional molds of secondary education are being broken, the problem of curriculum-making cannot be escaped. The need for passing current practices, methods, and technique of curriculum-construction under careful scrutiny is consequently apparent.

Agents Responsible for the State of the Curriculum

In every city the responsibility for the state of the high-school curriculum must be delegated either implicitly or explicitly to some agent or group of agents. A consideration of the technique of curriculum-making, therefore, might very properly begin with an examination of the agents by whom this function is discharged.

The facts for the senior high school from 109 cities and for the junior high school from 69 cities may be found in Table VI. According to this table, the responsibility for the state of the curriculum may rest with the state department of public instruction, with the city superintendent of schools, or with any one or combination of eighteen agents under the latter. If the returns for the junior and senior schools be combined, it will be observed that in fifteen out of a total of 178 instances the state department assumes sole responsibility for the curriculum and that in fifty-six the superintendent alone discharges this function. This means that in 107 instances authority over the curriculum is delegated to the various representatives of the superintendent in the city system. Naturally, the agent to whom this authority is most commonly delegated is the high-school principal. In 94 of these 107 cases he is reported as functioning in this capacity. However, as the table shows, he ordinarily has associated with him in this work, the heads of departments, the teachers of special subjects, supervisors, assistant superintendents, or other agents in the system.

The table reveals several relationships of some significance. The dependence on the state department for the senior-high-school curriculum is found for the most part in the cities having senior-high-

TABLE VI.—AGENTS TO WHOM RESPONSIBILITY FOR THE STATE OF THE HIGH-SCHOOL COURSE OF STUDY AND FOR ITS REVISION IS DELEGATED AS A DISTINCTIVE FUNCTION

(Data for the senior high school from 109 cities and for the junior high school from 69 cities.)

Agent	Senior High School				Junior High School	Grand Total
	1–499	500–1499	1500–	Total		
I. State department only	7	3	1	11	4	15
II. Superintendent only	17	8	5	30	26	56
III. Agents under superintendent						
1. High-school principal	13	31	20	64	30	94
2. Head of department	6	16	16	38	14	52
3. Teacher of subject	3	14	6	23	12	35
4. Supervisor of subject	2	6	8	16	15	31
5. Assistant superintendent	0	0	14	14	13	27
6. Department of research	1	1	3	5	7	12
7. Permanent committee	0	2	2	4	7	11
8. Director of the curriculum	0	0	2	2	2	4
9. Assistant principal	0	0	3	3	0	3
10. Deputy superintendent	0	0	1	1	2	3
11. Director of supervision	0	0	1	1	2	3
12. Associate superintendent	0	0	2	2	0	2
13. Subject committee	1	0	0	1	1	2
14. Supervisor of elementary education	0	0	0	0	2	2
15. Chairman of subject committee	0	0	1	1	0	1
16. Department of standards	0	1	0	1	0	1
17. Director of measurements	0	0	1	1	0	1
18. Recorder	0	0	1	1	0	1
Total	50	82	87	219	137	356

school enrolments of fewer than five hundred pupils. The larger cities have apparently secured a measure of freedom here that is denied the less populous centers. Likewise, the tendency for the superintendent to assume sole responsibility for the state of the curriculum is confined largely to the smaller cities or the cities having the smaller high-school enrolments. In the larger communities the superintendent is much more likely to delegate authority to his subordinates. Moreover, the number and variety of these subordinates, assistants, and special agencies must be highly restricted in the smaller cities. Between the junior and senior high schools there seem to be few significant differences.

A critical examination of the situation as reported from these cities raises certain doubts regarding the adequacy of the existing organization. The question which called forth the responses summarized in the table took the following form: "Do you have in your regular administrative organization agents other than the superintendent to whom responsibility for the state of the high-school course of study and for its revision is delegated as a distinctive function?" That as large a proportion of the cities as the table suggests actually have agents to whom this function is *distinctively* delegated is extremely doubtful. The more likely interpretation of the facts is that, where principal, departmental head, teacher, or assistant superintendent is mentioned, the particular agent in question merely carries a larger measure of responsibility than any other individual in the system. The probabilities are that in the great majority of cases the curriculum interest is but one among many and is a distinctly marginal interest at that. For example, the various studies of the high-school principal show that he is in actual fact an extremely busy individual, engaged in a multitude of tasks, and devoted for the most part to the routine aspects of his job. Technically, he may be regarded as responsible for the state of the curriculum in his school, but actually this responsibility is accorded very little of his time and energy. The matters receiving his attention are those immediate and pressing demands, such as the distribution of supplies, the handling of disciplinary cases, the pacification of irate parents, the adjustment of the complaints of teachers, and the preparation of reports, which must be met if the school is to function in its physical aspects. The state of the curriculum seldom takes the form of one of these demands. The curriculum does not insistently force itself upon the attention of teacher, supervisor, and administrator. Consequently, if the problem of the curriculum is to receive the consideration it deserves, it must be delegated as a distinctive function to some agent in the system. This means that some individual or group of individuals must accept the state of the curriculum as a focal, rather than as a marginal interest.

Criticism of the Curriculum: Its Source and Nature

Source of Criticism

The process of curriculum-revision necessarily begins with some expression of dissatisfaction with the existing program. Conceivably, this criticism may emanate from any source, from agencies within or forces without the educational system. The sources from which the criticism did come which led to the last revision, either general or partial, of the high-school curriculum in the cities investigated are indicated in Table VII. For the junior high school, reports were received from 57 cities and for the senior high school,

Table VII.—Immediate Sources of Criticism Which Led to Revision, Either General of Partial, of the High-School Course of Study

(Data for the junior high school from 57 cities and for the senior high school from 95 cities.)

Source of Criticism	Junior High School	Senior High School	Total
Superintendent of schools	53	72	125
High-school principal	42	70	112
High-school teacher	35	68	103
General supervisory staff	17	22	39
State legislation	8	15	23
College	0	12	12
Children	4	7	11
School board	5	6	11
Senior high school	9	0	9
Parents	3	5	8
Social groups	2	5	7
Press	1	3	4
Book companies	2	1	3
High-school inspector	0	2	2
Total	181	288	469

from 95 cities. Since no differences in the source of criticism between the general and partial revisions were discovered, facts for these two forms of revision were combined.

According to the testimony of those who reported practices from these cities—and they were presumably in most cases either the superintendents or their representatives—the criticism which led to revision came more frequently from the superintendent than from any other source. The superintendent was mentioned 125 times. His nearest rival is the high-school principal, with a score of 112.

The high-school teacher occupies third place. From these three sources came three-fourths of the criticism launched against the curriculum. Except that the senior high school is to be reckoned with in the one case and the college in the other, the sources of criticism are the same for both the junior and the senior high school.

Perhaps the most significant conclusion suggested by the table is that the high-school curriculum is relatively free from criticism arising from non-professional sources or at least that such criticism does not lead to curriculum-revision. Even the local school board rarely initiates criticism that bears fruit. The various minorities in the community appear on the whole to have but little influence. If this is a true picture of the actual situation, the responsibility for the improvement of the curriculum would seem to rest squarely on the shoulders of those who are professionally equipped for the task. But that this picture is entirely trustworthy may be doubted. The questionnaire was filled out by persons who were undoubtedly tempted to glorify the rôle which they had played in the process of curriculum-revision. Moreover, after the event, it is always very difficult to give a reliable account of the forces that produced any complex social phenomenon. This problem, therefore, requires further investigation.

Certain facts not presented in the table merit brief consideration. The sources of criticism varied somewhat among cities of different sizes. In the smaller systems the superintendent is a more important factor in initiating criticism than in the larger systems. In the latter the responsibility is carried in greater measure by the high-school principal, the high-school teacher, and the general supervisory staff.

Another question worthy of consideration concerns the major and minor sources of criticism. The questionnaire called not only for a report on the sources of criticism but also for a division of those sources into major and minor influences. When the situation is surveyed from this standpoint, the superintendent of schools is seen to play a yet more important rôle in the process of curriculum-revision. Thus, while he is reported as a source of criticism 125 times, he is described as a major source in 68 and a minor source in 57 instances. In the case of the high-school principal the relative emphasis is reversed. Out of a total of 112, he is rated as a major source of criticism but 45 times, and as a minor source, 67 times.

The corresponding figures for the high-school teacher are 30 and 73. Thus, according to his own estimate the superintendent is by far the most important factor in directing attention to the need for the revision of the high-school curriculum. An interesting commentary on this situation is found in an investigation[1] recently conducted by the writer in the high schools of fifteen cities. In this study the high-school principal was asked to indicate the agencies chiefly responsible for initiating changes in the curriculum. According to his estimate, he is the most important agency, with the teacher occupying second place, and the superintendent third. Apparently, much depends on the point of view!

Nature of Criticism

What was the nature of the criticisms which these various agencies advanced against the existing curriculum and which led to its revision? The answer to this question is found in Table VIII. Since no important differences between the smaller and the larger cities were discovered, the reports from all cities were combined. Data for the junior and senior high schools, however, are presented separately. The number of times each criticism was reported as a major or a minor criticism is indicated.

The basic criticism of the old program was that it was not adequately adjusted to pupil needs. This criticism easily leads in total frequency; as a major criticism it is mentioned more than twice as many times as its nearest rival. Almost every conceivable criticism is reported from one school or another. In some places the old course was regarded as too short, in others as too long; in some as too easy, in others as too difficult; and in 43 instances the old course had to be discarded because it was "out of style." Apparently, even a superintendent of schools hesitates to refuse to pay homage to the goddess of fashion. She seeks to exact her toll in education as well as in dress and social display.

Between the junior and senior high schools there are three interesting differences. In the former the inadequacy of the methods of instruction associated with the old course receives special emphasis. In accordance with its traditions this question of method seems less important in the senior high school. On the other hand,

[1] Counts, G. S. *The Senior-High-School Curriculum*, p. 127.

TABLE VIII.—MAJOR AND MINOR CRITICISMS WHICH LED TO REVISION, EITHER GENERAL OR PARTIAL, OF THE OLD COURSE OF STUDY

(Data for the senior high school from 92 cities and for the junior high school from 54 cities.)

Criticism	Senior High School			Junior High School			Total		Grand Total
	Major	Minor	Total	Major	Minor	Total	Major	Minor	
Old course unadjusted to pupil needs	34	37	71	21	23	44	55	60	115
Old course poorly organized	15	32	47	9	26	35	24	58	82
Old course uninteresting to pupil	7	26	33	5	20	25	12	46	58
Growth of high-school population	12	35	47	1	2	3	13	37	50
Old course out of style	5	18	23	6	14	20	11	32	43
Growth of knowledge	6	33	39	1	1	2	7	34	41
Old course taught by wrong methods	5	13	18	6	14	20	11	27	38
Old course too difficult	1	10	11	1	7	8	2	17	19
Old course too long	1	8	9	1	4	5	2	12	14
Defective articulation with elementary school	0	0	0	0	4	4	0	4	4
Old course too short	0	1	1	0	1	1	0	2	2
Old course too complex	0	1	1	0	0	0	0	1	1
Old course too easy	0	1	1	0	0	0	0	1	1
Total	86	215	301	51	116	167	137	331	468

in the latter the growth of the pupil population and the growth of knowledge are recognized as vital factors in creating the need for curriculum-revision. Whatever may be said regarding the growth of knowledge, the expansion of the school enrolment at the senior-high-school level during the last generation lies at the root of the need for a fundamental reorganization of the secondary-school curriculum.

Evidence on Which Criticism Was Based

One other set of facts concerning the criticism of the old curriculum will be presented. On what evidence was that criticism based? The data for the junior high school from 54 cities and for the senior high school from 90 cities are set down in Table IX.

TABLE IX.—EVIDENCE ON WHICH CRITICISM OF THE OLD COURSE OF STUDY WAS BASED

(Data for the senior high school from 90 cities and for the junior high school from 54 cities.)

Evidence	Senior High School			Total	Junior High School	Grand Total
	1–499	500–1499	1500–			
General knowledge of facts	21	30	21	72	40	112
Results of organized, but subjective study of situation	13	19	18	50	37	87
Results of objective study through tests by persons within system	13	10	11	34	27	61
Results of formal survey by outsiders	3	0	1	4	3	7
Total	50	59	51	160	107	267

This table requires little comment. For the most part, criticism is based on either a general knowledge of the facts or a subjective study of the situation. In but 25 percent of the cases is evidence derived from objective study. And the contribution of the formal survey by persons from outside the system is practically negligible. In both the junior and senior schools and in both large and small systems the conditions are substantially the same. Needless to say, any trustworthy criticism of any school program can hardly be prosecuted in the absence of accurate and objective knowledge.

THE TECHNIQUE OF CURRICULUM-REVISION

Agents of Revision

If criticism is to bear fruit in the revision of the curriculum, it must eventuate in practical steps looking in this direction. What agent or agents in the system serve as the avenues through which this criticism reaches the curriculum? By whom is the initiative taken which leads to revision? The responses of the superintendents in 92 cities for the senior high school and in 58 cities for the junior high school are summarized in Table X. In each case the report was supposed to describe the course that had actually been followed in the last revision of the curriculum.

TABLE X.—AGENTS BY WHOM THE INITIATIVE WAS TAKEN IN THE REVISION, EITHER GENERAL OF PARTIAL, OF THE HIGH-SCHOOL COURSE OF STUDY

(Data for the senior high school from 92 cities and for the junior high school from 58 cities.)

Agent	Senior High School			Total	Junior High School	Grand Total
	1–499	500–1499	1500–			
Superintendent	29	24	21	74	50	124
High-school principal	14	26	16	56	24	80
High-school teacher	7	21	11	39	17	56
General supervisory force	3	7	7	17	17	34
School board	0	1	1	2	4	6
Pupils	0	1	0	1	1	2
Assistant superintendent	0	0	1	1	0	1
Press	1	0	0	1	0	1
Public	1	0	0	1	0	1
Senior-high-school teacher	0	0	0	0	1	1
State department	1	0	0	1	0	1
Total	56	80	57	193	114	307

The general impression conveyed by this table is much the same as that conveyed by Table VII. In the latter the immediate sources of the criticism which led to curriculum-revision were described. For the most part, if the data presented in these two tables may be trusted, those individuals or agents who provide the criticism also take the initiative in the process of revision. In 124 instances, according to Table X, this initiative was taken by the superintendent of schools. The high-school principal comes second with a record of 80. The only additional agents having frequencies which place them in a position of any importance in this matter are the high-school teachers and the general supervisory force. Of course, in interpreting this table it must be borne in mind that the facts were furnished by the superintendent and might therefore be expected to give an unduly favorable account of the part which he plays in the process. In all probabilitiy the high-school principal is somewhat more active in the revision of the curriculum of his school than the table suggests.

Machinery of Revision

If the task of curriculum-making is to be prosecuted in an organized way, some sort of machinery must be set up. Rather detailed reports were received from the different cities describing the organization that had actually been used. Since the practices were ordinarily quite complex, and since they usually followed no single pattern in any city or institution, the facts cannot be satisfactorily presented in tabular form. A descriptive account will therefore be attempted. In this account, owing to the fact that the procedures followed in the junior and senior high schools were much the same, no comparison will be drawn between these two divisions of the secondary school.

The machinery for curriculum-revision may consist of a single individual, a small group variously constituted, committees of teachers working under different forms of leadership, or any combination of these three instruments. In very few instances is the burden carried by a single individual; but, according to the reports, it does occur occasionally in the smaller systems. When this procedure is followed, the individual bearing the responsibility is the superintendent or the high-school principal, usually the former. Dependence upon the small group is very common. This instrument was employed in the junior high school in 24 cities and in the senior high school in 45. When such a group is organized, it is almost always composed of members of the general administrative and supervisory staff, high-school principals, and high-school teachers. Only very rarely do experts or specialists from the outside find membership in this group. But the most common organization employed in these cities was the committee of teachers. In the junior high school such committees were used in 41 cities and in the senior high school in 49. By far the most frequent form of leadership provided for these committees was that of the administrative officer. Leadership was also frequently furnished by supervisory officers and somewhat less commonly by the teachers themselves. Persons from outside the system played but a very minor rôle on these committees. It should be pointed out in conclusion that these committees of teachers often work with or under a more general committee, which represents the various interests in the system and which discharges coördinating and correlating functions.

Method Used in Revision

What procedures do these individuals or groups follow in modifying the old program? Where do they get the materials with which they create the new curriculum? From what source do they obtain guidance in the selection and organization of subject matter? The answers to these questions are found in Table XI. Progressive practice elsewhere and committee discussion are the more important sources of guidance. Dependence on independent research is somewhat less common. Yet the evidence suggests that the revision of the curriculum is proceeding increasingly in the light of the results of investigation. The reader should, of course, observe that the

TABLE XI.—METHOD EMPLOYED IN THE SELECTION AND ORGANIZATION OF MATERIALS FOR THE NEW COURSE OF STUDY

(Data for the senior high school from 91 cities and for the junior high school from 57 cities.)

Selection and Organization Guided Largely By:	Senior High School			Total	Junior High School	Grand Total
	1–499	500–1499	1500–			
Progressive practice elsewhere	22	27	23	72	43	115
Results of committee discussions	14	24	22	60	40	100
Results of previous research, measurement, or experimentation	13	13	8	34	25	59
Results of research, measurement, or experimentation undertaken for the purpose	5	6	7	18	15	33
Orders from superintendent or his representative	6	4	2	12	9	21
Expert opinion	0	0	1	1	2	3
Total	60	74	63	197	134	331

several categories employed in this table are not mutually exclusive. Committee discussions, for example, might derive their inspiration and content from progressive practice elsewhere or from the results of research.

Obstacles to Curriculum-Revision

What are the major obstacles to curriculum-revision? In order to answer this question, the superintendent of schools was asked to indicate the factor or factors which had actually operated to restrict or limit the construction of an ideal curriculum. The responses to this request are reported in Table XII.

It would appear that there are five major factors. Arranged in the order of their importance, these factors are: first, the cost of ideal content or method; second, the training and present abilities of the teaching force; third, the character of the existing building or equipment; fourth, the character of existing textbooks; and fifth, the limitations of our present knowledge about the curriculum. The striking fact about this table is that the school is apparently hampered but little by the conservatism of the general public or by the interference of external forces. The great obstacles to curriculum-

TABLE XII.—FACTORS WHICH OPERATED TO RESTRICT OR LIMIT THE CONSTRUCTION OF AN IDEAL CURRICULUM

(Data for the senior high school from 79 cities and for the junior high school from 54 cities.)

Factor	Senior High School			Total	Junior High School	Grand Total
	1–499	500–1499	1500–			
Cost of ideal content or method	11	25	14	50	20	70
Training and present abilities of teaching force	15	17	9	41	27	68
Character of existing building and equipment	12	18	12	42	25	67
Character of existing textbooks	14	13	8	35	22	57
Limitations of our present knowledge about the curriculum	6	17	8	31	26	57
Conservatism of public	6	10	1	17	7	24
Conservatism of school board	2	6	2	10	3	13
Conservatism of administrative office	2	5	0	7	5	12
Possible exploitation of changes for political purposes	1	4	0	5	1	6
Influence of book companies whose textbooks would be displaced	1	1	0	2	0	2
Total	70	116	54	240	136	376

revision apparently reside within the school, in those interests which are vested in "things as they are." Under the restrictions set by the financial cost of change and the limitations of their own knowledge, the members of the profession seem to be given a relatively free hand by society.

Whether this is a true picture of the situation may be seriously questioned. The reader will observe that the conservatism of the administrative office is not regarded as an important obstacle to the construction of an ideal curriculum. Is this not probably to be traced to the fact that the administrative office was passing judgment on itself? If the questionnaire had been filled out by teachers, would the superintendent of schools have been given the same rating? And may the failure to feel the restraints of the general public not have been due to the essential conservatism of the administrative office? Conservatism is always a relative matter. If, for example, the conservatism of the superintendent equals that of the school board, the former is not likely to sense the bonds that bind him. Unless he is progressive and creative, society at large will not seek to curb his program.

The way in which the teacher hampers and influences curriculum-making in the high school merits special attention. With his training and experience he does constitute one of the great vested interests in the school. In this sense he is essentially conservative. But perhaps the greatest obstacle which the teacher presents to the development of an ideal curriculum centers not in the fact that he is conservative, but rather in the fact that he is a specialist. As a specialist, if he is energetic, he is not so much concerned about maintaining the *status quo* as in advancing the interests of his specialty. This situation is clearly revealed in the results of an investigation of the senior-high-school curriculum recently conducted by the writer. In this study 416 teachers of particular subjects, such as first-year algebra, third-year Latin, general science, civics, etc., were asked in the course of the description of the practices in these subjects whether in their opinion their particular subjects should be taken by more or by fewer pupils than take them to-day. The responses of these teachers are summarized in Table XIII. English is not included in this table because that subject is so commonly required of all pupils. All the other great divisions of subject matter are represented.

This table shows why subjects are being added to the curriculum much more rapidly than they are being abandoned. With the exception of the teachers of mathematics, practically all the teachers in these high schools feel that their own subjects should be more largely patronized than at present. Only rarely does a teacher favor a reduction in the number of pupils taking his subject. And quite likely such an individual is regarded as guilty of treason by his subject-matter compatriots. Most teachers are after numbers, are constantly seeking a larger place in the sun, and are prepared to oppose vigorously any effort to reduce the quantitative status of their subjects in the curriculum. If the high-school curriculum is ever to be revised in the pure light of educational need, one of two things must happen. Either the major problems of the cur-

TABLE XIII.—JUDGMENTS OF 416 TEACHERS AS TO WHETHER MORE OR FEWER PUPILS SHOULD TAKE THE SUBJECTS WHICH THEY TEACH*

Subject	Should this subject be taken by more or by fewer pupils than take it to-day?			
	More	Same Number	Fewer	Total
Latin	43	4	4	51
French	28	3	4	35
Spanish	22	3	3	28
Mathematics	17	13	18	48
Natural Science	55	11	2	68
Social Science	46	1	2	49
Commercial Subjects	48	8	5	61
Industrial Arts	32	5	0	37
Home Economics	20	0	0	20
Music	10	0	0	10
Art	8	1	0	9
Total	329	49	38	416

* Counts, G. S., *The Senior-High-School Curriculum*, p. 139.

riculum will have to be solved by a group of persons specially trained for the task or the high-school teacher will have to undergo a process of professional enlightenment commensurate with the scope of the responsibilities which he bears. At present, neither of these two conditions is fulfilled. Consequently, efforts at the reconstruction of the high-school curriculum take the form of partisan conflict and educational policy is determined by a balance of power among the vested interests.

CHARACTER OF PRESENT COURSE OF STUDY

Although the present investigation is concerned primarily with the practices of curriculum-making, something should be said regarding the general character of the existing course of study. An effort was made to discover the fundamental principle of its organization, the detail of its prescription in content, and the degree of its attention to the methods of instruction.

In Table XIV is presented a summary of current practice in the general organization of the course of study. Data were secured for the senior high school from 100 cities and for the junior high school from 62 cities. The excess of the grand total over 162 is explained by the fact that in many instances the course of study of a particular high school or city was organized in part about one principle and in part about another. According to this table, the general tendency is to follow tradition and organize the curriculum into separate subjects, such as algebra, Latin, history, etc. This tendency is somewhat stronger in the smaller than in the larger communities and in the senior than in the junior high school. In the more populous centers and in the lower division of the secondary school the curriculum has been more sensitive to criticism of conventional procedure.

TABLE XIV.—FORMS IN WHICH THE MATERIALS OF INSTRUCTION ARE ORGANIZED

(Data for the senior high school from 100 cities and for the junior high school from 62 cities.)

Form of Organization	Senior High School 1–499	500–1499	1500–	Total	Junior High School	Grand Total
Organization into separate subjects such as algebra, Latin, history, with acquisition of knowledge and skill as an important aim	28	36	28	92	55	147
Organization around large topics based on the social activities of the day	4	20	15	39	31	70
Division into socialized group work and individualized study and drill work in the tool or skill subjects	4	13	10	27	24	51
An activities curriculum with no division into subjects, and no provision for other than incidental learning	0	2	0	2	3	5
Total	36	71	53	160	113	273

The extent to which the present course of study prescribes the content of the curriculum and the ground to be covered is reported in Table XV. The more common practice seems to be that of following a middle course. The general ground to be covered is usually specified, but within these limits a considerable measure of selection is allowed the teacher. This tendency is best exemplified in the senior high schools of the smaller cities, least so in the junior high schools. In the latter, particularly, does the course of study recognize the needs of pupils at the various ability levels and specify rather precisely the minimal essentials to be mastered by all pupils. As in the case of the principle followed in the organization of the curriculum, so here the junior school appears to be less conservative than the senior institution.

TABLE XV.—CHARACTER OF THE CONTENT OF THE PRESENT COURSE OF STUDY

(Data for the senior high school from 102 cities and for the junior high school from 62 cities.)

Present Course of Study	Senior High School			Total	Junior High School	Grand Total
	1–499	500–1499	1500–			
Specifies general ground to be covered, but provides for some measure of selection by the teacher............	24	28	26	78	45	123
Specifies requirements for different classes of students, as bright, average, and dull, but provides for selection by the teacher beyond the requirements	2	11	13	26	30	56
Specifies precise minimal essentials and provides for choice by the teacher beyond minimal essentials............	7	12	8	27	26	53
Provides only standards and rich suggestions of materials, leaving it to the teacher to make selection of materials best adapted to bring children up to standard........................	2	10	5	17	11	28
Specifies in detail the precise ground to be covered, giving no option to the teacher........................	2	5	3	10	0	10
Provides general directions only, leaving it entirely to the teacher to determine what standards shall be attained and what materials shall be used.........	1	2	2	5	2	7
Total...........................	38	68	57	163	114	277

In Table XVI is reported the measure of freedom which the present course of study allows the teacher in the choice of methods of teaching. There seems to be no disposition on the part of those who make the course of study to prescribe the exact methods and devices to be followed by the teacher. Content is obviously much more fully prescribed than method. Although the methods which are regarded as best or desirable are prescribed in a general way in 96 instances, there are 74 cases where the choice of method is left entirely to the teacher. At this point there is a rather sharp contrast between the junior and the senior high school. The teacher in the latter is much more generally allowed complete freedom in the choice of method than is the teacher in the former. This difference, again, is in harmony with the traditions of the two institutions.

TABLE XVI.—MEASURE OF FREEDOM WHICH THE PRESENT COURSE OF STUDY ALLOWS THE TEACHER IN THE CHOICE OF METHODS EMPLOYED

(Data for the senior high school from 102 cities and for the junior high school from 62 cities.)

Present Course of Study	Senior High School			Total	Junior High School	Grand Total
	1–499	500–1499	1500–			
Prescribes in general methods regarded as best or desirable	16	17	16	49	47	96
Leaves choice of method entirely to teacher	16	22	15	53	21	74
Prescribes exact methods and devices to be followed by teacher	0	0	0	0	1	1
Total	32	39	31	102	69	171

TRAINING TEACHERS IN THE USE OF THE COURSE OF STUDY

In the degree that curriculum-making disregards the training of teachers it will be ineffective. If no provision is made for training teachers in the use of a changed or revised course of study, the old program is almost certain to persist. Changes made on paper remain on paper until they are translated into the habits and abilities of teachers. In Table XVII is reported the status of this important matter in the cities included in the investigation.

The most significant fact appearing in the table is that in the senior high schools of 54 of 101 cities and in the junior high schools of 18 of 61 cities no formal provision is made for training teachers in the use of the course of study, except as this function is discharged by the high-school principal. Of course, to the extent that all teachers are brought into the work of curriculum-making and revision through membership on committees, a measure of training is automatically provided. But such provision is undoubtedly far from adequate. It is, however, gratifying to note that the more extreme neglect of this training is confined largely to the smaller schools and that the junior high school shows a tendency to break with tradition and make more definite provision for training the teacher in the use of the course of study. If curriculum-making in the future is to be effective in the maximal degree, such provision must become general.

TABLE XVII.—PROVISIONS FOR TRAINING TEACHERS IN SERVICE IN THE USE OF THE COURSE OF STUDY

(Data for the senior high school from 101 cities and for the junior high school from 61 cities.)

Provisions for Training Teachers	Senior High School			Total	Junior High School	Grand Total
	1-499	500-1499	1500-			
Supervisory demonstration or instructive meetings	7	15	16	38	41	79
Visits of special supervisors	7	12	17	36	39	75
No formal provision except through supervision of principal	25	18	11	54	18	72
Classes for teachers held in connection with nearby training school, college, or university	5	12	12	29	29	58
System of instruction through teachers' committees	0	0	1	1	1	2
Professional study classes within the system	1	0	0	1	0	1
Total	45	57	57	159	128	287

APPRAISING THE COURSE OF STUDY

If changes in the high-school curriculum are ever to be controlled and directed intelligently, they must proceed in the light of precise knowledge. This means that provision must be made for the continuous appraisal of the existing course of study. Before an old program is abandoned, it should be appraised as accurately as the prevailing state of educational technique permits; and as soon as a new program is inaugurated, machinery should be set in motion for the purpose of discovering how it functions. From the day that a new subject is added to the curriculum, knowledge should begin to accumulate through which to evaluate it. That changes in the curriculum in the past have not rested on any such scientific basis, no one would deny. In large measure even the forces which produced these changes have remained obscure. Certainly subjects have been both dropped from, and added to, the high-school curriculum without the support of precise and trustworthy knowledge.

The situation as it exists in the cities studied is revealed in Table XVIII. According to this table, while few cities report that no appraisal is made, the great majority merely claim an informal appraisal by administrative and supervisory officers. This much would probably have been claimed by the school masters of any age. There is evidence, however, to indicate that here and there, particularly in the larger cities and in the junior high schools, steps are being taken to provide for a more careful appraisal of the curriculum. If such procedures become common, the time may be expected to pass when subjects are either added to, or removed from, the curriculum in the absence of definite knowledge in favor of such action. The course of study may yet assume a stability that is not derived from tradition and take on an elasticity that does not rest on hasty and superficial criticism.

TABLE XVIII.—METHODS EMPLOYED IN APPRAISING THE COURSE OF STUDY

(Data for the senior high school from 98 cities and for the junior high school from 60 cities.)

Method of Appraisal	Senior High School 1–499	500–1499	1500–	Total	Junior High School	Grand Total
Informal appraisal by administrative and supervisory officers	27	33	28	88	52	140
Appraisal through study of results of routine testing by research department	2	11	10	23	30	53
Formal special appraisal through use of questionnaire, measurement, etc.	2	6	3	11	13	24
No appraisal made	4	1	2	7	2	9
Total	35	51	43	129	97	226

CHAPTER VIII

PROGRESSIVE PRACTICES IN MAKING STATE AND RURAL SCHOOL COURSES OF STUDY

George A. Works
Cornell University, Ithaca, New York

Introduction

It has not been possible for the writer to make an evaluation of all of the state courses of study or of any considerable proportion of the rural-school courses prepared by local school authorities. This report can, therefore, make no claim to completeness in the sense that the procedures used in preparing courses are reported for all of the superior courses of study prepared by either state departments of education or by local rural-school authorities.

Fortunately, Miss Annie Reynolds, of the United States Bureau of Education, had made a study of state courses of study just prior to the preparation of this report. The results of her study were made available to the writer. The results of an evaluation of several hundred courses of study by the Bureau of Elementary Curriculum Research, Teachers College, Columbia University, were also available. In addition, inquiry was made of a number of students of the rural-school curriculum for meritorious curriculum studies that they might know about. The information drawn from these three sources was used in selecting the courses of study on which the procedures used in curriculum-making are reported.

Besides its incompleteness due to failure to secure information regarding all superior courses of study, this report is incomplete for another reason. The writer was not able in all instances to obtain reports regarding the methods used in preparation of the courses of study that were finally selected.

These reports on curriculum-construction do not include all the cases in which information on procedures used were obtained. In several cases the persons reporting on the technique used in building the courses of study stated that they had selected courses that appealed to them as being superior and adapted them to the conditions in their schools. In other instances the reports made on procedures were so brief and differed so little from those reported more fully by others that they have not been included as separate reports.

The main body of this chapter consists of reports of techniques used in making either state or local rural-school courses. In some instances the reports have been used essentially in the form in which they were submitted by the person who prepared them. In other cases the original reports have been modified to fit the purpose of the chapter. In still other cases the reports of techniques used have been gathered from printed reports or from the courses of study. If material modification was made in the reports originally submitted, or if the reports were based on material drawn from printed sources, they were submitted to some person familiar with the procedures used in making the courses for checking as to completeness and accuracy of statement. It is hoped that by these means all serious errors have been avoided.

Each of the reports immediately following was obtained by one of the procedures suggested above. The writer desires to express his appreciation to those whose coöperation has made possible the preparation of this chapter, especially to his colleagues, E. N. Ferriss and C. B. Moore.

Making the Connecticut Common-School Course of Study[1]

During 1922-24 the State Board of Education of Connecticut made provision for a complete revision of the curriculum of the public elementary schools. The work was a coöperative enterprise participated in by representatives of the State Department of Education, members of the faculties of the normal schools and committees of teachers and superintendents. The assistance of experts in curriculum-making from outside the state was secured for certain phases of the work. The activities of the several groups were coördinated by a Board of Review, of which the Commissioner of Education was chairman.

Two phases of improvement of the work of the schools were undertaken simultaneously. They were (1) revision of the normal-school curricula and (2) the preparation of suggestive courses of study for the elementary schools of the state. It was the desire of the State Department of Education to get the work of the train-

[1] Based on information furnished by Commissioner A. B. Meredith.

ing schools more closely integrated with the other phases of the professional training of teachers and to secure courses of study for the elementary-school period that could be used at least in the practice schools.

As a forerunner to the preparation of the courses of study and the teaching monographs, a "Basic Monograph" was prepared. The monograph includes the discussion of problems that are applicable to all the courses of study. They relate to:

1. The aims and purposes of education.
2. Desirable educational outcomes which should be kept constantly in mind by those who make and administer curricula.
3. The general principles governing the selection of subject matter in the several courses of study.
4. The general principles governing the organization of subject matter in the courses of study.
5. General facts and principles pertaining to the learning process upon which the detailed methods and teaching devices presented in the monographs are based.

"This monograph should be considered basic to an intelligent understanding and effective use of both the courses of study and the teaching monographs."[2]

In the last fifteen pages of the monograph the suggested topics are dealt with in simple language. Ample illustrative material is used. Most attention is given to the "principle of underlying method and teaching devices."

Supplementary to the Basic Monograph are the following:

A Course of Study in Arithmetic
A Monograph on the Teaching of Arithmetic
A Course of Study and Monograph on Handwriting
A Course of Study in Nature Study
A Monograph and Course of Study on the Teaching of Music
A Course of Study in Reading, including Literature
A Monograph on the Teaching of Reading
A Course of Study in Oral and Written English
A Manual of Physical Education for Rural Schools
A Course of Study in the Social Studies—History, Geography, and Citizenship.

[2] Page 3.

In general, the plan followed in the preparation of the courses of study has been to state the general aims of each subject in the elementary school. These general aims are supplemented by a statement of specific aims for each grade. Suggestions are made regarding the minimal achievement for each grade. No attempt is made to prescribe a detailed body of subject matter. Although a minimal course is suggested, the emphasis is placed on aims and on activities designed to attain the desired ends; and in the monographs, on suggestions with reference to methods of teaching rather than on the prescription of content as is the customary procedure.

With the exception of physical education, no special courses were prepared for the rural schools. However, the absence of detailed prescription of content gives a degree of flexibility that makes it readily possible for the capable teacher and supervisor to adjust the courses to rural conditions. The Division of Rural Education, the Division of Elementary Education, and the Division of Normal Schools, were intimately associated with the work of preparing the courses of study, and rural teachers and supervisors were members of each committee. They served as a means of securing a general adaptation of the courses to rural conditions.

In Connecticut the State Board of Education does not have the authority to prescribe courses of study. The acceptance of courses issued by this body is a matter resting with local school authorities. This means that they must be convinced of the superior quality of the new courses. The preparation of the new courses was accompanied by educational work that has resulted in their very general acceptance. The monthly meetings of teachers held by the supervising agents for rural schools during the school year 1923-24 were designed to prepare the rural teachers to use them. Similarly, meetings of city and town teachers were held in all parts of the state to acquaint teachers, principals, and superintendents with the available courses. The work with teachers in service was paralleled by the use of the new courses as the basis of instruction in the normal schools and in the practice schools associated with them. As a result, new teachers entered service equipped to use the new courses intelligently.

Furthermore, three experimental classes were organized in one of the normal schools in which problems arising in connection with the use of the courses could be given laboratory study.

The courses and monographs were ready in July 1924. Up to November 15, 1925, there had been distributed 55,000 copies. Nearly all of the 169 towns have requisitioned a sufficient supply to provide each teacher with the necessary courses and monographs. The report of the Director of Rural Education for the period 1922-24 says: "In view of the increased number of normal trained teachers entering the rural field and of the fact that all others entering this field have received six weeks' instruction based upon the new courses, and in view of the teachers-meeting work of last year, the rural schools are quite well prepared to use the new courses of study effectively from the beginning."

Developing the High-School Curriculum in Missouri

In 1925, Bulletin No. 1, Courses of Study in Junior and Senior High Schools, was issued by the Department of Education in Missouri. In the foreword the following statement occurs:

"The bulletin is intended to serve as a kind of background for the bulletins which will follow on the various high-school subjects. It should be of great interest and value not only to those teachers who are working on the course syllabi bulletins, but to all teachers and administrators who are interested in secondary education."

In many respects this bulletin is different from the basic monograph developed for Connecticut, but from the foregoing statement it is evidently intended that it will bear a somewhat similar relation to the courses of study being developed for use in the junior and senior high schools of Missouri.

The bulletin was prepared under the direction of a committee of three, representing the School of Education of the State University, the Department of Education of Missouri, and the high-school teachers of the state. There are three divisions to the bulletin:

Part I presents a large body of facts of significance in preparing courses of study. They relate to the ages and mental ability of the high-school pupils; the characteristics of the high schools in communities of various size in terms of pupil enrollment, number of teachers, program of studies, curricula, and wealth of communities. This part includes also a presentation of the facts relating to what pupils in the high schools of the state are now studying as contrasted with ten years ago.

The data on the typical Missouri high school in each class of community should be of very great value in preparing programs of study for those schools. The rural high schools are placed in three groups on the basis of size. In this phase of the study are given the data of most direct significance in making rural-school curricula.

Part II is a formulation of principles and methods of work to be used as guides in making the courses of study. These principles are the work of Dr. Thomas H. Briggs of Teachers College, Columbia University, and the several committees voted to make them the basis of their work.

"Part III contains the statement of objectives for each course of study. These statements were prepared by the chairmen after consultation with their committee members." The aforementioned committee of three persons, which was responsible for the preparation of the bulletin as a whole, took the statements of objectives as they came from the several committees and made such changes as they believed desirable. "Two general classes of objectives, the propaedeutic and the disciplinary, have purposely been omitted from all lists. It is admitted that all subjects have value as preparation for advanced work in various kinds of colleges and universities. It is also admitted that all subjects have some disciplinary value." This committee accepted the view "that each subject to be included in the program of study must have positive justification in terms of direct values for the majority of boys and girls educated in our junior and senior high schools."

The details of the preparation of the courses are in the hands of the several committees. These committees are composed of public school teachers and members of the faculties of the higher educational institutions in most cases.

Committees have been formed for the following subjects: English, ninth-grade citizenship, vocations, extra-classroom activities, world history and European history, United States history and Missouri history, sociology and economics, geography, mathematics, general science, biology, chemistry, physics, foreign language, commercial studies, art, music, home economics, agriculture, industrial subjects, and health and physical education.

In connection with the formulation of the objectives for each subject, a bibliography of professional references has been prepared that should prove helpful to the teachers of those subjects. The

State Teachers Association is coöperating with the Department of Education in the undertaking.

Making the Common-School Curriculum in Virginia[3]

The course of study for rural and elementary schools in Virginia was constructed under the supervision of a committee consisting of representatives of the State Department of Education and the State Teachers Colleges. This committee had some expert advice from persons outside the state.

The committee at its first session agreed to be guided by the following principles in its work:

1. "To furnish material for developing an ideal of good citizenship among the children of the state.

2. "To meet the needs of the school on the level which then existed.

3. "To aid in developing the teachers in the rural and village schools of the state. This last aim made it necessary to couch the course of study suggestions in non-technical language.

4. "To regard this course of tudy, not as a model or finished course of study, but as one which was needed in improving the content of instruction in the rural and village schools. After an interval of five years the course of study should be revised to meet the conditions then existing.

5. "To submit a tentative edition of the course of study to teachers, supervisors, and superintendents."

To facilitate the work and to give each member of the committee a chance to work intimately with those subjects with which he was most familiar, the elementary-school subjects were placed in the following groups:

1. Social studies, civics, nature study, history, and geography.
2. Health, hygiene and physical training.
3. English, reading, language, grammar, and spelling.
4. Arithmetic.
5. Arts, penmanship, music, drawing, home economics, and industrial arts.

A sub-committee consisting of two members of the general committee was formed for each of these five groups of subjects. Each

[3] Material for this section was furnished by Miss Rachel E. Gregg, formerly of the State Department of Education in Virginia.

sub-committee added to its membership from the faculties of the teachers colleges, and in case of health education from the State Board of Health.

The sub-committees submitted their work to the general committee for criticism. On the basis of the suggestions made, the subcommittees reworked their courses.

These courses were then put in tentative form and placed in the hands of local school authorities for trial. In case of the social studies the chairman of the committee visited a number of schools in which the courses were being tried, for conferences with teachers. In this manner and through written criticisms offered by teachers, supervisors, and superintendents, many helpful suggestions were secured by the committee. These were considered in the final drafts of the courses.

In the final form the course was printed and distributed in time for use in all the summer schools for teachers. As a further means of giving teachers an intelligent understanding of the courses, they were made the basis of the work in the institutes.

Curriculum-Revision in Wisconsin[4]

Purposes. Elimination of materials and methods which were obsolete. Reorganization of materials to fit present conception of educational endeavor. Better distribution of teaching energy through improved class organization.

Personnel. Members of the State Department of Public Instruction formed the committee on curriculum-revision. This committee was subdivided into small working groups, with a chairman who was responsible for the formulation of material and its presentation to the larger committee. The heads of departments in the normal schools were invited to participate in the discussion, to present curricula, and to criticise material under consideration. Final judgment was reserved for the State Superintendent and his assistant.

Method of Procedure. 1. Summer of 1921. The committee as a whole discussed at length the general objectives. Subcommittees worked upon definite portions assigned and sent out questionnaires to secure data with reference to acceptance or rejection of material

[4] This section is given essentially as reported by Miss Isabel Davidson, formerly a member of the State Department of Education in Wisconsin.

and to obtain proposals for new material. Mooted points were discussed vigorously, and compromises were affected where unanimity could not be secured. Material was then presented to the committee as a whole, and correlations were sought. This course of study was intended to serve as a guide for rural-school teachers, including those of the smaller villages and towns. The course of study for the state graded schools was, at that time, separate and distinct, though coördinated.

2. Autumn of 1921. A tentative, much abridged outline of study of the curriculum was printed on large sheets as a means of indicating the essential points in each subject, also as a means of securing reaction from principals, teachers, and laymen, upon the proposed plan.

3. Spring of 1923. A further revision of the course of study was made in which emphasis was placed upon *objectives* and *attainments,* rather than upon detailed subject matter or method. This revision indicated a spiral plan in the development of subject matter, made further eliminations in some subjects, and aimed to be suggestive rather than too prescriptive. This course of study is now the accepted course of study for the state graded schools, the rural schools, and those villages and towns not having a definite plan of their own to follow.

All members of the State Department of Public Instruction contributed to this revision through suggestion, advice, and helpful criticism, though one member was held responsible for organization of material.

Procedure in Carroll County, Maryland

Supt. M. S. H. Unger, of Carroll County, Maryland, writes as follows regarding the procedure in study-making in that county: "It is a process that goes on continually, both in written and oral procedures in the classroom, in teachers' conferences, and by circular letters, and the responses from the teachers and the chairmen of the committees of teachers working on specific matters and the lesson plans. At the end of each year we insert the most worth-while material into the course of study and eliminate from it the undesirable things."

Development of Rural Course of Study in Williams County, Ohio

Under the leadership of Supt. F. O. Russell, new courses of study are gradually being developed for the rural schools of Williams County, Ohio. The first course to be organized was in agriculture for the elementary schools. The committee working on this course consisted of one school patron, a country school teacher, a teacher of vocational agriculture, the county agricultural agent, and the county superintendent. This group gathered information bearing on the economic and social conditions in the rural communities of the county, and with the information gained as a background, formulated a course of study.

Following the preparation of the tentative course and previous to the opening of the school year, an institute of one week was held. A part of the program was given over to an interpretation of the course of study in agriculture and to ways and means of carrying it out in the schools. Mimeographed copies of the course were placed in the hands of the teachers for use during the year. The committee that was responsible for the formulation of the course followed up the teaching, called conferences, and prepared tests to assist the teachers in the measurement of the results of their teaching. These activities are arranged through the office of the county superintendent. This committee is also charged with the duty of making such modifications as experience in the schools seems to indicate are desirable.

A course in geography has been worked out by a procedure similar to that used in agriculture. During the school year 1925-26 a start was made also in the revision of the course of study in English.

The Adaptation of Courses by Teachers

Rural-school organization is such in most states that it is not possible for those locally responsible for rural schools to undertake curriculum-construction on any such scale as has been done in a number of cities in recent years. This point of view is illustrated by a statement contained in a letter from a county superintendent: "I might state that two years ago we made an effort to do some scientific work in this field, but found that we could not get very far because of lack of funds. We have no means for financing a proposition of this sort." In several instances local rural-school authorities frankly stated that they took the best courses they could find and adapted them to their conditions.

Course of study making in rural schools becomes largely a problem of adapting courses prepared by state school authorities to local conditions. Two reports on this phase are presented. The first of these is based on a report made by Dr. O. G. Brim in connection with the Texas Educational Survey. The second is a statement of the procedure in adapting a state program of agricultural instruction to a community's needs.

Studying Local Needs in Texas[5]

"The purpose of education is to promote the growth of the child. It does this by supplying for him the essential conditions of growth lacking in his normal environment. Education is to enrich the child's life with meaning. It can do so only by building upon his present experiences. It is to cultivate in the child abundant fruitful interests. This, too, demands knowledge of his daily life. It is to make him intelligent and efficient in his many activities and relations. One must know the child intimately and the world in which he lives, its limitations and its resources, if one would guide his education wisely; for the more intimately we know environmental forces, the more adequately can we use, supplement, or counteract them through experiences provided at school.

"Attention was called to this problem in discussing the relation of the school and community. It was discussed again at some length in connection with the data as to the degree and ways in which teachers and superintendents adapt the State curriculum to local conditions. Attention was called to the lack of any such intimate and meaningful contacts between subject matter of the daily lessons and the child's interests and experiences. It has been suggested that special curricula be provided for rural children. It was further suggested that special curricula be provided for Mexican children and for negro children. All these essential conditions of a vital and meaningful curriculum are dependent upon an intimate knowledge of the community, home, and personal life of the child.

---

[5] Texas Educational Survey Report: Courses of Study and Instruction.

"In order to give greater concreteness to the idea, to show its significance in specific instances, to stimulate such an undertaking by those who are responsible for constructing the curriculum, and to foster a greater interest in, and attention to, the child's life in every step of the educative process, an illustrative study was made of three communities. In reading these data one must bear in mind, the fact that, while many of these questions are extremely personal, they should be collected and utilized in an impersonal manner. An attempt to secure such information is justified because of its intimate bearing upon the success of the school.

"The communities selected were quite different in type, and were located in different parts of the state. It was the intention to add a negro community, a ranching community, and a general farming community from the northern part of the state, but this was not found practicable. Community (A) is a Mexican community from a southern border county. Community (B) is an isolated community of mixed foreigners in the central eastern part of the state. Community (C) is a progressive American farming community near one of the prominent cities of the state and having excellent access to varied school life and stimulating intellectual contacts. The differences are far greater than this formal report will show, but in prosecuting such a study teachers would become aware of these subtle forces and become sensitized to adjust school work to their needs.

"The child is a social product. He not only speaks the language of his home or community, but he adopts their standards of cleanliness, their level of morality, their habits of recreation and reading, their social attitudes and ideals. What kind of a community does a child live in when not at school?"

With the assistance of persons more or less familiar with conditions in the three communities considerable data were collected bearing on social aspects of the population; health standards; reading habits, sources, and facilities; musical opportunities; social attitudes and ideals of the adults; recreational and social life provided for young people; conditions affecting health; and appearance of the farmstead. In commenting on the materials collected in this manner Dr. Brim says:

"While it is difficult to point out specifically where each of these items would make a difference in school work or serve to modify the curriculum, much of it has a direct bearing. The data as to health standards and practices reveal a wealth of situations about which vital and profitable questions could be raised. These could be made the basis of class discussion. They would lead to a purposeful and meaningful study of textbook material. They would tend to eliminate the systematic study of physiology in favor of a study of practical problems of better living.

"Reading habits and resources offer further suggestions. Children are helped or handicapped by home conditions, by parental habits and attitudes toward reading. Not only the number but the quality of books at home should be known. The teacher should be familiar with the kind of books, papers, and magazines read; the topics discussed by parents, if any; the attitudes expressed; the encouragement the child receives.

"The rural child has a right to music. It is a possible source of permanent pleasure. The rural community provides little that would tend to cultivate an appreciation of it, or to satisfy one who already loves it, or to offer musical ability an opportunity to develop. Could the teacher and curriculum-maker visualize the problem of education as an enrichment of human life and then sense the emptiness of the rural community, there would be less emphasis upon a few formal 'essentials,' greater effort made to supply every school with a Victrola and records, and to educate the teachers to teach the children to love and appreciate good music.

"The data on social attitudes and ideals are pregnant with meaning for the rural teacher. The rural child imbibes these community attitudes and standards as the babe its mother's milk. His life is determined by them. The picture of this situation that one is able to put upon paper is so incomplete, yet the answers to such questions indicate the social spirit of the community, both between its several members and in these outside relations. As long as there is local indifference or bitterness among neighbors, it is practically impossible to realize the larger spirit of human brotherhood in the child. As long as outside local contacts are limited to purchasing things over a counter or standing as strangers on street corners, the social sympathy and understanding basic to a democracy is next to impossible. Once these details of the local situation were known and appreciated by the teacher, the work in civics would never descend to the formal recitation of facts about political machinery.

"Many of these items could not be directly discussed in school. But whether the items have a direct bearing or merely provide a basis for a more complete understanding, whether the situation is one that can be directly discussed or is one which must be approached by indirection, each adds to the effectiveness of a teacher's service. They picture the child's world. If education is a process of improving living from day to day by dealing with it rather than something arbitrarily attached, then the better this life is known, the more fitting will the help be.

"To gather these data so as to present a true picture of the world in which the child lives is an extremely difficult undertaking. That must be apparent to anyone. But difficult as this information is to secure, it should be the goal of every teacher to know her children and community as intimately as this study demands. In fact, the knowledge should be far more searching if the teacher is to succeed most effectively in stimulating and guiding the daily life of the child into a continual widening and richer future. It would be a most excellent thing for the rural children of Texas if every teacher were to make such a study of his community in a conscientious and sympathetic spirit and were to apply the knowledge gained to the reconstruction of school work."

Constructing the Agricultural Part of the High-School Curriculum at Trumansburg, New York[6]

In contrast to the non-agricultural part of the curriculum, which is determined by state syllabi, the agricultural part of the curriculum is prepared by the local teacher of agriculture, subject to the approval of the Division of Vocational and Extension Education. Reference of this responsibility to the local teacher is necessary since course-objectives must be determined in terms of certain local factors which differ widely in their effects upon local practice.

In the preparation of courses of study for pupils in agriculture, the factors determining the construction of the curriculum, whether for regular high-school pupils or for special groups, involve five main school problems: (1) determining the patronage area which will supply the pupils who will elect courses in agriculture; (2) locating and classifying the pupil personnel; (3) analyzing the

[6] This statement was prepared by Dr. R. M. Stewart, Cornell University.

conditions under which education must be obtained, if obtained at all; (4) determining and evaluating facilities and selecting appropriate methods of teaching; and (5) organizing the curriculum in the light of these problems.

1. *Determining the patronage area.* Practically 100 percent of the pupils enrolled in agriculture are non-resident, since agriculture is only incidentally appropriate to other than farm-reared boys. The field for the teacher's activities had to be determined. A study of the non-resident enrollment for a period of ten years showed clearly the area which the Trumansburg High School had been serving: a fairly large number of one-room rural schools, in fact, thirty-eight such schools, fell within this patronage area.

2. *Locating and classifying the pupil personnel.* Utilizing these schools as centers, the boys and young men were located by means of a topographic map, according to roads, farms, and school districts. Further, a record was taken of each as a basis of consideration of availability and fitness for instruction in agriculture. In this survey the number and ages of the girls residing on these farms were recorded, since the presence or absence of girls on a given farm would affect the relative opportunities on that farm for any older boys. The classification of this group of farm youths for purpose of instruction in agriculture was a fundamental problem.

Three groups, each of which presented two types, were easily discernible: (1) the high-school group; (a) those taking a non-vocational course in the high school, and (b) those enrolled in vocational agriculture—the group for which the main machinery of vocational instruction in agriculture has been set up; (2) the junior group, (a) those between ten and fourteen years of age who are not carrying junior projects in agriculture, and (b) those of the same age carrying junior projects—the group organized in keeping with the program of the Boys' and Girls' Club Work; and (3) the out-of-school group, (a) those under twenty years of age for which part-time education is appropriate, and (b) those twenty or over for which evening school work is designed—the group of young men who must receive their education largely on the farm, if at all.

3. *Analyzing the conditions under which education must be obtained.* The data recorded on each boy or young man fell into two main classes. The first class related to the many variable factors

that are peculiar to particular farms, such as principal trading centers, availability of local school facilities, the number of children in the family to be trained, the number of children in the school, and the opportunity for remunerative employment. The other class related to the more or less constant factors which the character of the agricultural resources revealed. Since the latter set of conditions is determinative of the major outlines of community need in agricultural instruction, a study of agricultural resources was made.

From a new soil map for the area, four soil types were located. The correlation between soil types and crop types became an interesting study, and the survey of crop and animal enterprises furnished the main foundation of curriculum-construction. From farm enterprise records taken on approximately half of the farms distributed over the entire area, the relative frequency and scope of each specific crop and animal enterprise was determined, thus revealing the importance of each one. For example, of 124 farm records, 88 farms, or 71 percent, raised wheat to an average amount of thirteen acres per farm; 118 farms, or 95 percent, raised hay, clover, and timothy to an average amount of 31 acres per farm; 116 farms, or 90 percent, had dairy cows, but with only five to the farm; 115 farms, or 89 percent, had poultry, averaging 160 birds to the farm.

Crop enterprises and animal enterprises were studied in the light of their frequency on farms for the entire area, frequency for each of the 'soil type' areas; also, they were studied to discover for their respective percents of the total farm business first in the area as a whole and then for the area of a given soil type. The purpose of this survey and its analysis, therefore, was to determine types of farming for the area, to locate distinctive areas for comparison with different soil types, and to locate the young men by sections and by types of farming.

Certain other factors which the survey revealed were utilized in making up the curriculum: the labor situation, means of transportation, the extensiveness of teaching resources, the length of the growing season, the financial conditions of farmers, and the interests of pupils. By inspection and special surveys, it was possible to check the local labor situation with standards for different types of labor and thereby determine (with other factors) possible combination of enterprises, such as tree-fruits major and hay-grain minor, or cash-enterprise major (beans, potatoes, cabbage) and livestock minor (horses, cows, sheep). Both surveys—personnel and agricultural resources—showed distances to market, types of roads, and connection with the main arteries for travel. A study of trading centers for the area and other centers, such as church, grange, and lodge, indicated tendencies to travel.

The growing season was found to be variable on account of diversity of topography, variability of soil, and the proximity of part of the area to Cayuga Lake. The elevation at Cayuga Lake is 400 feet. Running up to an elevation of 800 feet are found poultry and fruit; from 800 to 1200 feet roughly, the conspicuous crop is beans; from 1200 to 1800 feet, hay, pasture, and sheep become more conspicuous, while beans and wheat begin to disappear. The wide diversity of crops and animals raised and the great variation of soil and other determining factors, present a wider array of enterprises and a greater abundance of teaching resources than can be used in instruction. Thus, selection had to be made.

A study of the economic condition of the workers had significance in at least three directions: (1) in revealing the scope of enterprises which the farmers found profitable, as evidenced in the extent of the practices; (2) in discovering types of farmers whose records show accurately the profits of the business; and (3) in learning the methods of the best farmers in particular enterprises or in large scale farming. Though it is expected that young men would be interested in farming for other than economic reasons, a study of the supervised farm experience covering several years showed a growing tendency to select projects in the more profitable enterprises.

4. *Determining facilities and selecting methods of teaching.* Teaching in terms of farms and particular farm enterprises in natural settings is a growing practice in teaching agriculture. In determining the scope of curricular offerings, therefore, consideration of the most appropriate methods of teaching and the facilities for using such methods had to be made in advance. For example, whenever the field trip, the practicum, the survey, or directed study, was determined upon, the character of the curriculum was involved, since a method more expensive of time would thereby reduce the consideration given to other phases of content. Hence, availability of time, means of transportation, requirements for securing 'natural

settings' placed certain limitations upon the curriculum program. The presence, in the area, of farmers who had distinguished themselves in particular lines of farming added to the facilities of teaching in terms of the farms. As special equipment and supplies determined the feasibility of offering certain features in classroom studies, so also the presence or absence of certain types of farms and of coöperating farmers in the area for a given objective teaching situation affected the emphasis of such parts in the curriculum.

5. *Organizing the curriculum.* In the light of the foregoing considerations the following tentative curriculum was prepared for the high-school group by E. R. Hoskins.[4]

First Year	Second Year	Third Year	Fourth Year
Poultry or Sheep Field Beans Field Corn	Cabbage Potatoes Home Orchard and Garden	Horses Poultry Sheep Farming, Dairy Cows, Swine	Farm Management, and Agricultural Economics (covering all enterprises)
Wheat Sheep Horses	Poultry or Sheep Buckwheat Horses	Pastures and Mixed Hay Clovers Alfalfa Small Grains	Continuation of special animal and crop projects

Selecting soils and fertilizers for particular crops, saving manures } ————→ Maintaining soil fertility

Farm Shop ————→

Farm Machinery ————→

Farm power, Tractors, Gas Engines.

Farm Engineering ————→

In connection with this curriculum it should be noted that generally throughout the state the first and second years are alternated, likewise the third and fourth. Major and minor enterprises were so considered because of their relative importance in the patronage area, or because of the degree of pupil interest in them, possibly also because of the relative need for classroom instruction in them. Enterprises such as poultry or sheep were considered major for one year and minor for another, or major to certain individuals where projects were involved, and minor for others where

[4] Teacher of agriculture, who coöperates with the writer in the training of teachers of agriculture at the New York State College of Agriculture at Cornell University.

projects were not involved. To accomplish this with a group, the curriculum was varied, first to suit the special needs of groups of pupils and then, to emphasize a definite continuity of enterprises as those to be represented normally in the farm business. Related instruction consists of the unifying and integrating content which became 'service' materials to the enterprises, and these have been placed, as indicated, where they 'serve' best.

The most important crop and animal enterprises were placed in the first two years in order to serve the larger number of boys enrolled, since only about twenty-two percent of the boys entering agriculture complete the full four years. Certain enterprises which were considered as minor in the first year, partly on the basis of the relative immaturity of the boys and partly on the basis of limited opportunity or excessive financial risk, became major considerations for the second or later years when the educational aspects became more significant. Certain enterprises which were considered major during the early years of the curriculum because of their significance at that time, both for the vocation and for the education, became minor as the vocational purpose became dominant and the educational values involved became relatively negligible.

Certain 'service' subjects are conspicuous throughout the curriculum, particularly in the early years, which take on management aspects as the upper years are reached. Soils and fertilizers are emphasized during the first two years because of their significance for growing crops, shifting to a special management emphasis in maintaining soil fertility in the upper years. Farm shop, emphasized early to take care of repair and simple construction work incident to carrying on enterprises and handling machinery, shifts to the management problem of buying and caring for machinery, and to the problems of farm engineering in the upper years.

Integrating or unifying subjects, such as farm management and agricultural economics, were placed in the last year as a basis of organizing and evaluating the principles that were operating in the promotion of the several enterprises of the entire teaching program. This permits of a more or less uniform course for a diversified region. Further, opportunity was provided in the first two years for any specialization the pupil wished to make in his later years. The program is flexible so that pupils may find it adaptable to any section of the area, so that crop enterprises contribute to animal enterprises and animals to crops; and that soil fertility may be maintained. Choice of major and minor projects allows for adaptation to soil types and farming types. Provision is made for teaching in terms of human and agricultural resources on the farms in the area. Special instruction was provided in commercial fruit growing and commercial poultry for certain pupils who desired to specialize.

In preparing unit courses of instruction for the out-of-school groups, the major interests of the group were determined as far as possible in advance of instruction. Applying the principles of vocational instruction in agriculture for the regular high-school group as far as practicable, the teacher prepared three unit courses designed to embrace the special interests as expressed personally by these young men. In addition, since these young men were actually farming on practically a full-time basis, instruction was arranged in terms of the supervised farm practice which these men could undertake.

The organization of this Trumansburg High School curriculum in agriculture, based upon the knowledge of the community and its resources was designed (1) to serve a vocational purpose, (2) to express in its organization the principal and constant practices of farmers in the area, (3) to provide for flexibility, so that the individual differences of pupils may be recognized both in the method of studying the constants and in the selection and study of variable enterprises, (4) to regard the rate of mortality and to provide, therefore, for important things first, (5) to provide continuity and concentration (a) by 'service' and integrating studies and (b) by continuing individual projects over several years, (6) to emphasize, as far as possible without destroying intrinsic values, a sequence of enterprises economical to class administration, and (7) to utilize resources at hand as a basis of discovering the principles sought for in the teaching.

Evaluation of Procedures Reported in This Chapter

It is of fundamental importance that classroom teachers should be intimately identified with making the courses they are to use. Their daily contact with pupils puts them in a strategic position when it comes to judging the appropriateness of materials for use at any given period in the pupil's development. There is, however, a still further reason for utilization of the teacher in this work. One of the most important problems involved in influencing educational outcomes by means of curriculum-making is that of securing an intelligent attitude toward the use of the curriculum. In the past the prevalent methods used in making courses developed an unfortunate attitude on the part of the teacher toward them. She regarded them as something to be accepted in the form in which they were issued. They represented so many facts to be acquired by the pupils under her direction. For most teachers the course of study was static, instead of dynamic. So long as this attitude prevails, it is futile to expect the largest results from the efforts that are being made to develop curricula on more scientific bases. To secure the desired results, teachers must have an intelligent understanding of the curriculum. Participation in the making of it will do much to develop this attitude on their part.

A state department of education faces two problems involving different techniques when it attempts to develop the right attitude on the part of the teachers toward courses of study. They are: (1) its realization with teachers in service; and (2) its realization with teachers during the pre-service training period. In meeting the first problem the relatively limited area within which the teachers of a city work makes it possible to provide for a much larger measure of participation by them in the actual work of making the courses of study than is possible in case of a state. However, the procedures used in Connecticut, Missouri, and Virginia are suggestive of methods that give opportunity for classroom teachers to make their contributions in the original formulations. In Virginia provision was made for general participation on the part of the teachers by placing the courses in their hands in a tentative form. After experience in the classroom with the tentative courses, the teachers were then invited to make suggestions. This method is valuable especially when provision is made for conferences between those who formulated the tentative courses and the teachers who have given them a trial. This was done in Virginia with the course in the social sciences.

In the development of local courses teacher-participation can be carried much farther. The statement of the method used in Carroll county, Maryland, shows how by coöperation between teachers and supervisors the teachers are constantly contributing to the development of the courses. In this county the courses are mimeographed instead of being printed and they are kept in loose-leaf binders. This form makes it easily possible to insert modifications of the courses from time to time.

In Wisconsin the teachers did not assist in the preparation of the tentative courses, but elaborate provision was made for giving them opportunity to assist in putting the courses in a more permanent form. This method has a weakness. Most teachers are loathe to criticize a piece of work that bears more or less evidence of being completed. This procedure is not likely to secure the largest measure of participation on the part of the teachers, nor to stimulate the maximal amount of thought on curriculum problems.

In addition to participation in the preparation of the curriculum and in the revision of the tentative formulation, state departments of education have recognized the importance of preparing teachers to use the new curriculum through institutes, supervisory conferences, teachers meetings, etc. The procedure used in Connecticut is an especially good illustration. The development of new curricula for the normal schools and of new courses for the elementary schools were carried on simultaneously. Representatives from the normal schools were on both committees and the two pieces of work were coördinated through a director.

Too great emphasis cannot be placed on the fact that if course-of-study making and course-of-study adjustment are to be conducted most intelligently in the school system, there must be thorough preparation of teachers during pre-service training to meet these problems. Teachers who undertake such work as is described by Dr. Brim in the Texas School Survey or by Dr. Stewart in the development of the course of study in agriculture should have experience in it as a part of their pre-service training. This implies training-school facilities that shall furnish ample opportunity for prospective teachers to secure experience in the type of school in which they are preparing to serve.

Such studies as are reported by Drs. Brim and Stewart are also illustrative of a type of activity on the part of teachers that should be stimulated by constructive supervision. When teachers have made such a survey of the field as was made in the study reported by Dr. Stewart, it is very unlikely that they will take the attitude that has so commonly obtained toward the curriculum. Such work means genuine growth in ability to evaluate teaching content in terms of the needs of society and pupils.

The value of the expert is coming to be recognized in the preparation of state courses of study. In Missouri expert assistance was obtained to formulate the principles and methods of work. In Connecticut the work was in charge of an expert, and he had additional assistance in the development of the techniques needed in making certain courses. The importance of the expert is recognized to the extent that in some states definite provision is made by the department of education for research in curriculum-making.

The placing of curriculum-construction on a more scientific basis is certain to raise questions with reference to the best form for a state course of study. If such adaptations as are suggested by the studies of Drs. Brim and Stewart are to be encouraged, the state course will be much less concerned with detailed outlines of content than is now the case. They will, however, be concerned with showing teachers how to secure the significant facts relating to making courses of study and how to evaluate these facts in the light of educational objectives. Much more emphasis will be placed on objectives and activities, as has been done in the Connecticut and Detroit courses. In the development of this phase of curriculum-making the expert can render invaluable assistance. There is still much to be done in determining what is the best form for a state course of study.

Most rural schools are so organized locally that they are not able to employ the outside expert, as have many city school systems in recent years. Rural schools are more largely dependent on such leadership as can be furnished by local superintendents, supervisors, and teachers. This was shown in the replies sent to county superintendents as to the technique they used in course-of-study making. A number of them stated they adapted the best courses they could find to their conditions. This indicates the need for more activity on the part of the state department of education in formulating the right type of state courses and in showing school authorities how to adapt them to local conditions.

SECTION III

EXAMPLES OF PROGRESSIVE CURRICULUM-CONSTRUCTION IN PUBLIC SCHOOL SYSTEMS

CHAPTER IX

CURRICULUM-CONSTRUCTION AT DETROIT

STUART A. COURTIS
Educational Consultant, Detroit Public Schools, Detroit, Michigan

Scientific curriculum-revision has been carried on continuously in Detroit since 1910, the year when the first standard test was given in the public schools of the city. Mr. Charles L. Spain, at that time assistant superintendent of schools, upon reviewing the results of the first arithmetic tests, immediately undertook a series of research studies in this field. He used his conclusions as a basis for a partial revision of the existing course of study in arithmetic.

In 1914 a supervisor of educational research was appointed to take charge of the testing and research work, and the field of investigation was extended to include other subjects in the curriculum. Gradually, relationship with other supervisors and with other departments developed in response to the need for making the results of the research work available to those charged with curriculum-revision. Finally, the war-time emphasis upon the value of education, the opportunities for change and adjustment afforded by the advent of a new superintendent, war-time prosperity, and many similar factors coöperated to make rapid development possible.[1] The peak of this evolution was reached in 1921. Since that time the post-war financial depression, changes in personnel with the inevitable adjustments in organization, and many similar factors have operated to obscure more or less the unitary character of the development. To-day (1926) while the general policies and plans are still in effective operation and are still being adjusted to meet changing needs, the different divisions are operating under the changes in ideals, methods, and relationships which inevitably go with extensive changes in personnel. The present account, therefore, will so describe the development of the organization charged with curriculum-revision and the process itself as to present the basic ideals and practices as they were when most highly integrated.

[1]For a detailed account of the evolution in Detroit, see *Public Education in Detroit*, by A. B. Moehlman, Chap. XV, p. 202 (Public School Publishing Company, Bloomington, Illinois).

In November, 1916, by popular vote, a seven-man board of education, elected at large, was substituted for a twenty-one-man board, elected by wards on a political party system. The new board took office July 1, 1917, and the change in educational policies was noticeable at once. When in 1919 a change of superintendents occurred, the board took advantage of the occasion to outline its policies more definitely and to make extensive adjustments.

The board decided upon a highly centralized organization, democratically administered, and selected Frank Cody to put their plans into effect. Superintendent Cody, in turn, selected a group of specialists for his cabinet, delegated to them authority over various departments, set up, as policies for both the administrative and instructional divisions, the socialization and vitalization of school work, demanded facts in support of recommendations and insisted upon coöperative discussion of plans, and coöperative effort in achievement. The resulting policies and organizations subsequently adopted by the board are the products of such group discussion and action and cannot justly be credited to any one man, agency, condition, or circumstance. To those who participated in it, the progress made during this period will ever stand out clearly as an illustration of the benefits of "coöperation on a fact basis."

The distinctive elements in the new situation created, so far as they affected curriculum-construction, are four in number.

1. *Unity.* The conscious recognition in policy and action that education is one thing, not many. This is not a new ideal in theory, but few cities have put the theory into practice.

2. *Recognition of instruction.* The clear separation, in organization and activities, of the administrative and instructional functions. This separation at the time was unique in American education, but has since been widely copied.

3. *Machinery of coöperation.* The building up of organizations which make it possible for the various departments to operate and to coöperate more effectively as coördinate divisions of a unitary organism. Many features of the organizations developed were, and are, unique.

4. *Fact basis.* The enforcement of the policy of presenting evidence in support of recommendations or opinions.

Each of these will be discussed in some detail.

I. Unity

Because the board constituted the superintendent its sole executive officer, it was possible for him to bring representatives of all departments around a common table and to emphasize the fact that all departments must make the maximal contribution possible to the workings of each department. For the first time in the history of the Detroit schools, it became possible for each department to know at first hand what each other department was doing and to contribute directly criticisms and suggestions. For instance, the finance department was enabled to secure the coöperation of all other departments in the preparation of the annual budget, and each department had the opportunity of presenting its claims and supporting evidence before an unbiased tribunal. The critical element in the situation, however, was the insistence of the superintendent that conflicts of opinion be harmonized on the basis of facts. In all departments this led to repeated surveys and research studies to get the facts, and many appraisal studies to harmonize differences in interpretation. As a result, each department was obliged to formulate its own policies and plans more definitely than it had ever done before, came to know more about its own work and the inter-relations between its work and the work of other departments, and came to see education in Detroit as a whole. Naturally, the stimulating effects of such coördination and coöperation were felt all through each department, down to the lowest levels.

II. Recognition of Instruction

Analysis and discussion of the work of principals, supervisors, teachers, and other agents in the Detroit school system brought the fact to light that there was much overlapping in the functions of different agents. Accordingly, the different functions were defined and the various departments reorganized to correspond. Next, authority for a given function was delegated to the department in charge and that department was held responsible for the efficient exercise of the function. Since the department of administration was made responsible for the administration of the course of study, for certain types of supervision, and for contributions of criticisms and suggestions bearing directly upon curriculum-revision, it will be necessary to describe in brief outline the administrative machinery and its functions.

"Administration" was defined as: "That group of activities which deals with (1) the carrying out of policies that provide physical, financial, and educational conditions, under which pupil, teacher, principal, and supervisor may work to best advantage; (2) the provision of channels through which the course of study, general data, and instructions may be quickly and effectually placed in operation; (3) the provision of channels through which information about conditions in the schools may be promptly transmitted to the central office; (4) putting into operation standards of achievement; (5) the preparation of general data and reports; (6) research activities; (7) general publicity."

"Instruction," on the other hand, was defined as: "That group of activities which has to do with the actual improvement of instruction, as (1) preparation and development of courses of study and bulletins of methods of teaching; (2) examination and recommendation of textbooks; (3) demonstration teaching; (4) institutes and teachers' meetings for the improvement of instruction; (5) personal conferences for the interpretation of methods and of the curriculum; (6) classroom visitation and inspection; (7) setting up standards of achievement; (8) direction and supervision of the training of regular, probationary, and substitute teachers; (9) experimentation and instructional research."

The distinctive differences between the two departments can best be shown by contrasting the two words, "maintenance" and "improvement." Administrative agents are charged with the maintenance of the efficiency of instruction which involves:

(1) Knowing what the course of study contains
(2) Knowing the degree of efficiency in putting the course into effect that has been adopted as standard
(3) Knowing the standard method of achieving standard efficiency
(4) Knowing the standard equipment, supplies, and organizations related to the above
(5) Directing teachers in putting the above into effect
(6) Measuring the actual efficiency of instruction achieved
(7) Locating low points; diagnosing causes and applying remedies when this is possible
(8) Calling for assistance from supervisors in diagnosis and remedial work when defects exceed administrative responsibilities

(9) Locating and reporting high spots
(10) Discovering, formulating, and reporting difficulties or problems in need of scientific investigation
(11) Making suggestions for the possible improvement of instruction

It should be noted that this list of duties and activities relieves the department of instruction from all administrative responsibility. A teacher is responsible to her principal and to him only. A supervisor has no responsibility for any teacher's work nor for the appraisal of that work. He is set free for a specific purpose. That purpose is outlined in the definition of instruction. It is the *improvement* of instruction.

It should be further noted, that while the duties listed relieve the supervisor of administrative responsibility, they impose on a principal and his teachers the responsibility for detecting the defects in the existing order and for suggesting the most desirable points of attack for the supervisor's work of improvement of instruction.

The differentiation of instruction from administration is best comprehended from a list of duties paralleling those given for administration. Instructional agents are charged with the "improvement of the efficiency of instruction" which means:

(1) Constructing the courses of study
(2) Determining the degree of efficiency to be adopted as standard
(3) Selecting efficient methods of teaching
(4) Formulating standards of equipment, supplies, and organization
(5) Formulating tests and methods of measuring efficiency of instruction
(6) Formulating methods of diagnosis and methods of remedying specific defects
(7) Digesting reports of low and high spots from own or other systems
(8) Formulating for transmission, and arranging for the transmission to the system, high spots found in own or other systems
(9) Discovering, formulating, and solving all the instructional problems of the system.
(10) Making suggestions of problems for the improvement of the work of other departments
(11) Rendering assistance 'on call,' that is, when and where requested to do so

This list of duties is predominantly a list of research activities. Under this system, the supervisor will give approximately one third of his time to research, one third to the adaptation of the results of research to practical use, and the remaining third to assistance to agents who are actually using the products. The supervisor becomes almost wholly a research agent, and the goals of his research activities are better courses of study, better methods of teaching, and better methods of appraisal. Research requires time for experimentation and reflection, and this time is provided by freeing the supervisor from administrative responsibility.

III. Machinery of Coöperation

The essential characteristics of the organization developed under these definitions may be represented graphically by the diagram

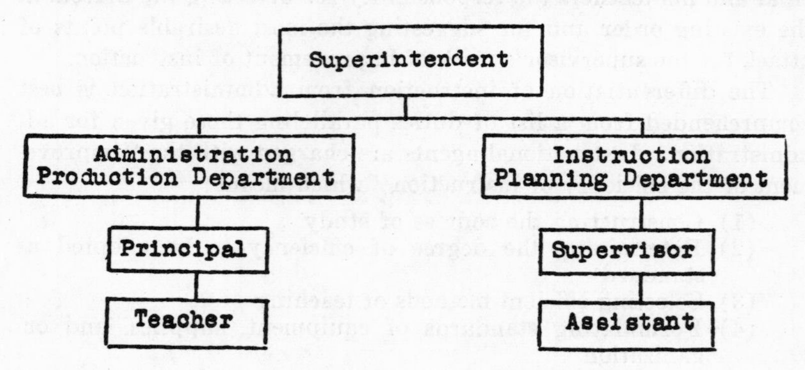

Note that there is no connection between the two departments except through the superintendent. They are independent, but coördinate departments, coöperating in the achievement of a single task, but specialized to perform a particular and non-overlapping portion of the task. Each is responsible only for its own work and each reports directly to the superintendent, whose responsibility is to maintain the coördination and balance between the two departments. It is the superintendent alone who can decide the many puzzling conflicts which necessarily arise.

With the development and nature of the administrative organization, this account would not be concerned, except that it has a very important and distinctive bearing upon the possibilities of coöperation of teachers and other administrative agents in curriculum construction.

The form of organization adopted for Detroit provides for a continuous system from kindergarten through college. There are four levels of administration—elementary, kindergarten through Grade 6; intermediate, Grades 7, 8, and 9; high, Grades 10, 11, and 12; and collegiate, Grades 13-19. Ideally, on each level there are District Principals[2] in charge of a building and having administrative supervision over a number of other schools of the same type in his district. Actually, the three colleges—Arts, Medical, and Teachers—have never been formally organized on this basis, although the three deans have met quite regularly in conference. On the elementary level, however, there are now sixteen district principals. The complete scheme of administrative organization may be represented diagrammatically thus:

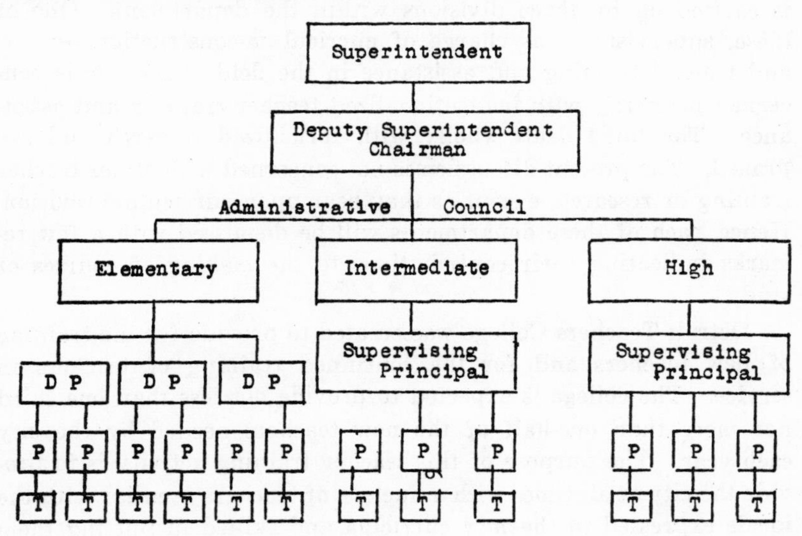

At a meeting of the administrative council, the interests of the entire system from the kindergarten through the high school are represented. The administrative council meets once in two weeks. Its meetings are followed by meetings of district principals with

[2] The title of the District Principals on the Intermediate and High-School level has been changed to "Supervising Principal."

their principals and by meetings of principals with their teachers. Administrative directions thus pass by a human chain directly from superintendent to teacher.

The organization, however, serves not only for transmission outward, but also for transmission inward. The opinions, criticisms, and contributions of any teacher, and of all teachers, may be, and are given vocal expression in the council through their administrative superiors. The organization thus provides formally organized machinery for putting a new course of study into effect and for collecting suggestions and contributions for its improvement.

The Department of Instruction has a similar organization, with only such modifications as are made necessary by differences in the work of the two departments.

The work of curriculum construction, assistance, and appraisal is carried on by three divisions within the department. One of these, supervision, has charge of curriculum-construction proper, and teacher training and assistance in the field. Another is concerned primarily with institutionalized teacher training and assistance. The third deals wholly with formalized research and appraisal. The present discussion is not concerned with either teacher training or research, except as they bear upon curriculum-revision. Hence, each of these departments will be dismissed with a few remarks indicating their contributions to the making of courses of study.

Detroit Teachers College was created to provide for the training of new teachers and for the continued training of teachers in service. The college is expected to provide not less than one third nor more than one-half of the new teachers needed by the city each year. The purpose of this teacher training activity is to provide the city at all times with a nucleus of teachers familiar with the ideals expressed in the new curricula and skilled in putting them into effect. Supervisors give courses in Teachers College and share in the preparation of the training curricula. Each advance made anywhere in the system is at once put into effect in the training schools and in the training courses. Graduates thus become demonstration teachers for progressive ideas and are an invaluable agency for the rapid modification of practice throughout the city.

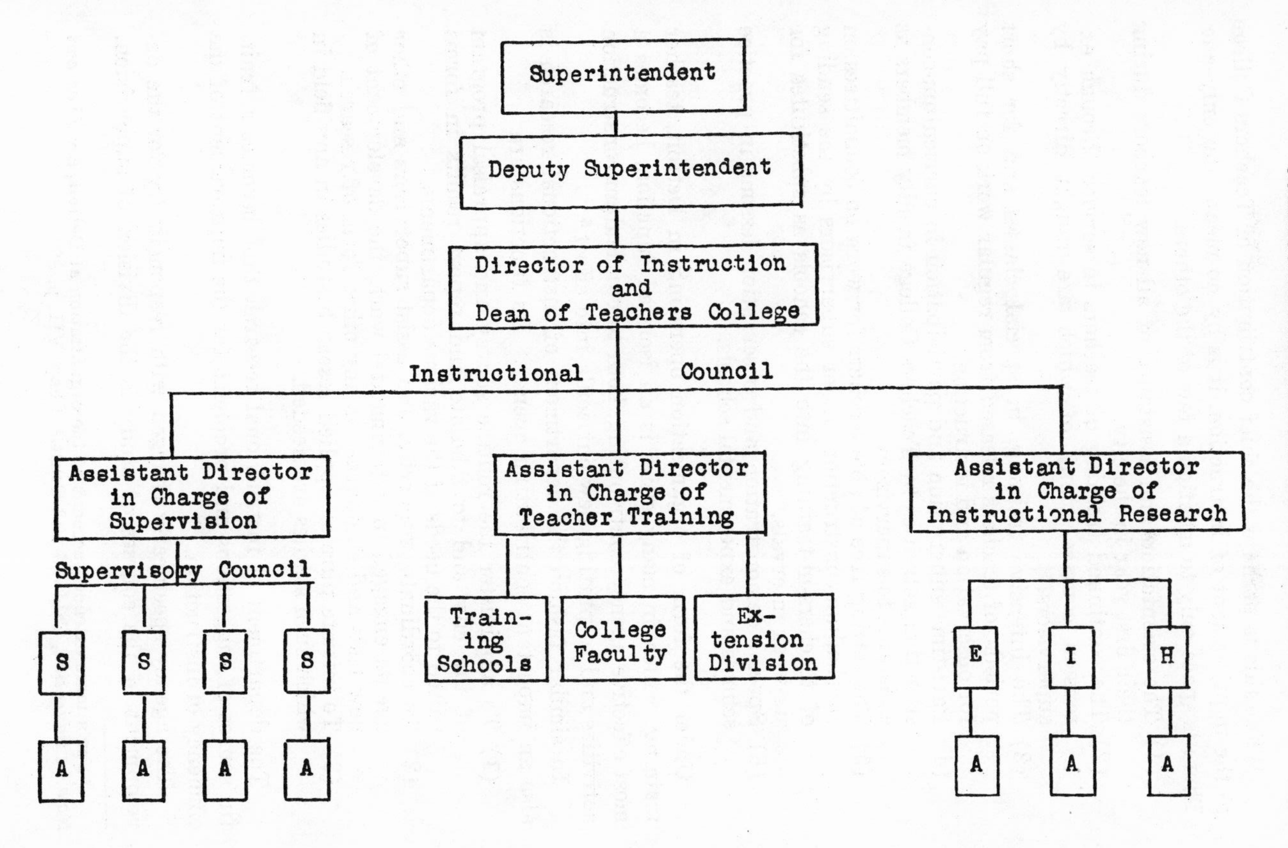
Superintendent
Deputy Superintendent
Director of Instruction and Dean of Teachers College
Instructional Council
Assistant Director in Charge of Supervision
Supervisory Council
S
S
S
S
A
A
A
A
Assistant Director in Charge of Teacher Training
Train-ing Schools
College Faculty
Ex-tension Division
Assistant Director in Charge of Instructional Research
E
I
H
A
A
A

While this is perhaps the chief contribution of Teachers College to the improvement of instruction, it is by no means the only one. There is space only to mention a few of the others.

(1) The orientation and assistance of all new teachers during their first year in the city.
(2) The continued training of teachers in service through extension courses, many of which are taught directly by supervisors.
(3) The intensive training, in special classes and for short periods, of teachers released from regular work on full pay for observation and instruction.
(4) Part-time supervision and participation in curriculum-construction activities by Teachers College faculty members as assistants to supervisors.
(5) The setting free of able teachers for work on committees on curriculum-construction under supervisors by the sending of teachers-in-training into the schools as substitutes for six-week intervals.
(6) Special demonstration and observation lessons in practice schools and experimental schools.

Under the form of organization operating in Detroit, teacher training, which in many cities is an isolated function, becomes a most effective agency contributing, both to curriculum-construction activities and to putting new curricula into effect.[3]

In similar fashion the department of instructional research is also an important contributing agency. Its functions are

(1) To administer the routine survey and appraisal program of the city and to tabulate and report results in forms suited to the needs of the various departments.
(2) To coördinate, supervise, and assist supervisors and other agents engaged in experimental work, the development of new tests and standards, or any other form of research.
(3) To initiate pure or applied research studies in any field in which such studies are needed.

The department of instructional research thus becomes a fruitful source of suggestions and problems for the improvement of the efficiency of instruction.

The agency specifically charged with responsibility for the development of the courses of study is the division of supervision.

---

[3] For a more extended account of the organization at Detroit, see *Then and Now in Education*, Caldwell and Courtis, Chap. VII, p. 98.

There are approximately fifty members of this department, besides as many more part-time contributing members in related divisions and departments.

"The subject supervisor," according to Mr. Spain,[4] Deputy Superintendent, "is an expert. He is the best informed person in the system with respect to existing conditions in his field and the person best equipped to solve the special problems which may arise. The supervisor is expected to be a constructive thinker, who stands ready to contribute the results of his creative effort for the benefit of the entire school system." As has been indicated, he is primarily a research agent.

The division of supervision is organized as a supervisory council and holds weekly meetings for the discussion of common problems. Plans for the development of courses of study, results of experimental work, completed courses, etc., all pass through the refining and integrating process of expert discussion and suggestion by specialists representing every phase of the work in the schools. Unity of aim and method and correlation between subject matter divisions are thus insured.

Development of a Typical Course of Study

This discussion of the machinery of coöperation would not be complete without a description of the organization in operation. Its uniqueness lies not in its organization, but in the way it makes possible the participation of the entire system in actual curriculum-construction. By way of illustration, the development of a single course of study from problem to solution will be presented. While no one actual course has exhibited all the phases to be described, each phase could be illustrated from an actual course of study, under ideal conditions, and all of them would occur about as follows:

1. The first phase is the definition of a problem. Suppose that the results of a city-wide survey proved the Detroit schools were doing poor work in spelling. The request would go out from the superintendent for criticisms of the existing course and for suggestions for its improvement. During the next month there would come pouring into the superintendent's office from every department facts about every phase of the work in spelling. This mass of material

[4] *Elementary School Teacher*, March, 1926, p. 501.

would be transmitted to the department of instruction for digestion. In the meantime, the distinctive contribution of the supervisor of spelling would be a survey of practices in other cities, especially of recent experimental studies. The best teachers of spelling in the system would be set free to form a committee which would work under the direction of the supervisor of spelling. If necessary, 'special' survey or diagnostic tests would be given in the city schools until the major aspects of the problem had been clearly determined and formulated. The results of the committee's work would be presented to the supervisory council, and to those members of Teachers College faculty interested in spelling, for confirmation and refinement. When the report of the findings went to the superintendent, it would be the joint product of all the educational forces of the city.

2. The second phase is experimental solution. Let us suppose that the evidence proves the defects in the existing practice are two: (1) lack of adaptation of words to grade and ability levels, and (2) lack of adjustment of methods of teaching to individual needs. With the findings and evidence the instructional department would submit to the superintendent at a cabinet meeting plans with estimates of costs (1) for a survey of children's spelling needs, and (2) for an experimental trial of a suggested method of individualization of spelling instruction. During the cabinet discussion all departments would become familiar with the plans and make their specific contributions. If the evidence was convincing and the experiment promising, the cabinet would approve the plan and authority would be given by the superintendent for the experimentation. The finance department would see that the necessary money for supplies, printing, etc., was available; the administrative departments would be prepared for requests for coöperation; the supply department would be ready to honor requisitions for the necessary supplies. A small number of representative schools would be put under the direction of the supervisor of spelling for experimental purposes, and the administrative forces in these schools notified to make any adjustments of time schedules, organization, content, methods of work, etc., the supervisor might wish to try.

3. The third phase would be active experimentation. Able teachers might be transferred to the experimental schools, special tests devised and given, special materials printed and tried. Throughout

this phase, however, there would be constant experimentation under the law of the single variable and constant appraisal of the results obtained. The final product would be, let us say, the discovery of a new method of teaching spelling and better standards of efficiency.

Meanwhile, other committees of teachers, under the direction of the supervisor of spelling, would have been busy collecting, through the coöperation of the principals and teachers of the city, the facts in regard to children's needs, differentiated in terms of age, grade, sex, intelligence, and social status. The product of their activities would be the material out of which differentiated courses of study might be made.

4. Construction would now pass over into the fourth phase, formulation. Again, committees would be formed and begin their labors of experimentation and trial. This time the emphasis would be upon preparing the material and methods in the form best adapted to use in the city schols. The product would be the desired new course of study in spelling.

5. The fifth phase would be: "Sale to the administration." On a given day the supervisor of spelling would come before the administrative council and present her material and evidence. Questions would be asked until the matter was understood, then further discussion deferred for one month to permit of administrative examination and criticism. During this month the material would be transmitted outward until every teacher in the system had inspected, studied, tried, and otherwise satisfied herself as to the possibilities or defects of the new plan. At the meeting at the end of the period, all the suggestions and criticisms from those who must do the actual work of teaching, if the new plan is adopted, would be presented. If the objections were not valid, the supervisor would be able to meet them with evidence collected in the experimental schools. If the objections were valid, the supervisor would withdraw her proposal, for further experimentation and modification. The modified plan would be re-submitted. The time would come eventually when all objections would be met. The project then passes into the sixth stage, training of administrative officers.

6. The superintendent would call for those district principals who had been convinced the method was an improvement to volunteer to try it out on a practical basis. Those principals who volun-

teered would organize and call upon the supervisor for assistance. It is to be particularly noted that with the 'sale to the administration,' the matter passes out of the supervisor's control. It is no longer a supervisory project, but an administrative project. Those who volunteer do so to make a contribution to the city's improvement, and they assume the initiative. They request the supervisor for demonstration meetings and standards of judgment and appraisal. For the next few weeks the group of volunteer district principals visit the experimental schools and observe the work of proficient teachers. The supervisor furnishes them with "items to observe," and they rate the teachers and compare their ratings. They are also furnished with appropriate tests and given practice in measuring the results of teaching. In the meantime a 'master key teacher,'[5] trained by the supervisor, has been established in the training schools of Teachers College and the new curriculum and methods put into the training courses of the students. Each volunteer district principal has also made a careful canvass of his district and selected an able teacher to be the 'key teacher' for his district. The key teachers from each district are sent to Teachers College and are trained by the master key teacher.

Eventually, the time comes when the volunteer district principals declare themselves competent and undertake to put the new method into operation in their districts. Their first task is to train their principals. Using their key teacher and the items to observe, they put their principals through the same course of training through which they themselves have passed. Each principal, when competent, then trains his teachers, sending them in one by one to observe the work of the key teacher. Soon difficulties arise and teachers begin to request the assistance of the key teacher. A special substitute is put in her place and she visits teacher after teacher 'on call.'

During this period of preparation, standard tests have been made ready and the department of instructional research now organizes large control experiments to measure the general effect of the new method, considering the schools of those who did not volunteer as controls and the schools of those who did as experimental schools.

[5] Proposed, but not in effect. At present 'key teachers' are trained directly by supervisors.

Each teacher and school conducts its own testing to see whether it has met the standards set by the supervisor from the results in the schools under her direction. The results of the tests in the various schools are sent to the department of instructional research and consolidated to obtain city-wide measures. Soon it is known where the work is going well and where it is failing.

Principals report to district principals and district principals report to the superintendent. Soon difficulties arise. The supervisor is called upon to visit schools and give assistance in diagnosis and remedial work. Little by little, the efficiency arises. New schools volunteer. The results are discussed in meetings, reported at conventions, published in magazines.[6] Eventually, the new method is adopted city wide, and the cycle is complete.

It should be particularly noted that the training of district principals and of principals is in administering and appraising the new method, not in teaching it. Administrative officers must know the aim of new courses of study; they must be acquainted with their content and the standard methods of teaching. They must be able to appraise the work of a teacher, to diagnose her defects, to assist her in various ways. They do not need to develop instructional skill. The training of administrators by supervisors is in administrative functions only.

IV. Fact Basis

The critical factors in coöperative, scientific curriculum-construction are, in our opinion, a conviction that education takes place in accordance with discoverable natural law, and the existence of machinery of coöperation. Detroit is fortunate in having both. The rank and file of its teachers have had direct personal contact with experimentation and research since 1910; the reorganization of the school system provided the machinery. The resulting competitive coöperation in making contributions to improvements is the logical outcome. Mr. Spain says: "Let it be assumed that all progress must be founded on a knowledge of the facts—on scientifically ascertained data. Research then becomes a function of prime importance, because a knowledge of the facts is a necessary prerequisite

[6] For instance, see "An experiment to determine the effectiveness of practice tests in teaching beginning reading," by Nila B. Smith, *Journal of Educational Research,* March, 1923, pp. 213-228.

to the successful performance of the other supervisory functions." Research has been the determining factor in Detroit's program of curriculum-revision.

Policy. The basic instructional policy adopted by the superintendent's cabinet as a guide for curriculum-revision was based on modern philosophical theories and formulated as follows:

"Education is to be conceived as a process of social heredity which results in the integration of personality and the maintenance of a progressive social order.

"The supreme function of the educational process is to be taken as the attempt to bring individuals to see life as a collective struggle for human betterment through conquest of nature (including man himself). The teacher is to educate children by stimulating them (through control of environment) to activities directed toward the achievement of vital and worthy purposes, and by interpreting such experiences.

"In general, democracy demands methods which yield a maximum of (a) self-direction, (b) self-appraisal, (c) self-control, (d) experience in working coöperatively with one's companions in the achievement of social ends.

"The fundamental and persistent problem of education is the individual. The one possible method of solution that will yield the results vital to a democracy, is self-education in a social, democratic environment, that will call out creative expressions of the personality of the individual in service to the group. That is, within the limits made necessary by school organization, the abilities of teachers, and the need for systematic work, the tastes and interests of children should determine classroom procedure rather than a fixed program, a textbook, logical organization or the will of the teacher. Except where individual desire conflicts with social needs or regulations, in passing from kindergarten to the upper grades children should have a larger and larger share in choosing what is to be studied, in organizing the plan of their work, in assigning lessons, etc. Control of children's activities should be exercised more through control of environment than through direct command, and class work should prove immediately and innately satisfying to the children.

"In other words, the spirit of education, and of the teacher should be service, not domination; assistance, not preparation;

guidance, not instruction. 'Service' is to be the keynote of the new era just commencing, and the spirit of service must permeate the work and relations of both teachers and children.''

The changes which have taken place in Detroit are in general accord with this policy. Large bodies move slowly and even to-day actual courses of study and methods of teaching fall far short of the lofty ideal set up as the goal of curriculum-revision. Nevertheless, in the successive revisions of courses of study that have taken place it is possible to trace great progress toward the ideal.

The fruits of research are illustrated most clearly in the curricular products which have been designed to individualize mass instruction in the fundamental skills—reading, writing, arithmetic, and English. Progress along this line has been exceedingly rapid and effective.[7]

The magnitude of the curriculum-revision undertaken at Detroit is best shown by summarizing the courses of study published from 1921-1925.

SUMMARY OF CURRICULAR MATERIALS

(Number of copies published)

Courses of Study		*Teachers' Manuals*	
English	7,000	Reading	4,000
Spelling	4,000	Writing	4,500
Arithmetic	9,500	Arithmetic	7,000
Social Science	6,000	Children's Museum	1,000
Geography	1,500	High-School English	1,000
Art	2,500	Health Education	10,500
Music	1,000	Music	2,000
Health	4,000	Library Standards	2,000
Nature Study	2,000	Total	83,000
Vocational Subjects	9,500		
Speech Improvement	1,000		
Code of Morals	3,000		

TEXTBOOK AND PRACTICE MATERIAL USED BY CHILDREN

Reading	408,550	Sight Saving	1,500
Writing	599,500	Safety Education	3,000
Mathematics	10,000	Vocational Subjects	152,200
Spelling	941,000	Teacher Training	7,400
Grammar	20,000		
Speech Correction	10,000	Total	2,153,150

[7] For a detailed account of such contributions, see *Adapting Schools to Individual Differences*, ''The *Twenty-Fourth Yearbook* of this Society,'' Part II, pp. 106-113, 191-198.

In addition to these formal printed documents, reference must also be made to the constant stream of mimeographed reports, directions, suggestions, and aids which constitute one of the most effective means of making vital information available to those who are to use it.

However, no mere aggregate of figures can express the really vital product of the system of curriculum-revision followed in Detroit. The product of most worth is the stimulating effects upon the professional attitudes and activities of the rank and file of the teaching corps, and the resulting transformation for the better in the benefits received by children from their educational efforts.

CHAPTER X

A UNIT-ACTIVITIES CURRICULUM IN THE PUBLIC SCHOOLS OF BURLINGTON, IOWA

E. M. Sipple
Headmaster, The Park School, Baltimore, Maryland, and formerly Superintendent of Schools, Burlington, Iowa

The purpose that directed the curriculum-study outlined in this discussion was to perfect an organization and to develop a suggestive instructional scheme that would place the more vital aims of the school in a commanding position.

The discontent with the prevailing curriculum-organization arose from practical problems of the classroom teacher. How can the teacher have a program that will challenge her daily to do developmental teaching without departing radically from the curriculum of the school? The answer seemed to me to be: in some organization that would remove the choppy classroom schedule from the teacher's desk without casting her upon a wholly uncharted sea.

The grouping of school work into activity units was suggested by Professor Harold Rugg in the course of a classroom discussion in a summer school at Teachers College. Out of this suggestion I formed a hazy plan of organization which the Burlington, Iowa, elementary staff and I thought about during the next school year. For three summers Professors Rugg, Bonser, Evenden, and Kilpatrick gave valuable assistance, offered much needed encouragement, and opened up the opportunity to study the problem under Teachers College influence.

For two years before receiving the suggestion of a grouping, or unit plan, the elementary staff, including principals, supervisors, and teachers, had been working with the writer upon the common problem stated in the first paragraph. We had taken the first important steps toward a coöperative solution to our problem. We had arrived at a place of mutual confidence. We had agreed upon fundamental educational beliefs, and had thus established a common point of view, including a formulation of the object of our search. Our beliefs may be summarized briefly as follows:

(1) School is a place for rich living. It is a place in which to have children carry on activities that will enrich their experiences from day to day, and that will thus prepare them for full living to-morrow by giving them broad living to-day.

(2) Living in either child life or adult life is not 'compartmentalized' into arithmetic experiences, history experiences, geography experiences. An approach to life conditions, therefore, demands the breaking down of artificial barriers set up by the usual school curriculum.

(3) Many of the so-called 'important facts' in various bits of subject matter have been glorified without justifiable grounds in terms of use.

(4) Subject matter offers rich summaries of how people have thought, felt and acted; and how they are now thinking, feeling, and acting under certain life conditions. The task is, therefore, to utilize this racial experience for the good of the children.

But does a real educational problem exist here? Are the vital aims not already in a commanding position in the usual classroom? Does not the usual curriculum-organization meet the demands of progressive education?

The test of a curriculum, or of any other part of school machinery, is its effect in the classroom. What, then, does the usual curriculum give to the classroom teacher for her daily guidance? It places before her a working schedule that looks something like this:

9:00 to 9:10 Opening Exercises
9:10 to 9:40 Arithmetic
9:40 to 10:10 Reading
10:10 to 10:40 Language

and so on with the other subjects of the grade.

I have assumed the favorable conditions of one grade in the room, and have not attempted to complicate the program by dividing the class into sections. Then, of course, the schedule would look still worse. The principle, however, would not be changed.

The teacher's daily schedule is an ever-present companion. It tells her what to do and when to do it. At 9:10 she is to begin arithmetic; at 9:40 she is to dismiss the class and begin with reading; at 10:10 she must dismiss this class and call a language class, although at that time she may be having a language lesson of the highest type.

Now, as society has become more complex, it has delegated more and more to the school. We do want all-round children. We want them to have music, art, nature study, and elementary science, thrift education, health education, instruction for duties as members of society, appreciations of the better things of life. We want many desirable contacts for them.

It seems to me to be a physical impossibility for the schools to continue to add small parcels of segregated matter to their programs as rapidly as the changing conditions of society and the shifting of problems to the schools demand.

The teacher is asked to do all these worthy things and to continue with the old-line school subjects still in an important place on the program. She is asked to use developmental methods of teaching. But such methods require opportunity for children to investigate, to think, to express themselves, to develop their own individualities. She has a right to ask: "How can I stick to a set program, have children do tasks in books on a schedule, and still meet the demands of progressive teaching?"

Although such a classroom schedule, based upon a subject-matter curriculum, does not state the method to be used by the teacher, it does indicate definitely that she is to have a recitation on a definitely isolated bit of subject matter at a set time. Certainly, good teachers often do violence to such a program and break over the boundaries. There is nothing in the program which suggests that a teacher use her own ingenuity, however. She must be more or less of a pioneer, a free-lance, to do it. The average teacher will do her best to teach the subject on time, with an apology for any variation. She will see that her pupils know the 'important facts.' (But who made these facts more important than any of a thousand not to be learned?)

The whole apparent demand on the teacher is in terms of dissected-out subjects. She has before her at all times the task of teaching geography, history, arithmetic. There is nothing to challenge her to find out what is happening to the children as human beings. She is asked to think in terms of school subjects. Her pupils are tested in their ability as subject learners. Such a teacher is encouraged to become a subject-matter specialist, rather than a specialist in human values. Specialists are needed, strictly scientific subject-matter specialists, who do not concern themselves with what people are going to do about their discoveries and developments. But they are not needed as teachers of children.

Scholars are required for the classrooms, to be sure, but first of all scholars who are students of life and its unfolding, who think of subject matter as a source of supply for bringing about such actions in the pupils as will affect their human behavior favorably.

Characteristics of the Organization

1. The Burlington organization causes the classroom time-allotment schedule of the single subject to disappear. There is no definite assignment of a number of minutes to any subject, except spelling and drill in the fundamental processes in arithmetic. The school day is divided tentatively into four parts, in each of which the work is based upon activities considered universally essential to the realization of important social objectives.

2. The program is elastic. Even the wide boundary lines that are established for guides may be totally disregarded whenever occasion demands. In practice this occurs frequently.

3. It frees the teacher and the pupils for developmental work without the necessity of a timekeeper, and without the fear of neglecting the learning of certain 'important facts.'

4. It calls for thinking in terms of use, rather than in terms of subjects. The teacher who fails to adjust her thinking will inevitably fail in a miserable way under this plan.

5. It demands the full utilization of subject matter. While it does in most cases tend to eliminate the single textbook, it at the same time demands wide use of textbooks and reference books of all kinds.

6. It gives mile-stones of progress. Teachers are not asked to build their own curriculum without guidance, yet they are given wide leeway so long as they keep their main objectives in view.

7. It suggests starting places and checking plans, but it does not prescribe any exact time limitations.

8. It gives opportunity for coöperative assignments. When in full operation, it makes the formal teacher-made assignment under penalty disappear completely.

Organization

The organization is based upon an attempt to answer the question: For what purposes in racial economy have these units of subject matter been preserved? The four activity units here outlined serve as a basis for a tentative answer. The units are:

- Language Activities:
  - Reading (Literature)
  - Oral Expression
  - Written Expression
  - Spelling
  - Writing
- Health and Happiness:
  - Hygiene and Natural Science
  - Physical Education
  - Music
  - Art
  - Inspirational Literature
- Social Science (Living Together):
  - History
  - Geography
  - Community Civics
  - Civics
- Mathematics and Construction:
  - Mathematics
  - Manual Arts (including Domestic Science)
  - Physical Science

Language-Activities Unit

Why does language work have a place in every curriculum? Civilized man desires to express himself in language forms in a pleasing and an effective way. Racially, here is a language activity.

Why reading? Good reading is simply communicating with those who have left their contributions in written or printed form. It puts the greatest characters of all past time and many of the best of to-day as our next-door neighbors. They are ready to answer inquiries or spend an evening with us, provided we have mastered certain accepted forms of expression. Again, here is a language activity. Spelling and writing clearly come under this heading. From this has developed one of the activity units, namely the *Language Activities Unit*. It includes reading (in the narrow sense), oral expression, written expression, spelling, and writing. One fourth of a day is tentatively allotted to this unit.

Health and Happiness Unit

Why hygiene and natural science, art, music, inspirational literature? One of the everlasting searches of mankind has been for health and happiness. Hygiene and natural science are clearly studies of life, of living, a summary of man's attempt to know life and enjoy health and happiness. What of art and music?

When a pupil makes a health poster, is he studying art or hygiene? When he studies colors and applies this to the interior of a home, is he using art or hygiene? When he studies music, including appreciation, is he mastering a certain technique, or gaining means and material for wholesome enjoyment and right emotional expression?

Considered in terms of racial economy, these units of subject matter seem to be a summation of the attempts of human beings to be healthy and happy.

If the teacher has in mind that her duty is to help children to gain information and to develop habits and attitudes that will make for healthy, happy living—if she keeps this as her teaching goal, will it not affect her work?

Here is a vast storehouse of human experience, human expression, for use. It offers a chance for enriched living. Why dissect it out into 20-minute or 30-minute parcels and put it before the teacher in this dead form?

One fourth of the day is tentatively allotted to this unit.

The Social Science Unit (Living Together)

The preceding units have included experiences largely individualistic. This unit is largely social. It includes the following: history, geography, community civics, and civics of more advanced nature.

People have been trying for thousands of years to live together. This has always given rise to difficult problems and to attempted solutions of those problems. The struggle of man from the abyss of ignorance, fear, and discomfort toward the mountain height of enlightenment, peace, and satisfaction is an intensely interesting human drama. His upward flights and foolish slips are alive every step of the way.

Shall we permit children to live in this battle royal, and profit by it, or shall we merely teach them history, geography, and civil government? Shall we allot 30 minutes for an account of what happened, 30 minutes to a study of where and under what geographic conditions something has happened (not necessarily associated with the 30 minutes of 'what'), and 30 minutes for consideration of how human beings live together?

Is not the real problem of the teacher to present situations that will aid children to grow toward socialized human beings, with a sane local and national patriotism and with a world-wide vision?

In the plan under consideration one fourth of the day is tentatively allotted to social science, a consideration of the problems of people in their struggle toward civilization.

The Rugg Social Science pamphlets furnish an excellent source of material for this unit in grades above the sixth.

Mathematics and Construction Unit

The fourth unit has not been fully developed. It would include mathematics, physical science, manual arts, and domestic science.

In actual practice the boundary lines between these various units naturally disappear after a project is under way. However, the objectives still give teachers bases for checking up on their work and for determining whether or not they are avoiding narrowing the activities down to their own personal hobbies.

A Fourth-Grade Project—Health and Happiness Unit

In a fourth grade the children began the discussion of the making of healthy, happy homes in the 'Health and Happiness' group of activities. What does it take to make a happy home? This question brought out the fact that right-acting people, clean and attractive surroundings, including interior and exterior decorations, are required for such a home. Pupils reported on types of homes in various lands in their interest to find how people live at home. The decision was finally reached to build a cottage and put their ideas into it.

The manual training teacher and the older boys had to work with the children to do some of the things that little hands could not handle. However, the children themselves drew the plans to scale, wired the house for electricity and actually installed the lights, made all the furniture, which was large enough for use, made the curtains, rugs, and fancy work, painted the house inside and outside, computed the cost of the various items needed for the house from the lumber to the finishing touches, made the purchases, wrote letters of appreciation to those who had given special assistance, and wrote discussions concerning the house. Among the articles written were: "Quarter Sawed Oak," "Wiring a House," "Sunshine Cottage."

As a climax, the pupils had a house party to which they invited their parents and the public. A large crowd responded, for the children had given a good deal of publicity through their own enthusiasm. The girls prepared the refreshments that were served at the party and acted as hostesses. The boys helped to explain to the visitors all the points of interest about "Sunshine Cottage."

The teacher had no worry about her time schedule. She and the class started upon the 'Health and Happiness Unit,' but the boundaries of this unit were so elastic that they soon went far beyond their natural limits.

Eighth-Grade Project—Social Science Unit

An eighth-grade class gave an original dramatization of the Constitutional Convention. They represented the various colonies, presented the arguments from different sections, and reproduced the convention as they conceived it.

When they were writing the speeches, organizing the convention, discussing material to present, the teacher did not have to watch the clock to know when to dismiss the civics class or the history class (which was it?) and call the English class. She did not even need to think of the time for the language-activities period. Some rather good language work was already going on.

The project did have a starting place in the 'Social Science Unit.' The unit plan of organization acted as a chart for guidance. It did not, however, limit the activity period to any number of minutes each day. That was left to the judgment of the teacher.

This started as a social science project. The major check for progress, therefore, was in terms of the unit primarily involved. All information was checked for accuracy. The arguments were seen to be the arguments presented in the Constitutional Convention.

During this activity, however, excellent language activity was carried on. Choice examples of argumentation were studied; outlines of speeches were made; speeches were written; public speaking was practiced under motivated conditions. The "Committee on Correct English" found errors to report. These formed the basis for corrective English, including the necessary study of grammar.

Why should this not constitute the major work in the language activities group?

Seventh-Grade Project—Language Activities

The two preceding illustrations show that language activities develop naturally from other activity units. However, a language project might start and end fairly well within the language-activity unit.

A seventh-grade class chose to present a dramatization of the "Great Stone Face." As a result of this choice, they had a number of things to do.

1. They had to be familiar with the story, to know the literature.
2. They had to have some conception of the purpose of the author to make their writing and their acting true to life as the author presented it.
3. They had to know the order in which the events occurred if they were to arrange the sources and the acts properly.
4. They had to understand the characters to represent them correctly.
5. They had to be able to say about what the characters would say in the various settings.
6. They had to write the play, including stage directions.
7. They had to choose the pupils who could act the parts of the various characters.

The activities involved in this production did not take the class far into any other unit. There was interpretation of literature. There was oral expression and written expression. There was correctional English work. All these came well within the language-activities unit, and one fourth of the day was adequate to meet any one day's requirements.

Of course, a study of the ''Great Stone Face'' made demands upon history and geography, but not to a degree that caused the project to carry over naturally into the Social Science unit. The teacher felt under no obligations to make any artificial correlation.

Tests

The space allotted to this paper will not permit an extended discussion of tests, or checks, for desirable measurable outcomes. Many of the most desirable outcomes can be seen and felt, but not objectively tested. However, standardized tests and teacher-made tests do have a place in the unit organization.

In the Language Activities it is not difficult to use tests to answer such questions as the following: Are the pupils able to express themselves pleasingly and effectively, their grade considered? Are they able to read effectively?

In all units, testing for knowledge and for ability to use knowledge and skills under testing conditions is easy enough. It is not difficult, for example, in the Health and Happiness unit to devise tests that will determine whether or not children know what a balanced diet is; what color combinations are restful and pleasing; what place music has in the life of the home and of the individual; how to assign art and music to places in life; what constitutes good living habits; what are some of the simple relationships of other life to human life; how to take reasonable health precautions; how to meet ordinary emergency or first-aid conditions; how to protect others from contracting colds and other communicable diseases;

how to have the home surroundings and the community surroundings clean and attractive and conducive to health and happiness.

In the Social Science Unit it is easy to find out whether or not children have the necessary information to meet the requirements for their age and development in answer to questions like these: What kind of person should one be to be classed as a best citizen of the school? Of the community? Of the nation? A wealthy farmer said: "I am absolutely independent of city people; I have everything my family needs right on my big farm." Was he right? Give reasons for your answer.

Children can be taught to answer questions under any sane plan of instruction, based upon any type of curriculum. Whether the answers are merely stereotyped answers to formal questions or whether they are expressions of experiences will depend upon whether the children have merely learned some facts or have enriched their point of view through school living.

The activities curriculum asks the teacher to see that her pupils enter into situations that at least have the elements of life in them, and then to watch closely to have them engage in purposeful activities of a worthwhile nature. It asks her not to be satisfied with formal tests, but to be alert every moment of the day in her contacts with children so that she may answer this question: Do my daily contacts with the children, my observation of their living, my careful study of them as human beings, lead me to believe that they are living richly, that they are growing broadly?

Difficulties and Dangers

Educational language is largely in terms of small segments of subject matter. Curricular and classroom schedules are so familiarly based upon subjects that the first difficulty is to think in terms of activities and human outcomes. The attitude and the thinking of the teacher are the foundation of the success attending a curriculum of this character. Here the plan stands or falls. A formal, subject teacher could never bring herself to risk omitting certain 'essential matter' in logical order.

It is a little difficult at first for a teacher to get her bearings. She is likely to 'flounder,' as she might do under any elastic program. A new teacher is lost for an exploratory period.

The technique of teaching demanded under a schedule based upon this organization is still comparatively new to most teachers. But it has unlimited room for growth, and this is in its favor.

The plan calls for teachers with confidence and with ability to launch out from that sacred shore—a definite program.

Teachers at first worry because of fear that important facts may not be learned in certain grades.

A teacher may neglect drill entirely. This would be a mistake. Drill should grow out of the program when properly administered.

There is a danger of becoming wrapped up in continuous movement and of neglecting to organize and summarize.

Familiar tests now current are made in terms of subjects. A testing program might easily destroy the whole plan. Special test forms, therefore, must be used to check for the larger outcomes that are testable.

Summary

Both the plan of the curriculum and the attempt to use it under public-school conditions are full of shortcomings. The scheme does, however, tend to encourage certain teaching conditions that seem to me to be sound.

1. It shifts the point of view of the teacher from subject matter to human activities, to enriched living. If it fails here, it fails completely.

2. It provides an elastic program for the teacher, and thus encourages her to carry on developmental work.

3. It sets out to have children engage in human activities of universal application.

4. It places high value upon subject matter, but assigns it to its rightful place—that of racial experiences to be fully utilized.

5. It modifies the familiar curriculum and the resultant classroom schedule rather radically, but it provides starting places and checking units within limits not unknown to progressive teachers.

6. It demands a continuously growing curriculum, with administrator, supervisors, teachers, and pupils contributing toward its development.

CHAPTER XI

THE PHILOSOPHY OF THE WINNETKA CURRICULUM

CARLETON WASHBURNE
Superintendent of Schools, Winnetka, Illinois

The Winnetka curriculum is based upon four hypostases: Every child has a right to master those knowledges and skills which he will probably use in life; every child has a right to live naturally, happily, and fully as a child; human progress depends on the development of each individual to his full capacity; the welfare of human society requires the development of a strong social consciousness in each individual.

It is a comparatively simple matter to determine what knowledges and skills are commonly needed. Scientific investigations of the demands of society in this field are well under way. It is becoming possible to build the knowledge-and-skill part of the curriculum upon research. The Winnetka schools have contributed their share to such research.

We, in Winnetka, have made an exhaustive study of the common allusions to persons and places in periodical literature, recognizing that in order to read intelligently a person must have familiarity with these persons and places.[1] We have made comparative analyses of the vocabulary studies of others, to determine what words children are most likely to need to spell.[2] We have made statistical studies of primary reading books to find what phonograms are most useful to children learning to read,[3] and have analyzed the 10,000 commonest words in the English language to discover the syllables

---

[1] Washburne, Carleton: "Basic facts needed in history and geography" and "Building a fact course in history and geography," Chapters XIII and VI, *Twenty-Second Yearbook* of this Society, Part II, 1923; Pendleton, Charles, and Washburne, Carleton, "The fact basis of a history, geography, and civics curriculum," *Journal of Educational Research*, October, 1923; Mohr, Louise, and Washburne, Carleton, "The Winnetka social science investigation," *Elementary School Journal*, December, 1922.

[2] Washburne, Carleton, "A spelling curriculum based on research," *Elementary School Journal*, June, 1923.

[3] Vogel, Mabel; Jaycox, Emma; and Washburne, Carleton, "A basic list of phonics for Grades I and II, *Elementary School Journal*, February, 1923.

which occur so commonly as to demand instant recognition.[4] With others, we have measured the speed and accuracy possessed by successful, intelligent men and women in various arithmetical processes, as a guide to the degree of skill children are likely to need.[5]

As a result of such studies of our own, and of studies of the same general type made by others, we have, as far as possible, built the knowledge-and-skill part of our curriculum on the known needs of society.

If a certain bit of knowledge or skill is necessary to practically every normal person, every child should have an opportunity to master it. There should not be excellent grasp for some, good for others, fair for others, and poor for still others—there should be real mastery for every child. The wide differences that are known to exist among children make it obvious that this mastery cannot be obtained by all children—or any group of children—in the same length of time and with the same amount of practice. Hence it is necessary to provide varying amounts of time and varying amounts of instructional material for different children.

To do this under ordinary public school conditions, the Winnetka Schools, following Frederic Burk's lead,[6] have developed their individual instruction technique. This consists of re-stating the knowledge-and-skill curriculum in terms of very definite units of achievement; preparing complete diagnostic tests to cover all of these units; and preparing self-instructive, self-corrective practice materials. When these three things have been done, it is not at all difficult to allow each child to work as long on any unit of the curriculum as is necessary to master it.[7]

The grade subdivisions of the knowledge-and-skill curriculum in Winnetka are based upon statistical records of the amount the slowest, normal, diligent child can accomplish in a year. We consider it unfair and demoralizing to set up standards which some

[4] Washburne, Carleton, "The commonest syllables," *Journal of Educational Research,* October, 1926.

[5] Washburne, Carleton, "Social needs in arithmetic," *Elementary School Journal,* September, 1926.

[6] Ward, Mary A., and others, "Individual system as developed in the San Francisco State Teachers College," *Twenty-Fourth Yearbook* of this Society, Part II.

[7] Washburne, Carleton, "A program of individualization," *Twenty-Fourth Yearbook* of this Society, Part II, and bibliography therein.

children are doomed never to meet. A normal probability curve of achievement in a common essential is an admission of flat failure on the part of the school or the teacher. To set a standard, presumably based on a social need, and then so to teach that very few children achieve it, that the bulk of them are consigned to mediocrity, and others to failure, is inexcusable inefficiency.

Each year, therefore, for the past six years, the teachers of each grade in Winnetka have met with me in May or June and gone over the accomplishments of all the children in each subject. The records of children proved by intelligence tests to be subnormal have been, for this purpose, ignored. So have the records of children who are known to have loafed, who have obviously not tried to get their work done, and of those who have been absent for more than two weeks. The records of all other children have been analysed, and if *any* normal child, with an I.Q. over 95, who has attended school regularly and worked diligently, has not reached standard in a certain subject, the standard has been immediately lowered. Or, if any such child has not been able to complete all the units of work assigned to his grade in any subject, uncompleted units have been pushed up into the next grade higher.

Conversely, if the slowest, normal, diligent child in a certain subject has completed more units of work than we had considered practicable for a year's work in his grade, additional units have been pulled down from the grade above and made a part of the lower grade's curriculum.

In this way, after repeated adjustments based on each year's careful record of every child's progress, we have gradually found, experimentally, how many units of work and what standards of achievement are attainable by all normal, diligent children in a year's time in each grade.

Attacking the same problem from another angle, we have made, or are making, grade-placement studies to determine what sort of material is suitable for children of various stages of school progress. One such study consisted of measuring the spelling ability of several thousand children in and about Chicago, then finding what commonly needed words were relatively easy to spell and what ones relatively hard, for children of each degree of ability.[8] Another

---

[8] Washburne, Carleton: "A spelling curriculum based on research," *Elementary School Journal,* June, 1923.

involved finding what books are read and liked by children of different ages and degrees of reading ability in thirty-four American cities.[9] Another, growing out of this, consists of analysing the measurable differences between books liked in various grades.[10] Still another consists of writing material for children of certain grades and known reading ability, then testing their comprehension; rewriting the parts that have failed to get across, and re-testing, until the material is made suitable.[11]

This whole field of grade-placement is relatively unworked. A curriculum is not scientific or efficient unless it is based on known needs *and* is so constructed as to involve the presentation of suitable subject matter in the right order and at the right stage of a child's development, as determined by research.

Through at least partially scientific selection of subject matter, through such scientific studies as we have been able to make of the best methods and times for the presenting of subject matter, and through the technique of individual instruction and progress, the Winnetka schools are finding that it is possible to teach the commonly needed knowledges and skills in about half of the school day—and to teach them in such a way that every normal child, temporarily at least, achieves mastery.[12]

This leaves half the school day clear—usually half the morning and half the afternoon—for the other phases of the curriculum.

Every child has the right to live naturally, happily, and fully as a child. In *human* life, childhood is in itself an important phase. *Biologically,* childhood may be mere preparation for the reproductive stage, and all life beyond that stage may be mere waste. But humanly, the whole span of life is worth while. The reproductive stage is often the stage of struggle and turmoil from which one looks back longingly to the care-free happiness of childhood or to the peace and contemplation of later life. Childhood in itself is a beautiful section of life, and children should be given a chance for free, full living.

---

[9] Washburne, Carleton, and Vogel, Mabel: *Winnetka Graded Book List,* American Library Association, 1926.

[10] Washburne, Carleton: "Measurable differences in books suitable for different grades," *Elementary English Review,* April, 1926.

[11] Still in progress—to be published.

[12] Washburne, Carleton; Vogel, Mabel; and Gray, William S. *A Survey of the Winnetka Public Schools.* Public School Publishing Company, 1926.

Homes are built primarily for adults. The mother who said, "Helen, go and see what John is doing and tell him not to," is quite typical. The present nursery-school movement is bringing to our attention the need for places built and planned for children. The playground movement has for years been trying to provide opportunities for happy child life.

We try to make the Winnetka schools happy, attractive places for children to be in. What Bobbitt calls the "play-level" of the curriculum has a respected place in our schools. We believe in colorfulness, coziness, hominess in our classrooms; in an opportunity for spontaneity. We want children to *want* to come to school.

There is, however, a more far-reaching purpose back of the activities of that part of the day which is freed from academic subject matter. We are attempting to develop each child's individuality, each child's special interests and abilities, as fully as possible. And we are trying to train him in the use of his own particular abilities for the welfare of others, to instill in him a fundamental sense of his dependence upon and responsibility for the group of which he is a part—a group which gradually enlarges until it embraces all mankind.

The group cannot progress—mankind cannot evolve—except as each individual develops and as each individual *varies* from the average. Schools in the past have been largely concerned with making people alike, with giving them the *same* knowledges and skills. There is a place for this—we don't want originality in spelling, for instance—but if we really succeeded in complete standardization of education, we would produce a race of Robots. And progress would cease. In so far as we can find and develop in each child, on the other hand, those capacities which are different, in so far as we can encourage self-expression and creation, we are making for human evolution.

Creative work consequently occupies a vital place in the curriculum of the Winnetka Schools. We are attempting to provide both stimulus and opportunity for each child to contribute something new. Instead of suppressing variation, we are trying to encourage and develop it, so that each child as an individual, different from all other individuals, may grow to his full stature.

No individual can develop fully, however, except as the society of which he is a part develops. Each individual must, for his own ultimate welfare, contribute to the welfare of the group.

The part of the curriculum most necessary in the present stage of human development, therefore, is neither the acquisition of knowledges and skills nor the opportunity for happy, childlike living, important as we believe both of these things to be. It is the attempt to give children a deep and abiding sense of the fact that in the world's good is one's own, and that in one's own is the world's. This is akin to what Bobbitt calls "large-group consciousness"—it is a realization of the interdependence of man on man, of the organic unity of the human race.

These terms all sound abstract and far out of the realm of childhood. They sound 'high brow.' Yet unless we can make them real in the lives of the coming generations, there is little hope for the survival of civilization. Mankind to-day is like an uncoördinated baby with a sharp knife in its hand. Science has given us knowledge which is as capable of destroying the race as it is of upbuilding it. And the spiritual development—the sense of social responsibility—of mankind has not kept pace with its knowledge. To help mankind to coördinate—to train it in coöperation while it is still in our schools—is our one great hope, and our greatest responsibility.

The worst of it is that the science of education has scarcely touched this aspect of education. We have to grope our way blindly. And meanwhile the baby has the knife!

The efforts of the Winnetka Public Schools to develop a social consciousness include provision for a wide variety of coöperative activities in which each child must merge his personal good in the common weal, and also many activities in which each child may develop fully his own individuality.

Dramatizations offer one field for coöperative activities; for the writing of the plays, the planning and making of the costumes and scenery, the advertising and managing of occasional public performances, give children opportunities to develop their own special capacities, and to contribute these to the group enterprise.

The preparation of the school paper—some writing for it, some drawing, some making stereotypes from the drawings, some carving woodcuts, some soliciting advertisements, some handling the business end, some setting type, some running the presses, some taking charge of distribution—give a large number of children a chance to develop their own particular abilities and at the same time to coöperate in a common activity.

Team games on the playground, ensemble playing in the orchestra or band, or in the harmonica bands of the lower grades—these and dozens of other activities are selected and planned with the primary purpose of training children to live socially, of making each child realize that the welfare of the group depends upon each member of the group contributing the best that is in him.

Another, and not dissimilar line of social development comes through our self-governing assemblies. The assemblies and the business meetings within each classroom are training in citizenship —training in social acting and thinking.

The social studies, which are often the basis for many of the socialized activities, probably offer the most direct training in social consciousness. Our history and geography from the beginning are world history and geography. Our emphasis throughout the grades is on the underlying unity of man. Both the factual side of the work in the middle grades and the problem side stressed in the junior high school are constructed and taught from the point of view of developing a social consciousness in the children.

Finally, the subconscious development of a social sense through the various activities, and the generalized social consciousness brought out in the treatment of the social studies, are made definite and personal through discussions both in class and between the teacher and each child, and through a system of rating each child's development.

The report card used in the Winnetka schools shows on one side the pupil's progress in mastering commonly needed knowledges and skills, on the other side his progress in developing certain attitudes and habits essential for social living. A section of this latter part of the "goal card" is reproduced herewith. The remainder of it deals, in the same way, with orderliness, work spirit, self-reliance, initiative, and special interests or abilities.

Each 6-week period a check mark is placed opposite the paragraph that most nearly describes the attitude of the child. This is done by the teacher in consultation *with* the child himself. We have found this rating helpful both to the child and the teacher. The child learns self-analysis and sees definitely an ideal toward which to work. The teacher is obliged to consider the attitude of each pupil and to see where each needs developing.

There are progressive educators who would have us merge our underlying principles in an "activities curriculum" so that chil-

Group Spirit	Period						Period					
	1st	2nd	3rd	4th	5th	6th	1st	2nd	3rd	4th	5th	6th
Has marked ability to co-operate with the group in both work and play. Shows consideration for others. Is helpful in all activities.												
Is able at most times to co-operate with the group and contributes his share to the betterment of the work or play activities.												
Shows the usual amount of ability to co-operate with the group both in work and in play. Shows an average degree of consideration for others. Is helpful when his own interests are not too greatly cncerned.												
Slow to co-operate with the group. Shows only a slight degree of consideration for others. Seldom is very helpful, often hinders.												
Does not co-operate with the group in work or play. Is selfish and violates the rights of others.												

dren's mastery of knowledges and skills would grow naturally out of childlike, social situations. This sounds good; but we seriously doubt whether it can be done without damaging each type of activity.

Socialized activities demand that the whole group work together. Knowledge-and-skill mastery requires that different children proceed at different rates. Some of the social problems children need to attack and some of the knowledges and skills they need to learn are not really childlike, and cannot therefore be taught through child-like activities.

Our observation has been that schools which attempt to develop all their knowledge-and-skill subjects from childlike activities, often do a 'sloppy' job in giving the children mastery of the tool subjects, and sometimes distort the so-called 'childlike' activities in an attempt to bring in knowledge and skills.

There seems no valid reason for supposing that all types of activity should correlate or that the same methods should be applied to all types of learning. It can be shown that children can master knowledges and skills happily and satisfactorily without tying these up to projects. And it has yet to be proved that children who do so master them are unable to apply them to life situations. Our own experience has been that if children are at the same time living full lives, and if the materials of instruction are so prepared as to show the children the relation of their knowledges and skills to real situations, there is no unusual difficulty about 'carry-over.'

Nor do we find any signs of split personality or divided self that some people have feared might result from giving children mastery of subject matter individually, and social training in groups.

The ordinary, natural life of any person is divided into different parts. At a certain time we eat breakfast. A little later we may be reading the world news. Then we may be doing our particular job. In the evening we may be amusing ourselves at the theater, or a dance, or in our home. These activities are unrelated. Each fills one need in our lives. And we don't suffer from the lack of correlation.

In Winnetka, we feel that the development of the social consciousness is too important a thing to be used as a mere means to the end of mastering knowledges and skills—or to be distorted in an effort to include all necessary knowledges and skills. Insofar as the socialized activities *incidentally* shed light on the tool subjects, or give application to these subjects, we are glad to recognize the relation. But we do not feel that we can safely trust to such incidental relationships to give our children the necessary mastery of the tool subjects.

It would be a mistake, on the other hand, to assume that in practice the knowledge-and-skill subjects, the creative activities, and the socializing activities are in water-tight compartments. While we feel that each requires different treatment in the curriculum, the children don't know that we are making any such distinctions. The school day, in actuality, shows a constant inter-play among all functions. The play activities, creative work, and socializing activities merge to such an extent as to be often undistinguishable the one from the other. When a socializing activity calls for certain knowledge or skill, the social and individual parts of the work merge. Certain parts of the day are largely, although not exclusively, devoted to individual mastery of tool and fact subjects. Other parts throw the emphasis upon self-expressive and socialized activities—upon group and creative work. But sharp lines are not drawn.

In our *thinking,* however, in our selection of subject matter and activities, in our equipment and planning, the three functions of the curriculum stand out in bold contrast. The underlying philosophy of the Winnetka curriculum demands that every normal child master the knowledges and skills he is going to need in life; that every child be given a chance to live happily and richly as a child; that every child be given an opportunity to develop fully his own individuality; and that all children be brought to the fullest possible realization that in the world's good is one's own, and in one's own good is the world's.

CHAPTER XII

THE DENVER CURRICULUM-REVISION PROGRAM

JESSE H. NEWLON
Superintendent of Schools
and
A. L. THRELKELD
Deputy Superintendent of Schools,
Denver, Colorado

The curriculum-construction problem in Denver is that presented by a large city. The task that confronts those who are responsible for the administration of large school systems is that of bringing curricula, as regards content, methods of teaching, and administrative procedures, as nearly as possible into line with the best educational knowledge and practice. The accomplishment of this objective requires an extensive and complex organization working scientifically. A large school system obviously cannot be given over entirely to detailed and extensive curricular experiments such as can be conducted in avowed experimental schools. But this is not to be interpreted as minimizing the importance of curriculum-experimentation within the schools. Some of the most important present-day methods and procedures in education originated in public schools. There should be centers of experimentation in every system.

Consistent with this policy, much experimentation has been carried on in the Denver schools. There have been trials of proposed courses of study, and one elementary school has been designated "the curriculum school." The importance of such experimentation in cultivating a scientific spirit among teachers is implied in what follows.

The Denver curriculum-revision program, which was inaugurated in 1922 and for which the Board of Education made its first substantial appropriation in May, 1923, has important characteristics which will be discussed under eight separate captions.

I. THE BOARD OF EDUCATION HAS RECOGNIZED THE IMPORTANCE OF CURRICULUM-REVISION BY SUBSTANTIAL APPROPRIATIONS FOR THIS WORK

In June, 1923, the Board approved the recommendation that $31,500 be appropriated for curriculum-revision work in the ensuing year. One quotation from the formal recommendation to the Board is pertinent:

"Curriculum-making is a first consideration in the successful administration of any school system. This is true because it has to do directly with instruction, and appropriations made for school support are in the last analysis for this purpose. It is, therefore, extremely wasteful and short-sighted for a community to spend large sums of money on its schools and at the same time fail to concentrate in an effective way on the problem of making appropriate courses of study. Just as one of the many considerations, attention is herein called to the fact that if 10 percent of the teacher's time is spent on non-essential and misplaced materials in courses of study, it represents an annual waste to the Denver taxpayers of $315,000 when calculated on the cost of the instruction item alone.

"Inasmuch as all appropriations for general control, coördinate activities, auxiliary agencies, operation of school plant, maintenance of school plant, capital outlay and debt service are for the purpose of being applied to instruction, it is legitimate to say that if 10 percent of the teacher's time is spent as above indicated, it actually represents an annual loss to the Denver taxpayers of $478,000 on the basis of the present budget. To say that a thorough-going revision of our curricula would mean a saving of at least 10 percent, due to elimination of non-essentials and misplaced materials and the substitution therefor of carefully selected and graded materials in the light of extensive studies that have been made, is putting it mildly. In all probability the saving would be much more than 10 percent. This is speaking in terms of dollars and cents."

A year later a second appropriation of $25,000 was made to carry on the work the second year.

In May, 1925, the Board approved the recommendation that a curriculum department be established, with an adequate budget, and placed under the direction of a specialist, his title to be Director of the Curriculum Department. In all, $100,000 has been expended under this program since the beginning of September, 1923.

The appropriations for the first two years and the budget for the new department have provided funds for the employment of specialists, for the employment of substitute teachers to relieve regular teachers for this work, for the employment of a clerical staff, and for printing. The Board and the community have thus frankly recognized the importance of the continuous study and revision of curricula and methods by the school staff under expert guidance.

II. The Extent to Which Teachers Participate Is an Outstanding Feature of the Program

In Denver the membership of the course of study committees is composed largely of classroom teachers, although some principals and supervisors are included. Classroom teachers have been chosen in all cases as chairmen.

During the first two years these committees worked under the general guidance of two specialists employed on part time for this purpose, members of the departments of education of the University of Colorado and the Colorado State Teachers College. The committees now work under the guidance of the director of the curriculum department, who has oversight of the work in all grades and departments and is concerned with principles and procedures applicable to all fields. Committees are also assisted by specialists in particular subjects who are brought to Denver for conference when work has proceeded to a certain point or when the most authoritative advice available is needed on a given problem. The committees are assisted further by a professional library at the Administration Building under the direction of a competent librarian, who has rendered invaluable aid in the preparation of bibliographies and in many other ways. Reviewing committees, composed of administrative officers and principals, formulate recommendations regarding general policies of administration and review the work of subject-matter committees, but the initiative in the actual work of the preparation of courses of study rests with the committees of teachers who actually write them. The whole program is carried out under the general supervision of the superintendent and under the direct supervision of the deputy superintendent of schools.

The considerations underlying this procedure are, first, that a course of study will function only to the extent to which it is understood by the teachers who are to use it, and, second, that a curriculum-revision program that involves every teacher in the study of curriculum problems and in participation in the process of determining what the content of course and method of instruction should be affords the best possible device for the training of teachers in service. A program of this kind, properly directed, will ultimately raise every fundamental issue pertaining to curricula and method for the consideration of teachers and administrative staffs.

Such a program must originate in the initiative of the local school system. It must grow from the inside out. Teachers, principals, supervisors, and all concerned with instruction must set about in an organized way to study ways and means by which the effectiveness of instruction may be improved. When teachers are studying this problem, they are studying the problem of curriculum-revision.

It is obvious that a 'felt need' for curriculum improvement exists to some extent in every school system. There is no school system that would claim that its present work is perfect, and in that very fact there is a logical, as well as a psychological, starting point for a program of curriculum-revision.

Granting that there is always the challenge to a school system to improve its instruction, the next consideration is that of marshalling all of the local educational resources in such a way as to procure their maximal contributions to the solution of the problem. This may be done by organizing the teachers in every subject into committees charged with the responsibility of working out better courses of study in their several fields. Likewise, supervisors, principals, and all administrative officers responsible for instruction should be organized.

The first big outcome of such a program is the discovery and definition of problems. This is, of course, a very significant step in any learning process. When the teachers have arrived at this stage, there naturally evolves a felt need for more assistance in the solution of problems than the local system can furnish from its own ranks. It is at this point that assistance from the outside should be considered.

This phase consists in bringing to the local organization, as far as it is practicable, the specialists who are authorities in particular fields. Each specialist should come prepared to do definite work with the committee or committees for whose assistance he has been called. He should be informed of the committees' problems before he comes, and then he should spend most of his time at the committee table. General lectures of an institute character are not a major need under this plan and should be held to the minimum. After the specialist leaves, he should be kept in touch with the committees' work, to the extent necessary to maintain an adequate follow-up plan of coöperation between him and the committees which he has assisted. All this calls for extensive coöperation between schools of education in universities and colleges and local school systems.

Such organization and procedure implies teacher participation on a very extensive basis. By this process teachers come to regard the courses of study as instruments to help them in the solution of the problems of their daily work. In other words, they come to appreciate courses of study because they see their practicability and usefulness, and in the last analysis the worth of a course of study is conditioned by the extent to which it is successfully employed by the teacher. No program of curriculum-revision can claim anything for itself if it fails at this point. Teachers must have a background for understanding and appreciating the courses of study which they are using if they are to use them intelligently. This background of understanding and appreciation is dependent on the maximal participation of which the teacher is capable in the construction of the courses. It is only by actively engaging in the process of curriculum-construction that a teacher can attain to his greatest effectiveness. There is no substitute possible for a maximum of teacher participation if teacher growth and effectiveness are to be provided for and if the best results are to be expected from classroom procedures. Since teaching is a professional job, the practitioner can be master of his profession only if he is conversant with the theories that underlie practice.

This point of view in curriculum-revision emphasizes the felt needs of the teachers as they arise in the everyday work of the schools. It is not a long story from the status at which the teacher studies curriculum-revision from the point of view of his felt needs to the status where he considers what should be taught from the point of view of the pupils' needs, and in the last analysis the pupils' needs are determined by life situations. What, then, are the life situations which face the pupil, and how may this or that subject best contribute to those situations, or can they contribute at all? If they cannot contribute, they should be eliminated from the program. The extent to which they can contribute determines the extent to which they should be taught. This gives us our basis for the selection of content and method.

III. The Administration Has Imposed No Pattern to Which Committees Must Conform in the Selection of Content and in the Organization of Courses of Study, But Has Encouraged All Concerned with Curriculum-Construction to Most Thorough Study and Consideration of These Problems

The actual launching of the curriculum-revision program was preceded by a year of study, in principals' meetings under the chairmanship of the superintendent of schools and in faculty meetings in the various schools under the chairmanship of the principals, of the general principles underlying curriculum-construction and some of the controversies that exist in this field. Effort has been made from the beginning to stimulate teachers to a continuous consideration of these problems, for those in charge of the program implicitly believed and still believe that it is better for a set of guiding principles to evolve from such study than that they be imposed arbitrarily on the committees in the beginning.

There are two ways of going about a curriculum-revision program. One is to begin by setting up the objectives to be attained in the various grades and subjects and by laying down a set of guiding principles to govern in the selection and organization of subject matter. To our way of thinking, such procedure is unsound. It is to a large extent reversing the procedure that ought to obtain in curriculum-construction, because it limits the activities and responsibilities of committees. The character of a course of study is to a large extent arbitrarily determined before the committee actually begins its work. This means the stifling of initiative.

In Denver we have followed the opposite procedure. We steadfastly refused to lay down a set of principles to guide committees in their work or to express our opinions as to what were the particular objectives to be attained in particular courses. On the other hand, we took the position that every committee should begin by making a survey of the writings, the experimentation, the practices, the controversies, and the unsolved problems of its field. Necessarily, before a committee can make an intelligent attempt at the actual construction of a course, the members must also become students of the principles and the philosophy of education. We have endeavored to create a condition in which it was necessary for every committee to make its own decisions as to guiding principles and objectives. It has been the function of those who direct the curriculum-revision program to criticise these proposals of committees. Every committee knows that all its work will be subjected to scrutiny and criticism.

We believe that under this procedure a set of guiding principles and objectives will emerge, subject of course to constant modification, that will be better than any that can be imposed or agreed upon at the beginning of a program; and that it is better designed to stimulate study, investigation, and participation on the part of teachers, whereas any other procedure tends to prevent it.

Nor do we consider it a defect if all committees should not be in complete agreement on such matters. A certain amount of variety is stimulating. The functioning of the curriculum department will insure that this variety will not become inimical to the unity which must obtain in the educational program of a school system, but will rather strengthen it by constantly stimulating study and growth.

It is evident that under such a procedure there will be a variety of outcomes. As a result of the influence of common study and of the general spirit that pervades the program and dominates those who are responsible for its direction, there will be a general similarity of outcome, but in the absence of a definitely imposed pattern or the will to impose such a pattern, variety is inevitable.

IV.—The Life-Situation Criterion Has Been Used Most Extensively in the Selection of Subject Matter and Activities

Most committees have attempted to determine content and activities on the basis of life situations. It seems unnecessary to attempt a definition of this widely used phrase. Nor is it necessary to go into a detailed discussion of how broadly the term "life situation" may be interpreted. From one point of view it may be argued that any situation which the pupil is likely to face at some time is a life situation for him which he should study. But pedagogically, the principle to be followed is that if the pupil cannot be brought to see it as a life situation for him, his work will not be motivated and therefore will not be effective.

Through working in a vitalized program of curriculum-revision, teachers come to appreciate this fact, and there is a tremendous effort to judge the value of an item of content for a course of study on the basis of whether its real worth can be made apparent to the pupil. Since teaching consists of revealing worth-while situations to pupils, quite as much as, if not more than, of merely dealing with situations which pupils already recognize, one finds committees that have caught this vision working out their courses of study in such a way as to show the pupil what and why he ought to study. Having arrived at an appreciation of motivation in their own work, teachers are willing to grant that it has the same value for pupils in their work. While it is extremely difficult to teach everything that must have a place in our schools to-day and at the same time give it genuine motivation, yet a program of curriculum-revision governed by the points of view that are here being discussed obviously makes progress in that direction. Life situations become the criteria by which subject matter and method are chosen. Subject matter and method become means to the end of the pupil's growth, instead of idols of worship to which all must conform. Purposeful activity, with ever-growing worth in purpose, becomes the keynote of the whole program.

A curriculum constructed on these principles must necessarily be in process of continuous revision. It is based upon a dynamic, as opposed to a static, conception of life. From one point of view, life situations are constantly changing; from another, the methods of meeting old situations are changing, so there is no place for a static philosophy of education, unless we are to consider education as entirely separate from life. The Denver program of curriculum-revision has been officially recognized as a continuous process through the establishment of a curriculum department which is to direct the program from year to year. New courses will continually evolve and old courses will be continually revised. There will be curriculum-revision as long as there is education.

A few illustrations will suffice to indicate how the Denver committees have applied these principles.

In the field of home economics for the junior high schools a survey was made of the activities in which the girls participate in the home. This job analysis, or study of a life situation, very greatly influenced the selection of content, methods of teaching, and the grade-placement of subject matter.

The committee that prepared the commercial courses for junior and senior high schools made a careful investigation of the commercial practices in the offices of Denver business and industrial concerns. The content of these courses was largely determined and methods of teaching were distinctly affected by this investigation. The intention was to create classroom situations as nearly as possible like those actually found in the business world.

The plan of a unified social science course was adopted for the junior high schools. This course, extended over a period of three years, is organized into large units, subdivided into problems or projects. Each of these large units deals with a civic or social problem with which the individual of to-day must be familiar in order to discharge intelligently his duty as a citizen or as a member of the community in his social or vocational relations. This committee is indebted to Dr. Harold Rugg and his associates for the study which they made of present-day civic problems through an examination of the problems discussed either in the press or in notable books, and problems listed by authorities in the field.

The committees preparing the Latin course of study for the junior and senior high school made a wide use of the results of the Classical League investigation of classical studies in high schools. It cannot be said that the Latin curriculum is based to any great extent on life situations, especially in the upper years. Tradition, college entrance requirements, the force of public opinion, as well as its educational values, explain the retention of such a subject as Latin in the curriculum. Since Latin is to be taught, the effort is made to make the study of it of as great value as possible to those who pursue it. The Classical Investigation attempted to determine what type of Latin instruction would best function in the life of the student. To a certain extent, the commission breaks with tradition as regards the selections to be read and the relative emphasis on the study of words, grammatical construction, and reading. In brief, the purpose of our committees was to make Latin of as much practical value to the individual as possible.

The course of study in spelling is, of course, based on life situations in that the words to be taught are determined largely as a result of recent statistical investigations. The same is true of the courses of study in the English language. Tradition is gradually giving way to scientific investigation in selection of content in this subject.

An examination of all the courses of study will reveal differences in organization with respect to the extent to which the life-situation criterion has dominated the committees and the extent to which traditional considerations have dominated them. There is more research for the guidance of committees in some fields than in others. The force of tradition is stronger in some fields than in others. Some committees are more conservative than others. It is our belief that this variety is more desirable than the rigid uniformity that is produced by a pattern set by the administrative staff, and that continued growth and this variety are inseparable. Only under such conditions can creative abilities be fostered and stimulated.

V. There Is a Variation in the Organization of Material for Instruction, with a Tendency Toward the Use of the Problem, or Project, Method Wherever This Method Is Applicable

Students of education to-day generally accept the proposition that the outcomes of instruction and the methods of instruction are indissolubly associated. Therefore, one of the most important problems that a course of study committee confronts is that of how subject matter shall be organized for learning. A number of Denver courses of study have been organized largely on the problem, or project, basis. In other courses this method is not used. The course of study in the social sciences for junior high schools is organized around problems, while the arithmetic course of study for the elementary schools is more traditional in its organization. Of necessity, drill is of great importance in the work in arithmetic. The life-situation criterion has influenced the selection of subject matter in this course of study. The problems of motivation have been kept constantly in mind by the committee in suggestions as to method, but it is obvious that the problem of this committee is different from that of a committee in the social sciences.

An examination of all the courses of study would reveal a wide variation, with a tendency to organize on the problem basis where the subject matter will permit.

VI. The Curriculum Is Interpreted to Embrace All the Activities of the School System

In line with this doctrine, those responsible for the direction of extra-curricular activities in the secondary schools are preparing manuals pertaining to these activities which will be, in fact, courses of study. In similar manner, manuals will be prepared descriptive of the administrative procedures in secondary schools that will be, in effect, courses of study for the guidance of those who are charged with the administration of these schools. This policy is based on the belief that the educative process is not confined merely to that which goes on within the walls of the classroom, but embraces every activity and every administrative policy of the school—in short, that the corporate life of a school is a matter of the utmost importance in the realization of the objectives of a system of education.

VII. The Program Is Based on the Assumption That in a Large School System Growth Is Dependent on a Due Recognition of the Force of Tradition and of Public Opinion, and of the Differences in Teachers in Respect to Types of Mind and Professional Preparation

It is feasible to carry out in such a school as the Lincoln School of Teachers College an entirely experimental curriculum and to make the school a laboratory of research. In a single public school or a very small public school system, under proper conditions, such a project can be carried out. In a large public school system such a program is impossible. The inertia to be overcome is too great, to say nothing of the practical difficulties involved and the folly of subjecting large numbers of pupils and teachers to the hazards of an entirely experimental curriculum.

In high schools the force of tradition is strongly in evidence—college entrance requirements must be taken into consideration. The schools ought to be progressive; they ought to go as far as possible in basing courses on sound educational theory and research, but it is frequently impossible to go the whole distance at one time.

It must be recognized that there is a difference in the types of minds of teachers. An extremely conservative teacher, unfamiliar and unsympathetic with the new point of view in the teaching of such a subject as Latin, might fail almost completely if asked to undertake a course of study embodying all of the modern thought in this field. Some teachers are better prepared professionally for their work than others. All these facts must be taken into consideration, and courses of study must be modified in accordance with them. This explains why an administration is sometimes justified in accepting a course of study in a given field which does not go as far in the embodiment of the results of research as the administration thinks it should go.

The teacher factor and the factor of public opinion must be taken into consideration. It is essential, however, that all departments of the school system be moving in the direction of progress, and the administration must supply the stimulation that will maintain this condition.

VIII. The Essence of the Denver Curriculum-Revision Program Is the Bringing into Coöperation All Forces That Affect Instruction in the Schools

Until comparatively recent years, it was not thought that classroom teachers could contribute much to the construction of courses of study. The practice was to place in the hands of teachers the courses of study that they were to follow. There has come a general recognition of the importance of the teacher. It is evident, however, that other factors are equally essential. The policy of delegating entirely to teachers the making of curricula would be as fallacious as was the policy of leaving the teachers entirely out of this process, and would likewise fail to take account of the indispensable contribution that must be made by research and by specialists who, by devoting their lives to the study of teaching in particular subjects, become authorities in their fields.

The problem of administration of a school system is that of creating machinery that will bring all these forces to bear on the construction of courses of study and will make possible their smooth and effective functioning. This problem is not a simple one, and its final solution has probably not yet been found.

CHAPTER XIII

THE ST. LOUIS PROGRAM OF CURRICULUM-REVISION

WALTER D. COCKING
St. Louis Public Schools, St. Louis, Missouri

In the spring of 1924 Superintendent John J. Maddox requested the principals of the St. Louis schools to state what they deemed to be the most pressing and urgent needs of the school system. By far the greater number of the replies indicated that the outstanding need was attention to the curriculum. Superintendent Maddox, therefore, immediately began to formulate plans looking to the complete revision of the curriculum of the public schools of St. Louis. He soon saw the necessity of having some member of his staff give full time to the work of outlining and directing the entire program. For this purpose, the writer was appointed as a member of the division of research, and the program of curriculum-revision was placed under his direction.

Plans were carefully formulated with a view to effecting a complete revision of the course of study from the kindergarten through the teachers' colleges.[1] The three steps involved in this program were: (1) the setting up of the aims and objectives for the school system as a whole and for the divisions of the system in particular and the determining of a program of studies and time-allotment to be followed in achieving these aims; (2) the determination of content in the various programs of study looking toward the attainment of the accepted aims and objectives; and (3) the installation of the revised curriculum in the various grades and divisions of the school system.

The first step was definitely undertaken in September, 1925. It was considered that the determination of aims and the setting up of a program of studies and time-allotment was the particular job of the administrators of the school system, namely, the principals. A committee was therefore appointed consisting of four prin-

[1] Although a great deal of work had already been done looking toward certain modifications in the curriculum, no unified attempt to treat the program comprehensively was undertaken until 1925.

cipals and the general director of the curriculum program. Each principal on the committee represented one of four divisions of the school system, kindergarten-primary, elementary, intermediate, and high school. The task assigned to the committee, which was known as the "Committee on the General Aim of Public Education," was the re-statement of the general aims of public education in the city of St. Louis.

The committee soon discovered that there was a dearth of practical materials bearing on the subject. There was found to be an abundance of educational philosophy, somewhat general in character, but few school administrators apparently have set forth in writing a statement of the specific aims of their school systems.

Early in its work the committee decided that it was useless to attempt any statement of aim which would be educationally sound without first coming to some agreement in regard to certain underlying principles which would guide the committee in its acceptance or rejection of proposed aims. The sixteen principles which were finally determined upon are here stated in the language which was most acceptable to the committee.

1. Self-activity is fundamental to learning.
2. While transfer of training may take place under certain conditions, it is neither automatic nor inevitable.
3. There is no desirable 'discipline' in doing what is merely difficult and distasteful.
4. Education serves both proximate and ultimate ends.
5. The universal interdependence of man is basic for education.
6. The welfare of society demands the optimal development of the individual.
7. Education represents an investment by society to promote the common welfare.
8. The school is only one of the educative agencies established by society, and the inevitable overlapping in duties and responsibilities necessitates mutual coöperation.
9. Schools serve two interests: those of the individual and those of society; wherever the two come into conflict, those of society take precedence.
10. It is the duty of the school to adjust itself to social progress.
11. The school should endeavor to give to all a common integrating body of functional knowledge, of habits, of ideals, and of appreciation.

12. It is the duty of the school to adapt the means of education to the needs of the individual, whatever may be the mental, physical, moral, or environmental conditions.
13. The need of the individual for two coördinate types of ability is recognized; unspecialized, to discharge common personal, domestic, and civic duties; specialized, to render expert service to society.
14. The fact of individual differences conditions the results that may be expected from the educative process.
15. Education includes teaching the individual to do better the desirable things of life that he would do anyhow.
16. Culture, as a desirable outcome of education, consists in the all-round development of those capacities and ideals which make for human progress; it includes social service, many-sidedness, democracy, physical well-being, development of spiritual life, aesthetic appreciation, well-mannered expression, insight, force, and idealism; it is altruistic, dynamic, and creative.

The committee then decided to formulate a statement of the general aims in terms of certain knowledges which should be attained, certain habits which should be fixed, certain ideals which should be reached, and certain appreciations which should be acquired. After this part of the work was completed, eight additional school principals were called into conference, two from each division of the system. This committee of twelve reviewed the work of the original committee and then resolved itself into four divisional committees. The task of the divisional committees was to state the specific aims of the four divisions of the school system previously named. In the statement of divisional aims, the committee followed the same form which had been adopted by the general committee.

After a tentative statement of divisional aims had been prepared, a reviewing committee of fifty principals was called, in order that the report might receive their careful, constructive criticism. After a certain amount of revision on the basis of criticisms received, the report was finally presented to all the principals, supervisors, and teachers in the system. The committees felt that it was especially desirable to obtain from classroom teachers thoughtful and constructive suggestions in regard to the aims which had been set up. Therefore, a mass meeting of teachers was called for the purpose of explaining the curriculum program to the teaching body and requesting that the teachers examine carefully the tentative report on general and divisional aims. Copies of the report were distributed at this meeting. During the following week, faculty meetings were held in the various schools and the report was freely discussed. Suggestions and criticisms from teachers were transmitted to the committee through the various principals. Thus, the statement of aims was subjected to continual revision in the light of opinions expressed by teachers, principals, and supervisors.

Before the final revision of the report was completed, the statement of general aims was submitted to school patrons. A special number of "School and Home" was published. In this number, the tentative report of the committee on general aims was printed. Parents were invited to make criticisms and suggestions if they cared to do so.[2]

Thus, before the committee's report on general and divisional aims was finally submitted to the superintendent of instruction for his approval, it had received the careful criticism of a large number of people whose positions and interests qualified them to express intelligent opinions in regard to the desirable objectives of public education.

The four sub-committees next turned their attention to the determination of a program of studies—or the offerings of the several divisions of the school system. They worked on the premise that a place in the program of studies would be found for a particular subject only when the subject could prove its usefulness in the attainment of the aims previously set up. When a tentative program of studies was finally agreed upon, the members of the committee directed their attention to the amount of time it would be necessary to give to each subject in order to achieve the particular aims which could best be realized through the content of the particular subject in question. When this work had been completed, the reports were presented to principals, supervisors, and teachers for consideration and criticism. The sub-committees then revised their reports in the light of the suggestions which were received. Thus, the first step, which is seen to be largely administrative in character, was taken.

---

[2] A number of copies of this number of "School and Home" were also sent to well-known educators throughout the country. Some very helpful letters were received in response.

The next step in the program involved the actual selection of subject matter. It was decided that this was the job of the classroom teacher, since the work obviously required a close and intimate knowledge of pupils and pupil activities. In selecting the teacher committees to work on the subject matter of the courses, an effort was made to use objective standards of selection. It was decided that the kind and amount of training that each teacher had had, what major and minor subjects in college, the number of hours work in educational courses, and the years of experience, together with the recommendation of his principal for specific units of work, should form the standards in determining committee selection. It was on the basis of these standards, together with certain conditions relative to personal fitness, that committee selection was finally made. Difficulties encountered in former curriculum enterprises influenced those in charge of the program to adopt the following principles in regard to teacher committees: (1) units of work to be done should be small and specific; and (2) committees should not be large.

Committees were appointed by grades for each division of subject matter; each committee consisted of a chairman and two associates. In all, 147 committees of three members each were appointed. The personnel of these committees was made up entirely of classroom teachers. One member of each committee was selected as chairman.

Other committees of supervisors and specialists were appointed to act in an advisory capacity with all the participating committees. The personnel of these advisory committees was as follows: All of the supervisors of the system; principals who had special interests and special training in certain subjects, and teachers who, through long and rich experience, could contribute much to the work of the committees.

By action of the board of education, on recommendation of the superintendent of instruction, chairmen of all participating committees were released from their other school duties to do full-time work on the curriculum. All three members of a committee carry the responsibility for the type of work which the committee decides to undertake, but the chairman who is released from his other duties does the research and the writing which are involved and carries out the details of such plans and methods as may be decided upon by the full committee. The final report of the committee is also written by the chairman. On February 1, 150 teachers were released for full-time work in this capacity. They are now housed in a certain division of the magnificent new Roosevelt High School, where a complete organization has been set up and equipped with an adequate clerical force for intensive work on the program of curriculum-revision. Once each week, the committee chairman meets the rest of the committee to report progress and to determine the nature of new work to be done. Each committee chairman has an individual desk and an adequate library at his disposal.

The first step, after these committee chairmen were released, was the organization of a 'training school,' with the director of the general curriculum program as 'teacher.' The matter of determining curriculum-technique was discussed and a common method of procedure was determined upon. Then the chairman of each committee undertook the task of compiling a complete bibliography on his particular phase of the subject. This bibliography consisted of books, pamphlets, magazines, bulletins of various kinds, courses of study which are in operation in other cities, and available reports of research in the subject. The chairmen also decided to undertake certain research projects which it was possible to carry on in the St. Louis schools and which would be helpful in the determination of the subject matter to be included. To aid them in this particular field, a research specialist has been assigned whose duty it is to confer with each committee chairman in regard to the best manner in which to set up and carry on the research contemplated.

One of the most important steps in the development of the program was the securing of an adequate library. In this particular, St. Louis has been very fortunate. An excellent source of aid was the regular teachers' library which is operated by the St. Louis Board of Education. As other materials are discovered which may prove of use to the curriculum committeees, they are purchased by the board of education and added to the teachers' library if they are not available elsewhere. The teachers' division of the St. Louis Public Library has been most helpful and coöperative in the securing of library materials. The entire resources of the library have been placed at the disposal of the committees and a daily delivery from the main department to Roosevelt High School has been arranged. A great deal of new material which has a bearing on various phases of the curriculum has been ordered.

Also, the Mercantile Library, a large private library in the city, has generously assisted in supplying materials for study. Authorities at Washington University have offered the use of their library facilities. Other libraries are coöperating by releasing for a short time many of their references on curriculum-study. They have been especially helpful by loaning to the committees copies of unpublished theses. All of the courses of study which have been published since 1920 have been secured and through them the committees are able to discover actual practices in relation to the various subjects. The belief is that the final report of the committees will, in general, be determined by three factors; namely, actual practice elsewhere, the opinion of authorities in the field, and the research which has already been done or which the committees may be able to carry on.

The work has now proceeded to the point where the committees are working on their tentative reports. When these have been completed, they will be presented to all of the teachers in the system for careful consideration. In the light of suggestions which will be received, the reports will be revised. Educational specialists will also be called into conference on the tentative reports after the committees have gone as far as they are able to go. In the light of suggestions received through these specialists, further revision will probably be made. During the summer, it is expected that final reports of the various committees will be printed in loose-leaf form.

Beginning with the opening of the school year next September, the new courses will be tried. In fact, next year will be 'try-out' year for these courses in the St. Louis schools. The committees already organized will meet from time to time to consider the difficulties encountered and the constructive criticism which will be received as a result of putting the courses to the test. Supervisors and principals will endeavor to secure a fair trial for all subjects under as nearly ideal conditions as possible. Service bulletins will be issued by the committees during the curriculum-organization to assist the teachers in interpreting what the committees had in mind in regard to the various courses, and to suggest appropriate materials and methods of procedure. In the light of these trials further modifications will be made. Undoubtedly, some sections will be entirely removed and others will be substituted, while in other instances only slight changes will be made. As a result of this year of experiment under practical conditions, it is hoped that a program for the continuous adjustment and modification of the school curriculum will be developed.

This gives, in brief, some idea of the plan of curriculum-revision which is now in process in St. Louis. Almost all the conditions in connection with the work are favorable. Principals and teachers declare that the revision is not only necessary, but urgent. They are giving splendid coöperation and are looking toward the early installation of a revised course of study. The board of education has been most generous in necessary legislative enactments to make possible the success of the work. The approximate cost of the school system for the entire program of curriculum-revision will be under $50,000. This is estimated on the basis of actual cost over and above the regular expenses which would ordinarily be incurred for school operation. It is hoped that the results of this program will be of value, not only to the city of St. Louis, but also to other cities and communities where similar need for a revision of the curriculum of school training is felt.

CHAPTER XIV

THEORETICAL FOUNDATION OF THE LOS ANGELES ELEMENTARY COURSE OF STUDY

Ethel I. Salisbury
Director of Course of Study, Los Angeles City Schools, and
Associate Professor of Elementary Education, University of California,
Los Angeles, California

Every carefully planned curriculum is based on a philosophy of education. This philosophy should be the sum total of all the findings of research and the best thinking of leading educators; for it extends into every classroom and determines the procedures there.

The philosophy which is to determine the curriculum in a city school system must harmonize and relate actual endless detail, take into account the human factor, meet emergencies, and deal promptly with the whole field of elementary education in answer to the urgent needs of a teaching staff. Elaborate scientific technique cannot be applied to every problem, but a study of conditions and those researches already complete must be used in making decisions.

There are three major tasks in the construction of curriculum for a city system: (1) to determine the ideals toward which all individuals should progress, (2) to survey actual conditions, and (3) to bring together the two by the introduction of the right type of activities.

Ideals Are the Goals

The outstanding objective of life is continuous progress of the individual toward increasingly enriched experience. Through experiences the individual should gain in power to understand and appreciate the meaning of life, to do that which is in harmony with natural laws and to use the knowledges and skills necessary for more complete satisfactions. These changes within the child are directed and guided by certain ideals of conduct held before him by the teacher, parents, and others.

These ideals have been determined by race experience. They may be classified under the headings: physical, mental, constructive, and social well-being. These in turn must be broken up into more specific ideals.

The ideal of physical well-being involves among other goals those of (1) perfectly nourished body, (2) normally functioning eyesight, and (3) correct posture.

The physical ideal necessitates progress toward a complete knowledge of what to do to maintain health. It should also develop an attitude which will lead the child to do what is good for right living at all times and places.

The intellectual ideal requires that the child learn to think and to remember and to do in the most efficient and economical way.

The ideal of social efficiency includes honesty, loyalty, courage, and many other qualities. The number is too extensive to list here. For a normal group of children, the social ideal demands also that the child master the skills of reading, writing, spelling, arithmetic, and spoken and written English. The social ideal is the goal toward which the child must progress if he is to live so both he and his fellows have the fullest and best expression of self. This implies the necessity of inhibitions. There must be not only an ability to lead, but there must be also an understanding of the ability to follow expert leadership and to fit in harmoniously with the group.

The constructive ideal is approached when the child learns to plan, to imagine before doing, to build, to create or invent.

Conditions Constitute the Starting Point

The ideals, then, are the goals. The condition of the child and his surroundings constitute the starting point. These include:

(1) The point of view of the community
(2) The wealth of the community
(3) Policy of the system
(4) Actual training and experience of teachers
(5) Measured efficiency of the children in each skill
(6) Estimated progress of the children in appreciation
(7) Previous training
(8) Home conditions
(9) Textbooks
(10) Equipment and supplies
(11) State laws
(12) Community needs, such as are revealed by accident statistics, forest fires, infant mortality, etc.

Normal Children. Children who do not vary widely from the normal can be educated in homogeneous groups. Here we have the usual classroom, in which it is possible to lead a large number of children together into a series of similar experiences which will profit all of them.

Deviates. But there are also many children who, owing to the handicaps of heredity and environment, deviate radically from normal conditions. These children must be provided for by a differentiated series of activities.

These are the children who are

(1) Variations above and below normal mentality
(2) Foreign speaking
(3) Blind
(4) Deaf
(5) Defective in Speech
(6) Crippled
(7) Psychopathic
(8) Poor
(9) Irregular in school attendance
(10) Malnourished
(11) Surrounded by poor home conditions

Activities Are the Only Means of Learning

Having arrived at the broader ideals of education and taken into account through observation, study, and a testing program the divergence between the conditions and the ideals, the next step is to determine the series of activities by means of which each child will progress toward the ideals.

There is a vast and confusing amount of detail in any comprehensive plan of education. There are hundreds of ideals, conditions, and possible activities—the scope is as broad as life itself. Course-of-study makers, therefore, can be of most practical service to the teacher by outlining the more inclusive ideals and by recommending those activities which are most useful in developing elementary abilities which lead to the desired goals. A description of some of the activities in detail, with an analysis to show how each may be guided to develop right habits and thoughts with the children is essential. In other words, the course of study should attempt to answer concretely the question: "What are the children to do?" This can best be done by describing activities that have been used with profit to the children and by showing when and how these may be used.

What is an activity? "An activity is the pursuit of an interest." The educative values of an activity depend upon the knowledges, habits, skills, and attitudes derived in the doing. It involves on the part of the child the following steps: (1) purposing, (2) planning, (3) executing, (4) judging.

Guidance is essential in order that the child be led into a variety of satisfying experiences which leave him eager for other richer experiences. So does he make progress toward the ideals.

Wise guidance must be conscious of both conditions and ideals. It must note the needs and abilities of children, discover the interests in which they are already engaged and then lead them into profitable activities.

When the circus is in town, the language, reading, writing, spelling, and social studies in certain classes may be related to an activity which has largest possibilities for the realization of intellectual or investigative ideals. The children will be stimulated to answer such questions as: "Why is the giraffe spotted?" "Does he have a voice?" "Why does he have long legs and a long neck?"

By observing, by searching in books and inquiring of authorities, the children derive such outcomes as knowledge of where to go for information and practice in searching for information, in discarding material beside the point, in comparing authorities, and in verifying facts. These are the ideals for emphasis in this type of activity.

But along with these, progress can be made toward social ideals if the teacher has them in mind. For example: the children can derive an appreciation of the keeper's concern for 'safety first,' regard for others who wish to see, coöperation in staying with the group rather than causing concern or delay, courtesy in keeping to prescribed paths.

In terms of skills, children may report their experiences and information gained to others, with outcomes in English, spelling, and writing. Reading is used in gathering information.

Less progress can be made toward physical ideals in an activity of this type. Children can, however, derive knowledge of appropriate clothing for the weather.

If the children make the circus out of materials, the teacher, having in mind the constructive ideal, will guide the work to guarantee such outcomes as appreciation of proportion, form, and color, and skill in handling materials.

This activity emphasizes the investigative ideal. Others may emphasize the physical, the social, or the constructive aspects. The ideals in the mind of the teacher determine the outcomes to be derived. The course of study must offer balanced rations in its suggestions for activities.

Besides giving attention to conditions and ideals, guidance must constantly apply psychological and biological laws to its procedure. Illustrations of these principles are: "Activities for the young child should involve the coördination of the larger muscles." "The interest span of little children is usually of short duration." "Little children are by nature spontaneous and need not be made conscious of educative values of their activities."

What Are the Activities Most Suitable for School?

Not all activities have sufficient value to justify their use in the school. Before the children are given time and opportunity to enter into certain activities, the teacher should ask these questions of herself: "Is the child sufficiently interested to acquire satisfaction in carrying out the plans?" "Will the activity lead the child into other profitable activities?" "Can the child carry the responsibilities involved?" "Is the time required for a successful culmination appropriate to the interest span of the child?" "Does the activity give practice on the essential skills?" "Is there an opportunity for social contacts necessitating specific acts of coöperation?" "Does the activity permit adaptation to individual differences?"

The specialized activities for the deviates are often similar in kind to those in which normal children engage, but they differ in the way in which they are carried out. Some of the specialized activities, however, vary radically to meet conditions. Among these may be mentioned the drills for those who are defective in speech, the reading of Braille by the blind, the following of a given diet and exercises for the malnourished, the handwork projects for the mentally defective.

What Is the Relation of Subjects to Activities?

The subjects of the curriculum which were originally confined to the skills have long dominated procedure in classrooms. Each subject has been taught by itself. Skills have been isolated and learned with no relation to their uses. But with the realization that normal learning involves many types of subject matter and that practice is more effective than drill, the tendency to minimize the lines of demarcation between subjects has grown.

Public demand has introduced so many subjects into the curriculum that it is impossible to divide the day's program on the subject basis. This fact has lead to a changed conception of their part in the curriculum. Subjects are logically organized bodies of content. In carrying out activities, subjects are, therefore, to be considered as sources of material from which to draw, rather than ends within themselves.

What Is the Relation of the Skills to Activities?

The series of activities planned for the child in school should involve practice on the skills. The teaching of the skills is a highly complicated process. In guiding the activities, the teacher must study individual differences, be conscious of certain ideals of performance, and at the same time apply a specialized technique dependent upon a working knowledge of many basic principles. It is part of any program of course-of-study-making to enunciate these principles and interpret them to the teaching staff as a whole.

Below are given some of the outstanding principles determining procedure:

Reading

1. It is economy of interest and effort on the part of teachers and pupils to delay teaching children to read until they have reached the sixth-year mental level.
2. Children who have not reached the mental age of six should be provided with a curriculum giving a rich language experience along with proper activities in manual arts, physical education, music, and free play.
3. The major need in life is for silent reading, rather than for oral reading.
4. Oral reading in primary grades is a great aid in building a reading vocabulary, because the familiar vocal symbol is associated with the less familiar visual symbol.
5. The reading vocabulary in primary grades should be within the speaking vocabulary.
6. Some method of sound analysis or method of phonetic approach should be taught in order that pupils may help themselves over confusion points.
7. Such analytical work should be begun after the child has a repertory of words and sentences meaningful to him.
8. The sound of the letters and phonetic elements should come chiefly through the experiences of reading sentences from which the child is deriving meaning.
9. As an aid to this, systematic drill should be given, emphasizing particular sounds which are needed in connection with the reading.

10. Systematic drills should be subordinated and related to actual reading.

11. Periods of relaxation should follow reading periods.

12. A normal child who is apparently a non-reader should very early have his case diagnosed by a psychologist and receive special help.

13. For the non-English-speaking child, the first step in learning to read is to get a speaking vocabulary of English.

14. The major experience by which the non-English-speaking child acquires a vocabulary is conversation with English-speaking individuals about things which mean something to him.

15. Rate and comprehension should be improved together. The nature of content, familiarity with the material, and mechanical make-up are factors influencing rate and comprehension.

16. The content of primary reading should be about things familiar to the child.

17. The ability to read is developed by reading—not by talking or being talked to.

18. Ability to dramatize a selection does not guarantee ability to read it. That is another ability.

19. Children should be guided in their selection of material. They should frequently be permitted to choose, within limits, the materials to be read.

20. The child's reading should include materials of various types: geographical, historical, arithmetical, emotional-description, poetry, etc.

21. Selections of literature which require an unwarranted amount of drill for mastery should not be taught.

English Expression

1. In life, the need for oral English is greater than the need for written English.

2. We learn to speak by speaking. Rules of grammar have little influence on the formation of speech habits, though they may help a mature student to correct bad habits.

3. In order to talk or write well, it is necessary to have something to say. Children should be given the greatest possible number of enriching experiences and be permitted frequently to choose their own topics for composition.

4. Oral expression should be the major part of the English expression in the primary grades.

5. The first goal to be reached in oral English in the primary grades is freedom and joy in expression.

6. Children should learn from experiences that the way to hold interest is to have something to say and say it well.

7. When a child has found his weak points, he should endeavor to overcome them by drilling himself along the line of his needs and noting his progress.

8. A rich vocabulary is necessary for adequate expression and understanding. Children should form the habit of adopting and using new words which fit their needs.

9. In all composition the emphasis should be laid upon quality, rather than quantity.

10. Much uncensored written work in other classes defeats the purpose of the English class in composition training.

11. If clear thinking and adequate expression are demanded in all school exercises, there will be less trouble with the 'sentence sense.'

The Responsibility for Curriculum-Making

If classroom instruction is to be influenced by curricula, these must be the result of democratic procedure. Trained leaders necessarily carry the heaviest responsibilities. They initiate the task, develop plans, organize, and direct. They state the ideals or objectives, enunciate the underlying principles of education, and interpret these with concrete illustrations.

Teachers and principals participate by developing new appropriate activities, and by trying materials and methods. Committees for collecting and for evaluating activities are made up of teachers, principals, and supervisors. By this means, understanding and support of the program are guaranteed, and the course of study is made a practical instrument. Such procedure develops interest and promotes the professional growth of the staff. Growing teachers, better materials, and more effective methods of instruction necessitate constant revision of the curriculum, and so the course-of-study program is a continuous process.

SECTION IV

CURRICULUM-MAKING IN PRIVATE LABORATORY SCHOOLS

CHAPTER XV

CURRICULUM-MAKING IN THE LABORATORY SCHOOLS OF THE SCHOOL OF EDUCATION, THE UNIVERSITY OF CHICAGO

Harry O. Gillet
Principal, University Elementary School
and
William C. Reavis
Principal, University High School
School of Education, University of Chicago, Chicago, Illinois

The Problem of Curriculum-Making

Curriculum-making has been one of the major lines of experimentation in the Laboratory Schools of the University of Chicago for the past fifteen years. In recent years it has occupied the attention of the department heads and special teachers almost to the exclusion of other lines of research. The schools have considered it one of their special functions to produce and test out in actual practice materials of instruction for classroom use. As a result, a technique of curriculum-making under laboratory conditions has been slowly evolved.

The Technique of Curriculum-Making in the University Elementary School

Curriculum studies are being made in every subject, but especially in arithmetic, history, geography, nature study, and elementary science, language, French, health, reading, spelling, music, and art. The school is organized and operated on a plan designed to encourage and facilitate such studies. Above the third grade the teaching is largely departmental. In all the grades music, drawing, and physical training and health are being taught by special teachers. The classes number from sixteen to thirty-two children. There are two or more groups for each subject in each grade. The teaching load is not too heavy. Most of the instructors are especially trained in one subject or a small group of related subjects. Library facilities are adequate. Requisitions for books and other materials are generously filled. Lesson sheets are typed and duplicated in large quantities.

Experimentation in the field of the curriculum is a coöperative enterprise, in which each teacher has a responsible share, but it is institutional, not individual or personal. An experiment is not undertaken lightly or impulsively. It must be worth doing in its promise of educational outcome. The teacher must show that she has surveyed the field of the subject comprehensively and critically, that she has definite objectives, and that she is prepared to use a scientific technique appropriate to this type of study. She must subject her work to rigid tests for effectiveness and must make formal as well as informal reports from time to time. The administrative and supervisory officers are kept in close touch with every phase of the project as it develops.

Between two and three years ago we began to make a radical and extensive revision of the course of study in history, geography, science, arithmetic, and grammar in the upper grades. The revision is still in process. It is in harmony with Superintendent Morrison's plan of unit organization and teaching, which has for its chief outcome an adaptation or a functional understanding on the part of the learner.[1] Its purpose is to teach ways of thinking as well as a body of facts, skills, and appreciations. It presupposes an ability and a readiness to direct one's study toward learning, an ability which even in its earlier development marks the pupil off from the primary stage of learning. Fairly conclusive evidence of ability or inability to study, in this sense, may be secured without much difficulty.

Observation and tests seemed to indicate that many children of our fourth grade had entered this secondary stage. Accordingly, it was deemed advisable to experiment with unit organization and teaching of subject matter in the several grades beginning with the fourth.

The following statement of general procedure in the case of history may serve for geography and arithmetic also. The plan was proposed well in advance. The superintendent presented and discussed the theory in considerable detail. He outlined a procedure for experimentation in the grades with appropriate and adequate study of the materials and technique of instruction and

[1] Morrison, Henry C.: *The Practices of Teaching in the Secondary School.* University of Chicago Press, 1926.

testing of the learning products. Later, he presented a set of topics to suggest appropriate units, together with what he had in mind for each. The teachers adopted the list tentatively and set to work to organize several of the units in detail. This involved defining the ends to be achieved in each case, searching out and reading a great deal of material, selecting what seemed most promising for the children's use, ordering sets of some books and extra copies of others, preparing the 'presentations' and the tests to follow, organizing and duplicating the study sheets to guide the reading, preparing questions to test understanding and mastery, and planning for adequate organization and expression on the part of the pupil. In due time the plan was put into operation in the classrooms. It is still operative on an experimental basis. Everything connected with it was, and still is, under constant scrutiny. The weekly meetings of the teachers of history serve as a clearing house of experience and promote coöperative effort. Study materials, tests, and test evidence are discussed and evaluated. Revisions are made. The materials to constitute the formal written reports of the experiment are surveyed. Twice in the year these reports are filed in the office of the research secretary, to become parts of the permanent records of the school.

In grammar in Grade VI, science in Grades IV and VI, and health in Grade V, the materials of instruction are being organized and taught on the unit plan. Since there is only one departmental teacher in each of these subjects, group meetings are not held, but the superintendent and the principal confer with the teachers individually from time to time with respect to the general plan and the details of procedure, and discuss the outcomes as they appear.

Revision of spelling lists is constantly being made. As a working basis, one of the scientifically determined spelling lists was adopted several years ago, with such modifications as the written vocabularies of our pupils seemed to warrant. Compositions are checked from time to time to determine the further changes to be made in our lists. Pre-testing, testing after teaching, and testing for retention after an interval, as well as an examination of the spelling in compositions, are bringing to light some evidence with regard to relative difficulty and grade-placement.

The instruction in French in Grades IV, V, and VI is directed chiefly toward a reading adaptation. To achieve this end, we have to provide a great deal of appropriate reading material. We have to supplement what we can find in print with some of our own preparation. It appears in mimeographed form for class use. We have prepared also considerable test material for experimental use.

In art there has been experimentation going on for several years to determine an adequate and well graded graphic vocabulary.

It is recognized that schools need more well selected reading matter in the middle grades, both as assimilative material in the several subjects of study and as a means of enriching the apperceptive background. The teacher in charge of the Elementary School library is accumulating a body of information about available books, children's choices of books, and some of the motives which influence their choice.

Not only must experimentation proceed along certain rather well defined roads and submit to rigid tests and impartial scrutiny, if it is to be scientific and lead to valid conclusions; it must also be accompanied by detailed records. We are accumulating such records. They are continuously in the process of making. In the last year they comprised more than two thousand pages of single-spaced typewritten material for the kindergarten and six grades. In general, a report includes a statement of the questions under investigation or the ends to be achieved; what was done, how it was done, and the materials that were used; the tests employed, the test scores for classes and individuals, and other evidence of the outcomes of instruction and study; interpretations of the evidence; and a critical discussion of the piece of work as a whole and as to its parts. The reports permit a checking of procedure, materials, and results, and form a basis for further work along similar lines.[2]

Curriculum-Making in Arithmetic in the University Elementary School

The procedure in the University Elementary School in organizing curriculum materials probably can be shown best by referring in considerable detail to a program in one subject—arithmetic. The course in this subject is divided into a primary section for the kindergarten and approximately the first three grades, and a secondary section for approximately the next three grades.

[2] These reports are available for use by qualified students who are working on problems of the curriculum and methods and technique of instruction.

The teachers of the primary section have under way a study of the fundamental mathematical understandings, skills, and adaptations which are prerequisite to a successful pursuit of the subject in the secondary period. They hold weekly meetings with the superintendent and the principal. A survey of the field resulted in the following tentative list:[3]

(1) The concept of number itself, which most children develop in the kindergarten period
(2) Figures as symbols for expressing number
(3) Combining numbers into other numbers
(4) Fractional parts
(5) The concepts of multiplication and division of numbers
(6) The concepts involved in the common measurements
(7) The primary spacial concepts
(8) The addition and multiplication combinations and the corresponding subtraction and division facts
(9) The conventions for expressing United States' money

Each was discussed in detail with respect to scope in the primary stage. Individual and class tests for each were worked out and presented for group criticism and revision and then were given in the several grades. The results were tabulated and brought to the meetings. The results suggested some refinements in the testing program and technique. Also they showed a wide range of pupil accomplishment and understanding. It was apparent that careful observation of little children in the process of getting these concepts, understandings, and skills would produce much of value to those interested in curricular materials and the ways in which children learn. Such observations are being made and recorded. They have an important place in the school records. The test scores indicated a teaching program also. A program of pupil experience, with materials in construction and other projects, is being carried on experimentally toward achieving some of the ends. Direct teaching is necessary to reach other ends. Tests are given from time to time to determine what remains to be done and the most effective means and materials to use. The reports are presented first in the group teachers' meetings, discussed, and then sent to the records room for permanent filing.

---

[3] Morrison, Henry C.: *Op. Cit.*, p. 208.

Experimentation in arithmetic in our Grades IV, V, and VI has centered of late in the organization of the subject matter into teaching and learning units. A study of the field of the subject with respect to the important thought-units initiated the project. These were listed tentatively after a period of group discussion. In preparation for classroom experimentation several of the topics were worked out in detail with reference to the purposes to be attained—namely, an adaptation or a functional understanding and a mastery of the mechanics. Tests for mastery of the unit "division," for example, ought to demonstrate the pupils' ability to recognize a division situation in a problem as well as to operate the mechanics of the process of division. Pupils may acquire this ability by directed study of appropriate materials. It is the teachers' task to organize the materials and direct the study. Our teachers' task in organizing materials for the topic "division," for example, is to provide for the long period of study and assimilation a large amount of graded problem material covering a wide range of division situations in real life, but within the children's comprehension and intelligent interest, and covering also all the difficulties in the division process. After the material is used in the classroom, it is modified as experience and tests direct. All the details of teaching procedure, the problem material, the tests and test scores are brought to the teachers' meetings for discussion and criticism. Finally, all is prepared for the permanent records although, of course, experimentation with respect to a unit may go on actively for several years. In the meantime there is accumulating a body of arithmetic curricular material that has been subjected to critical examination in all stages of preparation.

The Technique of Curriculum-Making in the University High School

In the University High School, curriculum experimentation is very largely restricted to department heads or instructors specially designated by the administrative officers because of competency in their respective fields and their ability to undertake research problems. The numerous preliminary steps which pertain to the training of participating members of the staff are thus obviated. A public school system is usually compelled to make such preparation before it is ready to undertake the production and formulation of curricular materials.

The department head or special teacher knows in advance the subject matter of the field in which he works; he is familiar with the criticisms past and current of the content, organization, and methods of teaching in his particular subject, understands the recommendations which have been made for the improvement of the curriculum, and knows the objectives which should control its selection and organization.

After a curricular study has been decided upon by the department and administrative officers concerned and its scope delimited, the following procedure of curriculum-construction is carried out: (1) the materials of the curriculum are selected according to definite objectives; (2) the materials are organized into pedagogical units according to psychological principles; (3) the curriculum is then tried under experimental conditions, *i.e.*, the teaching and learning are observed, performance of pupils is measured, and the results are evaluated; (4) the materials are reorganized in the light of the classroom evidence and are submitted to experimental teaching and learning again; (5) the process of teaching, observing, testing and reorganizing is continued until satisfactory results are obtained.

Unless entirely new curricula are being experimented with, the available materials of the curriculum under consideration constitute the point of departure. They are assembled and checked to see whether or not they can be defended, (1) on the ground of their immediate usefulness to the pupil in meeting the demands of his everyday life both in and out of school, (2) on the ground of their deferred social utility to the individual in meeting the situations of adult life.

As a result of the application of the foregoing criteria to the matter under consideration, a minimal amount of curricular materials will usually be secured. Using it as a structural frame work for the course, additional materials (called 'connective tissue' by Professor Charters) can be supplied either for purposes of vitalizing or completing the initial curricular structure.

In some schools the work of curriculum-construction stops when the materials have been collected, but in a laboratory school the experiment is merely started. The next step is to arrange and organize the materials, not logically as has too frequently been done, but according to psychological principles. To illustrate: In the traditional course in algebra which was organized logically, we find literal number, exponents, and signed number introduced in the early lessons or within the first two weeks of the course. The fact that the race required many hundreds of years to arrive at an understanding of these concepts received little consideration in the organization of the course. A psychological examination of the way the concepts are learned by immature pupils results in a different type of organization. The abstract concepts must be deferred until the pupil has developed, through intuitive mathematics, an apperceptive background for the abstractions which the logical organization thrusts upon him before he is ready to grasp or appreciate them.

By actual experimental teaching, the relative places in the course at which the respective materials can, and should be, taught are determined. The curriculum can then be organized with a greater degree of certainty regarding its suitability for pupils of a definite grade. Experimentation might well end at this point if the school were concerned only in bringing the pupil into contact with isolated experiences. The laboratory school, however, has a greater responsibility. It must see that the pupils thoroughly understand the experiences which the curricula contain. Otherwise, it is engaged in an ineffective and uncertain enterprise.

All the way through the processes of correlation, practice in arithmetical computation was provided for incidentally through problem exercises which involved computation as well as reasoning. At the same time, the algebra and trigonometry were interwoven with the geometry and arithmetic. First, only the simplest algebra was employed, but it was gradually increased in difficulty until it was finally encountered as an abstract science.

When what was considered to be a first course was constructed, it was tried in the different first-year sections by the different teachers of the mathematics department. Objective evidence was assembled and modifications were made each year until the materials reached a degree of perfection which warranted publication for more extended experimentation in other school systems.

In a similar manner other courses were developed for the whole field of secondary-school mathematics and the first year of the junior college.[4]

To insure the mastery of the curriculum under reasonably efficient teaching conditions, the experimenter goes on with his study of the organization of the materials of the curriculum until they are arranged according to psychological principles in pedagogical units which facilitate the attainment of mastery on the part of the pupil. Until the curriculum is organized in unit situations which permit adaptation and ultimate adjustment on the part of the pupil to the fundamental conditions of life, it cannot be fully justified.[5]

The experimenter with the curriculum must also examine his materials with a view of correlating his objectives with those of other departments. This may be illustrated by the very close correlation established in the University High School between the course on "Community Life and Civic Problems" and the "Beginning Course in English." The objectives of the two courses were so similar that a complete articulation was eventually effected and the latter course discontinued.[6] Economy in time is thus realized in the reorganization of the curriculum through the elimination of duplications. From the point of view of the laboratory schools this is one of the major objectives in curriculum-research.[7]

No experiment with the curriculum is regarded as complete, even if the ends described have been attained. The materials must be submitted again and again to the acid test of classroom use. Revision is a continuous process which must go on as the objectives undergo change. Hence, testing is an important part of curriculum-research at every step. Qualitative judgment is valuable, but it is not sufficiently reliable to be depended upon exclusively. It must be

---

[4] Breslich, E. R.: *First-Year Mathematics, Second-Year Mathematics, Third-Year Mathematics,* and *Correlated Mathematics for Junior Colleges.* University of Chicago Press. *Junior Mathematics.* Book I, 1925; Book II, 1925; Book III, 1926. Macmillan Company.

[5] Morrison, Henry C.: *Op. cit.,* pp. 35-48.

[6] For detailed account see, Hill, H. C. "Opportunities for correlation between community life and English." *School Review,* 30:Jan., Feb., March, 1922, 24-36, 118-126, 175-186.

[7] Morrison, H. C. *The Major Lines of Experimentation in the Laboratory Schools* (Studies in Secondary Education, I, pp. 1-19. Supplemental Education Monographs, No. 24, Department of Education, University of Chicago, 1923.)

supplemented with the results of carefully prepared tests designed to measure the pupils' ability to master the materials taught. Reteaching and reorganization must then take place in the light of the evidence thus obtained.

Experimentation with the curriculum in virtually all of the high-school subjects has been carried on in the University High School within recent years. Any one of the curricula might be selected as an example of the technique which has been described. Mathematics is chosen for the reason that it represents the longest experiment in the reorganization of curricular materials in point of time.

Curriculum-Making in Mathematics in the University High School

The experiment[8] to develop a curriculum in mathematics for the University High School began in 1903 with an extended classroom test of the plan of teaching algebra and geometry simultaneously. In the ninth grade algebra was taught three days a week and geometry two during the first semester, and during the second semester algebra two and geometry three. A similar plan in Grade XI was followed for advanced algebra and trigonometry. Although the scheme was claimed to be successful in Europe and was advocated by certain leading educators in this country, the experiment in the University High School proved unsatisfactory after a trial of two years and was given up. An experiment along the line of the correlation of high-school mathematics was next undertaken. This has continued up to the present time. In recent years a more scientific technique of curriculum-making has been developed and significant revisions of the course materials have followed.

The application of the fundamental objectives of present usefulness and deferred social values to the traditional materials of the mathematics' curriculum has enabled the experimenter to meet such potent criticisms of traditional mathematics as (1) the static character of the curriculum, (2) the logical organization of the courses, (3) the superfluous nature of some of the content, (4) the

[8] Breslich, E. R. "The Development of a Curriculum in Correlated Mathematics and Discussion of Aims, Values, and Results," *Studies in Secondary Education. I*, pp. 116-136. (Department of Education, University of Chicago, 1923.)

ungraded character of the materials, (5) the deductive method of procedure, and (6) the absence of function in the organization of the curriculum.

By eliminating from arithmetic, algebra, geometry, and trigonometry the materials challenged by the controlling objectives, a certain residue remained in each of the subjects. These materials were arranged in separate curricula in psychological order and organized in pedagogical units. The respective units were next enriched with needed materials from the daily life of the pupils. Inconsistencies were removed and as much content was retained in each unit as was needed to enable the pupils completely to understand it.

The next question to be attacked was: *How can any one of the curricula supplement the others?* This required a scheme of correlation or unification of the different curricula. The work of effecting a correlation according to psychological principles led to the adoption of intuitive geometry as the core of the first course of secondary-school mathematics. The basic materials of the curricula in arithmetic, algebra, and trigonometry were utilized wherever they were needed or were found to be helpful in the manipulation of the geometric materials. As the correlation proceeded and the materials of intuitive geometry were used up, geometric materials which employed informal reasoning were utilized in making the transition from the intuitive and informal to the logical demonstrative geometry of the later courses.

CHAPTER XVI

THE LINCOLN EXPERIMENTAL SCHOOL

Otis W. Caldwell
Director, Lincoln School of Teachers College
Columbia University, New York City

I. Conditions to Be Met by Improved Subjects and Methods

It has always been easier to discover shortcomings in educational endeavors and to indicate better things that may be done, than it has been to prove just how these proposed better things may supplant the deficiencies in current practice. Because of this fact, educational criticism and statements of educational philosophy and desired outcomes have often been clearly made without securing any large changes in educational practices. It probably is inevitable and also desirable that educational philosophy and criticism shall outrun practice. However, definitions of philosophy which are neither derived from experiment, nor followed by experiment, seem relatively ineffective, no matter how plausible they may appear to be. The period is rapidly passing when unsupported assertions about either philosophy or practice in education will be regularly accepted. Few educational workers would assert that we have a science of education as compared with the physical or biological sciences. But almost all believe that the persistent introduction of the standards and methods of scientific workers into the problems of education is producing very large returns and will sometime produce a science of education, even in a field in which personal opinion and group acclaim or professional advice have so persistently dominated. When the majority of fairly well-educated people know little of a new subject, the opinions of the few who know something of it are accepted as authority. Such acceptance of authoritative statement often has led the few to make assumptions in the field exceeding the foundation upon the known fact. Such has been the situation in education until a little more than two decades ago. So long as personal opinion alone was accepted as determining school subjects and school procedures, there was little opportunity for an experimental school. There might be schools to demonstrate one person's advanced ideas about education, but such schools were largely personal affairs, and in almost all cases each such school ceased to exist or became conventionalized when the forward-looking founder ceased his connection with it.

Education is now beginning a period of guidance by means of assembled evidence. A subject cannot properly be granted a place in the curriculum until there is a large accumulation of facts; until these are related to one another and their underlying meaning derived; until a body of principles of behavior and actions of things in the field have been formulated; above all in large measure the evidence, meanings, and principles found by one worker or group of workers must be the same as those found by others who may examine the same situations, if the subject is to be accepted as of proved value in education.

Until recently, the teachers in elementary or high schools would rarely have dared propose fundamental changes in the content or organization of the subject matter of courses of instruction as presented in the printed courses of study in textbooks. The subjects of study and their organization were determined chiefly by subject specialists. Even those who expounded educational philosophy did not secure large adjustments of subject matter, thus often leaving stated philosophy and classroom practice widely divergent. Such is still the situation to a large extent, but some important changes already made and indications of still more important ones give evidence of the trend of events. Also, teachers have improved in subject scholarship and in professional understanding. This improvement is as yet more conspicuous and more encouraging because of the direction in which it is leading, than because of the distance already covered. This change is, however, one of the very important elements with which experimental education now deals.

The Lincoln School directs its attention toward the curriculum in the endeavor to develop such changes in the subjects of study and in school life as shall more nearly secure the types of educational results now regarded as most desirable. Fortunately, the ten years since the school was announced, and the nine years of its active existence have developed no slogan of philosophy or practice. No one regards the school as founded upon any single type of educational thought or upon the educational philosophy of any one person. The causes are more substantial and much less personal than would be suggested by a slogan, or by any one person's educational philosophy. The determining influences would probably have produced some such school as this, even had those influences been unrecognized by all of the individuals concerned in the enterprise. Such causes have produced and will continue to produce other experimental schools of similar purpose, since these causes are partly inherent in the development of the types of public education which America has undertaken to make available to her young people. Such a large governmental unit, which offers education to all those of its people who possess ambition to achieve within the intellectual and vocational activities of a growing democracy, will need much careful experimentation to discover its most effective procedure.

In this connection it is sufficient to give brief mention of a few of the outstanding elements of the curricular conditions which were recognized as making an experimental school desirable. The past half century was unprecedently conspicuous for its growth and refinement in many branches of knowledge. Statements of what men knew or wished to know were promptly printed in newspapers, magazines, and books of popular technique and textbook nature. These publications were as widely distributed as the facilities would permit. Distribution of knowledge does not usually satisfy the human mind, but on the contrary, it arouses questions, stimulates thought, calls for development of more knowledge. Education is the great dissatisfier, the great arouser of ambitions and needs not previously known. Distribution of what is known is the surest way to increase the sources of supply of new knowledge. Thus, knowledge grew as never before, and refinements in classification, specialization, and accompanying terminologies probably developed more in the past half-century than in several centuries before. These refinements produced many branches of study, like those many small, leaf-bearing branches which grow out from the few main branches and supporting stalk of a forest tree. The specialists who knew the small, but important terminal branches urged their supreme importance for educational uses. The curriculum became filled with intensive studies of differentiated branches, often to the exclusion of any view or appreciation of the main trunk and its major branches, by means of which connection with the nutrient earth is maintained, by means of which physical support is secured, and by means of which the small leaf-bearing branches may receive light and thus be enabled to operate as working laboratories. It is obviously the finer branches with their food-making factories—the leaves—in which the most intricate constructive processes occur. It does not follow, however, that the intricate constructive processes are the topics most useful or most significant for those who try for the first time to interpret the significance of the whole structure.

As a further result of the worthy and most welcome growth in subject matter during the last half century, so many scholarly specialities have developed, each with high significance in its particular field, that it has become impossible for a general student or general citizen to have studied and to have gained the significance of each of these specialties. Furthermore, the attempt to teach a considerable number of special subjects without the more general foundational studies, has resulted in knowledge of the outlying specially developed fields without the centralizing unifying materials and principles from which these special subjects have grown and upon which they are supported.

For a score of years effort has been under way in different subjects to find the most significant portions of the general foundational studies and to reorganize the outstanding fields of knowledge into general foundational courses. This movement seems to have begun in the natural sciences, but is now recognized also in mathematics, social studies, and industrial arts. In principle and in purpose the movement seems to be essentially similar in these four divisions of the curriculum. In the sciences, effort was first made to organize topical groups with the subject matter secured from any special sciences which assisted in making the topics mean most to young students. In mathematics, general courses were organized, which used materials from arithmetic, algebra, geometry, and trigonometry, all applied to significant situations. In social studies, topics were selected and materials for their study were secured from geography, ancient and modern history, sociology, civics, and economics. In industrial arts, general shops have been built and equipped with various types of machinery, and courses organized which touch each of the major handwork vocations, thus giving pupils an insight into the nature of a large number of activities without pretending to develop refined technique in any.

The educational situation and the inferences from it are similar in these four divisions of study. An educational tendency may be derived and perhaps certain guiding conclusions may be cited. (1) The practice of using highly refined special subject matter as a proper foundation for introductory or general phases of education has not been proved effective. (2) Knowledge has become so refined and so specialized that the further advance of knowledge in the different specialties is likely to be made only by those who have done much study in the special fields concerned, with this study supported by good general foundations. (3) We need those types of general topics within the major fields of knowledge which are pertinent to the needs and living experiences of the majority of people; such courses are desired also as the earlier stages of scholastic, vocational, or professional education. (4) It is significant that general foundational topics represent the types of considerations which were outstanding in the leading divisions of human knowledge in the earlier stages of development of scholarship. In an earlier day synthesis and a measure of coherence were assured; now we must definitely plan to secure them. (5) Better scholarship is desired. The types of general courses suggested are in no sense designed to reduce scholarly standards. They are designed to use from the chief division of knowledge those types of thought and action which are meaningful to a larger number of people now and in the lives they are to live; and being meaningful, a larger amount of intellectual effort, exaction, and attainment are expected.

One major purpose of improved subjects of study is a higher degree and a larger quantity of dynamic scholarship. More personal effort with clearer understanding of its processes and purposes is one of the tendencies of modern education.

There are those who fear that introductory school subjects such as those suggested, and the types of school life associated with such subjects, will cause schools to lose their disciplinary value. Modern education breaks squarely with the older doctrine of discipline for discipline's sake. Extraneous discipline is sometimes unavoidable, owing largely, I am persuaded, to our inadequate knowledge of child psychology, teacher psychology, and subject psychology; but if arbitrary discipline is permanent, if growth is not rapid toward discipline in control and in achievement by and within the persons who receive it, it is relatively futile. Jails, homes for the dependents and the unfortunates of various kinds are instituted by society for the use of persons who have not developed the type of discipline which modern education is ambitious to secure. It is not, then, less discipline which modern education wants, but more. It is not the discipline which enables one to march mechanically with the crowd of soldiers at the command of the officer, but the discipline which enables the individual to accord himself with the group, because of his own knowledge that this is essential to effective endeavor. Modern education, then, demands severe discipline of person and in achievement, but on an individual and social level not previously required in educational activities. Much experiment will be needed to bring subjects of study and school procedures into accord with this objective.

II. Some Accepted Factors of Experimention, and Some Fundamental Guides from Current Philosophy and Psychology

It is unnecessary to elaborate the factors listed under this caption. They are not new, and are original only in the nature of the emphases on one point or another. While these points have been stated by others and on many occasions, we shall need to re-state them until they have been clearly proved sound or unsound as they work in the studies and experiences of daily school work. The really new thing is so to reorganize school subjects and experiences as to test these principles. For these reasons the following list is presented without elaboration at this point.

A. Summary Statement of the Conditions and Needs Related to Experimentation with the Curriculum

1. The curriculum was formerly made by individuals who rarely tried out proposed new materials by planned experiments, and more rarely checked their results by objective tests.
2. Experimentation is now in progress in many schools.
3. Many teachers are experimenting in schools of the usual types.
4. Why should schools be set apart for experimentation?

a. Experimentation requires a smaller teaching load, so that more exacting effort may be given to specific constructive endeavor.
b. Experimenters should usually do some teaching.
c. There is great need of mutual criticism by experimenters.
d. There is needed an institution in which progressive teachers may work for a time, after which they may return to the public school system.
e. There is need for salaries that can not now be paid to many experimenters in a public school system.
f. There is need of more clerical help than is ordinarily possible.
g. An ideal experimental school should be a part of a public school system. Why not have it?

5. An experimental school requires a composition of representative pupils. It should be representative of the types of pupils for whom the results of the experimental school are designed.
6. Improvement of the curriculum is necessary to enable educational practice to catch up with, or to correct, educational theory.
   a. Much theory has been announced, and many of the claims made have not always been proved in practice.
   b. Courses of study are often inconsistent with stated objectives.
   c. How are objectives usually determined?
   d. Stated ideals have outrun practice.

B. Some of the Accepted Factors in Psychology and Method Upon Which Experimental Work Is Based

1. Definite, intensive, and purposeful effort is essential to educational development; young, as well as older people, can be educated only by means of, and through, work; the quantity of worth while work in the school subjects and methods of study should be increased.
2. Children learn best when school life is real and engaging—not artificial and repulsive.
3. Children develop fastest when engaged most of the time in doing things they can do—not constantly failing in things they cannot do.
4. Children learn much, and naturally, from one another and school work should guide them in this kind of learning.

5. Pupil coöperation with teachers and with one another is essential to proper conditions for education, and this coöperation provides the only means of insuring that school life and life out of school shall be parts of the same whole.
6. People learn through all of their senses—touch, taste, sight, smell, hearing. Education has acted as if words as seen and heard are the chief means of education. The nervous system is the physical foundation of education and it is reached by way of all the senses. More experiences, as well as more careful thought development, are needed in the program of studies.

III. The Experimental School as a School

This question at once presents an antithesis. Presumably, an experimental school is established because of acceptance or development of certain beliefs or evidences related to a philosophy of education. Therefore, the school may reasonably be expected to manifest the types of pupil life and learning which the fundamental philosophy would seem to require. But this philosophy requires reorganization and readjustment of subjects of study, new types of pupil relations and endeavors, and these may be secured only slowly, and by trial and adoption or omission as developing evidence proves to be desirable. Thus, the antithesis—the school which should exemplify certain types of thinking about subjects of study and school life and which hopes to provide workers an opportunity to discover how these types of thinking and of school life may be developed is itself expected to be an example of the educational outcomes toward which experimentation is being directed. The antithesis must be accepted by an experimental school. It must, as fully as it may, be a working illustration of the best educational philosophy it can derive from observation, experience, and reflection, and from consultation with progressive thinking about education. In order that there may be preparation for later proper living in a democracy, there should be an effective school democracy in which all school members learn to live effectively. If seriousness, pleasure, and personal responsibility are expected as characteristics of adult lives, these qualities need to have abundant place in childhood and youth, and school should provide for them. If elements of individual personality are assets in adults, school life should save and develop them and not endeavor to subjugate or destroy distinctive worthy personal qualities. If there is danger of weakness and superficiality in scholarship, the experimental school must provide for, require, and test to insure raised standards. If education is the dominant agency in determining what the next generation shall do and think, an experimental school needs clear policies as to the road it proposes to take, whither it thinks the road leads, and what is to be done upon arrival.

IV. Experiments with the Subjects of Study Most Necessary

The subjects of study are the units about which most educational activities gather. Most effective school people believe, and no assembled evidence contradicts this belief, that if subject-matter work by pupils is engaging, effective, and is retained reasonably well, the school is good, no matter how little or much of the so-called 'special interests' or activities are engaged in; and conversely, when subject work is poor in quality and retention, and is repellant, the school is unworthy, even though winning football teams are heralded and the school annual is magnificent. Therefore, an experimental school must work primarily upon the adjustment of subjects of study. This is not a task that can be completed satisfactorily and then left, because each useful adjustment will probably open ways for others that are better. Before the Lincoln School was established, some of those who were asked to vote money for it were of the opinion that financial support for twenty years would enable the school to accomplish its tasks on curricular study. These far-seeing men have since volunteered the opinion that such experimental schools will always be needed, at least so long as men and women of successive generations continue to focus their thought and emotions upon the welfare of their children.

Different investigators must use different methods and varying degrees of exactitude, dependent upon the nature and possibilities of the problem. It is hoped that accuracy of evidence may increase and that personal feeling and bias may be minimized. In the long run, personal interests are best cared for when the evidence is clear and the conclusion sound. Three types of curricular studies are presented as illustrations. Two of the examples chosen deal with selection of subject matter. One deals with choosing subject matter and with its organization about certain activities. It will be understood that not only are these three very different from one another, but numerous other pieces of work, if presented, would differ still more widely from those here presented.

V. A Third-Grade Unit of Work

Some years ago Miss Nell Curtis, in her study of transportation, with a third-grade group, selected as a centralizing unit for the study, the facts regarding transportation which the pupils might observe upon the nearby Hudson river. This soon led to a study of boats—boats of to-day, of recent past, of remote past, and to discussion of possible future boats. In the study there then follows observation wherever available; reading about boats and their use in transportation; design and construction; measurement; artistic decoration; weighing and calculation of cargo; study of values, of distances from and to which materials are transported; composition and illustration of stories with pupil and teacher criticism on vocabulary, spelling, reading, form and quality; final drawings, painting or written records of all boat work done; bibliographies of reading or other work yet to be done; list of topics on which adequate data were not found; lists of further studies to which the boat work leads; tests to see if computation, spelling, and reading skills are developing.

In continuance of that work and built upon it, Miss Martha Groggel has been engaged in an endeavor to reorganize the Grade III procedure so as to make more effective the manual or industrial and the artistic interests of third-grade pupils, while at the same time attempting to care for all the other desired growths and attainments for which Grade III assumes responsibility. A chart is herewith presented which sets forth the whole unit of work as the result of two years' experiment by Miss Groggel.

VI. Junior-High-School Social Sciences

Few, if any, subjects of study better illustrate the tendency to keep crowding new, but unvalidated factual elements into the school courses, than history, geography, and civics. Dr. Harold O. Rugg and others have been engaged in the study of guides by means

A UNIT OF STUDY RELATED TO BOATS
THIRD GRADE

STIMULATION

In the spring of last year many of the boys of this group were interested in trains and other means of travel.

Many summer experiences with boats.

Wood in supply box cut in shapes suggestive of boats.

Bulletin prepared by the teacher.

Trip to see Half-Moon.

Trip to see boat models.

PROBLEMS-QUESTIONS

To construct boats that will look like a certain kind and with which children can play.

How do boats "go"?

Who first thought of making a sailboat?

How did people get the idea for different shapes for boats?

To know more about the people who traveled on the seas in early times.

To find out about the making of boats.

How many different kinds of boats do we have today and how is each kind used?

How did early people use their ships?

To find out about the different parts of a boat.

How do people know how much to put into a boat before it will sink?

SUBJECT MATTER CONTENT WHICH HELPED SOLVE THE PROBLEMS

INDUSTRIAL ARTS

Construction of boats: Making pattern, shaping hull, making sail, making keel, casting weight for keel, making rack for boat, and testing boat.
How boats developed from early times to the present day.
The difficulty involved in building a toy boat so it will balance in water.
Different kinds of sail boats.
The need for a keel on a boat.
Different methods of propelling a boat.
Modern inventions in connection with the propulsion of boats.
What makes boats float.
Different uses of boats today.

HISTORY

The Half-Moon directed interest to Hendrick Hudson and his ship.
Historic ships: Santa Maria, Mayflower.
Reference work, reading and discussions about:
Vikings: What color and kinds of clothing did they wear? What did they eat? What kind of houses did they have? What were their boats like? Did Vikings have stores? How did Viking writing look? Story of Lief Erickson. The gods of the Vikings. Their beliefs.
Phoenicians: Scenery, boats, people, trade, beliefs, clothing, cities, industries, etc.
Egyptians: Scenery, country, boats, beliefs, tools, writing, etc. Story of the building of Solomon's Temple.
Early Mediterranean peoples.

GEOGRAPHY

Pictures of boat from newspaper which interested children in world geography.
Geography related to countries studied.
Norway: Country, climate, people and occupations.
Phoenicia: Country, climate, people, trading routes, daily life of early people compared with that of today.
Egypt: Country, climate, trading, etc.
Map interest: Norway, showing ancient home of the Vikings.
The Mediterranean countries, showing cities of Phoenicia and routes on which the King of Tyre sent materials for Solomon's Temple.
Plasticene map of Mediterranean Sea and surrounding countries on which children sailed card-board models of early boats.
Globe in frequent use to locate places mentioned.
Outline world map, locating countries.
Interest in determining distances (reading scales on map).
How far is it from Norway to Phoenicia?
How far is it from Norway to America?
Building Lower Manhattan on floor with blocks to exhibit boats.
Map was drawn on floor; buildings in New York City that helped most with sea travel.

ARITHMETIC

Measuring for boat patterns and measurements in boat making.
Figuring the number of board feet used by class in building boat racks.
Arithmetic problems in connection with science experiment of water displacement and floating objects.
What is a gram?
What is a cubit?
Dimensions of Solomon's Temple compared with dimensions of the Lincoln School.
Children saw a cubit measure at the Museum.

FINE ARTS

Sketching and painting pictures of Half-Moon.
Sketching and painting boat models.
Drawing blackboard frieze showing history of boats.
Ten easel pictures showing story of Lief Erickson.
Cut paper pictures of boats.
Painting Egyptian boats seen at Museum.
Painting Viking pictures showing clothing.
Painting modern boats.
Making clay tablet.

COMPOSITION—LITERATURE

Stories written about the trip to see Half-Moon.
Stories of other trips by individual children.
Original poems about boats and the sea.
Labels and invitations for boat exhibit.
Written and oral reports about boats, Vikings, Phoenicia and Egypt.
Stories for bulletin, room paper, council news, or absent class members, telling of class interest and study.

READING

Reference material pertaining to topics under discussion, found in school library or at home.
Children's reading material: Lief and Thorkle, Viking Stories, Early sea people, Boat Book prepared by other Third Grade, material prepared by student teachers.

SCIENCE

How can we tell if our boats will float and balance? Try out in delta table.
Three experiments: Why do some objects float and why do some sink?
How do people know how much to put into boat before it will sink?

DRAMATIZATION

Play-Story of Lief Erickson, spontaneously prepared by class.

MUSIC

Old Gaelic Lullaby. Volga Boat Song. Sail Bonnie Boat.

PROBABLE OUTCOMES

DESIRABLE HABITS AND SKILLS

Better skill in sketching.
Better skill in handling brush and paints.
A beginning of the development of how to sew.
Developing the habit of making a pattern before constructing an article.
Developing skill in shaping wood by means of plane and spokeshave.
Developing skill in using gouge and mallet.
Developing skill in reading distances on map.
Rapid growth in map drawing.
Developing habit of reading the newspaper.
Better skill in measuring.
Ability to gather information on a certain subject and reporting to class.
Increased ability in writing.

ATTITUDES AND APPRECIATIONS

Economic:

An appreciation of the use of weights and measures.
What it means to construct a real boat that will float and balance properly.
Appreciation of the change in the lives of the people caused by the discovery of iron and the use of sails.
Appreciation of paper as a writing material.
Appreciation of the modern inventions in connection with the propulsion of ships.

Social:

What the early people contributed to the world.
The number of people and industry it takes to supply materials for the construction of one building.
Comparison of the ideas of fairness of the early people with the present day.

Recreational:

Developing a joy in painting, sketching and drawing.
Growing interest in reading books about historical peoples, inventions or boats.
Playing with boats made.
Interest in the construction of a toy-boat.
Interest in the construction of a real boat.
The pleasure in making maps.
The pleasure of playing with maps.

Aesthetic:

Appreciation of the beauty in line and construction of boats.
The adventure of the ship.

INFORMATION

Knowledge of the development of the boat from raft to steamship.
Who Hendrick Hudson was.
General idea of historic ships.
An interesting acquaintance with Vikings, Phoenicians, and Egyptians.
General geographical knowledge of the world.
What a cubit measure is.
Knowledge of how to draw maps.
Some idea of what makes objects float.
Some idea of how to make boats balance in water.
Some idea of how to construct a toy-boat.
How the early people made their clay tablets.
How to make a clay tablet.
The need for molds in casting metals.
Some idea of how iron is made into different shapes.

TOTAL PERSONALITY AS MODIFIED BY THE FOREGOING EXPERIENCES

NEW INTERESTS LEADING TOWARD FURTHER ACTIVITIES

Interest in world geography and travel.
Maps and actual distances between given places.
The time it takes to get to certain places.

Interest in silk through answering the questions:
What kind of clothing did the Vikings wear?
How is velvet made?

Interest in what clay is: How it is prepared for our use and how it was prepared by early people for making clay tablets.

Interest in the Egyptian and Phoenician alphabet and how our alphabet was developed from it.
The materials the Egyptians used for writing.

Interest in metals.
Interest in weight of different metals through casting of lead for keels.
How metals are shaped.

Interest in the construction of modern buildings through reading about Solomon's Temple and comparing it with the construction of the Lincoln School.

Interest in other phases of transportation.

of which to discover what materials in these fields are really needful and useful as parts of an educational program.

The program comprises studies of what to teach, studies of children's interests and capacities, studies of existing curricula and of the product obtained from them, studies of grade-placement, and studies of learning and of the organization of the materials of instruction. The program, initiated in the autumn of 1921, has steadily enlarged and matured. Its foundation is two-fold: the critical study of society and of child capacities and interests. Because of the difficulty of consummating the former task, and because of the dearth of completed work in the field, their energies to the present time have been concentrated largely on the study of society and the formulation of materials of instruction in terms of it. That is, they have first set up studies the object of which has been to delineate the chief characteristics of society.

These characteristics, psychological because of the need for their incorporation in the curriculum, are five-fold: (1) The insistent and more permanent problems of the economic, political, and cultural order; (2) the chief generalizations, the modes of relational thinking, upon a mastery of which the intelligent consideration of the problems of society depends; (3) the cue concepts, the fundamental notions which epitomize the connotational background that an individual possesses of the various aspects of the current order; (4) the detailed materials of the social science field—the great movements and themes underlying American life and how they came to be, the epochs through which those movements have revealed themselves, the focal persons, and events, and the corresponding important facts of time and place; (5) and here they touch the controlling goal of curriculum-making, studies of the directive attitudes and ideals that should dominate human conduct—attitudes, for example, of sympathetic tolerance, of critical questioning; ideals of honest conduct, of pride in craftsmanship, etc.

The foregoing types of studies all deal with the content of the curriculum, with what to teach and how to teach it. To make the program clear, in so far as it touches content, a number of topical studies have been developed.

Only one of these studies can be here presented as a type, and but a small part of it. Geography, and to some extent history, have usually called for large numbers of location facts. A study was devised to determine which of these facts, or what types of them are of use in school work.

Altogether, seventeen criteria were employed in determining the relative importance of the various location facts herein reported. The criteria were found to vary widely in scope of applicability and in validity. The first eight criteria listed and described below were combined to yield composite rank-order lists of cities, countries, sections and regions, states, islands, bodies of water, rivers and mountains. (The weighting given each criterion in this amalgamation is given in the appendix of the monograph which reports the study.) The criteria numbered 9 to 17 were used in constructing rank-order lists of other important types of locations. The seventeen criteria are as follows:

1. The statistics of clearing house exchanges; "bank clearings." Used to determine the commercial importance of cities of the United States.
2. Statistics of trade (exports and imports) of all countries. Used to determine the commercial importance of countries.
3. Statistics of population. Used for all cities and all countries.
4. Area of territory. Used for all countries.
5. Relative number of magazine articles published in 1919, 1920, 1922, 1923, dealing with various types of locations. Used for cities, countries, sections, islands, mountains and mountain ranges, bodies of water, and rivers.
6. Frequency with which writers in critical journals employed the location facts in their writings. Used for all types of location facts.
7. Frequency with which frontier thinkers used the location facts in critical treatises on contemporary world affairs and their historical development. Used for all types of location facts.
8. The data of preceding studies of newspaper and magazine allusions. Used for all types of location facts.

In addition to the preceding eight criteria, which were combined to yield composite rank-order lists of various locations, the following criteria were used to give measures of the importance of other specific types of locations.

9. Statistics of freight tonnage handled at United States ports. Used to determine commercial importance of ports of the United States.

10. Value of total commerce (exports and imports) of world ports. Used to determine commercial importance of ports of the world.
11. Number of miles of railroad track operated. Used to determine importance of United States railroads.
12. Total of operating expenses and operating revenue. Used to determine importance of United States railroads.
13. Percentage of world's output of important minerals. Used to determine importance of mineral-producing regions.
14. Amount of traffic carried over ocean lanes of trade. Used (in an approximate form) to determine important trade routes.
15. Percentage of population engaged in manufacturing. Used to determine important manufacturing regions.
16. Areas of dense population suggested as important location facts.
17. Areas of production of agricultural goods suggested (for reference) to determine important agricultural regions.

Based upon these criteria, lists of essential map locations have been developed. These include such topics as: cities of the United States; foreign cities in order of relative importance; countries in order of relative importance; sections and regions in order of relative importance; states of the United States in rank-order of importance; islands and archipelagoes in order of importance; bodies of water in rank-order of importance; rivers in order of importance; mountains and mountain ranges in rank-order of importance; United States ports and world ports in order of tonnage and value of commerce handled; railroads in order of units operated and combined expenses and revenue, and other topics covering a total of twenty-six detailed lists. Then follows a study of the specific facts within these lists which most need to be developed through practice exercises, and a list of forty-five practice exercises in map location.

VIII. The High-School Course in Biology

The course in biology is supposed to bear a close relation to many common topics of necessary interest, such as health, food production, and other factual or theoretical biological topics. Very few studies have been made which give desired evidence as to relations actually existing between this school subject and the use of its factual content by citizens. Dr. C. W. Finley and the writer designed a study to discover to what extent biological information is used in the daily press. Such a study might show nothing as to what biological information the public should receive or would like to receive, nor what known or unknown biological information the press would like to use if it were available, but merely what does now find its way into the daily press. Also such a study would need to be associated with others of similar purpose before any conclusions might be drawn regarding the content of the high-school biology course. It is nevertheless by the accumulation of such studies that we may secure evidence as to what may properly enter into the biology course.

Seventeen full months' issues of representative daily papers were secured. These were from leading cities of the United States. Each paper was carefully read and all articles using biological information were clipped and classified according to an elaborate, careful plan, including re-checking. The results, as set forth in tabulated form, are indicated by the three charts selected for the purpose.

While these are but samples of the results of the whole study, they serve to indicate the kinds of information secured. The number, size, and general distribution of the 3061 biological articles are given in the table and diagrams below.

As illustration of the distribution of health articles by papers, and by different health topics, the following table and diagram are presented. Also, since "germ diseases" is the single health topic to which the largest number of health articles pertain, a further table is given showing the distribution of articles relating to germ diseases.

The conclusion cannot be drawn that, since these biological articles have been found and since they are clearly grouped into certain definite headings, they are necessarily the topics toward which all high-school instruction in biology should be directed. It may be that there are types of available biological information which should be presented, but which are omitted in the newspaper articles. Doubtless, also, some needful biological information is as yet unknown to biologists, or possibly if known, has not been made available to the public press. Possibly, the press would publish, and the public would like to read, much more biological material

Main Topic	Number of Sub-divisions of Topics	Number of Clippings	Length in Inches	Average Length of Articles in Inches
Health	8	897	7,550	8.4
Animals	10	755	6,422	8.5
Plants	13	660	5,521	8.4
Food	7	533	4,024	7.5
Organizations of Producers	3	81	652	8.0
General Nature	3	74	843	11.4
Evolution	4	47	446	9.5
Fictitious	1	14	48	3.4
		3,061	25,506	8.3

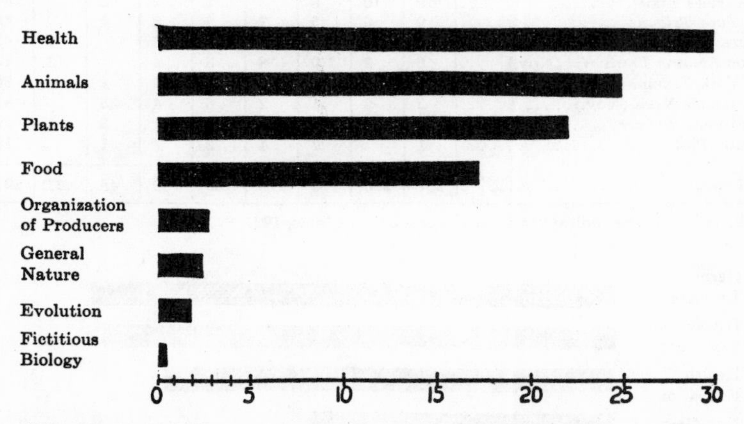

Distribution by Percents of the 3061 Articles Pertaining to the Various Divisions of Biology

of much wider range if it were made available. These are questions which the present study does not determine, but which should receive later attention.

It seems safe to conclude further that, since these types of biological knowledge are going to the public in such large quantities and over the whole country, the course in school biology should consider them as part of the legitimate materials to discuss in a course of study. Other evidences, when developed, should also be used in whatever ways those new evidences may justify. The biological articles listed are surely thought to relate to genuine public needs or interests, else the newspapers presumably would

TOPICAL DISTRIBUTION OF ARTICLES PERTAINING TO HEALTH

	Germ Diseases	Hygiene and Sanitation	Health Education	Non-germ Diseases	Dietetics	Drugs	First Aid	Physiology	Totals
*Kansas City *Star* (Nov.)	92	25	9	10	4	1	4		145
Boston *Evening Transcript*	19	8	30	14	5	1	3	3	83
Memphis *Commercial Appeal* (Nov.)	21	16	17	12		1	2		69
New York *Globe*	10	9	23	5	6	4	4	2	63
Atlanta *Constitution* (Nov.)	3	15	6	19	3	4	7		57
Chicago *Daily News*	4	20	11	5	1	6	3	5	55
Seattle *Post Intelligencer*	2	13	15	4	12	1	4		51
San Francisco *Chronicle*	6	7	12	4	5	6	3	5	48
Washington *Post*	3	21	6	6	5		1	5	47
Los Angeles *Times*	9	10	8	5	2	2	2		46
New York *Tribune*	9	6	5	7	6	8	4		45
Atlanta *Constitution*	12	14	8	5		2		2	43
Boston *Evening Transcript* (Nov.)	6	9	9	8	3	4		4	43
New York *Tribune* (Nov.)	6	6	4	10	4	4	1		35
Indianapolis *News* (Nov.)	3	9	4	2	6	4	3		31
Des Moines *Register*	1	7	5	2	1	4	3	1	24
Houston *Post*	1		7	1	2		1		12
Totals	207	203	179	119	65	52	45	27	897

*Unless otherwise indicated the papers are for June issue, 1921.

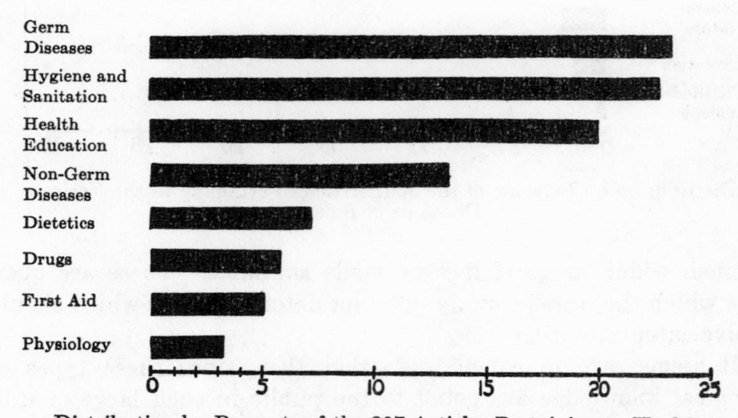

Distribution by Percents of the 897 Articles Pertaining to Health

not print them. Teachers may use many of these type articles, or others equally good, as cases of situations with which to conduct discussions or study of classroom problems in biological instruction. If biological study is to improve living and thinking, it

GERM DISEASES

	Number of Articles	Length of Articles
Smallpox	90	335
Tuberculosis	32	304
Treatment	16	92
Rabies	11	25
Yellow Fever	9	154
Diphtheria	8	57
Typhus and Typhoid	7	34
Bubonic Plague	6	117
Colds	6	56
Malaria	5	28
Sleeping Sickness	3	6
Influenza	3	5
Leprosy	3	10
Scarlet Fever	2	23
Lockjaw	2	18
Infantile Paralysis	1	36
Pellagra	1	16
Chicken Pox	1	8
Measles	1	8
Totals	207	1,332

needs anchorage in specific situations which are meaningful to the student.

VIII. LIMITATIONS UPON CURRICULAR RESEARCH

The three illustrations so briefly set forth, as well as all other dependable curricular studies, serve to show how slowly investigations may reasonably develop. The curriculum is very complicated and is built upon a small amount of really scientific evidence. No single investigation is likely to accomplish a large part of the reorganizational task; indeed most investigations as yet made have served to open the way for larger and further needful investigations. But even the small amount of facts already gained provides a new kind of guidance and a new kind of expectation for sound curricular development.

CHAPTER XVII

CURRICULUM-MAKING IN THE UNIVERSITY ELEMENTARY SCHOOL OF THE STATE UNIVERSITY OF IOWA

Ernest Horn
College of Education
and
Maude McBroom
University Elementary School
State University of Iowa, Iowa City, Iowa

The curriculum of the University Elementary School and the methods used in making that curriculum must be viewed in the light of the relation which the school bears to the College of Education and to the state at large. The school has three major purposes. First, it furnishes observation and demonstration facilities for the concrete study of the problems of elementary education by those who are in training for supervisory positions. Second, it affords a laboratory in which the faculty and students of the College of Education may study the problems of elementary education in a scientific manner. Third, it serves the public schools of the state directly as an agency for the production, publication, and dissemination of new curricula and methods, as well as a demonstration center where visiting teachers and superintendents can study. It is not the purpose of the school to afford opportunities for practice-teaching, but qualified mature students are permitted to teach in the school under experimental conditions. The instruction in the school is given by a regular staff of experienced teachers who are chosen because of their ability to do demonstration teaching and to teach under experimental conditions.

Before the school was first opened, in 1915, serious consideration was given to the possibility of demonstrating in the school a radically re-organized curriculum which should represent a new synthesis of values, a new grading, and may radical departures in method. This plan was abandoned in the belief that a radical departure from customary practice could not be readily utilized by public schools because of a lack of suitable textbooks, trained teachers, adequate courses of study, appropriate equipment, and intelligent support on the part of school patrons. It seemed better to devote the efforts of the supervisory and teaching staff of the University Elementary School to such reorganizations of present school subjects and to such improvements of teaching as can be expected to be taken over immediately or at least very soon by the public schools of the state. In other words, the school has interested itself in improvements which can be made with certainty in public schools, rather than with visionary possibilities which could be utilized by public schools rarely, and only in the future, if at all. Accordingly, the school has attempted to make its contribution by demonstrating to teachers and superintendents of the state and to students of the University, the most progressive and efficient courses of study in the prominent elementary-school subjects, as well as the most efficient methods of teaching these subjects.

Demonstrating the Contributions of Others

For the stimulation of the students and faculty of the University, as well as the teachers and supervisors of the state, the school has regularly organized parts of its course of study to demonstrate contributions made elsewhere or to make concrete the issues involved in important curriculum controversies. For example, certain units of Dr. Burke's individual instruction plan were demonstrated, studied, and tested. Many of the curriculum-practices and printed exercises developed by Dr. Courtis have been demonstrated and evaluated. The course of study in handwriting exemplifies that developed by Dr. Frank Freeman and Miss Mary Dougherty. Such demonstrations of the practices and proposals of the leaders in curriculum-construction have been an invaluable stimulation to the staff of the school, to the students in training, and to supervisors and teachers of the state. These demonstrations do much to prevent uncritical biases and the faults of indoctrination. They also show both staff and students the value of open-mindedness and coöperation in curriculum-construction.

The Use of the School as a Laboratory

The school is regularly used for the preliminary work which is necessary in formulating experiments conducted by the faculty and graduate students of the College of Education. All experiments are closely observed and the results carefully measured, not merely as a part of the experiment itself, but also to avoid wasting the time of the students. Critics of experimentation should keep in mind the fact that the introduction of any new method in a public school is a kind of rough experiment. In controlled experiments, however, poor results are quickly discovered, and the procedure used in the experimental method, if unsatisfactory, is abandoned.

The danger of drawing final conclusions from these preliminary experiments has been emphasized at all times. It is recognized that pupils, teachers, and conditions are not typical. Changes in method or in course of study are not recommended to public schools until the experiments have been repeated under public-school conditions. In all experiments, both in the University Elementary School and in the public schools, the greatest care has been taken to protect the pupils against any possibility of exploitation. No experiments are undertaken merely to satisfy curiosity. Curricular reorganizations or changes in methods are introduced only when they promise a definite improvement over what is now being taught in the schools.

The experimental work which can be carried on in the University Elementary School is very limited, not only because of the possible damage to the children themselves, but also because of possible interference of one experiment with another. The staff of the school and the students who experiment in it have kept in mind the fact that the school must be first of all a good school, and that to be a good school it must have, in the main, continuity of subject matter, point of view, and method.

Principles Which Have Guided the Making of the Curriculum

The staff of the school has held from the outset that the problems of the curriculum and the problems of method must be considered together. The chief principles which have been kept in mind in making the course of study are as follows:

1. The curriculum must be based on an analysis of the most important, the most universal, and most permanent values in life. Since curriculum-making in the University schools has proceeded by subjects, the first step has been to determine what is the func-

tion or functions of each subject in life outside the school. The second step has been to determine the chief knowledges, abilities, skills, attitudes, and appreciations which are needed in fulfilling its principal function or functions. The third step has been to determine the best grade-placement, the best organization, and the best method for developing these knowledges, abilities, skills, attitudes, and appreciations.

2. The course of study has been made, for the most part, by the joint efforts of the teaching and supervisory staff of the school, working in combination with the seminar in elementary supervision. All who participate recognize clearly that curriculum-making is the most difficult and technical task in the profession and that each step in making the course of study in any subject must be taken in the light of all existing scientific data, as well as under the guidance of the best expert judgment.

Every teacher of the school has realized that the traits which should constitute the objectives of the course of study are too important to leave to the chance interests of children or to such planning as the teacher may do from day to day and from term to term. The teachers believe that children and parents have a right to expect that no part of the course of study shall be introduced into the school until it shall have been perfected by the most critical and scientific analysis, and until satisfactory and appropriate methods of learning have been devised.

This does not mean that the course of study is inelastic or that the interests and present needs of children are neglected. That such needs and interests are utilized is clearly indicated in the third principle, which follows.

3. The needs and opportunities of children at each stage in their development have been constantly kept in mind, not only as one guide to method, but also as one criterion to be used for the selecting and grading of the course of study. Special emphasis has been placed upon the necessity of continually improving the conduct of each child in his present life outside the school. Situations which confront not only the child but also the adult are regarded as having a special significance in the organization of the curriculum. The entire staff has felt strongly the need for a more scientific analysis of the situations which confront children in life out-

side the school as well as in school. Important beginnings have been made in satisfying this need.

4. The value of each unit of subject matter is developed with the children with the utmost sincerity and frankness. It is recognized that children must be taught to distinguish large values from those that are smaller or even insignificant, and that to do this they must develop the same permanent standards of value which have always served thoughtful people.

5. For the reasons just enumerated, the school has labored hard to develop on the part of pupils a distaste for mere puttering, as well as for foolish, indirect devices. In the opinion of the staff of the school this attempt has been made with marked success. For example, the children are interested in working out such practical problems with their hands as are involved in making bird boxes and finishing furniture. They are not easily interested in concrete projects which have no usable outcome. The following example illustrates the attitude of the children toward devices: After a visiting demonstrator, by means of a song to the tune of "Katy," had attempted to interest them in the proper mastication of their food, one boy was heard to remark quietly to another as the class left the room: "How does she get that way?" This boy's language may not be all that could be desired, but his reaction to the device is sound.

6. The administration of classroom work and the general machinery of the school organization has been kept as simple as possible. The children have a very large and active part in the conduct of the school, but there is little of the formidable election of officers and drawing up of rules which so often accompany pupil participation in school government.

7. Pupils are at all times encouraged to work freely and under their own initiative, but with a strong sense of responsibility for getting something done, and for coöperating in a helpful way with the class group as a whole.

8. Pupils have been led to see the need for drill and for providing for memorizing important items. They share with the teacher the appraisal of each lesson, and coöperate in setting up plans for needed additional practice, and for such reviews as will guarantee the retention of important facts and principles for future use.

Conclusion

The staff of the school recognizes that the course of study is by no means perfect. Many basic problems are as yet unsolved. And yet, in spite of the limitations under which the school has worked in its attempt to render the greatest service to the College of Education and to the state at large, it is not unlikely that the present curriculum is superior to what would have been made, had a radical and wholesale reorganization been attempted. Critics of present courses of study in public schools often lose sight of the fact that the 'ideal' course of study has not yet been made, even in its rough outlines, and that very few of the accompanying problems of methods, grading, and equipment have been solved. Schools which have made extremely radical changes in their curricula do not at present seem to be doing as much for their students as do the best public schools through their improved courses of study, organized around the standard elementary-school subjects.

However, a valuable service could be rendered through the organization of an experimental school in which the course of study should be organized around the chief groups of activities and situations in life, without taking into consideration the present subjects which are now in the course of study. The staff of such a school should be given ample time to prepare for their work and should include a number of individuals trained in curricular research and in experimentation in learning. Moreover, little can be gained by founding such a school until the scientific analysis of life's values is more nearly complete than it is now.

CHAPTER XVIII

THE McDONALD COUNTY, MISSOURI, EXPERIMENTAL SCHOOL[1]

ELLSWORTH COLLINGS
College of Education, University of Oklahoma, Norman, Oklahoma

It was the intent of this experiment in a one-room country school that the chief variable should be the curriculum. One group of children, forty-one in number, called the "Experimental School," used a curriculum selected directly from their purposes in real life. Another group, called "Control Schools," used a conventional curriculum, known in Missouri as the "State Course of Study." In this experiment, the standings of the children for the year 1917 in the 'three R's' were determined by the use of standard tests for both groups. Four years later, in September 1921, the children were compared in their achievements in the common facts and skills. In 1921 the children of the Experimental School were also compared with the achievements represented by the National Standards.

The results in the common facts and skills at the end of the four years show that, of sixty-eight median achievement scores, the Experimental School was superior in all when compared with the Control Schools, and of fifty-seven median achievement scores, the Experimental School was superior in thirty-six when compared with the National Standards. These comparisons include measurements of the two groups in the following functions: penmanship; written composition; reading comprehension; American history information; geographical information; spelling accuracy; and accuracy in addition, subtraction, multiplication, and division. In other outcomes not subject to measurement by available tests, there are substantial evidences of very desirable changes in the attitudes of children and parents toward the school and education, in the conduct of pupils outside the school, and in many phases of community life. These are noted in more detail later. The school had changed from a "ragged beggar sleeping" beside the road into a veritable social center, active in the improvement of community life.

---

[1] From *An Experiment with a Project Curriculum.* The Macmillan Co., 1923.

The curriculum was selected directly from the purposes of boys and girls and was under continuous construction as the experiment progressed through the coöperative efforts of the supervisor, teachers, and pupils of the school. No use was made of existing courses of study, since this was an experiment in constructing a curriculum in terms of the purposes of boys and girls. The curriculum was classified under four kinds of projects: Story Projects, Hand Projects, Play Projects, and Excursion Projects. The daily program of studies included these four divisions and no more. The traditional school subjects were not taught, as such, to the boys and girls of the experimental school. The subject matter of these subjects received attention only when it contributed genuinely to a more effective realization of the purposes of boys and girls at the time. This use of subject matter does not mean, as sometimes interpreted, that children's purposes are utilized for the sake of teaching so much—say minimal essentials of reading, arithmetic, writing, history, etc. It means exactly the opposite. Subject matter is used for the sake of what it contributes to a more satisfying realization of child purposes. The purpose is primary and dominates in defining the activity that is to eventuate in its realization. Subject matter, as here interpreted, is the activity. In this sense, subject matter plays a very important rôle in child life; it is an intrinsic part of child life. With the Control Schools, exactly the reverse aim was practiced. Mastery of so much arithmetic, history, geography, spelling, writing, etc., within a certain specific time was the primary aim of these schools, and if child purposes were used at all, they were used as means for achieving this aim. Subject matter, in the traditional sense, was thus their primary aim.

In the development of the curriculum, the following principles were used as basic guides:

1. The school should further the continuous growing of boys and girls. The child receives from its ancestry a system of inborn tendencies which insure its growth under certain conditions. The child's active tendencies induce him to experiment with this world of things and people around him, and as a result of this active experimentation, the tendencies themselves undergo change—they grow. In playing Roly Poly, for example, he plays heartily into the game and begins active experimentation with the balls, bowling

at the Roly Polys, arranging them on the triangle, keeping score, etc. His purpose as his chief guide, however, defines his action in each instance—tells him his successes from his failures—and directs him in his observation, selecting, and testing of movements that enable him eventually to participate successfully with his other friends in the game.

The child undergoes two sorts of simultaneous changes as a result of his Roly Poly experience: (1) primary changes which have to do with specific habits connected with learning the technique of the game; and (2) concomitant changes which have to do with attitudes—attitudes toward experimenting with new things, toward variation and invention of new movements in the game, toward the teacher and other pupils as genuine co-partners, toward the game as a satisfactory activity, toward the school as a place for doing real things, toward the belief that it pays to try and to put forth effort, etc. Since these 'concomitant' outcomes, or attitudes, are projective, they lead the child on to further experimenting in the Roly Poly game or in other games and consequently to more 'primary' outcomes. It is in this fashion that the child continues to grow through a continuous building of habits, attitudes, etc. The most consistent function of the school would seem to be to provide an environment that furthers the continuous growth of its pupils—an environment that affords them practice in the selection and successful realization of purposes.

2. The teacher should guide boys and girls in the selection of purposes in real life. The function of the teacher in guiding boys and girls in selection of purposes is to provide a school environment suggestive of numerous and varied child purposes and to allow the child freedom under his guidance to select wisely these purposes.

The school environment probably most conducive to child purposes is similar to that of the better home. The outstanding feature of such a home environment is that it provides richly for social converse, observation of natural phenomena, and participation in various occupations and leisure activities. As such, it engages all of the basic tendencies—play, exploratory, communicative, and manipulative—of boys and girls. Following this lead, the first function of the teacher is to afford his pupils opportunity to continue their active participation in the real world about them—a world of games, sports, stories, natural phenomena, social converse, and occupations.

Since boys and girls pursue both individual and group purposes, selection is accordingly by individuals and by groups. In the former it is a coöperative matter between the individual pupil and the teacher, while in the latter it involves a group of individuals among whom the teacher is one. In group selection, each member, including the teacher, should freely suggest any purpose that he or she would like to have the group pursue. As the purposes are then suggested, one member should record them on the blackboard. The members of the group, the teacher included, should then discuss each in an informal manner, pointing out what they may get out of the proposed purposes, means available, and possibility of pursuing them. After this thorough scrutiny of the purposes suggested, the group should select one from the proposed list for group participation, a majority of the pupils controlling selection. Other purposes suggested and considered feasible should be recorded on the Project Bulletin Board. Then, too, as purposes are from time to time suggested, pupils individually or collectively should record them on this board as candidates for further consideration.

The criteria for selecting purposes are two: (1) practicability, and (2) the quality of 'leading on.' The criterion of practicability limits selection to purposes clearly conceived by the child and capable of guiding him in the processes of planning, executing, and judging. The growth of the child depends upon his ability to translate a foreseen end into pertinent means and to execute effectively these means. The criterion of practicability also proposes that purposes be selected with reference to available resources. This criterion proposes that the teacher guide boys and girls in the selection of only those purposes that lend themselves to successful realization in the sense that they can be carried through on the child level, by the use of resources that are available.

The second criterion of growth, that of activity that leads to further activity, proposes to evaluate fruitfulness of the child's purposes on the basis, first, of continuous action, and second, of branching action. The first of these criteria involves the selection of purposes which inherently possess the possibility of a continuous series of activities. An instance of such a purpose is Christene's purpose to make her doll an apron. This project did, in point of fact, suggest to her the purpose to make her doll a cap; the cap project suggested to her the purpose to make a pair of doll stockings; this suggested a doll rug; this, a chest for her doll clothing; this, a purpose to make her doll a new dress; this, to make herself a school apron; this, to study the different kinds of materials and styles for making aprons; this, the study of the sources of these materials. Inherently, the school apron project possesses the possibility and the probability of suggesting still other projects to Christene as she grows older. Thus, it is seen how the outcomes of one of her purposes suggest and prepare for succeeding ones.

As to branching action, the criterion of activity leading to further activity further proposes to limit selection to purposes that inherently possess the possibility and probability of suggesting other and different lines of purposes in the process of realization. Christene's original purpose to make her doll an apron is also an instance of such branching activity as the continuous activity developed. It led to the use of other materials, other processes, and other tools in what followed from it. Making the doll apron involved sewing materials and processes; the doll rug, weaving materials and processes; the doll furniture, woodworking materials and processes; the doll dishes, pottery materials and processes, etc. Christene's original purpose intrinsically possessed the possibility of continuous, branching activity. The very growth of the child depends upon the outcomes of one purpose ever suggesting and preparing for succeeding ones.

The criteria admit of two possible ways for initiating satisfactory purposes. In the first place, the pupil or pupils may suggest a purpose and the teacher may approve the suggestion on the basis of the proposed criteria; in the second place, the teacher may propose a purpose in the light of the proposed criteria and the pupil or pupils may accept the suggestive purpose. In either instance, the teacher is the sole judge of the final interpretation of the fruitfulness of proffered purposes on the basis of the proposed criteria.

3. The teacher should guide boys and girls in successful realization of purposes in real life. When the purpose has been selected, the teacher's function is to guide the pupils: (1) in working out plans for attaining it, (2) in executing the plans, and (3) in criticising the finished product. Here, as in the case of selecting purposes, the teacher should, by all means, allow pupils freedom in observing,

selecting, arranging, and testing means with reference to purposes set up. Planning, executing, and criticising should come from the pupils and not from some nicely drawn up procedure of the teacher. The fundamentals of guidance, here, are: (1) supplying sources of reference, materials, tools, apparatus, etc.; (2) suggesting indirectly by questioning ways of overcoming seemingly insurmountable difficulties that arise; and (3) approving or disapproving phases of the work in the process of realizing the purpose.

Results of the Use of This Curriculum Not Measured by School Achievement Tests

Reference has already been made to the results of this experiment as measured by school achievement tests. As one further summary of the achievements of the pupils, the results of the tests at the end of the four years of experimentation showed that the average equated time that it would take the Control Schools to equal the achievements of the Experimental School would be .382 of a school year. That is, to reach the average standing achieved by the Experimental School would require a little more than a third of a school year of *further* work by the Control Schools.

By a survey made by the writer, it was found that in twelve of the ordinary phases of conduct of pupils in life outside of the school studied in this experiment, standings were practically the same for both Experimental and Control schools at the beginning of the school year 1917. A very marked divergence in these phases of conduct of pupils is to be found between the schools for the 1921 measurements. The improvements in percentages shown by the 1921 survey in these functions for the two school groups, respectively, are shown in Table I.

From a similar survey of changes in the conduct of parents of the children in the two schools, improvements shown in 1921 in some of their activities are as presented in Table II.

The foregoing data, and many other data not here included, furnish concrete evidence that the isolation of the Experimental School from its community which existed before the experiment, had been, for the most part, broken down in the four years. On the other hand, the Control Schools had made very little progress during this period in overcoming their isolation, for the obvious reason

TABLE I.—PERCENTAGES OF IMPROVEMENT IN CONDUCT OF PUPILS OUTSIDE OF SCHOOL

Number of:	Percentages	
	In Exp. School	In Control Schools
Story books read in homes, in addition to school work	87.5	5.0
Children reading one or more newspapers in home	62.0	5.0
Children studying instrumental music	39.0	3.0
Children participating in community activities	100.0	0.0
Children engaging in social parties in homes	66.7	13.0
Children carrying on project work at home during vacation	69.8	6.7
Children reading six or more story books during vacation	70.8	7.9
Children reading one or more magazines in homes	65.8	22.5
Children practicing the ordinary health habits in homes	81.0	3.0
Children less attacked by common diseases	35.0	25.0
Children participating in games at home	84.9	30.0
Children saving ten or more dollars from earnings in vacation	68.0	2.0

that this weakness for the most part was inherent in the curriculum used in these schools. A study of the ordinary activities of life outside of the schools in the Control School districts reveals the very interesting fact that there is practically no correlation whatever

TABLE II.—PERCENTAGES OF IMPROVEMENT IN CONDUCT OF PARENTS

Number of parents	Percentages	
	In Exp. School	In Control Schools
Reading farm journals	96.0	3.8
Reading daily newspapers	56.4	6.6
Attendance regularly at night community meetings	75.6	25.0
Participation in community fair and play day	91.0	0.0
Testing seed corn	48.1	21.0
Testing milk of dairy cows	58.8	17.0
Changing from common breeds to thoroughbred poultry	31.0	7.2
Changing from mixed breeds to thoroughbred dairy cows	23.0	5.0
Less stricken with contagious diseases	20.0	4.9

between what people do outside of the school and what pupils do inside.

In practically every activity studied, the Experimental School improved more than fifty percent. This might be expected since the curriculum of this school was selected directly from the purposes of boys and girls in real life. The effective realization of these purposes not only influenced the immediate conduct of the pupils in life outside of school, but, in addition, reacted positively upon the conduct of their parents in the home and community.

CHAPTER XIX

FUNDAMENTAL CONSIDERATIONS UNDERLYING THE CURRICULUM OF THE FRANCIS W. PARKER SCHOOL

FLORA J. COOKE, Principal, and RAYMOND W. OSBORNE, Assistant Principal, Francis W. Parker School, Chicago, Illinois

GENERAL PRINCIPLES

The Francis W. Parker School accepts as its principal aim the training of character through vital social experience and for useful community life. It is our belief that the principle of coöperation, rather than selfish competition, should be stressed in all study and in every phase of daily living, and that in a wider application and acceptance of this principle lies our best hope for future betterment and progress. It is a far cry from the present attitude of the world about us to the acceptance of this idea of coöperation and to a system of education which would teach children from birth, actively, day by day, by precept and example, that fear and hate, greed and revenge, are not only wrong in principle, but utterly stupid because of the futility of their results. A system of education which is to develop the idea of coöperation among its pupils must teach them to observe fearlessly, to form judgment slowly, to maintain an eager open mind; must stimulate in each one a desire for thorough knowledge on which to base individual judgment and action; and must keep them constantly in contact with existing social phenomena wherever there are important happenings.

We believe it is the duty of the schools to emphasize much more than at present the preparation of youth for those demands which our country must soon make upon this generation, for definite knowledge of world affairs, for enlightened leadership from those who can lead, and for intelligent coöperation from those who must follow. We must break down the idea that it is sufficient to keep children busy and happy in an isolated and protected area, detached from the larger area of the world about them, with its pressing problems to be solved. Children can participate usefully and practically in selected civic and governmental affairs. They can consider intelligently certain world problems—especially those similar in nature or principle to those in small school communities which demand their loyalty and service.

In attempting to develop a curriculum which would utilize and develop the principle of coöperation throughout all the grades of the school, the 'social group project' has been found to be the best form of organization for our classroom practice.[1] We believe that this method of work tends to ingrain deeply in the child's experience those habits of thought and action, those satisfactions and joys, which come naturally from working intelligently with one's fellows to accomplish purposes which seem important to all the workers. A social group project provides abundant opportunity for original investigation, for creative effort and expression, and for individual and group enterprise, since, in working on such a project, the pupil has, in addition to his own interest, a shared responsibility for bringing back something of value to others.

This emphasis upon group work does not mean neglect of the individual. We believe that for purposes of development, children must be treated as individuals and not as a group. The individual must remain the pivot of our attention. But we would not have the individual center his own attention too much upon himself, his own attainments and progress, but have him find satisfaction in creative activity and achievement rather than in selfish competition for the first place in the class. We would not sacrifice the child to the group, but it is our opinion that he finds in the group the most natural and effectual stimulus to his best endeavor.

We believe that self-actuated work results in the greatest gain to the pupil, and therefore we seek to encourage self-initiated, individual, and small group projects, to foster special interests and to allow time for such activity on the regular school program. We should, however, avoid the danger of over-stressing unrelated individual work.

Since children differ greatly in power to grasp and retain, the amount of *drill* which individuals receive must always vary greatly in any group. Each child should have enough drill to give him adequate control of the tools of learning which he needs and no more.

---

[1] The limits of this article prevent further explanation of the meaning of the term ''Social Group Project'' as used in our school, but a full description, with many examples, is given in our publications, *Studies in Education*.

We would have the child from the beginning see the relationship between drill in the common essentials and the more creative activities which alone give to tool subjects their proper significance. In other words, we would have the skills in common essentials appear as felt needs, not extraneous goals, or objectives. If the child sees such relationship, he will welcome drill as a necessity in order to gain the skill which will enable him to save time in accomplishing his purpose. Technique, however valuable in real life, is not an end in itself, and any plan for gaining skill, isolated from its natural setting, is out of harmony with the process by which the child normally gains technique outside the school. In too many schools we see both teachers and pupils so concerned in getting control of tools that they have little time to use the tools for constructive and creative purposes.

We know from experience that the child does not have an opportunity to develop desirable habits of social usefulness under arbitrary dictation from the teacher or with high marks as the chief incentive. We realize that the principle of choice is a prime factor in a representative form of democratic government, and that training children to choose rightly should be continually stressed. We propose to fill every day with opportunities involving choice, both in academic work and in conduct, just as we plan to fill it with work involving interest, effort, initiative, and social responsibility. We cannot, however, go to the length of those radical leaders in education who would give the child the choice of subject matter and of activity throughout the day. It seems to us that the child has neither the wisdom nor the experience which will enable him to satisfy his intellectual hunger and supply his mental necessities, any more than he has the ability to select wholesome food and a balanced ration with which to nourish properly his body.

We believe that the teacher is responsible for creating a rich and stimulating environment, and for selecting the larger units of study which make up the curriculum. This is because the teacher realizes on the one hand the child's capacity, his natural interests and ability, and on the other, those great forces and ideas which have moved civilization forward, and he can select the fundamental experiences of the race which no child should lose. Our curriculum is classified under subject headings. The course of study is reference material for the teachers, but its underlying principles endure.

However, the projects in each field of learning vary greatly from year to year, according to the interests, maturity, and ability of the grade groups. The teachers of the school are further responsible for seeing that the child's experience in the school is unified, that certain threads of experience shall be traceable throughout the length and breadth of the curriculum; that is, that the skills and knowledge gained in one grade are used as far as possible in those which follow it. Colonel Parker says: "But knowledge is boundless and the pupils can get but a drop of the ocean. What knowledge can we present, then, in the years that we have them under our care and guidance? What rules shall govern us in the selection? The answer is not far to seek: Our selections can be entirely governed by what each pupil needs for his personal development. He needs that knowledge which will enable him to best serve his school and the world. The two answers are one: The needs of the school and the needs of the world are the needs of the individual.

We believe that the teacher is responsible for seeing that every avenue of a child's soul is open and in continual use; that as far as possible the day is filled with delightful work, hard work, worthwhile work; that in his early years the child has the opportunity to paint, draw, model, cook, sing, sew, dance; to construct, to read, and to write; and that he gains some measure of control over the fundamental tools of civilization—some experience in its occupations and arts which have brought mankind to the present level of society; and finally, that the teacher is responsible for seeing that the children's expression and effort result in satisfying achievement. There should be no such thing in the child's life as a sense of utter failure or of hopeless discouragement after he has put forth his best effort. In other words, the work should be within the capacity of the child—difficult enough to take all his energy and full of obstacles to overcome—but he should find all along the way that inspiration and impetus which only success and the sense of growing power can give him.

It goes without saying in this day and age that the use of standard and achievement tests are a part of our program, for the sake of the insight and knowledge which they throw upon the ability of the children, but not for classification of children into superior and inferior groups. In order to keep the teachers' attention upon all phases of children's development, in addition to the records of standard tests and measurements, other complete records are kept throughout the school. But more than ever we need to keep our vision clear to the value of those elements of life and education which *cannot be measured* and which give the highest aspiration and inspiration, which create in us standards of taste and attitude toward life which go far to protect us from any ugliness and sordidness in our environment. To this end children need to have daily contact with beauty in many forms, to live in an atmosphere in which beauty is considered a prime essential, from the point of view of both impression and expression.

We believe that creative expression[2] is fundamental to the child's fullest development, to his happiness and spiritual growth. All normal children have the right to live in a rich and stimulating environment, and to exercise to the full their powers of expression. Not everyone can contribute to the permanent beauty of the world, but it is the privilege of every school to create conditions which should arouse each child to express freely in some chosen form his own best ideas, inspirations, and emotions.

Technique of Construction

In the Francis W. Parker School the classroom teachers have always helped to determine and develop the curriculum. These teachers have been free to modify both content and method to fit the needs of particular groups of children. They have been encouraged to experiment, even radically to change the content of the curriculum, subject only to the condition that they be able to convince the faculty and the principal of the desirability of the experiment or of the value of the innovation that they wish to make. The resulting spirit of freedom and of coöperative responsibility has had a vital influence, not only in shaping the actual curriculum, but also in building up the spirit of the school—that intangible something which determines its individuality.

The curriculum as it exists to-day is the result of an evolutionary process constantly at work to refine and better to adapt the subject matter to the needs of the pupil. The strong personalities of many teachers have stamped it indelibly with their influence, and

[2] Volume VIII of *Studies in Education*, entitled "Creative Effort," presents the varied opportunities for creative work of this kind throughout the school. It is very fully illustrated by the work of the pupils.

it has grown by the coöperative study and effort of the teachers themselves, guided but not directed by the principals or department heads.

The gradual development of the curriculum under this principle is perhaps best illustrated by the course in history, in which the social aspects of history are stressed. The basis for the selection of subject matter is found in the varying characteristics, abilities, and stages of development of the children. Some vital period or chapter in the history of human progress, some typical race experience, illuminated with lasting achievement and characterized by high heroic action, is chosen for intensive study in each grade. The problems in each intensive experience demand initiative, invention, and creative imagination, and provide for contact with beauty in many forms. They give daily opportunity for a varied and satisfying achievement in self-expression. The knowledge content of the course performs two functions, furnishing an appropriate background for the children's own experiences and activities, and spurring them on to further questioning with stimulating information with which to face new obstacles and difficulties. The history course which has been developed through many years of use seems to lack chronological sequence and continuity. It is our belief that this criticism, while justified, is offset by the fact that the children live so intensively and joyously the typical experiences selected, presenting, as they do, universal life problems that they themselves unconsciously come to organize and classify their ideas and knowledge, with a resultant feeling of continuity and progress.[3]

A more consciously studied and systematic curriculum development is found in the course in science. Here, the teachers of the elementary grades and the science teachers, as a group, formulated and agreed upon certain fundamental controlling principles for the science work of the school, and then, with these principles in mind, critically examined the science work of each grade, both as a unit in itself and also to see if an adequate experience and contact with science materials was assured for the pupils in their progres-

---

[3] This course in history is printed as Volume VII of the Francis W. Parker School *Studies in Education*. The results of other curriculum studies are also presented in other volumes of this series. Especially to be mentioned are Volume V, "The Course in Science," and Volume VI, "The Individual and the Curriculum."

sion from grade to grade through the high school. The fundamental principles and experiences of science with which pupils should come in contact in the elementary school were agreed upon, and the attempt was made to place such topics in grades best fitted to pursue them, and to work out the experimental procedure best adapted to the pupils of those particular grades.

While the classroom teachers have had a determining influence in shaping and modifying the curriculum, it has been found useful and necessary to provide checks and limits to the individual interests and preferences of the teachers, in the form of definite minimal essential requirements for each grade in such tool subjects as English, spelling, and mathematics. Again, the formulation of these minimal requirements[4] has been done by groups of teachers under the leadership of the departmental specialists or principals. Some phase of this study is a constant faculty activity, and these so-called 'minimal essentials' are subject to repeated revision in the light of experience.

The development of large group projects, which is characteristic of our school practice, has had a vital influence upon the curriculum and has developed an extremely valuable type of correlation, in which the entire work of the grade centers. This may include the work of the special teachers in art, handwork, literature, etc., over a long period of time. For example, the work of the third grade for a considerable portion of the year is focused upon the development of Chicago. The problems studied are the social, industrial, and economic problems which the city has had to meet in its rapid development from a trading post to a great metropolis. The science work of the grade contributes to this central theme through studies of fur-bearing animals and fur-trading, through study of problems of water supply and purification, of simple pumps, and the elementary physics and chemistry necessary to the understanding of such problems. In their handwork the pupils make models of block houses and forts, of prairie schooners and freight cars. In their art they draw and model scenes typical of the stages of the development of the city. The stories of early explorers, of pioneers of the West, and of Chicago's leading citizens, are a large part of the

[4] These minimal essentials are stated in the school catalogue under each grade.

literature studied by the grades during this time. They write their own stories, and illustrate them with original drawings, so building up and writing their own history of the city. The needed drill in spelling and penmanship is motivated by their desire to write and make their histories neat and legible.[5]

The importance of training pupils to develop habits of social usefulness by constant opportunities for the exercise of choice in work and conduct, has been mentioned as one of the important fundamental considerations in curriculum-construction. In the upper grades, especially in the high school, such opportunities are found in the largest measure and of the most vital kind in those activities of the pupils that are commonly considered outside of the curriculum. We consider as vital parts of the curriculum the student government, with its various subsidiary organizations, the work of getting out the student publications,[6] "The Weekly" and "The Record," the school "Forum," which meets once a month in the evening and gives opportunity for development of individual interests in a socially useful way. The program provides regularly scheduled times for the conduct of these activities. In them flower much of the work of classroom and laboratory.

Finally, in theory and in practice, in incentive and result, in inspiration and in general content of curricula, we believe our once a week evening faculty meeting and our daily morning exercises[7] at which the whole school is assembled are the two features most necessary to any adequate or satisfactory functioning of the school's purpose. Through these media of organization we are brought into focus with, and become aware of, all that is best and most useful in the school; we sense its needs and opportunities; we learn to understand each other and to recognize the ability, the gifts and service of every member of the group; we give and take, lead and follow, and form the habit of balancing freedom with responsi-

[5] Another example of this type of correlation is the study of weaving as developed in the second grade. See *Studies in Education*, Volume VII, "The Course in History," Second Grade.

[6] Two booklets, "Student Government in the Francis W. Parker School," and "The Parker Weekly, the History and Organization of the School Paper," are available, and show the place these organizations have in the school. Both of these pamphlets were compiled and published by students upon their own initiative.

[7] See Volume II, *Studies in Education*, "The Morning Exercise as a Socializing Influence."

bility; we share, according to our capacities, in all the burdens and privileges which membership in such a community involves. The following quotation from Colonel Parker voices our belief that education which develops character is the only form which justifies a school's existence in a democracy and is the only valid test of a curriculum: "Character, constantly realizing itself in practical citizenship, in community life, in complete living, is the immediate, everlasting, and only purpose of the school."

CHAPTER XX

THE TECHNIQUE OF CURRICULUM-CONSTRUCTION IN THE HORACE MANN SCHOOL, TEACHERS COLLEGE, NEW YORK CITY

HENRY CARR PEARSON
Professor of Education and Principal of Horace Mann School
Teachers College, Columbia University, New York City

In the early years of its history, the Horace Mann School aimed to be both a practice and a demonstration school, but about twenty-five years ago practice teaching was abandoned and the school confined its attention to illustrating the best modern methods of teaching, with some emphasis upon experimentation in the newer methods of instruction. While the advent of the Lincoln School as an experimental station into the family of the Teachers College schools has more sharply emphasized the function of the Horace Mann School as a school of demonstration, it has never seemed wise or proper to abandon completely the experimental aspects of its work. Any school that gives up entirely its desire to venture into new fields will lose its progressive spirit and will thereby soon cease to be valuable as a place of demonstration.

The present aim of the Horace Mann School, therefore, is to demonstrate the best methods of accepted educational policies, to have an open-minded attitude toward successful methods employed in other schools, and to incorporate those methods into its own body of educational practice whenever scientific investigation shows that they may be wisely used. In a word, the Horace Mann School aims to be progressive, but not radical.

EARLY CURRICULUM-CONSTRUCTION

In the early days, the Horace Mann School was more closely identified with Teachers College than is the case now. Professors of various subjects in the College were supervisors in their respective fields in the school and often taught classes of children. This practice had many disadvantages as well as advantages. The several supervisors, being personally and vitally interested in pushing the claims of their subjects in the curriculum of the school, were often more successful than was wise in securing time and recognition for their respective fields. The result was an unbalanced curriculum. To remedy the situation, the principal of the school was given final authority in determining the materials that should enter into the curriculum.

In 1906 a comprehensive reorganization of the curriculum of the Horace Mann School was undertaken. This was a coöperative enterprise; each teacher made a special study of materials and methods of the work with which she was most familiar, and prepared written statements of this material for inclusion in the general curriculum. A committee, consisting of the principal of the school, Professor F. M. McMurry, and two teachers, attempted to modify and coördinate these reports from the classroom teachers so that they would fit properly into the general whole. The supervisors of the various departments concerned were consulted as experts and took an active interest in the preparation of this material. The result was a volume of over five hundred pages that was published in 1908. This curriculum was revised in 1912 and again in 1917.

Present Point of View on the Curriculum

It will be seen from what has been written that it has always been the policy of the Horace Mann School to secure the fullest coöperation of teachers, supervisors, and other experts in the organization of its curriculum. We have always felt the importance of having the teachers believe in the worth of the material that the curriculum indicates should be taught in the various grades. No curriculum will ever work its way into the life of the school except through the complete coöperation of the teachers in interpreting the printed statements.

Furthermore, the Horace Mann School believes that the methods of teaching exemplified in the curriculum should, so far as possible, be based upon the best experimental evidence. For example, when we were considering the advantages of formal versus informal methods in the primary grades, a thorough-going experiment was carried on for two years with two groups of classes. The results of this experiment gave us an idea of the proper procedure for our particular school. In a similar manner, when the course of study in spelling was under revision several years ago, a series of experimental studies was carried on for three years, which aimed to show the advantages of a class method of instruction as contrasted with an independent learning method.

Types of Curriculum-Construction

Since the last published statement of the Horace Mann curriculum appeared in 1917, there has been no attempt to rewrite the curriculum as a whole, but courses of study in various subjects have been made or are in process of construction.

1. Less than ten years ago, when it was decided that the course of study in spelling needed revision, a careful investigation was conducted among pupils of the Horace Mann School to find out what words were most commonly used in their writing vocabularies. This vocabulary study was subsequently checked against similar studies in other schools, until a Horace Mann list of words was selected which became the basis of our course of study in spelling. At about the same time, investigations were carried on in method, as has been mentioned before. More recently, a spelling notebook has been devised through the coöperation of graduate students and teachers of this school which will simplify the method of teaching spelling under classroom conditions. This represents in brief the methods that have been used in reorganizing our course of study in spelling.

2. Within the past two years a course of study in health education has been developed through the coöperation of Dr. Thomas D. Wood, of Teachers College, and his associates, assisted by teachers of the school. Suggestions for much of the material were received from a questionnaire that was sent to patrons of the school. Units of instruction employing this new material were taught by advanced students of Teachers College until the course of study was worked out in its present form.

3. A fusion course of study in the social studies is now being developed for use in our Junior High School. This piece of work has been under way for two years under the personal direction of Mr. Roy W. Hatch, of the Horace Mann School, and Mr. DeForest Stull, Associate in Geography in Teachers College. The material in this course is being tried under normal classroom conditions and

will appear in experimental form in a separate pamphlet within a few months.

4. A new course of study in elementary science is now in process of construction under the guidance of Mr. Gerald Craig. In this work Mr. Craig has been assisted by a large number of graduate students from Teachers College and by instructors in other institutions. Units of instruction in this course are being tried in various classrooms in order to determine their best placement.

5. A course of study in geography has been completed under the general direction of Mr. DeForest Stull and the geography teachers of the Horace Mann School. In this course of study, as well as in several others, we have availed ourselves of the findings of the Bureau of Curriculum Inquiry at Teachers College and have had the assistance of a large number of graduate students of Teachers College in various investigations.

6. Professor C. B. Upton, of Teachers College, who is supervisor of arithmetic in the Horace Mann School, is preparing a course of study in arithmetic. Professor Upton has had at his disposal the results obtained from the Bureau of Curriculum Inquiry of Teachers College and has had the assistance of a large number of his graduate students in mathematics. Professor Upton himself has been teaching classes in the Horace Mann School and carrying on intensive studies of method and material.

These illustrations of curriculum construction will serve to indicate in a general way how we are proceeding at present in the Horace Mann School with the reorganization of our curriculum.

CHAPTER XXI

THE PRINCIPLES OF CURRICULUM-MAKING IN THE BEAVER COUNTRY DAY SCHOOL

EUGENE RANDOLPH SMITH
Beaver Country Day School, Brookline, Massachusetts

GENERAL PRINCIPLES

In planning the curriculum at the Beaver Country Day School, several principles are felt to be fundamental. The first one is: *The work at each stage should fit the interests and abilities of the children concerned.* We believe that a child can work to the best advantage only if the work being done seems to him worth while, and if it is sufficiently well adapted to his powers to provide opportunity for hard work with the probability of success in accomplishment.

If the work does not seem worth while, and therefore does not arouse interest, the driving force from within will be lacking, and the work will be done only by virtue of some force from outside, probably furnished by teachers and parents. Such a condition is conducive neither to good accomplishment of school work, nor to the formation of the best habits of work.

Even the most difficult tasks, however, become enjoyable if the end in view seems to justify them; so the motives natural to children are taken into account, particularly in planning the social subject program for different ages. That the course should provide opportunity for hard work is evident. Improvement comes only through effort, and children themselves realize this enough to resent that which is too easy to challenge them.

On the other hand, tasks that are too difficult for accomplishment are discouraging, and instead of building up habits of efficient work, tend to break them down. The 'habit of failure' is one of the most serious that can be formed, not only because it prevents appreciation of joy in accomplishment, but even more because it breaks down the will to strive.

It may be said that there is no course possible that fits the abilities of a group of children so that each meets enough difficulty, yet does succeed. That would be true if the work were inflexible in its character. Although this carries us into the field of method, instead of curriculum-making, I think I must explain that we try to provide a range for individual contribution to any activity wide enough to allow for variation in ability to make such contributions.

But a course of study might, through interest, arouse the pupils to activity, might provide sufficient difficulty while still within their powers, and yet might be ill suited to them because of incompleteness.

We believe that all natural activities and responses of child life are within the scope of the school, and that a child should, between the home and the school, be given opportunity for expression and impression in all possible fields of development. The question of time in the curriculum will be dealt with later.

The second fundamental principle is: *The curriculum should provide a logical development for the child's future.* This, we believe, should be concerned much more with habits, skills, and means of getting information than with information for its own sake.

We do not find these two principles antagonistic, although we are quite ready to concede that no curriculum has yet been worked out to fit both perfectly. We believe that they work hand in hand, for unless a child lives a complete satisfying eleventh year, he is not rightly prepared for his twelfth year—and so for any stage of his development.

It is true, of course, that we try, to the best of our ability, to plan a logical series of steps that shall include mastery of the fundamental skills and knowledges that are indispensable in later life. It is easy, however, to swing to the extreme of making a beautifully logical scheme, viewed from the adult standpoint, that more or less completely fails to win the coöperation of the children for whom it was devised. It is also easy to overvalue our opinions of what is necessary as preparation for future study and for adulthood, unless those opinions have been scientifically formed and tested. The reports of various committees have been, therefore, the authority for our decisions in regard to many matters of logical order and content.

Perhaps I can best translate these statements of aims and difficulties into more practical form by saying that we try by our own observations and experiments, aided by all the information we can get from similar attempts by others, to decide what are the essentials for the education of our children, then we attempt so to distribute them through the school lives of the pupils that they shall answer the children's questions, supply their felt needs, stimulate them to go beyond the narrow limits of observation and investigation that might otherwise satisfy them, fit in with the underlying instincts and interests that are of varying strengths at different ages, and be, within reasonable limits of error, adapted to the thinking maturity of each age-group.

Another fundamental of our curriculum beliefs is: *The work of the children should not be entirely developed by subject-matter divisions more or less artificially built up,* and therefore more satisfying to the adult sense of order than are the natural groups suitable to children. Before the junior high school, and to some extent in that department, history, geography, nature study, current events, and civics are combined as far as possible into a single subject, from which is drawn much of the material for language expression, and to a much less degree for mathematics. While the study of literature can, and should, have many possible connections with this major interest, it must, of course, be carried on to some extent by itself, as must certain parts of mathematics that do not fit well into the larger subject.

The work done in this combined course should, we believe, also lead to expression through the arts and manual subjects. The children should draw much of their inspiration for the arts and skills, and much of their definite subject matter, if we may call it that, from the need to illustrate and express concretely what is being taken up in the academic work. This work, too, should lead them into moral and spiritual fields in a way to connect school life closely with the wider needs and ideals of the world.

To sum up this point, we are convinced that the curriculum, for the younger children in particular, should approach the blending of all interests that are so common in real life, instead of being artificially cut up into blocks designated as subjects. We realize, however, that there are limitations to such an arrangement. Special teachers must be scheduled for particular times; also, there are parts of each subject that refuse to fit into any coördinated scheme, and there are other parts that need emphasis that cannot be gotten easily in a subordinated portion of a larger project. Therefore, like most such principles, it must be applied with consideration for all the factors involved.

With a curriculum founded on such a centralized subject, a large part of each day can be left to the teacher and class to use as needs and interests dictate. There can, therefore, be a continually adjusted compromise between the ideal of the problem that includes all subjects, and the practical necessity of seeing that the tool subjects are mastered, or that some other need is met.

In the junior high school, there is much less complete combination of subjects, but social science, general mathematics, and general science are used both for survey purposes and as sources of material; English and foreign languages correlate with each other and with them, and to some extent the close relations of the elementary school are carried on through its first two years.

In the last four years of school (corresponding to the former 'high school'), however, we find no way satisfactorily to combine subjects beyond bringing out varying amounts of coöperation and 'cross reference' work between them. Perhaps at this stage, this is just as well. The maturity of the pupil justifies opening up to him distinct fields of human endeavor, requiring different methods of investigation and different methods of thought. Each subject should, if it belongs in the curriculum, contribute something to a student's mental power, his skills, his habits, or his breadth of vision, that could not equally well be gotten elsewhere.

The combination of, and inter-relation of, subjects seems to us to answer the question of time for an enriched curriculum. Much overlapping is saved by such a plan; the art and skill subjects contribute greatly to fixing the content of academic subjects, and often one investigation can serve two or more purposes, as when a pupil collects social science information, some of it possibly mathematical, organizes it, and finally presents it as a report that is subjected to English criticism.

For the thought subjects, in the primary and intermediate grades particularly, but to some extent throughout, the curriculum is a skeleton of minimal essentials; not, it is true, without suggestions for filling in, but nevertheless with much latitude left to teachers and classes, because the development of a strong interest sometimes forces the transfer of subject matter from one part of a year to another, occasionally even from one year to another.

Specific Arrangement of Subjects

Leaving this discussion of general principles, let us consider some of the more specific arrangements that result from them.

The social science central subject includes, as we have said, history, geography, civics, and current events. It might be said to be woven of two continuous threads of thought, one concerned with the pupils themselves, their surroundings, and their communities, from the smallest up to the United States and North America; the other taking up that which is more remote in time and place, and developing into a study of the world in general. In each one of the threads are involved the divisions already mentioned. The method for the study of those things immediate to the children, and particularly of those concerning their own country, is natural spiral as well as cumulative. The more important matters recur from year to year, each time with new and broader emphasis. The other thread is largely progressive, although of necessity repetition and enlargement must enter in from time to time. The thread concerned with the United States is thinner in the early stage, centering around holidays and other civic events, and coming often from likenesses and contrasts rather than from directly planned attack. Later on, it increases until it becomes the main thread, with the other as its adjunct.

In the three primary years, the children respond very strongly to primitive life, possibly because it is less complex and more easily understood by them than is present-day civilization, and so can be more easily used as material for imagination. Possibly also, because it to some extent parallels and interprets their own experiences in reaching out for the foundational things of life. This response is particularly strong in regard to the fundamental needs of food, clothing, and shelter. This second thread, therefore, takes the pupils into the lives of early uncivilized, or little civilized, peoples. Geography is accordingly little more than a condition of life until the third grade, where the more important land and water divisions and other geographical units become somewhat familiar.

The early civilizations, including those of Egypt, Palestine, and Greece, are used in the fourth year, with increasing consideration of geography in its relation to peoples and their problems. Much connection between this and the home-country thread comes out here through industrial and other comparisons. For example, the making of paper from papyrus may stimulate investigation of paper making to-day, clothing problems then and now may be compared, or the progress of the art of various countries may be traced.

In the fifth year, we found a very strong interest in the history of Europe, strongest perhaps in the period of chivalry. Consequently, Roman history is followed by mediaeval history and leads up to the European foundations for the study of United States history. The geography of Europe naturally accompanies its history, but since earlier Roman history gives an impetus for the study of Africa, that continent precedes Europe. The study of Africa, once started, naturally goes beyond what is needed for the Roman period and its general aspects are completed at this time.

The period of American exploration opens the sixth year, bringing in the continents of South and North America as a necessary accompaniment. The geography of the Oriental countries is studied almost as a separate subject, taken to complete the view of the world. Yet in many ways, it also connects with, and contrasts with, other parts of the social studies.

The first years of the junior high school probe rather deeply into present-day life, centering study about our own problems, but following our trade relations, our transportation, and our foreign affairs into all corners of the globe. It is expected that at the end of the eighth year the pupils shall have considerable knowledge and wide interests in regard to mankind, the conditions affecting his progress, and his problems, past and present.

The social sciences of the later years of the course are necessarily college preparatory histories, for which current outlines and textbooks are the foundation.

The mathematics is not hurried in the early primary years, coming in the first and second classes rather as a response to practical needs and game interests than as a superimposed task. Gradually, it takes a larger part in the curriculum, following the recommendations of various psychologists and committees and particularly the report of the National Committee. In this, as in all of the tool subjects, progress is regularly tested by standardized tests, which are used not only for diagnostic purposes, but also as a safeguard to the maintenance of curriculum standards and completeness.

The formal English is based on the usage necessary at each stage of progress: that usage is both oral and written, and comes partly from other subjects and partly from the inspiration of each pupil's reading in poetry and prose. Literature increases its proportion of the time as the pupils grow older. Oral English is required throughout the high school and much opportunity is given for presiding at meetings, writing and presenting plays, and other practical language applications.

The academic subjects for the last four years are to a large extent determined by college entrance requirements, although their content is sometimes modified or supplemented to suit individual or group needs. These requirements are, of course, considered as minimal essentials, rather than complete outlines. Some we would change if we could; for example, for many children, at least, we would probably increase the time given to social sciences, natural sciences, and the arts, at the expense, perhaps, of ancient languages.

In regard to the music, art, and skill subjects, much is still experimental, and much will always be undetermined, on account of the necessity of fitting them to varying needs. All pupils study music and at least one, often two, art or skill subjects. In addition, about half of the pupils take instrumental music at the school. In schedule-making, all such subjects are distributed through the day, partly for the purpose of relieving the continuity of academic concentration, instead of being grouped in the afternoon as subjects outside of the curriculum, and, therefore, more or less tolerated.

While this picture of our curriculum-making is of necessity very general, it indicates the flexibility of our procedure, and the principles that seem to prove themselves worth while. We hope that most of the open questions may eventually be solved by general experiment, but we should not wish to see a crystalized curriculum—or perhaps handling of the curriculum—even if it were efficient. There are so many varying elements in a group of children that the controlled flexibility of any curriculum-plan remains one of its most important attributes.

CHAPTER XXII

CURRICULUM-MAKING IN THE CITY AND COUNTRY SCHOOL

CAROLINE PRATT
Principal, City and Country School, New York City

In making our curriculum we have tried to follow the example which science has set, that is, given a group of children, we have put them in a certain 'set-up'—a set-up in which we think they stand a chance to develop their potentialities. This set-up is in the nature of an hypothesis and has come out of what we think we know of children—not school children, just children. In order to avoid school children, we began with those younger than school age, from all sorts of homes. Then we began to discover things and to modify or enlarge our set-up. This form, or hypothesis, or set-up (and I refer here to everything external to the children which stands to influence them) is the curriculum, or the form within which the school purpose operates.

It is obviously impossible to discuss these forms, which have arisen incidental to the purposes of a school, in any great detail. They are forms within forms, which arise and are abandoned as the individuals operating within them change. At times they are scarcely recognizable, at times they are obvious. Some of them are recorded and become paper formulations. Some of them establish themselves in an individual and some of them result from the experiences of a group. Because these forms are incidental to our situation they should not be taken over by others. They are sure to be misfits. All that they can do for others is to indicate a method of work.

Our set-up or set-ups are in the nature of tentative formulations to be discarded or retained. For example, we began with first a four- and then a five-year-old group, and so on, until we had covered the groups through seven years of age. The results of this experimenting by the trial and error method became, after several years, a paper formulation which we have used to test our procedure. It is also the general formulation of our record-taking: *Practical*

Activities (eventuating in industry), *Play Activities* (eventuating in art), *Special Training,* and *Organization of Information* are the four general headings. They are fairly useful if taken tentatively. They help us in our discussion of our programs, in recording them, as well as in keeping a balance in the programs themselves. We are not unmindful that play and work belong together; some of our teachers find it unnecessary to make any distinction between the two.

This formulation is by the teachers. There is no 'social' organization in the adult sense—where the formulation is made by those operating under it. This formulation by the teachers is intended to secure, however, not only the opportunities for individual development, but those for social development as well, and here I use the term 'social' in the adult sense; that is, we secure for the children opportunity to develop ability in collective formulation. In the "Play and Work Activities," for example, the children have the greatest freedom in formulating collectively and learn to do this through experiencing.

These two things, the formulations by the teachers and within these the formulations by the children, are going on side by side and check each other constantly. We call these forms "programs." They are in fact what we can indicate as curricula.

Merely as illustrative of method, rather than by way of suggesting a program for eight-year-old children, it might be to the point to treat our eight-year-old program historically.

We had a group of children, all of whom had had at least a year's experience in the school, most of them two years, and some of them even four. They were full of energy, with strong individual drives. They had evidenced considerable collective formulation as seven-year-olds through their building of a play city as well as in their dramatics. Our eight-year-old programs up to this point had been treated by the trial-and-error method. Taking both the incoming children and what we had found out about children of this age into consideration, we concluded they needed a stabilizing job which would be likely to appeal to the whole group. Miss Moore, who was to have the group, was particularly fitted to give the right kind of help to the children, because of her experience as a teacher combined with a business experience. She suggested that the 'Eights' take over the buying and selling of the school supplies. There was an immediate happy response to this throughout the school—especially from the office and Miss Moore set about studying the possibilities in the situation. I speak of this "happy" response, because I think the success of such an undertaking depends upon how far the group job can be made to appeal to the school as a whole, how much of reality it carries with it.

Miss Moore had the records of the children's previous experiences in the school to consult, the teachers who had had these particular children, and the teachers who had had Eights in the school, as well as her own experience with Eights. Before she made any formulations, she knew something of what she had to meet, both as to personalities and as to attainments. Her formulations contained the possibility of taking over all supplies or only part of them. She outlined the possibilities of a related program, including history, geography, arithmetic, and science. She presented this to the whole group of teachers in the spring, and receiving our approval, she kept the program in mind during the summer and was ready for work when the children returned October first.

Up to this point, we had not consulted the children, I admit, and I might also say that we place not too much confidence in their word of mouth refusals or acceptances of new undertakings at this age. They do not know what the possibilities are, even if they think they know whether they wish to undertake them. What we rely upon in our selection of these jobs is our study of the behavior of the children in their previous work. Because they live in a large community and a small one as well, and because the small community has undertaken to use and make understandable and vivid the large one, they have come through eight years of living with a fairly uniform body of information and experience. We merely assumed that they would be able to run a supply store. That our Eights have done this for three successive years acceptably suggests that our hypothesis for these children under these circumstances has been fairly correct. When the opportunity to have the store was finally offered the children, they all accepted it with great enthusiasm.

Unless we can understand how tentatively the formulation is held by the teacher up to this point, it is difficult to understand the degree of collective formulation or, indeed, individual opportunity which comes the children's way. This externalization is bound to condition them. One has to accept that. But we have found a degree of safety lies in analyzing the school situations for opportunities for the children to function as a part of the school and then watching for opportunities to enrich and enlarge their experiences. This secures to the children opportunity to experience within a simple, but a very real, school form. Our experience would indicate that operating under these simple forms secures the children opportunities rather than interferes with them.

Miss Moore's formulation contained what she saw as geography, arithmetic, science, and history in running a school store. This is the part of the program which she held in mind most tentatively. It was, and always is, to clear her own thinking that the teacher makes these first formulations at all. In making these paper formulations one always runs the risk of falling in love with them. When this happens, the whole school is more or less victimized, and I might say that nothing causes greater consternation when it is discovered.

In starting a new store the first thing that confronted the children was how to get the supplies. The actual cash had to be secured from the office in the form of a loan. They played with the situation more or less because they knew their parents had paid the office for school supplies. They took it seriously as well, for they did not suggest using their profits until the loan was paid back. In fact, their chief interest in their bookkeeping was to find out how soon they could make a payment on the loan. Having secured the money, the children investigated wholesale and retail houses at first hand. In some cases they interested dealers to the extent that they sent representatives to the class to give them exact information about the supplies they dealt in. These representatives, as well as the people who waited on the children in the stores, found inquiring minds to deal with. The children raised such questions as: how quantities are taken care of and were introduced to storerooms; where they got the materials and were told about manufacturing; how the materials got to New York and were told about water and land routes. They went back of these questionings, consulted maps, made maps, and took more trips. They built up a larger and different field of information than they had been familiar with before.

Within this 'store' formulation, the children individually and collectively planned and abandoned plans. They made their own forms, abandoned them, and tried over again. Their individual planning sometimes eventuated in something that was carried out by a group, sometimes in individual forms such as come out of pottery or shop materials or the use of drawing and painting materials.

Miss Moore recorded her program, as she went along, under the four headings stated above. When she had the leisure and the time to study her record in perspective, she came to the conclusion that the program had been valuable from the 'job' point of view and from that of enrichment and also that a good deal of progress had been made in the acquirement of the 'tools,' but she found the program weak on the side of dramatic and spontaneous play. As she had an opportunity to take a younger class another year, she turned over her record and her conclusions to Miss Stott, who took the eight-year-old class the next year. Miss Stott knew pretty well both the weakness and the strength of her program before she undertook it. She had the advantage of having known the children in a lower group. Also, she had worked on what we call the "play programs," the programs of the younger groups where spontaneous play dominates. The job side of the program had been splendidly cared for, so she decided to watch for opportunities in dramatics. Before the close of the year she went to the Sevens and asked them whether, as Eights, they would care to run the school store. But the children were ahead of her. They had been talking about it for some time and accepted without question. They discussed with her, together with a committee of the Eights, whether they would take over the counter and other fittings of the former group, after looking them over critically. They had several group meetings to decide upon these weighty matters. There was something of a hitch in the negotiations, as a result of the Eights' desire to sell their appurtenances and the Sevens' burning wish to make their own.

Miss Stott and her group took up a somewhat different line of geographic and historic inquiry. She searched for descriptive material which would contain something of the personal in order to give the children a sense of the life of the people they came in contact with. She found this in literature, in first-hand accounts, etc. The children, themselves, discovered a good deal through conversation with people at home and trips to museums with interested parents. The result of this treatment was more dramatic, spontaneous play with such things as costumes, stage sets, and properties.

Up to eight years of age the children have been dealing with the kind of information which they can get themselves. This has come about through a very distinct effort on our part to utilize the earlier years to the limit for motor and sense experiences. It is not that we distinctly keep books away from the children, but that they are so busy orienting themselves in their own situation that there isn't the time for book searching. But at eight the children are making more urgent inquiries into the past and the distant, and a new sort of research comes into being. The teacher has to show the children gradually how to get at what they want to know. They have played with what is going on about them as long as they care to, and they seem to show a distinct desire for what lies beyond the application of their mode of research to the here and now. From the side of opportunity for collective formulation, the children must have on tap a great deal of related information. At this stage the collecting of such information devolves largely upon the teacher, though it is a part of her intention to whet the children's appetites for more remote information and get them interested in making their own researches.

Miss Stott was particularly alert in supplying the children with related descriptive information, as her record shows. Having children who for several years had been learning to make use of related information in spontaneous play, they swung into using the new matter quite easily and were launched upon a new play experience which required a great degree of collective formulation.

The children played day after day with their information about Indians and white settlers, about lumbering camps, etc. This required social forms and re-formations. It required all the collective formulations available in individuals. Miss Stott did what she thought was necessary to secure the children opportunity to formulate through experiencing what they took to be the lives of people remotely associated with their own lives. If they lacked information to 'carry on,' she brought this up for discussion. If some children were not being used, she brought out what they might produce. One came across them building and playing in the yard, dramatizing in the gymnasium what they took to be Indian and white settlers' lives, dancing out their feeling for lumber jacks, making crude Indian things in the shop and modelling room to be used in their play, as well as stage sets in their classroom. All this stimulated individual effort toward contributions to the general play, but it served also to stimulate the individual child to produce for his individual satisfaction. It is interesting to watch composition in music, in painting and drawing, in modelling, going on side by side with this general dramatization. The teacher expects this, and her formulation provides for it with every group.

I have tried to give a picture of how a group program is in the process of developing. I hope my illustration has not conveyed the idea that a set program is likely to come out of such experimentation. Unless we can keep our efforts free from this, our method is a failure. I am distinctly trying to present the *method* of an experimental school, not its results in formulation. I should never advise a teacher in another school to try to run a school supply store, for example, except as the most tentative kind of an experiment. I believe a school store would be a failure unless the whole school were committed to it. This can be brought about only through a sense of the school as a whole which every teacher connected with it should have.

We seem to be working out a 'project' method, perhaps. The essential difference between our method and any project method with which I am familiar lies in the fact that ours is not merely a school method. It is a method which can be applied to adult social undertakings and is often applied to informal undertakings. It is a method of learning to live and work together. I have requests from teachers at times to forward to them a history or a geography project applicable to a certain grade. We do not have history, geography, nor yet shop projects. We do not even think in these obvious school terms. The shop, the laboratory, the library, are places to go to work on something which applies to the general program of the particular group or possibly to something which is going on outside the school.

The project method may carry the schools a step in the direction of better integration of the human organism, provided this is its aim and that this aim is kept in mind in working out the curricular details. But it may quite as easily promote disintegration. The very naming of a project, "history," "geography," or "arithmetic" suggests something machinelike, something which by the mere pressing of a button may be made to work automatically. Because an organism is complete in itself, because it is not run from the outside as a machine is, all effort to treat it like a machine tends to disorganize it, tends, indeed, towards the disintegration of the individual as a whole. All our efforts in curriculum-making might be summed up as an attempt to make it possible for every child to have integrating experiences in school so that he may tend to become an integrated individual. As his experiences are concerned with others of his kind, he tends to integrate as a social being as well.

CHAPTER XXIII

THE WALDEN SCHOOL

Margaret Naumburg
Founder of the Walden School, New York City

The Walden School finds itself between two opposing tendencies of the experimental school movement. On one side are those who stand for the exaggerated *laissez-faire* policy of individual development, believing that freedom consists in the removal of all restraint, however destructive this policy may be to the life of the group. But the majority of the progressive schools, discounting the difficulties of individual adjustment, prefer to emphasize the importance of a genuine socialization of both class groups and entire school plants. Now, the Walden School, unable to subscribe wholly to either of these policies, affirms an element in both of them. For it believes in the social function of the school towards the creation of a more harmonious and equitable future society, and it believes in the development of individual potentials as the swiftest means of insuring just such a socialization.

Our agreement with progressive schools in general may be summarized as a positive acceptance of the physiological, psychological, and sociological data revealed by modern science. This acceptance leads all progressive schools to some form of revaluation of both group and individual energies in education. It overthrows the immutability of the old-time fixed curriculum. And, for us in particular, it makes necessary the consideration of children in terms of their three-fold nature, as organisms needing a unified and balanced development of physical, emotional, and intellectual powers.

To realize, in a definite educational form, the simultaneous balance and opposition between group and individual forces, a new type of school organization had to be built up. This was possible in the Walden School because it began life with a single class of pre-school children. The earliest groups entered at two, three, and four years of age. Along with them the school was able to grow in a slow organic way from its original roots. As these children advanced to greater maturity, the school organization and program grew in proportion to their increasing needs.

In those days, the school, consisting of nursery, kindergarten, and elementary groups, was evident only as an incomplete form. And the impression went forth, and persists to this day, that it was founded, and has remained, as a school for young children. In this guise it naturally appeared to the outsider who, seeing it in the first phase of its expansion, was uninformed as to the purpose and intentions which underlay its existence. Until that original nursery group had, through its own growth, carried the school forward year by year, first through the primary, then the intermediate, and now into the period of the high school, no complete school could exist. For, by the very terms of its life the Walden School has grown up with its children.

In a genuinely experimental school the relation between the special school organization and the curriculum is immediate and close. To those accustomed to the use of more formal school programs, it may seem difficult to envisage a curriculum that cannot be isolated from that particular school organization with which it grew. But the process of developing the program of such an experimental school is exactly the reverse of the traditional method. Instead of preparing a curriculum to place in a school organization, our school started with the attitude of allowing a form to evolve from the needs of the children. It must be remembered, however, that our chief aim was to develop the three-fold nature of each child, individually. We believed that, given such a development in process, the social aspects of education would follow naturally. So that, though we emphasized the child's needs, we did not indulge them, but, on the contrary, we sought to direct them with this aim in mind. And in order to realize our intentions, it was evidently necessary to find teachers with creative spirit, rich background, and a technical preparation which was at once thorough and elastic. Or, when these were not available, then it was necessary to train them along with the growth of the school. With this approach, the Walden School started and soon began to develop a flexible form in which the possibilities of a new program could be explored.

The first five years of the Walden experiment convinced us that what had been a theory was indeed a fact. We brought into relief, among other things, the necessity for exact emotional adjustment and integration in each child. Given such an integration, we quickly discovered that children of two, three, and four years of age needed no serious suggestion or pressure from adult teachers in order to become socialized. From their own inner needs, they themselves sought and created activities. Similarly, we discovered that if children lacked emotional adjustment, if they were not helped to function in all three aspects of their being, if the chief interests and creative powers of each child were not studied individually and given an adequate expression at every age period, then their capacity to develop socially was hindered; a child would then not function fully in the social life of his own school group. In short, the first few years of experimentation justified our attempt to create a form in which the possibilities of a new program could be determined.

In order to do so, certain special conditions of school organization seemed necessary. A brief survey of this environment, as an approach to the technique of the Walden curriculum seems now in order. An all-day school was established for two reasons. First, that every phase of the children's lives might be carried on in a world of their own, where they might work and play and sleep and eat together, learning thereby to share community interests, without neglect of their personal growth, through study and creation. And secondly, the all-day plan made possible a more significant and balanced arrangement of the city child's day, by substituting the control of sympathetic and interested teachers for the misguided efforts of maids and governnesses. Furthermore, this plan made possible the wider use of outdoor life in special trips and play schemes.

In the early years of the school it was realized that such diverse activities required much space, and that quiet work and individual play were interrupted by louder and more active group movements. Two classrooms were therefore allotted to each of the school groups below the high school. A group teacher for every class, including the high school, stood in close personal relation with all the boys and girls of her own group. Many special teachers were also introduced as the children grew older. But these trained specialists, creative in their chosen fields of arts or science, supplement the efforts of the group teachers. Their work centers in special laboratories, shops, and studios. Whenever possible, the children go to these extra rooms for special studies. Considerable modification of this procedure occurs, however, in younger groups, where special teachers, when introduced at all, tend to visit in the elementary classrooms.

The classes in the Walden School are limited to sixteen boys and girls. Had the groups been larger, we could not have dealt unhampered with many of the educational problems we wished to solve. We have come to the conclusion that this number is about right in holding the balance between real group life and individual development. But this does not mean that the type of organization and curriculum now established in the school would not be applicable in principle to schools far larger, as the active interest of certain public-school organizations already proves.

But although sixteen is a small class, the Walden School regards any *chance* combination of sixteen children in a group as too large and uneven a unit for their best development. For, in our free school environment variability in capacities, interests, and disabilities of even sixteen children showed up clearly. And so the school set itself the problem of discovering the best way to help these children, whatever their particular endowments or limitations, to make the best use of their powers in both personal and social adjustment.

Based on the fact that no sixteen children have the same degree of ability or speed in any given subject, every group is divided, in each of the class subjects, into two or three sections, according to their capacities. In all subjects surprising variation was discovered as to speed, grasp, type of interest, and method of attack, among children of various age groups.

When classes were subdivided into sections of five to eight children of similar abilities in the three R's, languages, science, music, etc., there was a perceptible increase in general development. Clearly, the briefer periods of more concentrated work in these small groups carried the children ahead with greater speed and interest in their studies. But while sub-group work became a regular part, when needed, of the technique of class organization, it did not supplant the use of full group meetings in any class. For sub-group and general class meetings were of equal importance, but in different ways. It would be impossible to detail the experiments made in sub-dividing children in each class according to subject-matter ability. There is an attempt at every age to adjust every subject to the interest span of a particular group. For example, in the younger classes we found that periods as short as twenty minutes, several times a week, gave the best results in such subjects as music and nature study; and for the same reason, in a ten-year-old group science laboratory work would perhaps last an hour and a half, English an hour, and French a half hour. In the high school, Latin periods are half hours, English an hour, biology one and a half hours, and painting two hours. Then, the length of the periods of each subject is, of course, correlated with the number of times it occurs in the weekly program. The technique of this type of school organization is certainly not easy to carry out. But the results in terms of life and development have more than warranted the added effort required.

For the teacher, this subdivision of her group into small sections is extremely useful. It allows her time for individual teaching, wherever it is needed. In the younger groups, the use of the second of the classrooms becomes most important. For, while the teacher is occupied with a sub-group in arithmetic, the rest of the class may be at work in the adjoining room preparing a play, planning a trip, writing stories or finishing required work, on their own initiative. In the upper classes one regular classroom suffices a group, because all sub-groups in special subjects repair to laboratories and studios for work, leaving their own room free for use by the rest of their group.

On its program the Walden School carries many more subjects than do most schools. Having begun in the younger classes with great emphasis on personal creative expression, it continues to encourage special work in the arts and sciences. But from each child a minimum of required work is expected in all the regular school subjects, whatever his chief interests or abilities may be. And though the school questions seriously certain standards set by college requirements, not because they are too high, but because they are empty, it undertakes, nevertheless, to meet them, while widening the scope of these subjects, as well as by adding many others. But although in this way the school is able to prepare those children who wish to enter college or professional schools, it at the same time provides a greater opportunity for the discovery and development of their individual capacities.

The approach to subject matter is, of course, implicit in any discussion of curriculum. It is impossible, however, in this brief compass, to give more than our general attitude. Progressive schools generally feel the need of a more unified and more significant correlation of subject matter. They agree to attempt a revision of subject matter by inclusion of material more stimulating and more closely related to the lives of children; they all try to introduce better textbooks and special equipment. They seem equally anxious to improve the methods and approach of teacher to child: all of which seems important, but not enough. For, however fresh and interesting new subject matter may be, the Walden School believes that this material must be presented in such a way that the children themselves assist to a certain extent in the sifting and selection of the year's work. In almost any general subject, such as biology, history or English, the field is large and varied. There are, therefore, opportunities for many approaches. And the Walden School tries consciously to suggest these and encourage the children to take a hand in their selection. When a subject has been defined for a term's work, the individual boys and girls of the intermediate and older groups are definitely encouraged to undertake original research work of their own, for which due credit is given.

The problem of presenting subject matter to the best advantage involves an alteration between periods of intense concentration under the constant supervision of the teacher, and periods wherein the child, having mastered sufficient technique, is allowed to work independently. In order to meet this condition and to encourage a certain specialization along lines of chief interest and greatest ability, certain places in every child's program are marked "free periods." This does not mean that the child is free to do nothing. He is free to choose on which of all his school subjects he prefers to spend more than the required minimal time.

In the foregoing, the general aim and attitude which crystallized in the Walden experiment have been outlined. It may be well to summarize here. This experiment is based on the consideration of the child as a three-fold organism to be led to integration by 'positive channeling.' Thus, the rounding out of personality becomes a means of true socialization from within the group. We have come to know that the real group life of children cannot be directed by adults from above. For the moving center of socialization in a school lies not within the will of the teacher, but within the wishes and impulses of the children. These we have sought to direct according to our aim. That the responsibility for the socialization of children does not lie solely within the province of teachers or schools, but must be the final result of the complete functioning of all individuals in a school, is evident even in a class of children as young as three years, in the Walden School.

CHAPTER XXIV

SOME FEATURES OF CURRICULUM-MAKING IN THE ELEMENTARY SCHOOL OF THE UNIVERSITY OF MISSOURI

C. A. PHILLIPS
University of Missouri, Columbia, Missouri

The University Elementary School is an integral part of the School of Education in the University of Missouri. It consists of a kindergarten and the work usually included in the first six grades in an elementary school. On account of the capacity of the building, the enrollment is limited to about 120 children. We do not have a specially selected group of children; any child may enter until the limit for a particular room has been reached.

The school has three major purposes: (1) It must be a superior school for the service of the children who attend. (2) The school attempts to provide good conditions for observation and demonstration for those University students who elect to prepare themselves for the work of elementary schools or for supervisors in elementary education. (3) Its third function is to offer limited opportunity for research in curricular problems and supervision for graduate students in education and for the members of the faculty of the School of Education.

It is a state supported institution. In some particulars, this is a limitation on the activities in which the school may engage. Since the objectives for elementary education have not been scientifically determined, we do not care to make any final statement concerning the purposes to be achieved in elementary education. Likewise, since there is no thorough scientific technique for curriculum-construction, whatever one might say at this time is only tentative.

At the present time we make sure that our children meet all the ordinary standards of the country in the fundamentals in elementary-school subjects. We have found that it is not difficult to do this and at the same time to offer the children very useful and elaborate experience based on significant projects. Because of the small numbers in our groups, we are able to provide for individual instruction in such a way as to take care of the major interests of all of our children. For some time we have been featuring projects from the local community which offer interesting and real situations for the children. In time, we hope to evaluate and grade those projects in such a way that they will contribute more largely to the life of our children than we are able to make them do at the present.

Among the more important projects which we are using may be mentioned the following: a bank, dairy, creamery, shoe factory, hospital, ice-plant, packing house, wholesale grocery, greenhouse, printing plant, the State Capitol.

In a general way, our procedure is about as follows: Before we make the excursion, two or three days are spent by the class acquiring such general information about the project as is necessary for an intelligent observation. Very often, members of the class can furnish initial information directly from personal experience, and additional facts may be secured from our library to make the visit successful. It may be added that we have a well-selected library which the children are free to use at all times. Before the excursion is taken, the children are ready with numerous questions which may be answered during the excursion. It is our custom to take a stenographer along so that we may have an accurate account of the questions raised, with the answer which was furnished by some expert connected with the institution. The teacher of the children always accompanies the group, and commonly also the principal or director of the school. During the visit the children are encouraged to raise numerous questions concerning the institution visited. They keep their own notes so they will have accurate information when they return to the school. After the return to the school, the whole experience is made the basis for a number of lessons, to clear up the significant aspects of the excursion. Finally, the children complete the experience in oral and written composition. These written compositions, along with the complete account of the visit by the stenographer, constitute the basis for the curriculum. In this way, from year to year, the subject matter for local projects is accumulated.

In order that our treatment of local projects may be more concrete, we submit one example. This is an account of an hour and a half visit of the sixth grade to the Boone County Trust Company, an institution with a modern organization and equipment, with footings of more than two million dollars.

Mr. Reuther, the treasurer, conducted the party about the building. He took the party to the directors' room first. The questions that follow were asked by the children and answered by Mr. Reuther.

Directors' Room

Q. Who are the directors?

A. Mr. Bright, who is president, and the men who direct the bank. The directors do not own the bank, but simply manage it.

Q. How many are there?

A. We have fifteen directors.

Q. How do you get directors for a bank?

A. They are elected by the stockholders. Once each year we set aside a day on which we elect the directors; they in turn elect the other officers of the bank. We have a president, two vice-presidents, a secretary and a treasurer, and numerous other employes, tellers, bookkeepers, etc. In all, we have nineteen people at work in the bank. The officers are really responsible for the management of the bank.

Q. Do stockholders get salaries?

A. No, they do not get salaries, unless they happen to be officers also. Stockholders are paid dividends on their stock out of the earnings of the bank.

Q. How often do you have directors' meetings?

A. We have a directors' meeting of the full board once each month, but we may have other meetings also. We have a meeting of the chief officers of the bank every afternoon at which time the special work of each officer, if there is anything unusual about it, is called to the attention of this executive committee. We also use this directors' room for special meetings for different organizations who have anything to do with city affairs. The city school board holds its meeting in this room regularly.

Special Telephone

Q. What is this? How does it work?

A. This is a special telephone. There are two lines running from here to the various desks down in the bank below. When Mr. Bright, the president, or anyone else here, wishes to speak to some one down in the bank, he can push one of these buttons and connect up with the individual phone downstairs. Then the conversation can be carried on in the same way as you would on any other phone. It is a mere convenience to save time.

Clock

Q. What about this clock?

A. This is a regular Western Union clock. It is supposed to keep perfect time—at any rate it is connected with the Western Union Telegraph Company and is regulated in every way by their time.

Scale

Q. Do you weigh gold on this?

A. No, this scale is used to weigh our mail so that we can tell how much postage to put on it.

Tellers' Windows

Q. What is a teller's window?

A. These windows are the places where people bring their money to deposit it. The teller takes the money and gives the owner of it a deposit slip. At the close of the day's business, each teller separates his checks according to banks. Some checks are drawn on the different banks in this town—these are called "clearing checks;" other checks are drawn on different banks all over the United States. In the evening, the teller makes a total of his checks to see if his deposits are equal to his credits. He takes all the checks of our own depositors and turns them over to the bookkeeper. The checks on the town banks are bunched up and to-morrow morning all the banks, thru their representatives, have a meeting. We trade checks with each other. In case one bank has more checks than the other one, the difference is paid by drafts. In the case of out-of-town banks, we make a list of them with this machine. The list includes the date of the check, name of the person it is drawn on, the amount, and the name of the person who endorsed it. We make two copies of this list, the original sheet goes to St. Louis and we keep the duplicate. Finally, these checks are sorted and go to the Federal Reserve Bank, which in turn sends them to the different towns.

Money Counter

Q. What is this machine used for?

A. This machine counts pennies, dimes, nickels, and quarters. By turning a crank the machine adds up; when it comes to a certain number it stops. (Mr. Ruether takes a handful of quarters and drops them in the slot. The machine was set for forty quarters, so when forty quarters were dropped, the machine automatically stopped. Thus it had counted $10.00.)

Depositors' Ledgers

Q. What are these big books used for?

A. This is a depositor's ledger. Everyone who has an account in here has his own personal sheet. Whenever a check is given by the depositor, it is charged up to him and as soon as the check comes through the teller's window, or through the clearing, or the mail, then it is charged to the individual account. (Ledger sheets were shown to each of the children of the group.)

Bookkeeping Machines

Q. What is the use of this machine?

A. This is a bookkeeping machine. It is run by electricity. The operator starts with the balance on hand, then shifts to the amount of the check, amount of deposit, and the balance on hand is shown at the end. (The children watched the machine operate.)

Paid Machine

Q. What are you doing with this machine?

A. We call this a "Paid" machine. After checks have been paid and charged, we take them to this machine and it marks them "Paid," giving the date. The date tells exactly the day the check was charged. After the checks are canceled in this manner, we sort them and file them in the vault. Each person who has an account with us will have his own compartment in the file. At the end of the month, we sort out the checks for each individual and they are attached to his statement which comes off his ledger sheet. Each depositor has a statement furnished him at the end of the month.

Wooden Checks

Q. What is a wooden check?
A. If a fellow writes a check on this bank and hasn't any money here, we call that a wooden check.
Q. What do you do about it?
A. We send for him and he must make the check good, that is, he must bring in the amount of money to cover the check or give his note for it.

Main Vault Door

Q. Who closes this door?
A. Only the one who knows the combination. It has a time lock on it; that is, it locks at a certain time. We set the clock at the time it is to open.
Q. What about Sunday?
A. Well, we set it for as many as three days.
Q. What would you do after four days?
A. We would have to come down at the end of the third day and reset it. This door weighs 15,000 pounds, or 7½ tons. It cost $5,000. It is made out of solid steel.
Q. What was that bell?
A. There is a bell that rings every time anyone goes into the vault.
Q. What is in the vault?
A. In this vault are our safety boxes. Customers rent boxes and each customer receives two keys. Neither key opens the lock, both must be used in order to get in the box.
Q. What if someone loses his key?
A. The only thing we can do is have the lock broken and get a new one. We do not have any duplicate keys.

Inner Vault

Q. What's in here?
A. This is the place where we keep our money at night, under a combination lock. This vault is built out of 18-inch concrete. It has steel bars running in the concrete both ways every five inches.
Q. Where is the money?
A. Most of the money is now out in the tellers' cages, however, we have some in here. (Mr. Ruether reaches in and brings out a sack.)
Q. What's in the sack?
A. Gold.
Q. How much?
(Children say: "Oh, about a thousand, maybe a million.")
A. No, there is $3000 worth of gold in this sack. The gold pieces are $2.50,

$5, $10, and $20 denominations. (Children are shown the different sizes of money.)

Q. How heavy is it? May I hold it?

(All the children are allowed to handle the sack of gold and express their surprise at its weight.)

Bonds

Q. Show us some bonds.

(Mr. Ruether reaches into the inner vault and takes out a package of bonds, holding it up to the children.)

Q. What kind of bonds are these?

A. These are 4½% Liberty Bonds.

Q. How many are there?

A. We have here $65,000.00 in different kinds of liberty bonds.

Q. Show us the different sizes.

A. This is a $5,000 registered liberty bond. All bonds are very much alike, except for color. A $100 bond is golden, $50 bond, brown, etc. These bonds do not belong to the bank. They belong to our customers and are here for safe-keeping.

Q. What do you mean by registered bonds?

A. In the case of the United States bonds, "registered" means that the treasury department signs the bond with your name on it and no one but you can get the money on it. In case you should sell a registered bond, it will be necessary for you to sign the bond in the presence of some bank official, or postoffice official. Every six months, the treasury department sends the interest on it directly to you. By registering your bond, you are absolutely protected from theft. If some one should steal it, he would not have anything. It would only be a scrap of paper to a thief.

Q. Are there other kinds of bonds?

A. Yes, there are municipal bonds, school bonds, railroad bonds, industrial bonds—in fact, many, many kinds of bonds.

Q. Have you any of them here?

A. No, just now we do not have any bonds except government bonds. We have some school bonds, but they are in St. Louis at the present time.

Paper Money

Q. We want to see all the different kinds of paper money. (Mr. Ruether went to a teller's cage and brought back a number of bills—$1, $2, $5, $10, $20 and $50. The children examined the bills carefully.)

Q. What is the biggest bill?

A. $1000 is the largest we have, but I think there are some $10,000 bills. Some of these bills are silver certificates; some of them are gold certificates.

Interest

Q. How do you figure interest?

A. Here are some books, three of them, from which we figure our interest. Of course, the best way to figure interest is the long way and it is the surest; then we can check it with one of our books, if we want to. (Here Mr. Ruether took concrete examples and showed the children how to figure simple interest and compound interest by means of the books. Special attention was called to the fact that some interest is figured on a 360-day, and some on a 365-day basis.)

Checks

Q. How many kinds of checks are there?

A. The ordinary bank checks, certified checks, and travelers' checks. (Children say: "Oh yes, we know about the ordinary checks, but what about travelers' checks? Mr. Ruether went back into the bank and brought out travelers' checks of various denominations. The list included $10, $20, $50, and $100 denominations.) This is a $10 one. Such checks are bought when travelers make long trips where they do not know anyone. The check has the owner's signature on it. In order to get the money on it, he signs it again in the presence of some bank official who pays him the money. We issue travelers' checks in the name of the Bankers Trust Company of New York. They can be cashed anywhere in the world.

Q. What are they good for?

A. It's better to have them than to take so much money along, as they would not be good when stolen. Only the person who actually owns them can use them, except by clever forgery.

It is obvious that there are numerous important lessons involving interest, exchange, stocks and bonds, which come directly out of this experience. In like manner, other projects for the various grades are studied, as was indicated in another paragraph. We are hoping to build up some of the major features of the curriculum for the University Elementary School by this sort of procedure.

We are employing one other plan to secure material for our curriculum—that is, to find out children's dominant interests at the various places in their development by directing their activities in connection with these interests. This is being done at the present time in connection with the various features of handwork. In the lower grades the children are allowed to choose projects in connection with cutting paper, weaving, and sewing. An expert has been helping the fifth-grade and sixth-grade girls to determine exactly what they can do with projects in hand sewing and machine sewing in a year. In the same manner, an expert has been working with the boys of these grades to find out exactly what projects in handwork they can complete in a satisfactory manner. We expect that the finished projects from these experiments will help us to determine what normally may be expected of children at this level of progress.

CHAPTER XXV

THE EDUCATIONAL PRINCIPLES OF THE SCHOOL OF ORGANIC EDUCATION, FAIRHOPE, ALABAMA

MARIETTA JOHNSON
Director, School of Organic Education, Fairhope, Alabama

We believe the educational program should aim to meet the needs of the growing child. We believe that childhood is for itself and not a preparation for adult life. Therefore, the school program must answer the following questions:

What does the child of any particular age need to minister to the health of his body, to preserve the integrity of the intellect, and to keep him sincere and unselfconscious of spirit?

The answers to these questions will constitute the curriculum of the school, and as we grow in understanding of the nature and needs of childhood, the curriculum will change.

We believe that all children need music; therefore we give the younger children singing and dancing and singing games and all sorts of rhythmic work. As the children grow older, this work becomes folk dancing and folk singing, with reading of notes, singing harmonies, and learning to play an instrument at about ten or twelve years of age.

Time is given to dramatics throughout the school life.

We believe that all children need creative handwork. This is the fundamental method of thinking. Therefore, all sorts of material are provided for self-expression. For the very young children, merely making things of clay and sand and using blocks may be sufficient. Later, this develops into real projects, using tools and art and craft materials. The creative handwork continues through all ages up to college. We believe it should continue through the college program. Handwork should grow out of, or be related to, work in history, literature, etc., as far as possible.

We believe that all childhood needs stories. The stories for the very young children would naturally take the form of folklore, and fables, and fairy tales; later on, the form of history, literature, and geography, after learning to read at about eight or nine years of age. This reading work would also result in composition and the study, perhaps, of grammar in the high-school period. The literature, history, and geography stories begun in the early years, would be replaced by the study of history, literature, and science as such in the high-school and college years.

The speech centers are developed very young. A child may learn a language other than his own at an early age, whereas he should not be obliged to read his own until he is eight or nine years of age. We would, therefore, give the children some experience in using a foreign language, such as Spanish or French.

All children need fundamental conceptions of number. The work of measuring, weighing, estimating, counting, begun in the early years, would naturally require the use of figures at about eight or ten, when the mechanics of number would be acquired with great delight. Later, the applied problems, and still later, the abstract problems, which are enjoyed during the high-school and college years.

In order to preserve unselfconsciousness in growth, no grades or marks should be given and no intellectual tasks set by the teacher. The children should be grouped according to chronological age. The teacher should provide suitable work for the group, with individual variation where necessary. The child should not do as he pleases; he does not know what is good for him. In order to preserve the unity of his intellectual and emotional life, intellectual work should accompany and follow sincere interest and desire, and the reward for all learning should be the inner satisfaction and the consciousness of power which comes through understanding.

All children should have free play, so every daily program should include much time in the open, much time in free, self-prompted occupations, and some time to dream. The fullest social association should be given.

We believe that education is life, growth; that the ends are immediate; that the end and the process are one. We believe that all children should have the fullest opportunity for self-expression, for joy, for delight, for intellectual stimulus through subject matter, but we do not believe that children should be made self-conscious or externalized by making subject matter an end. Our constant thought is not what do the children learn or do, but what are the "learning" and the "doing" doing to them.

We believe all children need Nature—not so much for facts as for experience and attitude. The Nature walks and talks of the little children would develop into serious Nature Study, gardening, and science of the older groups.

Every schoolroom must be a health center. In the measure that the school provides activities and exercises which tend to produce a sound, accomplished, beautiful body, an intelligent, sympathetic mind, a sweet, sincere spirit, it is educational. In the measure that it does not, it is not educational, however informational it may be.

We believe that society owes all children guidance, control, instruction, association, and inspiration—right conditions of growth—throughout the growing years until physical growth is completed. No child may know failure—all must succeed. Not "what do you know," but "what do you need," should be asked, and the *nature* of childhood indicates the answer.

CHAPTER XXVI

CURRICULUM-MAKING IN LABORATORY OR EXPERIMENTAL SCHOOLS

F. G. Bonser
Teachers College, Columbia University, New York City

Among the numerous private schools and schools connected with universities and teacher-training institutions are several which have given very definite attention to the making of curricula. With few limitations legally prescribed, with small groups of pupils, and occasionally with funds adequate to secure the best teachers and special workers available, such schools have an opportunity to initiate and test experimentally variations in curriculum-making not usually possible in public schools. Resulting from requests sent to such schools, statements of procedure in curriculum-making were prepared by the following and are published in this volume:

Beaver Country Day School, Brookline, Massachusetts
City and Country School, 165 West 12th Street, New York City
Francis W. Parker School, Chicago
Horace Mann School of Teachers College, Columbia University
Lincoln School of Teachers College, Columbia University
McDonald County, Missouri, Experimental Country School
University of Chicago Laboratory Schools
University of Iowa Elementary School
University of Missouri Elementary School
Walden School, 36 West 68th Street, New York City
School of Organic Education, Fairhope, Alabama[1]

Each of these schools differs from the others in some rather distinctive ways, and all differ from general public school practice in several respects. Yet, with all of the diversity found, there are significant resemblances in purposes and methods.

Common Purposes in Laboratory Schools

All of these schools agree in very considerable measure in their purposes:

(1) To provide for the interests and needs of individual children.

[1] The description of the work of this school was received after Professor Bonser prepared Chapter XXVI.—*Editor*.

(2) To utilize the play, dramatic, constructive, and exploratory impulses of children, thus encouraging creative expression.

(3) To develop methods of coöperative activity in school classes and groups.

(4) To utilize the conditions and activities of the environment and the experiences of pupils as points of departure and means for further educative experiences.

(5) To permit much freedom to the teacher in selecting and adjusting work to the conditions and needs of pupils.

(6) To break down the barriers of subjects which interfere with true learning through correlating or integrating their elements in life-like experiences.

In general, these schools emphasize play, practical activities, creative expression, group coöperation, and the use of environment and current questions as sources of stimulation and means of growth to a degree not common in public schools. Reduced to lowest terms, there is evidence of but little difference in the fundamental objectives of these schools. All are striving to develop the traits of behavior which constitute efficient individual and social life. Differences are chiefly in methods of selecting and organizing curricular materials and of teaching, rather than in purposes to be achieved. Tests and measurements of the current type are reported by most of these schools, but the purposes stated for their use vary. In the Beaver Country Day School they are used "for diagnostic purposes and to maintain standards," in the Francis Parker School, "for insight into pupils' needs, not for classification of pupils into inferior and superior groups."

In each of these schools, the school staff itself—its principal or director, its supervisors, and its teachers—is responsible for the curriculum. Since the principal or director usually has the privilege of selecting teachers, a reasonably uniform point of view may be secured in each respective school if the principal desires this. All within the given school contribute to develop the curriculum and to perfect the methods and techniques of teaching which the point of view requires.

Outstanding Differences in Curriculum-Making

By contrasting the McDonald County, Missouri, Experimental School and the City and Country School of New York City on the one hand, with the Francis Parker School and Iowa State University Elementary School on the other, we perhaps have the sharpest points of diversity brought out.

In the rural experimental school in McDonald County, Missouri, the program and the curriculum are classified under four heads: Story Projects, Hand Projects, Play Projects, and Excursion Projects. Through group or class conferences in which the teacher is an active participant, the projects are chosen. Then, whatever is needed to carry these projects through is used, while the teacher helps in the finding and using of such aids from arithmetic, geography, history, the arts, and so on. Nothing is presented from the 'subject' except as it is found useful in some project. Out of the needs for techniques and skills arise supplementary projects for the development of these—the facts and processes of arithmetic, the mechanics of English, spelling, penmanship, and so on.

In the City and Country School, the selection by the teachers of large activities comes first. The content of the subjects which will probably contribute to these activities is outlined by the teacher of a given group as a program and presented for approval to the staff. When so approved, the children, accepting the activity, help to work out the details through the year. The program is tentative and is adjusted as the work evolves. A record is kept and may be used in subsequent years for whatever of value it includes. The buying and selling of school supplies as a large activity given in some detail in the report of this school illustrates procedure. The play city is another illustration. The program, on paper, to facilitate procedure is under four heads: Practical Activities, Play Activities, Special Training, and Organization of Information. The activities developed under these heads and the records of work for each seem to constitute the curriculum of this school, as far as a paper statement of its content is made. As the report states, the "set up—everything external to the children which stands to influence them" is regarded as the curriculum, or "the form in which the school purpose operates."

In the City and Country Day School the teachers select the large activities and the probable subject matter needed in advance, while in the McDonald County Experimental School the teacher and the children together select the projects and develop the subject matter from day to day or week to week, as the occasion requires. In this respect the two schools distinctly differ. In both schools, however, the work is based upon activities as the point of starting and the determining factor in the selection of subject matter. Neither school teaches 'subjects' as such.

In contrast with these, let us look briefly at the methods of curriculum-making in the Francis W. Parker School of Chicago and the Elementary School of the University of Iowa. In both schools the curriculum is, in a very considerable measure, made in advance. In both it is organized on a subject basis. In both it is made by the joint efforts of the teaching and supervisory staffs. In both there is provision for adaptation of the work to the needs of children by their respective teachers. In the statements of both schools there is reference to provision for appropriate drill—Iowa by "leading children to see need for it;" Francis Parker, "in relationship to needs for creative and adjustment activities."

In the Francis Parker School, what is called the "social group project" is used as the basis of organization for classroom practice. The principle of choice is employed, but not to the extent of giving the child the choice of all subject matter and activity. "Adult wisdom" is used in selection and direction. Given the paper curriculum, teachers and children together select the large units of activity and correlative subject matter through which the curricular purposes are achieved. In the Iowa University Elementary School "freedom of the pupils to work is encouraged—but with responsibility to get something done." In both schools teachers may make changes in the curriculum for their respective groups whenever they can secure the approval of the staff for such changes. At Iowa a change undertaken carries with it responsibility for experimental procedure, including records and the testing of results to evaluate the change. In the Francis Parker School great emphasis is placed upon creative expression and social group coöperation.

In their departure from public-school procedure in curriculum-making by subjects, in advance, and with the assumption that the work will be developed in a rather systematic way, these two schools are much less divergent from common practice than the McDonald County Experimental School and the City and Country Day School. In order of divergence from least to greatest, the four would seem to take this sequence: Iowa University Elementary School, the

Francis Parker School, the City and Country Day School; and the McDonald County Experimental School. The Iowa University Elementary School recognizes specifically, as stated in its report, its obligation to the schools of the state to serve them as a demonstration school that will aid them in improving their practice, and as a laboratory for testing the validity of changes proposed before they are put into operation in the public schools. While the Missouri country school is a public school, it was permitted to develop its work with complete freedom in its method of curriculum-making and teaching.

Curriculum-Making in Other Schools Reporting

In the Beaver Country Day School, the curriculum seems to be organized on a subject basis, but with an integration of subjects not usually found. In the elementary school, most of the material of the subjects is in a "combined course" of history, geography, nature study, current events, and civics. From this course is also drawn much of the material for language expression and, to a less degree, of mathematics. This combined course should also "lead to expression through the arts and manual subjects." For the younger children, "we are concerned that the curriculum . . . should approach the blending of all interests that are common in real life instead of being . . . cut up into blocks designated as subjects." With such a curriculum there can be time each day for the teacher and class to use as needs and interests dictate. The work is presented as a compromise "between the ideal of the problem that includes all subjects and the practical necessity of seeing that the tool subjects are mastered, or that some other need is met." In the high school there is less complete combination of subjects. The curriculum as made in advance is "a skeleton of minimal essentials," with teachers free to fill in appropriate materials as needed. Here the teacher becomes largely responsible for the actual curriculum, but with an obligation to cover the minimal essentials stated in advance.

The Walden School "finds itself between two opposing tendencies, . . . the exaggerated *laissez-faire* policy of individual development . . . and the socialization of both class groups and entire school plants," and so, "unable to subscribe wholly to either, . . . affirms an element in both." The curriculum was not made in advance, but evolved with the school. The interests and needs of children, provision for the development of creative powers, and flexibility in programs are all stressed, and the organization has developed to give full opportunities for securing these values. That the curriculum is organized on a subject basis is not specifically stated in the report, but subjects are occasionally mentioned warranting the inference that they are the basis of the plan. "Each group is divided into two or three sections in each subject on the basis of interests and needs." "Children are definitely encouraged to take a hand in the selection of materials within subjects defined for a term's work." Each child has free periods in which he is free to choose on which of the school subjects he will spend more than the required minimal time.

The University of Missouri Elementary School seems to have changed its principles and practice somewhat in recent years. That a subject organization has some part in the plan may, perhaps, be inferred from the statement: "We make sure that our children meet all the ordinary standards of the country in the fundamentals in elementary-school subjects." Projects from community life are used. "In time, we hope to evaluate and grade these projects in such a way that they will contribute more largely to the life of the children than we are able to make them do at the present." The excursion method is very prominent among these projects. Another source of curricular material is provided by learning the children's interests in hand-working activities. The appropriate special departments of the University are coöperating in this study to find out what can be done with most satisfaction. The report seems to rate highly the development of the community projects as a source of curricular material, describing an illustrative project in some detail. Records made of these projects by the children with the aid of the teacher, and by a stenographer, "constitute the basis for the curriculum," accumulating subject matter from year to year.

The Laboratory Schools of the University of Chicago have curricula organized on a subject basis. "Curriculum studies are being made in every subject." "The school is organized and operated on a plan designed to encourage and facilitate such studies." "Experimentation in the field of the curriculum is a coöperative enterprise in which each teacher has a responsible share, but it is institutional, not individual or personal." All work in revision is subjected to rigid tests for effectiveness before it is adopted. Such revision is in harmony with a plan for unit organization which has for its chief outcome "an adaptation or a functional understanding on the part of the learner." "Its purpose is to teach ways of thinking as well as a body of facts, skills, and appreciations." The report indicates a plan of curriculum-study which attempts to subject every item of revision to conditions of organization and validation that are thoroughly scientific.

The Lincoln School of Teachers College, Columbia University, has no paper curricula. The staff of the school have in mind certain general objectives, with many common elements and with some elements that are quite diversified. By coöperation of a very close and practical kind, a unity of progress for pupils is maintained, while at the same time a great variety of experimental procedures are under way, with a wide range of freedom for each teacher. It may not be correct to say that here a revised curriculum is evolving, but rather to say that here many units of revised curricular materials are developing. To say this in another way, there is no one formulation of an educational philosophy toward which all work is directed in its conformation, but rather every unit of curricular content is considered in terms of its specific effects upon the growth of the learner. The aim is to select material, organize the procedures in teaching, and test the results of the work with scientific precision and accuracy. A basic principle of the school's conduct is that of keeping the way open to continued experimentation and evaluation of practice in every field in which values are not already scientifically established. It welcomes in its staff those with various forms of educational philosophy and psychology who are really open minded, instead of attempting to unify or crystallize its curriculum under the formulation of any one philosophy. It attempts, both in principle and practice, to keep all of the conditions as favorable as possible for experimental work that is scientific.

The Use of Scientific Method in Laboratory Schools

To proceed scientifically in selecting and validating curricular materials, at least three steps are necessary: (1) the development or choice of acceptable criteria or standards for selecting materials; (2) the organization and presentation of the selected materials to children under conditions as exactly comparable as possible with those of other similar children using different materials; and (3) testing results to find the outcomes of the teaching of the selected materials and comparing these with the outcomes from the materials used by the control groups.

The report of the McDonald County, Missouri, Experimental School is specifically an account of an experiment for an elementary-school curriculum as a whole. The experiment was conducted along lines as thoroughly scientific as could be brought to bear at that time. The school selected its material on the basis of clearly stated principles; it tested its results by the best methods then known, and it compared its outcomes with those of other schools using different materials. While some of the techniques used at the time might be regarded as inadequate to-day, it used the best known methods at that time. The Iowa University Elementary School, the Laboratory Schools of the University of Chicago, and the Lincoln School of Teachers College all indicate that they are employing the most thoroughgoing scientific procedure in making revisions in curricula.

Apart from these illustrations, we find very little contributed by these other so-called 'experimental schools,' of which those included in the reports are types, that satisfies the demands of scientific procedure to complete validation. Bases of appraisal in most of them are subjective and philosophical, rather than scientific. In a large, general sense, each such school as a whole may be regarded as an experiment. On the other hand, very few such schools have undertaken work in a way to give scientific validity to the results which they report. They all more or less well demonstrate that they can give children an education that meets the tests applied to public schools. They maintain that additional values are realized that are not secured by children in public schools. General observation and the critical application of certain principles of education quite commonly accepted affirm many of the claims made. Yet some of the values maintained for these schools are still matters of controversy. With our limited facilities for scientific determination of values, this uncertainty is more or less unavoidable. Probably some uncertainties will always exist, and even be desirable. But to be uncertain is neither necessary nor desirable in those matters for which we have devised or can devise means of scientific procedure and measurement.

For a full quarter of a century several schools of the general type included in this list have been at work. That they have exerted and are exerting very great influence in improving school practice can not be doubted. They have usually grown up as a means of expressing and demonstrating some point of view in education derived from the recent contributions of educational philosophy and psychology. But the 'set up' is usually not inclusive of a full scientific procedure. There is provision for no testing of results in comparison with results from control situations which will afford objective evidence of measurable differences in achievement, if such exist. Both the amount and value of achievements claimed, rest upon assertion rather than upon incontrovertible evidence.

Has not the time come when these schools should feel an obligation to undertake to justify their practice by scientific procedure? While no one school could go far in a short time, every school could begin by working with small units of curricular material each year and conducting scientific experimentation with such units to the point of complete validation. Each could add something to our stock of positive knowledge about curricular materials and remove just so much from the realm of opinion. By the use of a worker trained in scientific procedure in each school, such schools could do much to help in the guidance of their own practice and contribute also to the problem of curriculum-making in the public schools. In schools devoted to the exposition of any particular philosophy of education, such procedure should not hamper their work. Rather, it should continuously help it. No wholesome philosophy of education is opposed to facts. The best way to strengthen any point of view is to support it by tested evidence. If scientific evidence is not in accord with the philosophy, then the philosophy must necessarily be modified to include the meaning of the facts. Scientific truth is never at variance with eternal truth.

For schools to do splendid work and in a few years to discontinue or revert to conventional practice with no record of measured results for the work attempted is wasteful and deplorable. Because of their relative freedom from limitations, many schools operating under private auspices or as parts of schools of education may introduce variant materials and practices not elsewhere possible. For this reason, they are often the strategic places for testing proposals far removed from current practice. If they would do this in a scientific way, giving results whose validity would be beyond question, they would stand as very highly useful experiment stations for advancing the cause of education as a whole. If what they prove to be scientifically valid and worth while is developed under conditions not possible at present in public schools, then such modifications in securing as many of these values as possible under public-school conditions could be made. But first of all, the validity and worth of the changes proposed should be established.

By reference to the General Statement of the Committee (Part II of this Yearbook), it will be observed that the general trend of the work of curriculum-making in the laboratory schools reporting is in the direction of the conclusions there expressed. Some of these schools far outrun the limits of the 'next steps' upon which there is agreement. That they are able to do this and to venture far into untried regions of curriculum-making and methods of teaching is most fortunate for the progress of education. But with this opportunity and privilege should go an obligation and a responsibility to render an accurate and scientific account of results. Such schools should not be content to affirm on the basis of casual observation and opinion that their work brings about desirable results thus and so, but should feel an obligation to prove it by evidence which no one can successfully challenge. That instruments of measurement are not yet available for testing values in all fields is true. However, by using all of the means of evaluation now known, and by giving concentrated attention to the problem, much more is possible in validating procedures and results than has yet been attempted. That some of the schools have made successful contributions that are scientific should stimulate and encourage all to use scientific method both in curriculum-making and in the development of correlative techniques of teaching.

SECTION V

MISCELLANEOUS CURRICULUM STUDIES

CHAPTER XXVII

REVIEW AND CRITIQUE OF CURRICULUM-MAKING FOR THE VOCATIONS

W. W. CHARTERS
School of Education, University of Chicago, Chicago, Illinois

The building of curricula by the functional analysis method has been carried farther than elsewhere in the field of the vocations. Not only has a greater number of vocational studies been made, but many of the techniques which have later been used in other subjects were first worked out in the vocational field.

The explanation of this condition lies in two directions. On the one hand, the trades are relatively simple in their operations, and are relatively superficial, so far as the theory underlying practice is involved in the use of good methods. In order to be a satisfactory plumber or carpenter, one does not need to have a great mass of so-called 'fundamental' information on which to base his practice. It is undoubtedly true that the knowledge of chemistry or of engineering would be extremely useful in research into the problems of these and other trades, but this research is for research workers rather than for the tradesman.

On the other hand, the support given to vocational education through the Smith-Hughes Act (under the administration of the Federal Board for Vocational Education) has led to concentrated and continued attention to the problem of building courses of study which will fit the student to handle the problems of his trade in the most efficient way. This interest shows itself in at least two ways. First, some funds are provided by the Federal Board for research into curriculum-organization; and second, many of the Smith-Hughes officials situated both in Washington and in the outlying states have sufficient leisure and clerical assistance to make it possible for them to work out courses of study on the functional basis.

In describing the application of the method of functional analysis to the trades and to the vocations, attention needs to be called to several considerations. In the first place, any curriculum which is built upon job analysis must take into account the personal qualifications necessary for success in the vocation. Each vocation has its own 'personality profile.' The machinist, for instance, needs to possess in a rather high degree the qualities of accuracy and speed, together with other qualities such as honesty and coöperativeness. The efficient carpenter will need to be neither so accurate and rapid, but he should possess neatness, let us say, to a greater degree than the machinist. Since these traits are so fundamental, it is essential that they be recognized in the curriculum for any vocation.

Not only must the traits be determined, but the activities which are performed in the occupation must be analyzed. This analysis may be based on duties or on difficulties. That is to say, we may list the duties that the worker must perform, or we may list the problems that he meets. Specifically, we may enumerate the duties for which a salesman in a department store is responsible, or we may discover the points at which salesmen in department stores fail to meet the requirements of the vocation. The duty analysis is more complete. The difficulty analysis concentrates attention upon those duties which cause trouble and assumes that the duties which do not cause trouble may be learned incidentally while on the job.

When the duties or difficulties have been listed, the next step in curriculum-construction is to collect the methods by which the duties are performed or the difficulties are met. These methods may be collected upon what is called a 'practice' level—that is to say, the empirical methods of performing the operations may be collected. It is, however, a part of the job-analysis method to carry the study farther by the introduction of the theory upon which the methods are based. This theory may take the form of principles underlying the methods or of auxiliary information, meaning thereby information that one needs to have in order to understand the methods. The introduction of the theory, as we use the term here, tends to make the tradesman into an engineer and to render him more intelligent and efficient in the use of the methods of his trade.

When the raw material which we have been describing has been collected, a third problem remains, namely, the arrangement of this material in proper instructional form. This involves the grading of the material on the basis of the difficulty and ease of learning in relation to the maturity of students. It requires a consideration of the appropriate amount of practice exercises and of other devices which will make the conditions such that learning will be easy and efficient.

In describing a number of the studies that have been made in the vocations, we shall need to bear in mind all the foregoing points. We shall consider (1) the attempts that have been made to determine the traits of the vocations, (2) difficulty analyses, (3) duty analyses, (4) the collection of methods of performance, (5) the derivation of the theory in the form of principles, auxiliary information, or related subject matter from these methods, and (6) the methods used in arranging the material in proper instructional order.

Before proceeding to a detailed examination of some of the outstanding and typical studies, attention should be drawn to the fact that there is a distinction between a description of an occupation and a job analysis of an occupation. Several such descriptions have been made. These include such studies as the following: The United States Department of Labor has worked out descriptions of many occupations, such as slaughtering and meat-packing, street railway work, glass manufacturing, cane-sugar refining, and flour milling.[1] These were prepared chiefly for the United States Employment Service in the latter part of the second decade of this century. The Federal Board for Vocational Education has made similar surveys of occupations such as the junior commercial occupations[2] and the pottery industry.[3] The University of California, in connection with the State Board of Education of California, has made such analyses as of the work of juniors in banks[4] and the house carpenters' trade.[5] A description of the occupation of hotel-

[1] They appear as United States Department of Labor bulletins, under the general series title of "Descriptions of Occupations." Separate bulletins are prepared for slaughtering and meat-packing, street railways, glass, and so forth.

[2] *Survey of Junior Commercial Operations.* Government Printing Office, Washington, D. C.: Federal Board for Vocational Education, Bulletin No. 54, Commercial Education Series No. 4, June, 1920.

[3] *A Survey and Analysis of the Pottery Industry.* Government Printing Office, Washington, D. C.: Federal Board for Vocational Education, Bulletin No. 67, Trade and Industrial Series No. 20, June, 1921.

[4] Jessup, Eva, and Blanchard, Clyde. *An Analysis of the Work of Juniors in Banks.* Berkeley, California: Division of Vocational Education, University of California and the State Board of Education, Bulletin No. 4, Part-Time Education Series No. 5, May, 1921.

[5] Stier, Leslie G. *Analysis of the House Carpenter's Trade.* Berkeley, California: Division of Vocational Education, University of California and the State Board of Education, Division Bulletin No. 12, Trade and Industrial Series No. 1, March, 1923.

keeping has been worked out by L. S. Hawkins for the American Hotel Association of the United States and Canada. This is a description of an occupation made by a private organization in coöperation with the Federal Board for Vocational Education.

The distinction between a description of a vocation and a job analysis of the vocation is one of completeness. The description, being chiefly made for purposes of selection and vocational guidance, indicates merely the outstanding duties and qualifications of a vocation. The job analysis, when used for instructional purposes, must necessarily include not only the outstanding duties and qualifications, but all the duties and qualifications as well.

We shall now proceed to a consideration of some typical studies.

Few trait analyses have been attempted. One of the most complete is the analysis of the traits of secretaries.[6] The method utilized is described in detail in the book containing the report of the investigation. In general, it consists of securing from experts a statement of the traits which in their opinion explain the success or failure of people in the occupation. Traits are defined in terms of trait actions. When a sufficient number of experts have been interviewed, the material obtained from them is thrown together in the form of the trait list, and the profile is made for the occupation: that is to say, the relative importance of the traits is determined by more or less objective means.

By the use of the same method, a similar study has been made for the profession of pharmacy, a report on which is now in press and may be secured from the McGraw-Hill Publishing Company under the title: *Basic Material for a Pharmacy Curriculum.*

In the trade analyses the traits are not explicitly determined.

An early study attempted to determine a course in manual arts upon the basis of home repair. It was assumed that students might be taught to be proficient in making repairs around the home. With this in mind, L. R. Fuller made an extended study of home repairs in the Middle West.[7] He discovered the relative frequency with which these repairs were carried on by laymen, and for the most frequent of the jobs he determined what tool processes were in-

[6] Charters, W. W., and Whitley, I. B. *Analysis of Secretarial Duties and Traits.* Baltimore, Maryland: Williams and Wilkins Company, 1924.

[7] Fuller, L. R. "Manual arts based on home repair." *Journal of Educational Research,* 1921.

volved. He was then able to describe a course in manual arts in terms of the processes used in home repair. This study was not, however, carried through into textbook form.

In the strictly vocational fields the first study to attract attention was Allen's analysis of the machinists' trade.[8] In this study Allen listed the jobs carried on by the machinist and described a type job specification and the objectives for each job. In addition to this, he derived the auxiliary information necessary for the learner to understand the operation. This provided a detailed statement of the mathematics, drawing, and science needed for a complete understanding of each operation. In the same bulletin he gathered together into courses the mathematics, drawing, and science derived from his analysis. Specifically, Allen presents the raw material for shop practice and for each of the so-called 'related' subjects. This material the instructor is expected to arrange in proper pedagogical sequence and into it to insert the necessary 'connective tissue.'

Allen's technique was used in later bulletins issued by the Federal Board for Vocational Education on brick-laying (Bulletin No. 95), paper-hanging (Bulletin No. 102), and the railway boilermakers' trade (Bulletin No. 69). The State Board for Vocational Education of Idaho also used this technique in an analysis of the auto mechanic's trade.[9] The State Board for Vocational Education of California has made analyses of several of the trades. For instance, an analysis was made of the plasterer's trade in which the same technique was used, with modifications.[10] Particularly interesting are the instruction sheets.

The United Typothetae of America made an analysis of the printing vocation and in 1924 issued a revised set of standard apprenticeship lessons. Another survey of the same sort resulted in a course of study in tile-setting, which was worked out under the direction of the Associated Tile Manufacturers (Beaver Falls, Pennsylvania). This course is important because it represents the best

[8] *Outlines of Instruction in Related Subjects for the Machinist's Trade.* Federal Board for Vocational Education, Bulletin No. 52, Trade and Industrial Series No. 13.

[9] *Analysis of the Auto Mechanic's Trade for Idaho Schools.* State Board for Vocational Education, Boise, Idaho.

[10] *Analysis of the Plasterer's Trade.* Division of Vocational Education of the University of California and of the State Board of Education, Berkeley, California. Division Bulletin No. 15, Trade and Industrial Series, No. 3.

technique known to-day for building a curriculum for a trade. This technique is described by Mr. L. S. Hawkins, the investigator, in the *Journal of Educational Research* for May, 1926. Briefly, the method used was this. The trade of tile-setting was divided into thirty-nine jobs, nineteen of which were basic and twenty special. The curriculum for each job was prepared in the following way. An expert tile-setter, a young college man, and the investigator met in conference. The tile-setter was asked to explain to the student how to perform the job. Thereupon, the student wrote down the tile-setter's description. The latter was then asked to read the typewritten report and decide whether the method was stated as he meant to describe it. When it had finally been written in a manner satisfactory to the tile-setter, the student was told to perform the operations under the observation of the tile-setter, but without assistance from him. After this had been done, the lessons were again revised. The series of nineteen lessons were then taught in Dunwoody Institute to twenty tile-setting apprentices under the direction of the tile-setter. After a further revision, the material was released for national use.

An analysis of the garment-cleaning occupation was worked out by the National Association of Dyers and Cleaners. The results are set up in the form of a course of study for beginners by C. C. Hubbard.[11] It is of interest, because, in addition to providing an analysis of methods of performing the jobs, it gives a great deal of theoretical information, such as a dictionary of trade terms, formulas, tables of weights and measures, tests, and other information of that sort.

As a variation in the form of arranging the material, Selvidge and Christy's study should be noted. The conventional method of teaching the operations of a trade is to list the jobs in the trade in the proper instructional order upon the basis of ease of learning, types of difficulty, or kinds of materials used. In the application of this method the operations involved in each job are taught incidentally as they occur. Selvidge and Christy, however, in their analysis of sheet-metal working[12] have analyzed the basic unit

[11] Hubbard, C. C. *The Instructor in Garment Cleaning.* National Association of Dyers and Cleaners, St. Louis, Missouri, 1924.

[12] Selvidge, R. W., and Christy, Elmer W. *Instruction Manual for Sheet-Metal Workers.* (The Selvidge Series of Instruction Manuals). Peoria, Illinois: The Manual Arts Press, 1925.

operations used in this trade and find them to be thirty-eight in number. They proceed on the assumption that, if a student learns these thirty-eight operations, he has mastered the alphabet of sheet-metal working, and that all he has to do thereafter is to make the proper combinations of these operations in order to perform any one of the jobs of the trade.

This modification of teaching procedure is significant. It indicates a return to methods which were discarded twenty-five years ago by the theorists in education. Under the criticism that to learn the elements without a recognition of their uses destroyed interest, educators ceased teaching the alphabet and taught interesting sentences. Music teachers no longer began musical instruction with the scales; instead, they introduced their pupils to tunes. It was felt that the old so-called 'logical' method produced less interest in the student than did those methods in which the student used his material immediately. Now we find these thoughtful professional men reverting to the discarded method. They feel that, if the elements are taught, combinations can be easily learned; and we may assume that interest in the process will be developed from the interest that the pupils have in the vocation. This is a very interesting change in present procedure by a return to earlier procedures.

The plumbing trade has prepared a standardized course of training for apprentices based upon a job analysis.[13] This course was compiled by the National Trade Extension Bureau of the Plumbing and Heating Industries. The course, as issued, includes materials to be placed in the hands of apprentices in shop work and also the scientific information necessary to proficiency in the trade.

In the case of paper-hanging, both the Federal Board for Vocational Education and the trade itself worked out a series of lessons. The Federal Board prepared raw material, using Allen's method,[14] while the vocation threw this and other material into teaching form.[15]

---

[13] *Standardized Course of Training for Apprentice Plumbers.* Evansville, Indiana: National Trade Extension Bureau of the Plumbing and Heating Industries.

[14] *Paper Hanging.* Washington, D. C.: Federal Board for Vocational Education, Bulletin No. 102, Trade and Industrial Series No. 29, May, 1925.

[15] *Paper Hanging.* Wall Paper Manufacturers' Association, 461 Eighth Avenue, New York City, Bulletin No. 102A.

In the field of agriculture not so much has been done in the use of the job-analysis method. The Federal Board has, however, prepared some courses, among them an analysis of the management of a farm business,[16] an analysis of a corn-growing enterprise,[17] and an analysis of a poultry enterprise.[18] This material was worked out along the line that Greene developed in his sheep husbandry curriculum, described in *Curriculum Construction.* In these studies less attention is paid to the auxiliary information and greater latitude is allowed the teacher and pupils, since the operations in agriculture are less definitely standardized and routinized than are the operations in most of the trades.

In home economics five interesting studies may be reported. An outstanding piece of work is published under the title: "Home Economics Conference of State Supervisors and Members of Teacher-Training Staffs." The material is published in mimeographed form by the Federal Board for Vocational Education. The conference was held in Minneapolis in 1922, and consisted of twelve state supervisors and trainers of teachers, who met, with Anna E. Richardson as chairman, under the leadership of Charles R. Allen. Those objectives of the conference with which we are concerned were the listing of a sufficiently large number of jobs to form the basis for a classification of the homemaker's responsibilities, the preparation of 'lay-outs' for a number of detailed jobs, and the outlining of short courses of instruction to meet definite needs. The Allen technique for the industries was applied to home economics.

The University of Missouri has published a bulletin on "Related Art for Home Economics Classes," by Miss Lila M. Welch. It discusses the points at which art applies to the problems of home economics. When these points of contact had been determined, the material was arranged in the form of students' problems, and the subject matter and methods of procedure were tabulated.

---

[16] *Analysis of the Management of a Farm Business.* Government Printing Office, Washington, D. C.: Federal Board for Vocational Education, Bulletin No. 88, Agricultural Series No. 16, October, 1923.

[17] *Analysis of the Management of a Corn Growing Enterprise.* Government Printing Office, Washington, D. C.: Federal Board for Vocational Education, Bulletin No. 101, Agricultural Series No. 24, May, 1925.

[18] *Analyzing a Poultry Enterprise.* Government Printing Office, Washington, D. C.: Federal Board for Vocational Education, Bulletin No. 75, Agricultural Series No. 11, June, 1922.

Attention should be called to a study of the series: "Memoranda on Home Economics," published by the State Board of Vocational Education, Springfield, Illinois, and entitled *Planning for the Course of Study,* by Ada H. Hess. In this study a list of the abilities and characteristics that should be developed by the girl in her year's work has been compiled.

A fourth study has been made by the Denver public schools. This is known as "Course of Study Monograph, No. 12," entitled *Home Economics,* and is applicable to the high school. In the preparation of this material check lists were utilized to discover the activities carried on in the home by high-school girls.

A fifth study was made by the Home Economics Division of the Iowa State College and is entitled *Job Content for Management Responsibilities.* It makes use of a revised form of the technique developed in the first home economics study referred to above. It is in mimeographed form. Other studies are being made, but the writer has been able to find none in permanent form and available for distribution.

The foregoing material is confined to the trades and industries for whose fostering the Federal Board for Vocational Education is governmentally responsible. Many other studies have been made by other agencies. In the field of retail selling a large number of studies have been made by the use of the job-analysis method. Miss Ringo, of the Research Bureau for Retail Training, University of Pittsburgh, made an analysis of the duties of buyers and floormen, upon the basis of which she constructed an executive training course for department-store executives.

A great deal of use has been made of the 'difficulty analysis.' Specifically, an analysis of the selling difficulties of sales-people in department stores which revealed some sixty weaknesses was used as a basis for the collection from expert sales-people of methods of handling these difficulties. This material was thrown into the form of a book called *How to Sell at Retail,*[19] and later was condensed into smaller compass because the sales-people were not greatly interested in reading a 'thick' book. The same method was applied to the preparation of language lessons. Twenty-five thousand

[19] Charters, W. W. *How to Sell at Retail.* The Houghton Mifflin Company, New York, 1922.

errors were collected in the city of Pittsburgh, and the most flagrant of these became topics of instruction in lessons prepared for department-stores sales-people. One other illustration may be mentioned. A list was made of the difficulties encountered by executives in handling people in commerce and industry. Methods used by experts were collected and the material was organized into a volume called *Personal Leadership in Industry*.[20]

A modification of job analysis was made in the case of the collection of material for merchandise information in department stores. The values which customers look for in purchasing were used as control elements in collecting information about materials and methods of manufacture to be taught to the sales-people.[21] These control elements were used as a basis for twenty textbooks in a merchandise manual series. A description of the technique used by Misses Ringo, Dyer, and Kneeland in these manuals is found in the Proceedings of the Third Annual Meeting of the Executive Board of the Research Bureau for Retail Training, Carnegie Institute of Technology.

In the retail field Miss Kneeland made an interesting attempt to derive the psychology of salesmanship from *How to Sell at Retail*. The investigator proceeded on the assumption that one could definitely determine the content of the psychology of retail selling by asking why the specific methods used in retail selling were efficient. As a result, one hundred fifty facts or principles of psychology were listed. The material was used as the basis for a course on the psychology of salesmanship for department stores.

The studies thus far described have all been studies on what can be called the 'trade level.' It will be of interest to note some applications of the method to the much more difficult professional fields. These we shall now proceed to describe.

The study referred to above in connection with the analysis of secretarial traits presents as well a duty analysis of a vocation that may or may not be called a 'profession.' A list of eight hundred seventy-one duties performed by secretaries were col-

[20] Charters, W. W., and Craig, D. R. *Personal Leadership in Industry*. The McGraw-Hill Book Company, New York.

[21] Proceedings of the Third Annual Meeting of the Executive Board of the Research Bureau for Retail Training, Carnegie Institute of Technology, Pittsburgh, Pennsylvania.

lected by the interview method. These were later checked by seven hundred fifteen stenographers and their frequency determined. Not only was the total frequency ascertained, but also the frequency for different occupations of employers, such as insurance men, engineers, advertisers, doctors, and so forth. Furthermore, a fairly satisfactory technique was worked out to discover which of these duties could better be learned on the job than in school, as well as to discover those duties which are less difficult to learn and therefore need have no attention paid to them in school. No recorded investigation has been made, however, into the course of study that would be needed in teaching these duties and traits. A statement of what, in the opinion of the writer, should be the next steps in building a curriculum upon the basis of this analysis is found in *The American Shorthand Teacher* (Volume I, No. 1, September, 1925) in an article entitled "A functional secretarial curriculum."

In 1923 Strong and Uhrbrock published a study in which they sought to determine a curriculum for executives in the printing vocation.[22] By the interview method they listed the duties of ninety-four executives in ten different printing establishments located in two large cities. When these duties had been listed, they then proceeded to make a study of what was needed to perform these duties when properly evaluated. They used committees of the faculty of Carnegie Institute of Technology to work out the materials which in their opinion, and upon the basis of the duties to be performed in the executive positions, were the essential elements in each subject. This study was carried through to the formation of a definite schedule in terms of semester-hours for the training course for printing executives.

For the last three years a study has been under way to determine a curriculum for colleges of pharmacy, based upon an analysis of the traits and duties of pharmacists. The investigation has been administered by a staff consisting of a director and several pharmacists, who worked in conjunction with an advisory committee composed of prominent faculty members from colleges of pharmacy. This staff was assisted by a large number of experts in different

[22] Strong, Edward K., and Uhrbrock, Richard S. *Job Analysis and the Curriculum.* (Personnel Research Series.) Williams and Wilkins Company, Baltimore, 1923.

fields of pharmaceutical education, such as physiologists, chemists, botanists, and the like. A comprehensive study of the duties of pharmacists revealed the fact that progressive members of the profession perform twelve types of duties. Subsequently, each duty was analyzed to discover what information was needed to perform it. When the study had been completed, it was found that some fourteen objective bases had been used for determining the content. While it was impossible completely to eliminate subjective opinion as to the content of the curriculum, the opinions could be much more accurately drawn than otherwise because of the presence of these fourteen objective bases.

The report of the pharmacy study is now in press and will be issued during the spring. As soon as it is completed, it will be accepted by a committee of the colleges of pharmacy who will use it as a basis for determining the new course of study in the professional phases of pharmacy.

Some four years ago an analysis of women's activities was undertaken at Stephens College (Columbia, Missouri) for the purpose of determining the required courses in a curriculum for women. The study has been completed, and the results are now being published. The traits of home-makers were determined by the methods used in the other studies described. The activities of women college graduates who were home-makers or were unmarried and in vocations were secured by means of diaries carried on for a week by each of several hundred women. This material was classified into twenty-three groups of activities; those which were common to both the married and unmarried women were held to be indicative of the required content of the course.

The groups of activities were the following: foods, clothing, physical hygiene, mental hygiene, communication, reading, recreation and play, social relations, civic relations, personal study, schooling, reproduction, religion, music, art, literature, nature, gratification of random interests, increasing the circle of interests, free associative thinking, introspection, increasing the income, and participation in vocations.

Later, each of these divisions was sub-classified according to the nature of the material. One illustration may be given. Under "foods" are found the following types of activities: the care of food, the disposal of waste, eating, preparation of foods, preparation of menus, the preservation of foods, the production of all foods, the selection of foods, serving, managing, financing, training, and equipment. The study was not, however, concerned primarily with the subdivisions. Its main purpose was to secure a list of major classes in which all the activities of women could be included.

These classifications were run for both the home-makers and the unmarried professional women. Upon this basis the required subjects in the course of study for women were determined by the simple process of finding which of these groups of activities were common to both classes of women, and by considering further which of these common activities would yield to school instruction.

As a result of this comparison, the following, in the opinion of a few judges, would be the required subjects in a curriculum for women. The first to emerge was the subject of clothing, because it appeared that the activities of married and unmarried women were about equally divided. (Parenthetically, foods would not be a required subject, because the unmarried women were primarily concerned only with the selection of foods, which would ordinarily be classified under the next topic to be discussed.) It is quite apparent that the care of health and the understanding of the rules of health should be a required subject. This would involve a determinable amount of service physiology—an amount sufficient to explain the reasons for the rules of hygiene. Likewise, it was quite apparent that a course, whatever its name, which would include the facts, methods, and habits of mental hygiene is of equal importance to both types of women. This subject would constitute a new type of course in individual and social psychology which would assist the woman in becoming master of herself and of social relations.

Obviously, on this basis a course of English composition, both oral and written, would be required. Specifically, about twenty percent of the activities collected had to do with some form of communication, such as conversation, writing, and telephoning. It was likewise evident from an examination of the material that a course which might be called 'social science' should be included. This course would involve a study of social, economic, and political problems centering around the civic organizations, and ranging all the way from a consideration of the milk supply of the community to the World Court. Similarly, attention would have to be given to the topic which in the classification is called "reproduction." Such a study would deal at least with questions of mating and marrying, and in part would be closely related to the subject of physical hygiene, already discussed. It is possible that this material should in some way be woven into the subject of psychology for women, mentioned above.

Both the married and unmarried women were found to secure a great deal of satisfaction and comfort from the appreciation of art, literature, the drama, and nature. Therefore, a course dealing with the aesthetic elements of life should be included. There should be added to this a group dealing approximately with ethics, religion, and personality, and having an ethical and philosophical core, rather than the psychological approach in mental hygiene.

Finally, upon the basis of this examination it appeared that there should be included a course on financing from the consumer's point of view. Such a course should deal primarily with the problem of getting the highest qualitative satisfaction from a determinable amount of income, and should have as its aim the development of an intelligent consumer.

If one reads over the classification of women's activities mentioned above, it is apparent that no consideration is given to personal study, the gratification of random interests, free associative thinking, and participations in vocations. The reason for this is that these are by-products of a college education, and direct instruction in them cannot be given. The dangers of introspection are cared for in mental hygiene. Increasing the income is largely a matter of academic interest to graduates of colleges who are not engaged in vocations. The training of children is not a required course because the unmarried professional women obviously have little to do with this, except as it is included within the vocation of teaching. The training of children will become an elective subject for those who are preparing to be wives and homemakers.

Such a curriculum would constitute the so-called 'cultural core' for women in all vocational schools and in colleges of liberal arts. It assures to each woman a consideration of the quite fundamental activities with which all women within the national group are concerned. It provides for the social sciences, for participation in local and national affairs, for physical health and mental happiness, for communication, for a philosophy of life, for contacts with, and an appreciation of, the beautiful in life, and for a systematic and economical selection of the materials used in a qualitatively high type of living.

Summary

The following observations can be safely made concerning the foregoing studies:

1. A considerable body of technical information and methods has been worked out in the vocational field.

2. Comparatively little attention has been paid directly to the analysis of traits and qualifications.

3. Some very fine examples of analyses of occupations can be found.

4. The analyses which have been made in the field of practice are more complete than those in the field of theory, although several examples of methods of deriving the theory from practice are presented.

5. The instructional order and the arrangement of the raw material have not been worked out with the same degree of thoroughness as has the raw material itself. This is due to two facts. In the first place, the people who are interested in working out the raw material have less interest in its pedagogical arrangement. In the second place, we have only recently secured the raw material, and time has not been available to do as much work as is desirable upon the pedagogical presentation of the material.

CHAPTER XXVIII

CURRICULUM-RECONSTRUCTION IN THE COLLEGE

F. J. Kelly
Dean of Administration, University of Minnesota, Minneapolis, Minnesota

Most of the chapters in this yearbook discuss the curriculum from the point of view of the method of its construction. It would be interesting to discuss college curricula from the same point of view. However, both because this is the first discussion of college curricula to appear in the Yearbooks of the National Society, and because curriculum-revision in the light of modern psychological and sociological developments has made so much less progress in the colleges than in the elementary schools and in the high schools, it seems more useful to devote this chapter to a discussion of recent reconstruction of the college curricula, rather than to a discussion of how college curricula are constructed.

With the growth of extreme specialization and emphasis on research in the graduate schools of this country, there has been a tendency for college teachers, trained in these graduate schools or in German Universities, to magnify specialization as a function of the colleges of arts and sciences.

To be great authorities in their chosen fields, to be great productive scholars, has come to be the dominant ambition of members of college faculties. To be great teachers, to be interested in students first, and in their subjects second, has come to be *passé* on most college campuses. On this account, the prevailing technique for making college curricula was described by Robert L. Kelly, Executive Secretary of the Association of American Colleges, speaking in 1923 as Chairman of the Association's Commission on the Organization of the College Curriculum, as follows:[1]

> It is unnecessary to attempt to account for the confusion which has arisen through the former method of curriculum-building, a method, as our investigation shows, which is still the dominant one. A careful scrutiny of the program of study of most of the colleges indicates that they are constructed very much as a tariff bill is constructed in the Congress of the United

[1] Bulletin, Association of American Colleges, April, 1923, page 71.

States. The final result is the outcome of strains and tensions, of concessions and exchanges as between departmental representatives. The evidences that unifying principles are actually functioning in the development of the college curriculum are difficult to discover.

Fortunately, a revival of interest in curriculum-construction on a sound scientific and pedagogical basis has been taking place of late all over the country. The last decade has seen many significant changes. But even to date, curricula which have resulted from the struggle by departmental specialists on the faculty for recognition of their particular fields of subject matter are in vogue throughout the country as a whole. It would seem more useful, therefore, to go at once to a discussion of the modifications now finding their way into college curricula than to devote time to variations in the methods of constructing curricula.

The absence of standardization in American education manifests itself in higher education, the same as in the lower schools. There are no federal laws defining degrees. "Diploma mills" have flourished for decades, some of them having no college buildings. Diplomas of identical names issued by regularly established colleges have very different meanings in respect both to kind and quality of educational training which they imply. It is manifestly impossible, therefore, to treat the subject of the college curriculum as if it were a standardized thing.

Certain forces have operated, however, to bring about a large measure of similarity among college curricula. These forces are growing stronger each year. The American Medical Association goes far in determining medical school curricula all over the country. The Association of Dental Colleges, the American Bar Association, the Association of Pharmaceutical Faculties, do the same for the curricula in the schools they influence. Standardizing agencies such as the Association of American Universities and the Association of American Colleges set up certain definitions affecting colleges of arts and sciences and in some cases decline to recognize colleges which do not conform to the stated requirements. Through the influence of these agencies and many others, there has come to be a sort of framework common to all American higher education.

Interest in curricula of higher education has lately found expression in studies of far-reaching importance. The study of medical education made in 1910 by Dr. Abraham Flexner for the Rockefeller Foundation served to revolutionize medical education. The study of dental education just completed by Dr. William J. Gies, with a subsidy from the Carnegie Foundation for the Advancement of Teaching, is a comprehensive investigation likely to modify greatly the curricula of dental colleges. Dr. W. W. Charters, with a subvention from the Commonwealth Fund, is just now completing a study of curricula of schools of pharmacy. Mr. W. E. Wickenden is directing a most comprehensive investigation of engineering education for the Society for the Promotion of Engineering Education. This study is financed mainly by the Carnegie Foundation for the Advancement of Teaching. Other recent nation-wide investigations in progress include a study of Latin and a study of modern languages, each promising to yield values precious to the student of college curricula. Four books representing more or less careful studies of the college of arts and sciences as an institution have appeared within the past two years: *College,* by John P. Gavit; *The American Arts College,* by F. J. Kelly; *Tendencies in College Administration,* by Robert L. Kelly; and *A Study of the Liberal College,* by Leon B. Richardson.

So much interest in the curricula of higher education as these studies indicate would lead one to expect widespread agitation for curricular changes among college faculties. Such is found to be the case. The general sense of satisfaction which characterized most colleges only a few years ago has given place to a feeling that the whole scheme of college education should be critically examined. Experiments with new courses and changed curricula are taking place in many colleges. The chief purpose of this chapter is to set forth briefly some of the more significant of these changes. Nothing approaching a complete survey of the hundreds of American colleges has been possible. The following report is based upon a study of the more important literature on the subject, and upon replies to letters written to thirty of the colleges known to be most active in one or another phase of curriculum-reorganization.

Important and striking though they are, it will not be possible to include in this brief report changes in curricula of professional schools. Their development is having a profound effect, too, upon the curricula of colleges of arts and sciences from which they have mostly sprung. The first two years of many colleges of arts are occupied largely with pre-professional courses, and a large fraction of students leave the arts college for the professional school at the end of two years. However, I must confine myself to a consideration of changes in curricula of colleges whose primary purpose is liberal, rather than vocational or professional. Such an institution I shall mean hereafter when I speak of a "college."

In the last century of its development the curriculum of the American college has passed through two distinct periods: (1) the period of the fixed curriculum—not so much dominated by a demand for a common body of knowledge as for a training through mental discipline; and (2) the period of free electives, developed in response to the doctrine of interest.

The present typical college curriculum, a third stage of development, represents mainly a reaction from free electives. Certain fixed requirements, few in number, such as English and physical education, serve to assure to everyone the absolute essentials. In addition, the college curriculum must assure breadth and scholarliness and must be adapted to differences of ability among students. Breadth is the object of the regulations for 'distribution;' scholarliness is the object of the requirements for 'concentration;' and recognition of individual differences accounts for such recent developments as sectioning classes on the basis of ability, honors courses, and the like. Curriculum-reconstruction now going on in colleges can best be discussed, therefore, under these four heads: (I) specific requirements; (II) broadening study, or 'distribution;' (III) specialization study, or 'concentration;' and (IV) adaptations to differences of ability among students.

But first, three striking examples of curricular adjustment intended to influence all these factors, but not easily analyzable on this basis, are worthy of notice and study.

1. Antioch College, at Yellow Springs, Ohio, has a six-year curriculum, half industrial labor and half study. Students pair so as to hold the industrial job by terms of five weeks each, getting the prevailing rate of pay, living as other workmen live. The job is regarded, however, as an organic, indispensable part of the student's education, as vital a factor in his 'culture' as his 'book learning.'

2. Pomona College, Claremont, California, has just announced its plan to develop a group of small colleges essentially independent of each other, rather than to develop a large college.

3. Yale has had for the past five years a unique organization known as the "Freshman Year." In order to secure a more intimate association between teachers and freshmen, to improve the quality of instruction, and to provide for suitable curricular adjustments, a separate faculty was established and charged with the full responsibility of the freshman year, much as if it were a separate one-year college.

These three examples are worthy of intimate study. Space will not permit a discussion of them in this report, however, which must take up the developments under the four headings mentioned above.

I. Specific Requirements

One of the conditions which has proved most embarrassing to colleges is the changing relationship between colleges and the secondary schools. While this changing relationship affects somewhat all aspects of the college curriculum, it is felt most keenly in its effect upon the attainment of a common body of knowledge. Thirty years ago, the curricula of high schools and preparatory schools were dictated almost wholly by the colleges. A fixed curriculum prevailed in the high school. The college determined what it should consist of. The work of the college could be built upon a common content brought from the preparatory schools.

College domination of high schools has largely broken down—particularly west of the Atlantic states. While colleges may with certain limitations set their own entrance requirements, it is not practicable in most cases to be in conflict with the high-school graduation requirements in essential respects. This fact is responsible for one of the greatest group of changes in college curricula in recent years. To-day most of the content of high-school courses must also be available in college. In 1912 the prescribed courses in the admission requirements of the 125 colleges on the approved list of the Association of American Universities was 73 percent of the total admission requirements. Eight years later, in 1920, that percentage had dropped to 45.[2] It is probably even less

[2] Furst, Clyde. *College Entrance Requirements.* Bulletin of Association of American Colleges, No. 2, Vol. VII, p. 16.

now. It is obvious, therefore, that specific requirements in the college curricula must be stated in terms of a combination of secondary-school units and college credits.

The difficulty inherent in this situation is very great. It is even further intensified, however, by the facts (1) that the high schools themselves are very dissimilar, and (2) that many courses offered in the high schools are not intended as preparatory to college, and many students pursuing them do not at the time ever intend to enter college, but do enter just the same. Altogether, this tendency of the high schools to become the "people's colleges," ends in themselves, and not essentially preparatory to any higher unit in the educational system, is the most perplexing problem faced by college curriculum-makers. It has forced upon them, as Koos[3] points out, the realization that there is much in common between the purposes or aims of the high school and of the first two years of the college, and that there is no logical reason for the abrupt break now experienced between the high school and the college; that much of what constituted the curriculum of the college only a few decades ago, is now available in the high school; that the age of entrance to college is about two years older than it was a century ago; that colleges, with their highly trained faculties of specialists, are putting into the four-year course an amount of specialization undreamed of earlier when colleges were devoted to general training; that this specialization period is viewed largely from the point of view of its vocational significance by the students, even where the college disclaims any such purpose.

Three movements affecting the problem of specific requirements will be mentioned.

1. The Junior College

One of the most striking curricular developments of this generation is the junior college, a curriculum of two years' extent. Their numbers are increasing rapidly; without doubt more than one hundred have now been established in the United States. Some are separate institutions; some constitute an upward extension of the secondary school with which they are associated; some are organized within a larger college, normal school or university. Wherever organized,

---

[3] Koos, L. V. *The Junior College Movement.* Ginn and Co., 1925.

the dominant purpose, aside from its pre-vocational function, seems to be to dovetail with, and to round out, the general training begun in the high school and to avoid the scattering which has largely destroyed the unity of the first two years of the typical college—particularly the large college. With the belief that intensive specialization is the function of the university, the advocates of the junior college, with its faculty in sympathy with the purpose of general training for participation in civic and social life, hold that a separate organization of the first two years of college work is called for. By careful coöperation with the high school and by avoiding highly departmentalized courses, unity may again be restored and a common culture achieved. With a clarified purpose dominating both the choice of subject matter and method of teaching, as well as the training of the teachers, it is held that the doctrine of interest will again become more operative. Whether or not these claims prove valid, time will tell. While there are other factors involved, the movement to establish junior colleges is gaining momentum largely because of faith in these claims.

2. Changing Traditional Requirements and Distinctions

Changes in Course Requirements. No complete survey of recent changes in specific requirements is possible here. The action of Rockford College will illustrate the sort of changes being made. In 1920 the four units of languages required were reduced to two, and in 1925 the requirement of two units of Latin for the A.B. degree was accepted "as desirable but not always essential." Also, in 1922 freshman mathematics ceased to be absolutely required for first-year students, and the entrance requirements in algebra were reduced from one and one-half to one unit.

Barnard College this year removed all prescribed subjects unless needed to give a student "a command of written and spoken English, the ability to read at sight with ease at least one foreign language, a healthy body, and a knowledge of hygiene."

Miami University has voted to discontinue "the fixed requirement of one year's study in either Latin, Greek or Mathematics."

Without citing other cases, the tendency illustrated by these actions may be summarized by quoting from the report of the Commission on the Organization of the College Curriculum of the Association of American Colleges which was made at the conclusion of a nation-wide survey in 1921, thus: "There is a marked *tendency* toward student registration in the modern subjects."

Making the A.B. Degree More Inclusive. The humanities were first to occupy the field of the college curriculum. The natural sciences fought their way to recognition, but students making any of the sciences their major study were commonly admitted, not to the A.B., but to the B.S. degree. As other new subjects have been admitted, such as education, home economics or business administration, the common practice has been to include them among the subjects leading to the B.S. degree. Consequently, there has been a feeling that the A.B. degree represented the 'all-wool' culture. In an attempt to recognize a wider range of student interests without this apparent discrimination, a tendency is discernible to include the whole range of subjects in the A.B. fold. Dartmouth, for example, has recently abandoned the B.S. degree. Rockford College has also dropped the B.S., and President Maddox writes: "The A.B. has been retained to unify the aims of the curriculum. Students may take an A.B. with a major in English or in Home Economics." A recent study by Mr. Horace P. Rainey[4] has revealed that independent teachers colleges now so rapidly going upon the four-year basis are using the A.B. as the principal degree to which their students are admitted on graduation.

3. General Courses

The most significant movement intended to correct in part the effects of too early departmental specialization and to bring back in some degree unity of the student's intellectual world, is the development of general courses for the early years of the college. Committee G, of the American Association of University Professors, reported in 1922 the results of a survey of Initiatory Courses for Freshmen,[5] revealing that fourteen colleges had begun to make use of this device to orient the student more effectively in his college environment and to initiate him to the spirit of genuine studentship.

---

[4] "A problem of teachers colleges," *Educational Administration and Supervision*, December, 1925.

[5] *Initiatory Courses for Freshmen.* Bulletin of the American Association of University Professors, October, 1922.

Antedating these initiatory courses, there had appeared in many colleges freshmen lectures and other "orientation courses," the purpose of which was chiefly to aid the student in making social and educational adjustments, such as the making of schedules for study, the use of the library, the proper safeguards to observe in his new living quarters, ideals and customs of the college community, and the like. These courses usually carried no credit, but were often required. Not many of these earlier courses sought new arrangements of old teaching materials, nor cut across departmental boundary lines, nor sought to unify the study of the basic facts and principles from all the aspects of a broad field such as the biological sciences or the social sciences. This remained for the more recent development, the first illustrations of which are described in the report just cited. This development is so important that a few of the more significant cases of such general courses must be briefly described. They fall under five types, according to the subject matter included: (a) courses not limited by any conventional departmental lines, (b) the social studies, (c) the natural sciences, (d) philosophy, and (e) the fine arts.

(*a*) *Orientation Courses Widely Inclusive in Scope.* Perhaps the best illustration of an orientation course which disregards all group and department lines is the one in operation for the last three years at the University of Minnesota. This course is "intended to assist the student to a synthesis of his present knowledge, to orient him in the world of nature, of man, and of organized society; and to arouse in him a consciousness of his relationships and a realization of his responsibility." It uses materials from the fields of the natural sciences, the social sciences, philosophy, and psychology. Only a limited number of students are allowed as yet to elect the course, and careful study is being made of the results. In spite of the breadth of the field covered, each instructor carries his section of students throughout the course.

Other illustrations of very general orientation courses are the "History of the World and Man," at Grinnell College, and "The Art of Living," at Connecticut College.

(*b*) *"Contemporary Civilization* (*Columbia College*). While other colleges have courses more or less like "Contemporary Civilization," as for example, "Civilization" at Leland Stanford, "Citizenship'' at Dartmouth, and ''Man in Society'' at Chicago University, the course which has had most adequate test is the one on contemporary civilization now running its sixth year at Columbia. What it is, as well as some of the evidence as to its success, are so well told by Dean Herbert E. Hawkes that I quote from an address he delivered before the Alumni Council of Amherst College, November, 1925:

> Five or six years ago a comprehensive and, carefully wrought orientation course was introduced in Columbia College as a required course for freshmen. It does not aim to cover all of the ground from chaos to Coolidge, but it does aim to 'hit the high spots' and to introduce the student to the kind of social and economic problem which the intelligent student of to-day might desire to attack. It is presented with the coöperation of the four departments of economics, philosophy, history, and government. The instruction in this course is exceedingly difficult, at any rate for the teacher, since each instructor carries his men throughout the entire year, in many cases over material which has to do with scholarly fields which are not his major interest.

Careful study of the results of this course has convinced the most skeptical members of the Columbia Faculty that the course has great value.

(*c*) *''The Nature of the World and of Man''* (Chicago University). Dean Ernest H. Wilkins, of Chicago University, describes this course as follows:

> ''The Nature of the World and of Man'' runs through the autumn and winter quarters of the freshman year. It is a coöperative course, with about twenty different men participating. It begins with the primal notions of chemistry, physics, the origin of the earth, the earth as the home of life, etc., and brings the story of life up through the different fields of the physical sciences to the point where man is defined as man.

Dartmouth's course on ''Evolution'' is another good example of cutting across science department lines. One essential difference, however, is that the Chicago course is limited to about the highest tenth of the class, while the Dartmouth course is required of all freshmen. An elective sophomore course on ''The History of Science'' is being offered this year for the first time in Columbia College. These will serve as types of the efforts—all too uncommon as yet—to unify around some principle the materials from several science departments.

(*d*) *"The Introduction to Modern Thought"* (University of Washington), an elective course for Freshmen, and *"An Introduction to Reflective Thinking,"* a course for the superior freshmen at Chicago, illustrate a third field which is yielding to the demand for unification. The Chicago course is described as "a definite attempt to teach the student how best to use and develop his own thinking powers."

(*e*) *"The Meaning and Value of the Arts"* (Chicago University) and *"The Introduction to the Fine Arts"* (University of Washington) represent the rarest attempts in the field of general or orientation courses. Here is an effort to bring out the common principle in such fields as architecture, sculpture, painting, music, and literature. It has had relatively little trial as yet. Its beginnings are hopeful, and if it can succeed, it will satisfy a most urgent need in education.

These will illustrate the rapid development going on in establishing general, or orientation, courses. Naturally, no agreement has yet been reached with respect either to the content of the courses or to the method of conducting them. In some places one teacher carries his section of students throughout the course, while in other places many teachers coöperate, each offering his particular aspect of the subject to a given group of students. In some places the course is required, in some places elective, and in some places limited to selected students. It seems safe to predict, however, that out of all the experimenting now being done, a partial solution will be found for the problems faced by the student who has come out of an elective course in the high school with little training in how to study, and enters an elective course in college where the work is in the hands of specialists in a score of highly differentiated departments. When the first two years of college, actuated by the new purpose, includes a group of these general courses, it seems likely that students will get a better understanding of "the meaning of the human story," and will acquire something more of a "common intellectual world."

II. Distribution

The broadening function of the college curriculum is achieved usually by a combination of required subjects and group requirements. These group requirements are usually completed during the first two years of the college. By the device of group requirements students are still obliged in many cases to take the subjects which have been dropped from the required list. For example, where German may have been required at one time, the group requirements may now specify a modern foreign language. Probably little is gained by such a change.

Because the distribution function is such an important aspect of the college curriculum it seems worth while to examine critically the operation of the group system, the method chiefly used to acccomplish it. Colleges usually divide their score or more of departments into from four to eight groups. One typical arrangement of four groups may be illustrated by Dartmouth's requirements:

> (1) One year of English. (2) A year course in each of two of the following: Modern language, ancient language, mathematics; (the modern language chosen must be a continuation of that presented for admission.) (3) A year course in each of two of the following: mathematics, physics, astronomy, chemistry, biology, physiology, geology. (4) A year course in each of two of the following: history, economics, political science, sociology, philosophy, psychology.

Work in seven departments is thus required, with quite a range of choice in the natural sciences and in the social sciences, but a very narrow range in the foreign languages and mathematics. It seems that the subjects valuable primarily as tools are still regarded as most essential for the distribution function at Dartmouth.

Another typical group arrangement may be illustrated by the requirements in the College of the University of Kansas: Five semester credits in each of six of the eight following groups: (1) Ancient languages—Greek and Latin; (2) modern foreign languages—German, French, Spanish, Italian; (3) English, including journalism and public speaking; (4) biological sciences—botany, zoölogy, anatomy, bacteriology, physiology, and entomology; (5) mathematics; (6) physical sciences—chemistry, physics, astronomy and geology; (7) philosophy and psychology; and (8) social studies—history, political science, economics, and sociology. From this array of departments and the range of choice permitted, little in common can be expected among the students. Courses cannot be studied nor taught from the point of view of the need for a common body of knowledge. Instead, each course is the beginning course of one of these highly differentiated departments, taught in general from the standpoint of a foundation for more advanced courses in the same department.

Exceptions may be noted here and there, where teachers have organized the courses in the interest of the student seeking breadth. At Antioch College, for example, two types of elementary courses are maintained in mathematics, physics, and chemistry—the one for those students who will not progress further in the field and who want the course as a part of a liberal education, the other for those students who are going ahead with scientific or engineering work. On the whole, however, these elementary courses taken to satisfy group requirements are poorly adapted for liberalizing students, but are well adapted for the beginning of specialization.

During the study[6] which I made of a dozen of the better liberal arts colleges three years ago, I talked with many of the student leaders as well as with members of the faculties. From these students I got the nearly unanimous verdict that many of the courses which were pursued merely to satisfy group requirements seemed to them of little value. While student opinion may be discounted somewhat, the students with whom I conferred were, in the main, those who were rated as leaders by faculty members or by the student body as a whole.

In the same study, a questionnaire was returned by 546 graduates of the twelve colleges, chosen at random from the classes 1910 to 1914. These alumni had been from eight to twelve years out of college. Among the questions answered were the following:

(1) What courses did you take in college which you would not take now if you were just beginning your college course?
(2) What courses would you take in place of the above?
(3) Leaving out the courses which have been of distinctly practical or vocational value, recall the college course which you prize most highly of all the courses you have studied.

Answers to these questions, as tabulated on page 59 of my study, reveal a general absence of appreciation of the subjects of mathematics and foreign languages, but a keen appreciation of social studies, especially philosophy, psychology, and English literature.

[6] Kelly, F. J. *The American Arts College.* The Macmillan Co.

It is freely acknowledged that alumni are not always able to render judgments upon such questions with due recognition of the more subtle values of the courses studied. On the other hand, if this sampling is representative of competent alumni opinion, I do not believe we can much longer, either by specific requirements or by group requirements, demand the study of those subjects which seem to alumni to have so little value.

Practices with respect to group requirements vary from college to college from the free choice of a half dozen beginnings in a half dozen out of a score of unrelated departments to well considered attempts to unify the distribution studies around some body of principles common to student interests. While the college world as a whole, if judged by college curricula, has scarcely recognized as yet this need for unification, there is widespread discussion of the point among college teachers. The increase in general courses discussed above is largely in response to this demand to correct this lack of unification. It seems likely that the distribution function will ultimately be achieved in large part by a number of these general courses, each covering an essential field of human interest. At present, however, attention may be given profitably to a type of distribution which uses departmental organization much like that prevailing in colleges generally, but which endeavors to provide a maximal degree of unification.

Rather than to choose partial examples from many colleges, it seems more useful to cite more fully the plan of a single college. For this purpose, Reed College, at Portland, Oregon, is chosen, partly because my limited survey has not revealed any college where it seems to be more effectively done, and partly because it has been the avowed purpose of Reed College from its beginning to build up coöperation among the departments in recognition of the unity of interests of the individual student. I shall, therefore, quote freely from the Reed College Bulletin of April, 1925, in order to give as much as possible of the actuating purpose as well as the curricular arrangement of studies.

In Reed College the curriculum comprises these four divisions, of which the first three are used to accomplish the distribution function: (1) Literature and Language, (2) History and Social Science, (3) Mathematics and Natural Science, (4) Philosophy, Psychology, and Education.

Students may elect either of two alternative groupings for their first two years, according to whether their interest tends more to Letters and Social Science or to Mathematics and Natural Science.

The primary significance of this curriculum can best be understood from explanations given in the Reed College Bulletin:

A CORRELATED AND INTEGRATED COURSE OF STUDY

The student is encouraged to look upon his work as forming one course of study, not a group of courses of study. He is made to feel that with his freshman year he enters upon a four-year course, all the various parts of which are closely bound up with one another.

THE FIRST TWO YEARS

During the freshman and sophomore years all students pursue a unified course of study, with correlated reading and conferences, and with special provision for students primarily interested in science and mathematics and those primarily interested in letters and social science.

The course of study deals with the fundamental bases and historical backgrounds of contemporary life. These are seen in the biological heritage of man, in his achievements in literature and art, and in his progress in coöperative effort and group action.

Independent Study. In order to accustom the student to independent work which will be expected of him in the last two years, and to encourage initiative, it is provided that in the freshman and sophomore years, instead of taking one of the elective courses, the student may devote a portion of his time (not more than one-fifth, and ordinarily less) to additional, individual study in connection with one of his regular courses, under the guidance of an instructor.

It is recognized that success in the last two years, during which the student will be thrown upon his own resources, depends upon the thoroughness of his preparation during the first two. A decided effort is made, therefore, to place him in the hands of the most experienced professors on the college staff at the moment when he begins his studies.

THE FRESHMAN YEAR

The course in "History and Literature" is intended to provide the background for an intelligent appreciation and understanding of the foundations of our contemporary civilization.

To this end, besides the lectures and small group conferences and papers in history and literature, supplementary study is required in one of the following fields: the development of political institutions, that of economic institutions, cultural history (music and art), and the history of philosophic and scientific thought. This work, which is correlated with the main stream of the course, is carried on by reading and discussion in special conference sections.

[The purpose of each of the other introductory courses—mathematics, general biology, chemistry and physics—is similarly set forth as study primarily for cultural rather than for specialization ends.]

THE SOPHOMORE YEAR

The study of the development of civilization is continued with one of the social sciences, chosen by the student, occupying the dominant place held in the freshman year by history, although the background given by the study of modern history is required of all students. The student is not allowed to lose sight of the intimate connection of what he is studying during this year with what he has studied in the previous year. Again, as in the freshman course, the coöperation of instructors calls constant attention to the close relation of historical, political, economic, social, and literary facts and ideas. Finally, the great problem of contemporary society presents itself; the reconciliation of the essential unity with the necessary individual, national, cultural, religious, and racial diversity of mankind.

Students in the Letters-Social Science Group take modern literature in addition to history and one of the social sciences, devoting approximately one-half of the work of the year to this course of study. Students in the Mathematics-Natural Science Group take, together with the history, either a social science or literature, giving thus slightly more than one-quarter of their time to this work. The program of study, aside from this, varies according to the special interests and needs of the student.

These quotations will serve to set forth the spirit and purpose in force at Reed College to achieve the broadening function of a college education. A brief visit to the college served to reassure the writer that the spirit set forth is an actual and dominating force in Reed College. The spirit and purpose there found are what an ever-increasing proportion of colleges are accepting as the goal of the distribution part of their curricula, and the plan in force at Reed College is at least suggestive. It represents a practicable plan which has had a considerable trial and appears to have overcome certain difficulties of departmentalism which have been claimed by many colleges to be well-nigh insurmountable.

III. CONCENTRATION

With the rapid expansion of knowledge and the increase in the modern need for specialization, college curricula which a century ago were given largely to general training now give from one fifth to two fifths of the time of the four-year course to what is called 'concentration.' Along with a general background of culture, a college man is supposed to have a fairly thorough mastery of one subject or field. This mastery is the primary purpose of the last two years of the college.

Concentration is achieved in three ways:

(1) A major sequence of studies in a given department, supplemented sometimes by a minor sequence in a related department. (To carry further the distribution function which is the chief purpose of the first two years of the college, minor sequences in departments unrelated to the major department are sometimes required.)

(2) A specialization curriculum, the component parts of which are taken from whatever departments are found to be offering courses needed for such specialization.

(3) A field of concentration, made up in large part for each student separately, the essential assumption being that the field mapped out may be concerned, not alone with content covered in college courses, but also with much that lies outside of college courses.

1. The Major Sequence

Of these three ways, the one prevailing by far most commonly, is the major sequence of courses. While practice differs widely, probably the majority of colleges require from twenty to thirty semester-hours to be taken in the major department. Each department is allowed considerable latitude usually in placing restrictions upon the courses acceptable for the major. In 1921 the typical major found by R. L. Kelley in his wide survey[7] was twenty-four semester-hours. His figures were drawn largely from the group of smaller colleges in which the major is probably somewhat less than it is in the larger colleges.

There is discernible no marked tendency to change the extent of the major, although few instances of increase have been noted. A number of colleges report, however, a change in the relation between majors and minors, these changes being in the direction of placing responsibility for the make-up of both major and minor in the hands of the major professor or advisor. Dean Helen Luft Manning, of Bryn Mawr, writes: "Last year the group system which required two major subjects of every student was changed to a system of the single major subject with allied work. Whereas

[7] *The College Curriculum*, by R. L. Kelly, Executive Secretary of The Association of American Colleges, in Bulletin of the Association, March, 1921.

forty semester-hours had been required for the completion of a group, fifty semester-hours are now assigned to the major and allied courses.''

The new major requirement at Dartmouth reveals very effectually, the tendency mentioned. A quotation from the regulations in force for the first time this year will show the break down of the strict departmental sequence and at the same time indicate the enlarged responsibility of the major department in mapping out the whole group of courses making up the concentration:

> In junior year five courses shall normally be carried. Of these, one or two shall be in the major subject, as the major subject may prescribe. In addition, one course shall be in a closely related department, the range of choice to be given the student being prescribed by the major department. All departmental plans for the major shall, however, be subject to the approval of the Committee on Educational Policy.
>
> In senior year the number of courses normally carried by all students shall be four. Of these, two year courses shall be in the major subject. In addition, the time of a student which would ordinarily be assigned to a fifth subject shall be devoted to special work which shall be prescribed by the major department. This work may consist of an additional regular course in that department, or of such special supervised work not in regular courses as may seem to the department best adapted to meet the requirements of the major.
>
> The major work shall be planned as a unified, coherent whole; and shall not consist of a series of unrelated courses.

This Dartmouth major tends clearly in the direction of a unified major in place of the customary requirement of a given number of semester-hours chosen from more or less unrelated courses offered in a given department. The unity of the Dartmouth major is further attested by the requirement that students must pass a comprehensive examination over the whole major at the close of the senior year. This type of major approaches the purpose of the third plan of concentration to be discussed a little later, under ''Field of Concentration.''

2. A Specialization Curriculum

In the tendency to use a curriculum made up of courses picked from any department which can contribute to the purpose, we see the influence of the vocational motive. All the professional schools associated with arts colleges in university organizations have largely fixed curricula to accomplish their professional purpose. There is a definiteness and coherence to such curricula that the usual major sequence lacks. There is an esprit developed among students who are pursuing such curricula that seems to be absent among those pursuing less unified sequences.

Partly to obtain these advantages, and partly to recognize that there is a genuine vocational motive actuating a considerable portion of junior and senior students in the arts college, the practice has arisen in a few places of stating the concentration requirements in terms of a series of curricula among which the students choose. While some department, in most instances, represents the core of each curriculum, courses from many departments are likely to be chosen. This type of arrangement calls for a clear understanding of the object in view in selecting the various courses to compose the curriculum, and that object is frequently vocational. For example, a curriculum designed to prepare for landscape gardening would probably have botany at its center, but a sequence in botany would by no means constitute such a preparation. Courses in design, in soils, in sanitation and surveying, would have to be fitted in with botany to constitute a suitable curriculum for landscape gardeners.

As would be natural to expect, this sort of concentration study has been received more favorably among the state supported schools than among endowed institutions. The University of Oregon may be cited as having gone far in the direction of developing specialization curricula in the arts college. There, the college does not use departmental majors, but lists a large number of curricula, named according to the ends in view. In a recent letter, Acting Dean James H. Gilbert said:

> The major professors, in consultation with the Dean of the College, have formulated compact correlated groups of courses, which in some cases have perhaps gone too far in the direction of rigid prescription. In the administration of these prescriptions, however, the major professor allows the student to depart from the prescribed work wherever a good reason for non-conformity can be offered.

From this it is evident that, while the statement of the curriculum is made up in each case from the point of view of function (just as the medical school curriculum is) and without regard to individual student interest, the officials try to take the individual's interest into account when administering the regulation.

3. Field of Concentration

Except for those colleges—a rapidly increasing number—which have made special provision for honors courses for superior students, Harvard University probably presents the best example of the field of concentration as distinct from the major sequence or the specialization curriculum. At Harvard the practice is to map out a field for mastery without too much regard for the content of courses in the department or departments involved. The distinctive feature of the plan is its demand for a mastery of a field, which mastery calls for a degree of independent study not so essential in other plans. Such a plan of concentration study has been naturally accompanied at Harvard by the development of the tutorial method of instruction as an aid to students in covering the field mapped out, and of comprehensive examinations over the fields at the conclusion of the study. The Harvard tutorial system, begun in 1914, along with the preceptorial system introduced into Princeton in 1905, marks the yielding of large group instruction to the needs of individual students. As such, it is so important that a brief account of how the system at Harvard is working after about ten years' trial is quoted herewith:[8]

> During the academic year 1923-24 there were in the Division of History, Government, and Economics 23 tutors and 608 men receiving tutorial instruction. The tutors were of all ranks from instructor to full professor, 10 giving full time to tutorial instruction, the others part time. The quota of students per full-time tutor was 30-40, and the time given by the tutor to the work averaged about 20 hours per week. Most tutorial instruction is given in individual conferences, lasting from a half-hour to an hour, though students having a similar interest and attainment are sometimes met in groups of two or three. The primary task of the tutor is to give the student such guidance as will enable him to prepare himself for the general examination, which, being a comprehensive examination in some large field of human knowledge, is not defined or covered by the student's courses. The work of the tutorial conferences was originally conceived as supplementary to that of courses, and such is still,

[8] *The Preceptorial or Tutorial System.* Report of Committee G. Bulletin of The American Association of University Professors, Nov., 1924, p. 47.

on the whole, the case; but inasmuch as the tutor's aim is to guide the student to a comprehensive knowledge of the subject, this end can often be best secured by a deepening and correlation of the content of his courses. The method employed by the tutor is that of informal discussion and the correction of written work. He seeks to arouse the student's interest, to stimulate his critical powers, to make him intellectually self-reliant, and to introduce him to the tools and materials of study.

Here, then, is a type of concentration study which sets out to develop intellectual independence. With the aid of a tutor, a student undertakes the mastery of a comprehensive field of knowledge. Unlike the major sequence, the essential thing is the unity of the whole field. No part may be learned and straight-way forgotten, as may be done at the completion of the separate courses in the major sequence plan or in the specialization curriculum plan. To be sure, either plan of curriculum organization, if accompanied by tutorial instruction and comprehensive examinations, would approach the values of the Harvard plan, as was pointed out in connection with the Dartmouth major. Nevertheless, the mastery of a field is essentially a different endeavor from the mastery of a series of courses whether these are arranged in major sequences or in specialization curricula. The intellectual qualities sought to be developed by this mastery are the choicest outcomes of college education.

IV. Adaptations to Students of Differing Abilities

College enrollments have increased with unprecedented rapidity in recent years. At the same time, the colleges have lost largely the control over the preparatory schools and must admit students of all degrees of fitness for college study. These two things have served to emphasize the fact that the sort of curriculum and method of teaching which may be best for the student of average ability and average preparation may not be best for the student of superior ability, nor for the student of inferior ability. The last fifteen years have witnessed a rapidly accelerating movement looking to adjustments of all kinds in the interest of individual differences among students.

Parallel with this movement has been the development of psychological examinations—and more recently, placement examinations—and student personnel offices in colleges. These have led to an increasing understanding of what these differences among students really are and have aided in the working out of adjustments to meet these differences. It must be acknowledged, however, that colleges have made but a mere beginning in either measuring the differences or devising suitable adjustments to them. Two most significant adjustments are worthy of consideration in a discussion of college curricula. They are the sectioning of classes and honors courses.

1. Sectioning Classes on the Basis of Ability

To a greater or lesser extent, this simple and sensible adjustment is now being given a trial in about half the best colleges of this country. No extended report is in order here, because the subject has been so ably and fully reported upon by Dean C. E. Seashore, of Iowa, in 1923[9] and again in 1926.[10] With the aid of the National Research Council, Dean Seashore has made extensive surveys of this practice, visited many institutions, and is now taking a leading part in deriving placement examinations on the basis of which sectioning can be more effectively carried out. In the 1926 report, replies from one or more departments using the sectioning plan in fifty-five colleges are quoted. While great variations in the methods of handling the problem exist, and while a wide variety of difficulties are encountered, it is surprising with what unanimity the departments report their experiences as satisfactory on the whole. Among the desirable results commonly experienced, the following may be noted: (a) bright students work more independently and diligently; (b) work suited to the slower students can be offered; (c) failures are reduced.

2. Honors Courses

The importance of stimulating students of superior ability to do, both in amount and quality, work of a high order is granted by everyone. That our American educational system, from the kindergarten to the University, tends to be adapted to those of average ability, is also universally conceded. This fact tends to penalize the student who is of superior ability. The farther he is above the norm, the greater is the penalty he pays. Yet democracy, almost

---

[9] Bulletin American Association of University Professors, October, 1923.
[10] *Ibid.*, February-March, 1926.

more than any other form of political organization, calls for high-class leadership. It is of utmost importance, therefore, that some means be devised whereby the student of superior native ability be trained to his maximum. The movement for honors courses, now growing so rapidly in American colleges, promises to strengthen greatly our system of higher education.

In April 1925, President Frank Aydelotte, of Swarthmore College, reported the results of an exhaustive study of honors courses.[11] In this bulletin the plans in use in each of the institutions are set forth in detail. It is therefore unnecessary to report upon them here. Honors for superior students are earned in three ways that may be described briefly:

Honors for High Average Marks. Graduation with distinction, *cum laude, magna cum laude,* or *summa cum laude* is frequently granted students whose average marks are up to a certain high standard. Occasionally, assignments involving independent study are required of students who are candidates for this graduation with distinction. In general, however, this is a way of rewarding those who do the same work as the rest of the class, but do it better.

Honors Based on Special Work Undertaken in Addition to the Regular Program. To make clear this type of honors course, I can do no better than to quote from President Aydelotte's report, page 11, as follows:

> There are almost as many different plans for honors based on additional work as there are institutions offering them. The extra work required is usually collateral reading and investigation done outside the ordinary courses of instruction. Sometimes, this work is done in vacations; more often, it is done in term time. The purpose is to make the student do something more than merely to meet the requirements of his courses. It is intended that he shall read between courses, that he shall rise from a mastery of separate details to some grasp of a subject as a whole. By intensive work on special topics, it is further intended to give him some experience of first-hand knowledge, some practice in dealing with original material, some training in independent investigation.

Honors Based on Work Superceding the Regular Requirements. In these special honors courses we have the most distinctive contribu-

[11] *Honors Courses in American Colleges and Universities,* by Frank Aydelotte. Bulletin of the National Research Council, Vol. 10, Part 2, Number 52.

tion of the past decade to higher education. A special course of study is designed for those who are qualified to do a superior and independent quality of work, the results to be tested in the end by a comprehensive examination. These special honors courses usually take the place of concentration study described earlier and generally operate in the junior and senior years. Further descriptions of them may best be gotten from President Aydelotte's report:

> In most of the colleges and universities considered in this section, students who have been granted permission to read for honors are excused from all or most of the ordinary requirements of class attendance, semester examinations, mid-term tests, and the like, and are left in freedom to spend all their time in preparation for the comprehensive examinations at the end of the course. In a few cases these comprehensive examinations are held at the end of each year over that part of the work covered during that year.
>
> While special classes or lectures are not usually found to be necessary for honors students, there is nearly everywhere provision for giving them individual supervision and instruction. In some cases this is done by the English tutorial system. In other cases, honors students in a given subject meet weekly in small seminars where they receive something like the same amount of individual attention. It is, I think, the usual experience that honors work can be well conducted only by the older and better trained men in the various departments.

It seems needless to give details as to plans in any individual institutions. Probably the best illustrations of honors courses can be found at Swarthmore, Smith, Dartmouth, Columbia, Chicago, Reed, and Stanford.

Summary

Recent curricular changes in colleges have been occasioned in the main by efforts to correct the disorders which grew out of the elective system and have been hastened by the rapid increase in college enrollments, thus bringing in a less selected body of students, and by the breakdown of the college control over high-school curricula and methods. Adjustments to bring about a better common body of knowledge have been in the direction of coördinating more closely required courses with entrance units, and in the introduction of general courses in place of elementary courses in the several college departments. The former tendency has resulted in the development of the junior college; the latter has stimulated increased coöperation among college departments and centered attention upon the distinction between the liberalizing and specializing functions of college instruction.

While the group system is still the prevailing method of assuring distribution of student electives, certain examples of a more effective unification of the first two years are appearing. A program of studies, a *table d'hôte,* is coming to take the place of a number of unrelated courses, a cafeteria. Each course in the program is prepared and taught in harmony with the purpose of the whole program.

For the specialization function, the one-time freedom of choice among departmental sequences is being more and more restricted. Emphasis upon vocational function is leading in the direction of well worked out curricula, organized around each department. Emphasis upon the need for intellectual independence and increased scholarliness is leading to the use of fields of concentration. This latter is revealing the need for individual assistance in study, the tutorial method, as a supplement to, if not a substitute for, class instruction. It is responsible, also, for the rapid increase in the use of the comprehensive examination covering the field of study in place of the examinations, term by term, covering each of the several courses.

Finally, with the development of the scientific method and quantitative measurement in education, psychological examinations have given impetus to the demand for treating individual students according to their differing abilities. This has resulted in widespread sectioning of classes on the basis of ability, and the introduction of honors courses for the superior students. By these methods it is hoped that better justice may be done those students who depart from the norm, and America may be able better to capitalize the fully developed capacities of her superior citizens.

CHAPTER XXIX
CURRICULUM-MAKING BY THE STATE LEGISLATURES

J. K. Flanders
State Normal School, Oswego, New York

An exhaustive search has been made of the constitutional and statutory law in each of the forty-eight states to discover the legislative enactments, in force in each of the three years 1903, 1913, and 1923, which would affect elementary-school instruction. The purpose of the study was to ascertain the extent to which legislators are dictating the course of study and the trend of such recent legislation. No cognizance was taken of court decisions or state board rulings. Only a brief summary can be presented here.[1] The findings have been classified under sixty headings and arranged in these eight groups:

I. Nationalism
II. Health and 'Prohibition'
III. Conservation of Life and Property
IV. Practical and Cultural Subjects
V. Humaneness
VI. Fundamental Subjects
VII. Religious and Ethical Subjects
VIII. Miscellaneous Subjects

Since a high percentage of the approximately 2200 prescriptions embody some sort of unique or exceptional provision, it is not to be expected that other investigators would always agree with the classification which the writer has made. 'Prescription' has been used, as a matter of convenience, as a general term to include not only positive mandates and direct prohibitions but also permissive legislation in the few instances where this has been regarded as of special significance; for instance, Bible reading and foreign language.

I. Nationalism

The term "Nationalism" is here used to denote a group of subjects, the dominant purpose of which is to foster local, provincial,

[1] Fully reported in the writer's *Legislative Control of the Elementary Curriculum,* Teachers College Contributions to Education No. 195, Columbia University, New York City, 1925. This contains a complete list of references to the various laws.

and national pride and patriotism. Seventeen items are listed under this head, and Table I shows that the total number of prescriptions for this group has more than doubled in the twenty years from 1903 to 1923.

TABLE I.—PRESCRIPTIONS WITH REGARD TO NATIONALISM

Item	Number of States in Which Prescribed			Increase		
	1903	1913	1923	1903 to 1913	1913 to 1923	1903 to 1923
Days of Special Observance	20	33	42	13	9	22
Flag Display	17	29	39	12	10	22
History of the United States	30	32	35	2	3	5
All Instruction in English	14	17	34	3	17	20
History of the State	13	20	25	7	5	12
Civil Government	13	17	24	4	7	11
Constitution of the United States	9	9	23	......	14	14
Foreign Language	11	11	15	......	4	4
Constitution of the State	9	10	14	1	4	5
Citizenship	1	1	14	......	13	13
Patriotism	......	1	12	1	11	12
Flag Exercises	3	4	10	1	6	7
Government of the State	2	5	7	3	2	5
Government of the United States	1	3	3	2	......	2
Patriotic Songs	......	1	3	1	2	3
Declaration of Independence	......	......	2	......	2	2
German	4	3	2	(−1)	(−1)	(−2)
Total Number of Prescriptions	147	196	304	49	108	157

Under the item "Days of Special Observance" is indicated the number of states in which at least one day was required by law to be observed with special exercises in the public schools. School holidays upon which no sessions are held would affect the amount of available schooling, but would not necessarily have any effect upon the content of the curriculum. In 1903 there was a total of thirty-four days of special observance in twenty states; in 1923 there were one hundred twenty-four days in forty-two states. Practice varies widely. Michigan and Montana each required the observance of seven different days, while six states required none at all during the period covered by this study. Fifteen days which may be classified chiefly as commemorative of the birthdays of national heroes and as memorial days for national events show an increase in twenty years from a total of eighteen days in eight states to eighty-one days in twenty-eight states. At the same time, five days which may be classed as conservation days have increased from a total of sixteen in as many states to twenty-eight days in twenty-five states. Temperance Day, developed entirely during the last decade, is now found in fifteen states.

The legislative requirement that a flag of the United States be procured and displayed in, on, or near every public school in the state, is the item classified under the heading "Flag Display." While not a subject of instruction, it is considered of sufficient interest to justify the isolation. The increase in the requirement in twenty years was from seventeen states to thirty-nine. No legal provision for a flag, in any of the three years under discussion, was found in the five states Georgia, Kentucky, Louisiana, Missouri, and North Carolina. The law in South Carolina pertains only to the state flag. The first law requiring flag exercises was enacted in New York in 1898, immediately on the outbreak of hostilities with Spain.

In most instances the prescription for teaching the history of the United States is found in the same section with the other fundamental subjects and no special emphasis is given to it. This was uniformly true in 1903 and 1913, and in a majority of the cases in 1923. However, in a number of states in 1923 supplementary laws are found and the prescription is more detailed and specific. An extreme case is that of Wisconsin, where a censorship of history textbooks was established in 1923 by a law which provides that—

> No history or other textbook shall be adopted for use or be used in any district school, city school, vocational school or high school which falsifies the facts regarding the war of independence, or the war of 1812, or which defames our nation's founders, or misrepresents the ideals and causes for which they struggled and sacrificed, or which contains propaganda favorable to any foreign government.

Upon complaint of any five citizens, filed with the state superintendent of public instruction, that any history or other textbook contains any matter prohibited by the foregoing subsection, that official must arrange for a public hearing within thirty days; and within ten days after the hearing must make a finding upon the complaint. Any textbook found to contain prohibited matter shall be removed from the list of adopted textbooks and withdrawn from use prior to the opening of the following school year. State aid shall not be

> "paid for the support of any district school, city school, vocational school or high school during any year in which any such textbook is used in such school after the finding of the state superintendent."

This law would seem to give fullest opportunity for the operation of local prejudice and ignorance. Other states have laws which doubtless work to the same end. In Oregon no textbook shall be used which "speaks slightingly of the founders of the republic, or of the men who preserved the union, or which belittles or undervalues their work." In Mississippi "no history in relation to the late civil war between the states shall be used in the schools of this state, unless it be fair and impartial." In Texas a textbook in the history of the United States must be adopted in which "the construction placed upon the Federal constitution by the fathers of the confederacy shall be fairly represented." It is hardly probable that a book which satisfies Oregon as giving sufficient credit to the "men who preserved the union" will at the same time be regarded by Mississippi as "fair and impartial," or that a book which meets the requirements of Texas will at the same time be acceptable to Wisconsin. Such laws must inevitably foster sectional misunderstanding. In the teaching of history or science or any other subject, truth does not change at state boundary lines.

The marked increase, during the last decade, in the requirement that all instruction in the elementary schools should be in English is doubtless an outgrowth of the nationalistic spirit engendered by the World War. The language in which the law is couched in different states, the lack of uniformity and of set phrasing, would seem to indicate a genuine widespread popular demand for such legislation. Closely allied with this, in fact frequently embodied in the same law, are the provisions regarding the teaching of foreign languages. The prescriptions in 1903 and in 1913 were all permissive; in 1923 one provision was mandatory and four were prohibitory. German has been tabulated separately merely as a matter of interest. It was specifically mentioned in four states in 1903, in each case the provision being permissive only. The two provisions in 1923 were prohibitive. Of course, these explicit provisions tell only a part of the story. German would be affected by the provisions regarding the teaching of foreign languages generally, just as the teaching of foreign languages would frequently be affected by provisions requiring that all instruction be given in English. A comprehensive understanding of this whole matter could be secured only by an examination of court decisions in the various states and of the rulings of educational boards of control.

No clear-cut line of demarcation can be drawn between the various subjects dealing with the form of government and the duties of citizenship. When one state requires "civil government" to be taught and another the "government of the United States and of this state," the mandate in each case can be fully met by courses which are exactly alike or by those which have very little in common. A course in "civics" may stress governmental forms or just ordinary neighborliness; the same is true of "citizenship." It is manifestly impossible, on the basis of the law alone, to establish a classification whose terms will be mutually exclusive. The increase in the requirements regarding the duties of citizenship has been especially marked in the last decade; also, the requirements regarding the constitution of the United States. In 1903 and 1913 the constitution of the United States was a required subject in nine states; in 1923 it was required in twenty-three states. In the two earlier years the provisions occur, in the main, merely as items in a list of required subjects. In 1923 we find not only a marked increase in the number of states requiring the teaching of this subject, but also a larger number of laws devoted exclusively to it. A number of these laws quite obviously follow a common pattern. Eleven states embody the same provisions, which are similarly expressed; nine of these laws were enacted in the year 1923. The teaching of the constitution of the individual state, when required, is commonly to be found in the same section with that for the Constitution of the United States. The following law of South Dakota, with its time-specification and penalty clauses to insure enforcement, while somewhat extreme, illustrates the trend of recent legislation.

> In every educational institution in this state, whether public or private, one hour each week in the aggregate shall be devoted to the teaching of patriotism, the singing of patriotic songs, the reading of patriotic addresses, and a study of the lives and history of American patriots. It shall be the duty of all instruc-

tors, and of all school officers and superintendents, to enforce the provisions of this section and any person who shall fail, neglect or refuse to enforce its provisions shall be deemed guilty of a misdemeanor, and upon conviction thereof shall be punished by a fine of not less than five nor more than one hundred dollars, or by imprisonment in the county jail not less than five nor more than thirty days, or by both such fine and imprisonment. It shall be the duty of the superintendent of public instruction to revoke the certificate of any instructor in any school in this state, who shall fail, neglect or refuse to enforce the provisions of this section.

II. Health and 'Prohibition'

Next to Nationalism, this group has had the largest increase during the twenty-year period. A study of Table II will show that the gain is in those subjects which deal with physical well-being, with personal and community hygiene.

Table II.—Prescriptions with Regard to Health and 'Prohibition'

Item	Number of States in Which Prescribed			Increase		
	1903	1913	1923	1903 to 1913	1913 to 1923	1903 to 1923
Stimulants and Narcotics	47	45	43	(−2)	(−2)	(−4)
Physiology and Hygiene	46	45	43	(−1)	(−2)	(−3)
Physical Education	5	7	25	2	18	20
Physical Examination	1	13	21	12	8	20
Personal Hygiene	1	2	12	1	10	11
Communicable Diseases	1	8	9	7	1	8
Sanitation	.....	2	7	2	5	7
Accident Prevention	.....	3	5	3	2	5
Tobacco	1	4	4	3	.....	3
Placards	.....	2	2	2	.....	2
Total Number of Prescriptions	102	131	171	29	40	69

"Physiology and hygiene," "stimulants and narcotics" might well be regarded as a single subject; as a matter of fact, in the law they are joined in a single statement in the great majority of instances. It is probably safe to say that no other subject of the curriculum has received so much legislative attention as this composite one. From the various enactments one might infer that "stimulants and narcotics" is regarded as our most important branch of learning; not only is it more widely prescribed, but it has received more extensive and more specific legislation than any other. It is our nearest approach to a national subject of instruction; it might be called 'our one minimal essential.' Numerous devices are resorted to in order to give force to the laws which require these subjects to be taught. Provisions are common regarding one or more of the following: the use of an approved textbook by the pupils; the teacher to pass an examination; the normal school to give special training; definite reports that all provisions of this particular law have been complied with; fines and forfeitures for neglect or failure.

Some sort of legislative requirement falling within the field of physical education was found in five states in 1903, in seven states in 1913, and in twenty-five states in 1923. The remarkable increase shown within the last few years is undoubtedly due in large measure to the special interest aroused during the period of the World War. Only one state made provision for the physical examination of pupils in the public schools in 1903; in 1923 this provision was to be found in twenty-one states. The provision in most cases was not comprehensive. Sometimes, it applied only to the larger cities; sometimes, it required an examination only every second or third year; frequently, the examination was limited to tests of sight and hearing, although several states included an examination for physical defects; usually, the examination was to be made annually. Probably the requirements would not, in a single instance, meet standards which would be regarded as adequate by authorities in school health work. Nevertheless, the showing is remarkable. An increase of twenty states was exceeded in only three items: "flag display," "days of special observance," and "fire drill." Quite obviously, there has been a widespread interest in this field, owing, doubtless, to a growing realization that a child's mental need cannot be met while his physical need is ignored. Some of the states provide that no pupil shall be compelled to submit to physical examination whose parent or guardian objects. The tender solicitude which is thus shown for the wishes of the parent regarding the body of his child is in striking contrast with the absence of any such consideration in numerous laws whose obvious purpose is to indoctrinate the child's mind. Doubtless the explanation is, in effect, the same; in each case there is to be found an aggressive group influencing legislation to further its own particular ends.

No hard and fast line can be drawn between what is called "personal hygiene" and the hygiene which is included with, and has been considered as a part of, physiology and hygiene. That something substantially different was in the minds of the law-makers is indicated by the fact that, in the majority of cases, "personal hygiene" is in addition to the hygiene which is joined with the provision for stimulants and narcotics. It is variously expressed in different states as "health," "the laws of health," "the proper care of the body," "personal and community health" and "safety," and is frequently included with physical education or sanitation. Instruction regarding communicable diseases is usually grouped with health education. Safety-First campaigns show their effect in legal requirements for the teaching of accident prevention.

The use of placards has been required in a few states to aid in instruction regarding stimulants and narcotics, cigarettes, the prevention and cure of tuberculosis, and thrift and industry; these placards to be kept conspicuously displayed in each schoolroom throughout the state.

The growth in legislation intended to improve individual and community health conditions is especially noticeable in the last decade. As already stated, the greatest stress is put upon the teaching of the effects of stimulants and narcotics. Regarding this prescription, the law is outspoken and mandatory. It is fortified by numerous provisions to secure its enforcement, the evident aim being that it shall be "taught to and studied by" every pupil in every grade. There has been a slight falling off in the number of states requiring the teaching of this subject; and the particular states where the decrease has taken place have not, as a rule, enacted laws calling for a broader health program. Still, for the country as a whole, the balance shows a decided gain for general hygiene. It would seem probable that, more frequently than formerly, the effects of stimulants and narcotics are considered as a minor topic in a large and important subject rather than as something special and isolated. It would seem probable, also, as a consequence, that the teaching has become more truthful.

III. Conservation of Life and Property

It is perhaps somewhat surprising, in view of the disastrous and fatal school fires which have occurred, to find that fire drills are not by law required in all of the states. In 1923 they were required in slightly fewer than half. The increase was somewhat more marked in the first decade.

Table III.—Prescriptions with Regard to Conservation of Life and Property

Item	Number of States in Which Prescribed			Increase		
	1903	1913	1923	1903 to 1913	1913 to 1923	1903 to 1923
Fire Drill	1	14	22	13	8	21
Fire Prevention	.....	6	17	6	11	17
Thrift	.....	.....	4	.....	4	4
Total Number of Prescriptions	1	20	43	19	23	42

Fire prevention has shown a more rapid increase during the second decade. Time requirements in this subject are very common. It is a frequent practice to place the responsibility for planning the course upon state officials entirely outside of the education department. Sometimes, the preparation of a book which is "to be read by the teachers" in instructing their pupils is also made the duty of such officials as the State Fire Marshal or the Commissioner of Insurance.

IV. Practical and Cultural Subjects

The most outstanding gain in this group was that of agriculture during the first decade, when twelve additional states prescribed that it be taught; the other subjects show only a slight growth.

No time specifications were found for any of these subjects. Frequently, there were exceptions or limitations which would make the teaching of a subject necessary in only a part of the schools of the state. Quite obviously, there has been less concern regarding the teaching of these subjects than was the case with a number of others, such as the observance of special days, the display of the flag, the teaching of fire prevention, of patriotism, the constitution, and stimulants and narcotics.

TABLE IV.—PRESCRIPTIONS WITH REGARD TO PRACTICAL AND CULTURAL SUBJECTS

Item	Number of States in Which Prescribed			Increase		
	1903	1913	1923	1903 to 1913	1913 to 1923	1903 to 1923
Agriculture	5	17	19	12	2	14
Drawing	9	9	10	......	1	1
Music	3	5	8	2	3	5
Household Arts	1	4	7	3	3	6
Industrial Arts	1	4	6	3	2	5
Bookkeeping	5	4	4	(−1)	......	(−1)
Exhibitions	......	......	3	......	3	3
Cotton Grading	......	1	1	1	......	1
Art	......	......	1	......	1	1
Total Number of Prescriptions	24	44	59	20	15	35

V. HUMANENESS

The three subdivisions of humaneness have been treated separately as an aid to more intelligent analysis, because they are fairly distinct and important aspects of the subject and are not always found together. Time requirements are very common. Laws regarding animal experimentation are invariably prohibitory.

TABLE V.—PRESCRIPTIONS WITH REGARD TO HUMANENESS

Item	Number of States in Which Prescribed			Increase		
	1903	1913	1923	1903 to 1913	1913 to 1923	1903 to 1923
Humane Treatment and Protection of Animals and Birds	8	15	17	7	2	9
Importance of Animals and Birds	1	6	11	5	5	10
Animal Experimentation	3	7	8	4	1	5
Total Number of Prescriptions	12	28	36	16	8	24

In Oregon we find this interesting provision:

They shall be taught the true relation of the human to animal life, the value of life, and the cowardice of needless killing or any act of cruelty to man or beast, inculcating a love for truth, justice, and that beautiful generosity that makes the strong supporters, instead of oppressors, of the weak.

VI. Fundamental Subjects

In view of the persistent adverse criticism of "fads and frills" in the school program it is, perhaps, a little surprising to learn that the fundamental subjects have received from the peoples' representatives such scant consideration, compared with many of the other subjects. Barely three fourths of the states have a direct, specific mandate.

Table VI.—Prescriptions with Regard to Fundamental Subjects

Item	Number of States in Which Prescribed			Increase		
	1903	1913	1923	1903 to 1913	1913 to 1923	1903 to 1923
Arithmetic	33	36	36	3	.....	3
English	33	36	36	3	.....	3
Geography	33	36	36	3	.....	3
Penmanship	32	36	36	4	.....	4
Reading	33	36	36	3	.....	3
Spelling	33	36	36	3	.....	3
Total Number of Prescriptions	197	216	216	19	.....	19

Time requirements and other special provisions to make sure that these subjects receive proper attention are almost never resorted to. It is apparently assumed that they are adequately provided for. The laws, throughout the twenty years, show no noteworthy change. North Dakota has this unique provision:

> Each pupil in the common schools as they shall become sufficiently advanced to pursue the same, shall be required to devote at least fifteen minutes practice in writing each day during the school year.

VII. Religious and Ethical Subjects

The provisions listed under the heading "Sectarian Doctrine" include not only direct prohibitions against sectarian instruction and the use of textbooks which are sectarian in character, but also prohibitions against sectarian control of public school money and against public support of sectarian schools. There has been no significant development during the twenty-year period. Apparently, the intention to keep public education non-sectarian has been, throughout, widespread and generally accepted.

TABLE VII.—PRESCRIPTIONS WITH REGARD TO RELIGIOUS AND ETHICAL SUBJECTS

Item	Number of States in Which Prescribed			Increase		
	1903	1913	1923	1903 to 1913	1913 to 1923	1903 to 1923
Sectarian Doctrine	39	39	38	......	(−1)	(−1)
Social and Ethical Outcomes	14	16	16	2	......	2
Bible Reading	10	10	15	......	5	5
Manners	7	6	8	(−1)	2	1
Morals	4	5	7	1	2	3
Total Number of Prescriptions	74	76	84	2	8	10

Of the prescriptions regarding Bible reading, one was mandatory in 1903, two in 1913, and eight in 1923; there was no increase in the number of permissive laws. The term "Social and Ethical Outcomes" is here used to denote various virtues, attributes, and qualities the "teaching" of which was required. A composite list of the qualities and habits desired would include the following:

Benevolence	Justice	Piety
Chastity	Kindness	Politeness
Cleanliness	Love of country	Promptness
Economy	Manners	Public spirit
Frugality	Moderation	Purity
Gentility	Moral courage	Refinement
Good behavior	Morality	Regard for others
Honesty	Morals	Respect for labor
Honor	Neatness	Sobriety
Humanity	Obedience to parents	Temperance
Industry	Order	Truth
Integrity	Patriotism	Truthfulness

A corresponding list to be avoided would include Falsehood, Idleness, Intemperance, Profanity, Vulgarity. Certain other objectives and outcomes are enumerated, such as "the true comprehension of the rights, duties, and dignity of American citizenship," "their own responsibilities and duties as citizens," "the principles of free government." North Dakota amended her list in 1911 by adding to it "international peace," a change worthy of note because of its exceptional character; we have here an express recognition by law-makers, when dealing with instruction in the public schools, of a world which extends beyond the boundaries of the United States. The following was adopted in Arkansas in 1923:

> *Whereas,* Training in morals and patriotism is important to child life and education, and to the welfare of the State, and
>
> *Whereas,* The prevalence and persistence of crime and immorality indicates a lack of such training in our present-day citizenship, and
>
> *Whereas,* The present course of study for our State public schools does not provide especially for such training; therefore
>
> Be It Enacted by the General Assembly of the State of Arkansas:
>
> Section 1. That a course in morals, manners, patriotism, and business and professional integrity be, and is hereby, included in the course of study for the State public schools.
>
> Section 2. That the State Textbook Commission is hereby authorized to adopt suitable textbooks on such subjects, for use in the public schools.

There has been very little change in the number of prescriptions in this group during the twenty years. The gain was somewhat larger in the second decade. The most significant change is the increase in mandatory legislation regarding the reading of the Bible. Whether this growth has been due to a popular demand or to an aggressive campaign by a small zealous group is, of course, not evident from the law. The legal provisions found in connection with these subjects illustrate with especial clearness a characteristic which is common to much of the legislation affecting the curriculum; namely, a tacit disregard of the laws of learning and an implicit faith in the efficacy, for character formation, of mere exposure to ideas. Those who promote the sort of legislation that is found, for example, in connection with "Morals" and with "Social and Ethical Outcomes," appear to be actuated by the assumption that desirable habits, attitudes, and ideals can, with certainty, be imparted by the written or spoken word.

VIII. Miscellaneous Subjects

Table VIII indicates that this group of subjects has not been regarded by our law-makers as very important. Elementary science shows the most growth.

Table VIII.—Prescriptions with Regard to Miscellaneous Subjects

Item	Number of States in Which Prescribed			Increase		
	1903	1913	1923	1903 to 1913	1913 to 1923	1903 to 1923
Elementary Science	2	4	6	2	2	4
Algebra	3	2	3	(−1)	1	......
Metric System	1	1	1	......	......	......
Forestry and Plant Life	......	1	1	1	......	1
Dictionary	......	......	1	......	1	1
Darwinism	......	......	1	......	1	1
Land Designation	1	1	......	......	(−1)	(−1)
Total Number of Prescriptions	7	9	13	2	4	6

Doubtless the provisions concerning Darwinism are of greatest interest. Not as much legislation was found regarding this as the writer had been led to expect from the publicity given to various bills which have been before legislatures in recent years. In 1923 there were two states with legal provisions directly affecting evolution. Florida had a concurrent resolution in opposition to teaching "as true, Darwinism, or any other hypothesis that links man in blood relationship to any other form of life." In Oklahoma,

> No copyright shall be purchased nor textbook adopted that teaches the "Materialistic Conception of History" (*i.e.*) the Darwin Theory of Creation vs. the Bible Account of Creation.

This law prohibits the adoption of a textbook, but apparently would not prevent the imparting of information directly by a teacher or the use of supplementary books of reference.

General Trends

The following twelve subjects show a gain of twelve states or more; that is, a gain equal to or exceeding one fourth of all the states:

1. Flag Display
2. Days of Special Observance
3. Fire Drill
4. Physical Examination
5. All Instruction in English
6. Physical Education
7. Fire Prevention
8. Agriculture
9. Constitution of the United States
10. Citizenship
11. History of the State
12. Patriotism

Fourteen items were added to the list of prescribed subjects during the twenty years; of these, six were introduced during the last decade. Among the individual subjects an increase in number of prescriptions is the rule. Very few of the items show a net loss. Individual states have occasionally amended the law so as to eliminate the requirement of a particular subject, but this has usually been more than offset by new prescriptions in other states. In the main, a subject once required continues to be required and to spread to other states. From Table IX it will be seen that there has been a total increase of three hundred sixty-two prescriptions, or of about 65 percent.

TABLE IX.—SUMMARY

Topic	Number of Prescriptions			Increase		
	1903	1913	1923	1903 to 1913	1913 to 1923	1903 to 1923
Nationalism	147	196	304	49	108	157
Health and 'Prohibition'	102	131	171	29	40	69
Conservation of Life and Property	1	20	43	19	23	42
Practical and Cultural Subjects	24	44	59	20	15	35
Humaneness	12	28	36	16	8	24
Fundamental Subjects	197	216	216	19	.....	19
Religious and Ethical Subjects	74	76	84	2	8	10
Miscellaneous Subjects	7	9	13	2	4	6
Total	564	720	926	156	206	362

No merely quantitative statement, however, will show the most significant aspect of the recent legislation, namely, the change in the character of its provisions. The recent enactments are, on the whole, more definite and restrictive. They embody more detail. Recent legislation reveals an increase in assurance on the part of the law-makers. Apparently, they are more conscious of their authority and more determined to insure the realization of their will. Time-allotments are much more common than they were twenty years ago and there has been a decided increase in the number of provisions imposing a penalty for failure to carry out a particular mandate. Responsibility is more definitely fixed. It is much more common than formerly to specify that an approved textbook must be used and that the teacher shall have had special training for the imposed task. In addition, the duty may be placed upon the teacher to include in her monthly report a statement that this special law has been complied with, her salary being withheld until she does so, and a similar obligation may be placed upon the administrative officers. Sometimes, also, state aid must not be paid to a community that has failed to carry out the provisions of one particular law. "This device is a powerful weapon. There might be twenty different laws creating obligations which rest upon a community and that community might fully meet nineteen of those obligations. If she should fail in the twentieth, she would forfeit not one twentieth of her share of the state fund but twenty-twentieths of it. This practice is such an effective means of forcing a local community to do the bidding of the central authority, especially when a large portion of the support comes from the state, that it could easily develop into virtual dictatorship."[2]

It must be acknowledged that coercive measures and time-specifications are still the exception rather than the rule. The situation is alarming, not so much because of the distance we have traveled as because of the direction in which we are going. The tendency, as has been pointed out, is not only for laws affecting the curriculum to multiply, but for them to become more mandatory and definite. If the process which is well under way keeps on, it is only a question of time when the curriculum will be fully determined by the members of the state legislature.

Legal provisions in the different states regarding the teaching of a given subject are not infrequently similarly phrased. 'Model'

---

[2] Flanders, J. K. "*Lawmakers Encroach Upon the Schoolmen,*" The New York *Times,* September 6, 1925.

laws are promoted by certain national organizations and by groups, often small, but interested and resourceful. Evidences of this are to be seen in connection with Bible reading, stimulants and narcotics, the constitution of the United States, and some others.

The issue is clearly drawn: Where should responsibility for the choice of the curriculum be placed? Is the curriculum to be worked out by professional experts in terms of the child and the community, their nature, and their needs or is it to be determined through haphazard legislation by educational laymen in response to special pleading?

CHAPTER XXX

A CRITICAL APPRAISAL OF CURRENT METHODS OF CURRICULUM-MAKING

HAROLD RUGG
Teachers College, Columbia University
AND
GEORGE S. COUNTS
School of Education, University of Chicago

I. INTRODUCTION

The story of curriculum-making in American schools is now before us. The historical backgrounds have been sketched, the social and educational forces at work have been considered, the major features of conventional procedure have been outlined, the more significant progressive practices have been described, and the chief trends and tendencies have been traced. The data for a critical evaluation of the contemporary situation are therefore at hand.

The need for such an appraisal is evident. A nation-wide movement for the study and revision of the school curriculum is under way. In the elementary school, in the secondary school, and even in the college, there is growing dissatisfaction with the existing program. As never before in our educational history, the problem of the selection and organization of pupil activities and the materials of instruction is engaging the thought of schoolmen. The reasons for this movement are many. The growth of American civilization, fundamental changes in the social order, the extension of the period of compulsory education, and the unprecedented expansion of secondary and higher education have all made necessary the reshaping of school programs. At the same time the development of a scientific attitude and technique in education has made schoolmen increasingly critical of conventional practices. But, whatever the causes, the movement for curriculum-revision is here.

The strength of this movement has been indicated in the preceding chapters. That more than one thousand school systems in the United States are continuously engaged in the task of curriculum-revision is a conservative estimate. A year ago the officers of the Bureau of Research of the National Education Association reported that over three hundred school systems were coöperating actively with them in curriculum-revision. Month by month this number is being augmented. The writers know personally of more than two hundred additional systems which are making use of experimentally reconstructed materials. Sixty percent of the school officials replying to our question blanks reported that the overhauling of their courses of study was being vigorously prosecuted. It is evident, therefore, that in the public school system the central position of the curriculum and the need for its reconstruction are clearly recognized. Furthermore, scores of suggestive innovations, based increasingly on thorough-going experimentation, are being introduced into both private and public schools. At least a dozen laboratory schools, several with a quarter century of history behind them, are devoting themselves wholeheartedly to the discovery of new materials, the investigation of the abilities and interests of children, the extension to progressive teachers of opportunities to experiment along unfamiliar lines.

All of these facts reveal an awakened interest in the curriculum and suggest that the revision of the curriculum is becoming a fairly continuous process. As schoolmen realize that pupil activities, and the materials of instruction which arouse them, play the central rôle in all education, they see that the curriculum is not a matter for occasional and sporadic attention; they see that the construction of the materials of education must proceed without interruption. This much, therefore, the agitation of the past few years has conspicuously secured. Interest in the curriculum and activity in curriculum-revision have been generated in abundance. But interest, however intense, and activity, however fervid, are not enough. Our appraisal is much more concerned with the productivity than with the initial momentum of the movement.

II. Inadequacy of Current Methods of Curriculum-Making

Definite evidence of the existence of a gap between the school curriculum and American life, on the one hand, and between the curriculum and the capacities, interests, and development of the child, on the other, is presented in the earlier chapters of this volume. Although this gap, of striking proportions a half century ago, was slightly reduced by movements for the administrative reorganization and the scientific investigation of the school curriculum which have developed during the past thirty years, the articulation of the school with society and the learner remains far from perfect to-day. Does the activity for curriculum-revision now evident in public schools give promise of a further and marked reduction of this gap and of a thorough-going reconstruction of the curriculum through a balanced recognition of the factors of child learning and the conditions of American life? Does present procedure in curriculum-revision provide the technique for the fundamental reconstruction of the school curriculum in terms of child growth and institutional life? To both of these questions we must give a negative answer.

Partial, superficial, and timorous "revision" rather than general, fundamental, and courageous reconstruction characterizes curriculum-making in the public school. For the most part, the job is being conceived too narrowly and attacked by inadequate methods. The responsibility for curriculum-making is commonly borne by committees composed of teachers and administrators who are already over-burdened with work. As a consequence, the existing program is always taken as the point of departure, and attention is centered on the addition of new materials or the subtraction of old materials from the established school subjects. Thus curriculum-making becomes a process of accretion and elimination. There is little, indeed almost no movement, under way in public schools to initiate curriculum-making from the starting point either of child learning or of the institutions and problems of American life. For over fifty years, tinkering has characterized the attack on the curriculum. In most centers the situation remains essentially unchanged. Although less completely than in the past, *scissors and paste still dominate* the methods actually employed. Our survey presents convincing evidence that in most school systems courses of study are prepared through direct copying of other courses of study. In both content and organization, they are derived from existing outlines, textbooks, and syllabi. And careful scrutiny of these models for imitation in turn leads to the conviction that they themselves were made by unscientific, indeed, by unthoughtful, methods. It is undoubtedly true that this imitating of what is called "progressive practice elsewhere," this utilization of "committee discussion'' *does* raise slightly the level of the school curriculum; but the gain through such *a priori* and uncritical methods must represent only a small fraction of the progress that could be made if more thorough-going procedures of reconstruction were employed.

The statement that these general methods employed are unscientific scarcely requires qualification. The specific practices, however, in the various school systems of the country represent great diversity. With the exception of a mere handful of school systems, curriculum-revision seems to issue from a vague feeling of the need for ''doing something about it'' on the part of superintendents, principals, and teachers. With the same few exceptions, the work itself is not directed by specialists, professionally trained and experienced in the manifold tasks of curriculum-making. We find almost no evidence that those who are revising our school curriculum are definitely conscious of the hiatus between the content of the curriculum and the modes of living and the problems and issues of contemporary civilization. If they are aware of this condition, their vision is obscured; accurate knowledge of the social situation and clear-cut ideas of procedure are seldom focussed upon the problem. Neither is there revealed clear understanding of the need for the re-departmentalization of school subjects and for the general introduction of creative activities into the school.

III. The Practice of Adding and Dropping Subjects

Modification of the school curriculum, elementary or secondary, consists of the century-old practice of the introduction of new subjects of study and the dropping of old ones. The curriculum of American schools has developed by just this method. The procedure may be well illustrated from the history of secondary education. To the Latin and Greek of the Latin Grammar School have gradually been added numerous subjects, such as algebra, geometry, rhetoric, physics, and chemistry, organized on logical and academic lines. More recently, the elaboration of the curriculum has also consisted in the organization of separate and relatively narrow subjects, such as history, geography, manual training, home economics, nature study, and others. Slowly, with the passage of time, subjects wax, wane, and disappear.

Our survey shows that this is still the chief mode of modifying the materials of instruction. Greek, Latin, algebra, and ancient history disappear from the 'required' program of the high school. English, civics, vocational guidance, problems of American democracy, and social studies, take their places. That the exchange has slightly raised the efficiency of American schools nobody will deny; but that the organization of the new materials has provided an adequate program is a thesis which few would care to defend. The crux of the matter is that while the high school has developed a technique for adding new subjects of study, it is sadly in need of a technique for dropping old ones and for viewing the problem of curriculum-making as a whole. Consequently, a serious difficulty inheres in this very practice, for subjects are being added to the curriculum three times as rapidly as they are being dropped. The result is a crazy-quilt of unrelated subjects, rather than an orderly series of developmental activities, meanings, generalizations, and problems. The present curriculum is an aggregation of disparate units rather than an integration of activities about a central educational purpose. And within each subject, academic form and logical arrangement, instead of learning and natural relationship, still thoroughly control the organization of the materials of instruction in the high school. At the elementary-school level, while the program has been much more sensitive to current discoveries concerning learning and child growth, tradition still lays a heavy hand on the curriculum. Not only does revision take place through the gradual addition of new subjects and the occasional subtraction of old ones, but detailed changes within the school subjects themselves are effected only by the same expensive means of accretion and deletion.

IV. Obstacles to the Systematic Reconstruction of the Curriculum

Why has curriculum-making to the present time been so partial and haphazard? Why has it consisted of revision by accretion and elimination rather than of systematic reconstruction? What have been the chief obstacles to the fundamental reorganization of school programs?

The forces operating have been many, but we shall direct attention to four. Perhaps all of these might be grouped under the single category of "vested interests." In the first place, the present interests and abilities of the teaching and administrative staffs have constituted an all but insuperable obstacle to genuine curriculum-revision. For this situation teachers and administrators are, of course, not to be censured. If the science of curriculum-making may be said to be born, it is still in its earliest infancy. Only occasional persons here and there throughout our great training centers have been equipped for the task. In the second place, traditional content and academic modes of organization are entrenched in existing text-books and courses of study. The nation-wide adoption of these text-books and guides to instruction has created powerful vested interests. Publishing houses and authors of widely used materials and methods naturally resist the demand for modification. These forces, with interests vested in the conventional program, are fundamentally conservative and serve as formidable obstacles to change. In the third place, there is the conservatism of the institutions engaged in training our elementary- and secondary-school teachers. Because of the strategic position of these agencies, this constitutes one of the most retarding influences. They are still dominated by an adherence to traditional subject organization, to "scholarship," to "discipline," to "learning." In considerable measure they have remained uninfluenced by the changing psychology of child learning.

Finally, operative chiefly upon the high-school curriculum, there is the influence of the entrance requirements of our eastern colleges and, to a lesser degree, of colleges in other parts of the country. For this situation the history of education offers but few parallels. Through their entrance requirements a small number of private institutions of great social prestige still exert a stranglehold on the curriculum of a fairly large proportion of our secondary schools. Books are written to fit the prescriptions of certificating and examining boards. Teaching is constrained to follow the outlines of text-books and examinations, and, indeed, to set as its goal the passing of examinations. Thus, in the secondary school the academic tradition is perpetuated by the domination of this ideal of preparation for a higher level of scholastic education.

V. Tendencies Toward the Re-Departmentalization of the Curriculum

The present situation as regards curriculum-making has now been viewed and in some measure appraised in its general aspects. The merits and demerits of conventional procedures have been considered. It remains to examine certain of the more hopeful tendencies and to present in broad outline the technique to be employed in the fundamental reconstruction of the curriculum. Among the more promising efforts at reorganization are those which point towards the re-departmentalization of the program.

Although the starting point of curriculum-revision is the school subject, although this procedure ordinarily consists of the rearrangement by committees of materials within school subjects, nevertheless there is a discernible tendency to break down certain barriers which have been erected between departments of knowledge. In some instances the subjects of the school curriculum are being enlarged. This movement is revealing itself in the more widespread organization of the "general" courses of instruction. Our investigations show, for example, that hundreds of school systems have reorganized history, geography, and civics in the junior high school to form a broad department known generally as the "social studies." Arithmetic, business practice, mensuration, constructive geometry, algebra, the function concept, graphic methods, statistics, are being organized into "general mathematics" courses. Physiology, hygiene, physical training, and athletics are being brought together into a single department. The various skills and processes dealing with oral and written speech, reading and literature in the upper grades are being integrated into one division of subject matter. Even the boundaries between these larger departments are being partially obliterated by the organization of courses which are frankly designed to discharge the function formerly delegated to two different departments. (For example, English and the social studies.[1])

It is through the experimental design and development of new textbooks and syllabi, chiefly in our laboratory schools, that the movement toward re-departmentalization of the school curriculum is

[1] See the work, for example, of Mr. H. C. Hill of the University of Chicago High School.

manifesting itself. No more significant measure can be found, however, of the *progressive spirit* of the school administrators and teachers than their widespread willingness, even at personal sacrifice to make use of these new materials of instruction. But this progressive spirit is insufficient to create the new curriculum. The experience of the past fifteen years in the scientific and experimental construction of school curricula presents convincing evidence that this movement for re-departmentalization is proceeding no more rapidly than new materials are prepared in textbook and syllabus in laboratory centers.

Under the hampering conditions of public-school administration, the manifold teaching and supervisory duties involved in the sheer operation of a school system practically prevent the teacher and administrator from engaging in the task of organizing new materials and methods of instruction. The latter tasks can be consummated only by persons specially equipped and released for that purpose from the hectic duties of teaching and administration. Although most of the work is still being done in private institutions, the development of laboratory schools within public-school systems[2] is one of the most encouraging tendencies of the times.

VI. The Influence on the Public-School Curriculum of the New Emphasis Upon Pupil Activities

Since the days of Francis Parker's regime at Quincy, an increasing number of students of education have insisted that the curriculum be organized around a nucleus of child activities. The adaptation of instruction to child growth, the adjustment of school procedures to learning capacities, emphasis on creative self-expression, have been the slogans of educational innovators. What impression has this conception made upon the school curriculum? Does our survey of contemporary practices in curriculum-revision reveal a distinct tendency to organize the curriculum of the public school about a core of pupil activities?

To this question no single answer can be given. In the high school, the movement has left no mark; in the elementary school, its influence may be traced here and there. Within the school sub-

[2] Witness, for example, the important beginnings which have been made in public-school systems like Detroit, Winnetka (Illinois), Denver, Los Angeles, and other places.

jects there is a marked tendency to make learning active rather than passive. There is some evidence of the introduction of constructive activities into the various subjects of study. There is an increasing use of excursions, field trips, observation of the physical world, map and graph making, individual pupil research, vivid open forum discussion, and extra-curriculum activities. But practically all of this utilization of child activity is *within* the confines of the established school subjects. Except in rare and isolated instances, initiating and creative activities have not become the center of organized school curricula. With the exception of a handful of laboratory schools like those whose practices are described in Chapters XV to XXVI of this volume, the chief outlines of the curriculum are still traced in terms of reading, arithmetic, language, nature study, history, geography, current events, etc. Indeed, there is almost no critical discussion available in educational literature or even in the publications of the laboratory schools of the psychological relation between so-called "activities" and the school subjects.[3] Printed discussion at least has not appeared to show that school people have thought through the relation between activities and school subjects (as obviously in the case of reading and certain aspects of arithmetic), or of how the constructive and creative activities—the so-called "projects"—can be organized to produce the outcomes which are supposed to inhere in the established branches of instruction.

Nevertheless, one gain is evident. The curriculum is being vitalized because of a gradual change in the conception of learning. Under the stimulus of psychological investigation, the writings of Professor Dewey, and the dynamic guidance of conspicuous leaders in our training centers, learning as memorizing subject matter is giving way to a conception of learning as living. As our own theoretical statement puts its: "Meaning grows only through reaction. . . . No formulated scheme of assimilation, made in advance and handed out complete by the curriculum-maker, can, of itself, be sufficient. . . . The curriculum should be conceived, therefore, in terms of a succession of experiences and enterprises having a maximum of lifelikeness for the learner." (Part II, Sec-

[3] Partial treatments of the matter, however, are found in highly suggestive publications like Katherine Keelor's *Curriculum Studies in the Second Grade*, Bureau of Publications, Teachers College, Columbia University.

tion VI of the General Statement.) This necessarily means that the curriculum-maker must have much greater regard than formerly for the activities of children.

VII. The Contribution of the Laboratory Schools

In Chapters XV to XXVI of this volume and in voluminous additional writings, the leaders of our experimental schools have recently described their practices and the theories upon which their programs are based. What are the chief merits and demerits of curriculum-making in these schools? Have they fulfilled the hopes which led to their establishment? Because of the conscious dedication of these institutions to educational experimentation, a critical examination of their procedures is peculiarly appropriate.

Perhaps the first comment to be made is that there is no one type of experimental or laboratory school. In curricular organization they range all the way from schools organized almost definitely on a "subject" basis (for example, the F. W. Parker School of Chicago, the University of Chicago Laboratory Schools, and the Horace Mann School of Teachers College) to occasional schools like The School of Organic Education of Fairhope, Alabama, the City and Country School, and the University of Missouri Elementary School (in its original organization) which are organized almost completely without reference to the conventional school subjects. Between these two extremes stand laboratory schools like the Lincoln School of Teachers College. In these schools the curriculum of the lower grades, while organized in part around certain "centers of interest" (some workers would call them "projects"), provides at the same time a definite place in the school program for certain so-called "school subjects." Critical comments upon the curricula and the methods of curriculum-making in these schools must, therefore, take account of this diversity in practice.

In at least four respects the achievements of these schools have been conspicuous. In the first place, learning is based much more completely upon the interests and drives of children than in the rank and file of public schools. The laboratory schools are "child centered" schools. They are essentially work schools rather than listening schools. In them children are almost constantly active.

There is little evidence of *ennui.* Retardation and early elimination are rare. "Failure," in the academic sense of having to repeat a grade or mark time, almost never occurs. Not content to fit children either to activities or to subjects, these schools accept the obligation to provide activities in which the child *can* engage.

In the second place, these schools *are* discovering "centers of interest" through which an understanding of the various aspects of life may be fostered and a variety of types of creative self-expression may be effectively organized. For example, the work of those who are developing creative music in the school constitutes little short of a real curriculum discovery. Their organized curricula[4] present systematic schemes of suggested activities which *can be utilized under conditions of mass education in public schools.* Through curricular plans of this type definite suggestions are given the teacher for developing situations which stimulate children to *make* music, to write poetry, to draw pictures, and to express themselves in writing. At the same time vital incentives are provided for reading, and even for the learning of certain principles in the physical sciences. Work of this character does, indeed, provide a real center, not only of interest, but of dynamic learning. And since the experience of these pioneers is organized in the form of reading and other printed materials, available for use in fairly large classes, it is of unusual significance to curriculum-makers in the public schools.

In the third place, these schools are developing a creative environment for the child. Perhaps their constructive contribution is best revealed in this achievement. In the words of Professor Cizek, the Vienna art teacher, the tone of these schools is described as "taking off the lid;"[5] and Mearns has recognized the major task of the school to be that of setting up the "drawing out environment." "Poetry cannot be taught or even summoned; it can only be permitted," is the characteristic dictum of the protagonists of the creative activities curriculum. In such schools specific prescrip-

---

[4] For example, see the work of Satis N. Coleman, *Creative Music for Schools* (in Grades III to VI inclusive).

[5] See, for example, *The Child as Artist: Some Conversations with Cizek.* Children's Art Exhibition Fund, Greenwich, Connecticut; also the April-June, 1926, issue of *Progressive Education,* "Creative Expression Through Art;" also Hughes Mearns, *Creative Youth,* Doubleday Page Co., Garden City, Long Island, N. Y.

tions of materials to be read are not made. The only requirement is that the child read *something.* He is surrounded with fine examples of artistic writing, drawing, music, dramatization. He takes part in vivid class discussion of the artistic merit of contemporary writings. In contrast with the analytic, mechanistic, regime of the school ''English'' class, this program establishes the informal atmosphere of the Robert Frost Club.

In the fourth place, these activity schools are making actual contributions to the theory and practice of curriculum-making. They are demonstrating the rhythmic basis of both appreciation and understanding. Furthermore, they are definitely experimenting to discover how to use the naive rhythmic capacities and tendencies for development in children. This is conspicuously illustrated in the organized bodily rhythm work of the F. W. Parker School and the City and Country School. It is also illustrated in the more systematic creative music of the intermediate grades.

So much for the constructive contribution of the child-centered schools. Is there another side to the picture? In what respects are these schools failing to live up to their opportunities? What are the outstanding demerits of their program of curriculum-making? Are these schools experimental in any genuine sense?

It is our opinion that the chief weakness of these schools is conspicuous intellectual waste. *Child activity is regarded altogether too frequently as an end in itself, rather than as a means to growth.* Criteria through which child activity may be evaluated are seldom set up. The fundamental purpose of education is the all-round growth of the child and the induction of the learner into the life of society. Educational reformers have tended to emphasize too much mere physical activity; to assume that because children are attentive, profitable growth is thereby certain to take place. On the contrary, true growth is measured by enlargement of experience, broadened vision, a widened and integrated background of meaning, increased power of generalization, enhanced artistic appreciation, creative self-expression. An outstanding weakness of the activities curricula is found in the fact that these dynamic activities in which the children engage are not definitely and systematically employed as educational instruments for the development of ideas and for generalization. This is apparently traceable to an inadequate psychological analysis of the theories and programs of these schools. The analysis of child activities and child learning is a complicated psychological undertaking. There is little evidence that the proponents of the activities curriculum have produced an intelligible and defensible analysis of the *way* in which growth in grasp of meaning, power of generalization, appreciation, and creative expression proceeds through activity. In certain quarters there has even been a tendency to attribute magical educational properties to the activities of children.

Careful observation recently in six of these experimental schools convinces the writers that habits of prolonged attention are not being adequately developed. Timed observations prove that the attention span and interest span of pupils in these schools are amazingly short. The activity basis of the work too often manifests a random character; it lacks continuity and sequence. The program has been derived too largely from spontaneous and casual interests. "Follow the child," has too frequently been the slogan of this movement. A more trustworthy guiding principle would be: "Direct the child into those channels of activity which, from the vantage point of mature psychological and educational experience, give promise of maximal development." In the language of Dewey, "There is no spontaneous germination in mental life." (See Chapter XII of Part II.)

Not only is there a critical need that the leaders in laboratory schools go through the mental travail of a fundamental psychological analysis of their activities; there is a conspicuous need also for a more complete orientation for the task of preparing the total school curriculum. The grade curricula of these laboratory schools consist essentially of series of more or less stimulating, but unorganized, units of work. They lack continuity and progression. The great goal of education is *maximal child growth at minimal expense.* Clearly, if maximal growth is to be guaranteed, the various stages of child development must be visualized in advance and reproduced in carefully planned developmental curricula. That is, the activities and materials of instruction employed in each of the school grades must be conceived as *units in a total scheme.* To leave to the spontaneous and casual interests of children, or even to the spontaneous and casual interests of free lance teachers, the development of the curriculum, is certain to produce precisely what it has produced in most of these schools—stimulating, interesting, but more or less random activities, lacking continuity, and unorganized with respect to a total scheme of development. In short, the result will be educational waste. In not a single laboratory school which has been examined by personal observation and studied through its written theory has there been discovered an analysis showing that the grade or year increments of the curriculum are based upon thoughtful design and definite prediction as to maximal growth.

Finally, in retrospect, after thirty years of curriculum-making in laboratory schools, one of the most regrettable wastes lies in the lack of definite scientific information concerning the results of these fine dynamic types of education. After a quarter century of work there are almost no measured records of the output of these schools. In only rare instances have these laboratory schools set up machinery for obtaining eye-witness accounts and measured records of innovations in the content and organization of the curriculum. Although teaching and the critical study of child learning are two fairly distinct sets of processes, the laboratory schools have assumed that the teacher could carry on both at the same time. The result has been that such accounts as we have of learning and teaching processes in these schools are casual and retrospective—not systematic and objective. Most of them are stimulating accounts of what teachers *think* they had produced in growing children; indeed, of what they *hoped* they had produced. That these suggestive accounts of a rich educational environment, casual though they may be, are valuable, goes without saying. But to be of real service in curriculum-making they must be based upon definite and systematic measurement, controlled experimentation, records of eye-witness observations by persons of real insight into child learning and masters of psychological and experimental techniques. The truth is that there are almost no *controlled* experimental studies now under way in the laboratory schools of America. In view of the unusual progress that has been made in the past decades in the development of the necessary techniques,[6] and the large sums of

[6] The reader will find an interesting agreement with this appraisal of the chief weaknesses in the laboratory schools in a recent pronouncement by the outstanding leader of the movement for a child-centered curriculum. (See quotations from Professor Dewey's article, *Individual and Experience* in Chapter XII of Part II of the Yearbook.

money which have been made available for the development of experimentation, this neglect of the use of scientific methods of appraisal is to a marked degree indefensible.

VIII. A Program of Administrative Procedure Based Upon Recent Practical Developments in City Systems

Returning now to a consideration of the situation in the public schools, let us center attention on certain guiding principles to be drawn from some of the more recent developments in city systems. Up to this point in the discussion the appraisal of methods of curriculum-making has given small grounds for optimism. Is the contemporary situation necessarily as hopeless as the routine procedure of the rank and file of schools might lead one to conclude?

We are convinced that it is not. The character of curriculum-making in progressive cities has changed markedly in the past half dozen years. Already in a few systems blind copying is being supplanted by comprehensive professional attempts to reconstruct the program of studies. The leadership of Denver, Detroit, Los Angeles, Springfield, St. Louis, and a few other of the larger cities, together with the creative work of Winnetka (Illinois), Burlington (Iowa), and a handful of compact school systems, gives great promise for the future. This experience suggests that a practical program can be organized which will markedly improve the curriculum of our urban schools.

The present writers have recently observed these practices in operation and have coöperated with a considerable number of public-school systems in the attempt to evolve an effective and trustworthy technique of curriculum-making. On the basis of these experiences a tentative practical program of administrative procedure can be outlined in a series of steps. That this formulation is subject to modification with the widening of experience is obvious. But such a formulation is a necessary tool for perfecting the program.

The fundamental desideratum, the first step in any sound program of curriculum-revision, is the development of a research attitude toward the problem on the part of those in responsible charge. The superintendent, the supervisory staff, the board of education, the teachers, must come to recognize that the task of curriculum-making is technical, professional, complicated, and difficult in the extreme. The successive chapters of this yearbook have illustrated vividly the obstacles in the way of effective curriculum-making. First and foremost, therefore, the building of an effective program in any community must wait upon the emergence in the community of a thoroughly professional and research attitude toward the problem. Once this attitude is established, the board of education will be in a mood to make possible the second step.

This second step is the provision of adequate funds for the *continuous and comprehensive* prosecution of curriculum-construction. This involves the creation of a separate and autonomous Department of Curriculum-Construction, coördinate in budget, leadership and authority with the Department of Supervision, the Department of School Buildings, or the Department of Educational Measurements. Indeed, the nucleus of the instructional work which very generally constitutes the major portion of school administration will be the Department or Bureau of Curriculum Construction. The first need, then, is the recognition of the professional character of the task, and the second is the appropriation of adequate funds for the creation of a central, autonomous department of curriculum-making.

The third step to be taken is the employment of trained and experienced specialists in curriculum-making and the organization of these workers under the direction of an executive officer. The latter should report directly to the superintendent and have control over the general function of instruction. Our survey shows that there is now no single agent trained in the science and art of curriculum-making who is responsible for the continuous and comprehensive construction of the materials of instruction. In all medium sized and large cities—indeed, no small city or town should be excepted from the rule—curriculum-making activities should engage the full time of at least one trained specialist.

The fourth requisite is that the specialist in charge of curriculum-making must be given adequate facilities for the development of his work. The department should be housed in a central building together with the other instructional and supervisory officers. The close coördination of the work of these various agents is essential. A professional library of curriculum books, scientific monographs, bulletins, textbooks, syllabi, and city and state courses of study should constitute the minimal equipment for such a department.[7] That it should be provided with adequate clerical and statistical assistance is a principle so fundamental to successful administration that it would scarcely require mention were it not honored so frequently in the breach.

The fifth step involves the organization of committees of workers under the coördinating direction of the special department of curriculum-construction. Practical curriculum-making is an enterprise of almost endless detail. Who is going to do the work? In an ideal situation (not actually to be found now in any school system in the United States) the task would be done by a technically trained research staff of specialists, clerks, statisticians, educational psychologists, and teachers. Practically, in the present undeveloped state of curriculum-making, it is impossible to finance such a program of specialists even in the larger cities. Actually, therefore, most of the work of preparing courses of study, syllabi, or outlines of study will be done by groups of teachers. In practice, the fifth step will consist necessarily of the organization of committees of principals and teachers.

Apropos of the use of teachers in curriculum-construction, one conclusion comes directly from the recent experience of Denver, Detroit, Springfield, St. Louis, Winnetka, and other systems. This conclusion is that adequate funds must be appropriated to release from all classroom duties those who are doing the detailed work of preparing courses of study. Someone has to perform the laborious tasks of assembling and organizing materials, preparing, criticizing, and revising outlines, selecting books, phrasing objectives, and illustrating methods of teaching. The conclusion is perfectly clear that this will engage at intervals the full time of at least two persons in each of the chief departments of the school, the social studies, reading, English, elementary mathematics, etc. Furthermore, teachers who are released from the classroom must be selected in terms of intelligence, technical training in curriculum-making, understanding of child learning, and general research attitude. They should be chosen for professional rather than for political

[7] The conspicuous examples of Denver and Detroit in their new practices illustrate what can be done in the development of adequate library facilities.

reasons. The utilization of selected teachers in the department of curriculum-construction according to some sabbatical arrangement might well serve as a fine incentive in elevating the professional standards of the teaching and administrative staffs.

This brings us to a consideration of a sixth need. As the work proceeds through the assembling of materials, the broadening of the characteristic outlines of the entire curriculum, and the arrangement of the order of activities and topics, technical advice will be needed. The experience of Denver and other cities points very clearly to the need of utilizing outside specialists. One of the most difficult phases of curriculum-making is that represented in the task of keeping the total problem in view and of seeing each special task in proper perspective. This is peculiarly the function of the central curriculum office, but even the workers in this office are often tempted to regard topics, subjects, grade or year materials, as separate and isolated units. Hence the need for frequent checking up by those removed from the details of the task and free from entangling alliances with the existing program.

Seventh and finally, this need for maintaining an overview, for seeing the curriculum as a whole, has important implications regarding the formation of the groups which are to do the detailed work. Recent experience points very clearly to the conclusion that the number of committees working on the problem of the curriculum should be small. In the first place, there should be a general coördinating and correlating committee composed of the director of curriculum-making and others who are equipped to view the problem in its entirety and qualified to adjust the conflicting interests of the groups of specialists. In the second place, the separate and specific subjects of study should be merged to form larger groups of related subjects. Witness, for example, the organization of committees on the social studies, rather than on history, geography, civics, economics, etc. In the third place, the inherent weakness in recent committee procedure consists in the organization of committees in terms of grades and the various levels of the school system. To guarantee continuity and real development there should be one committee on social studies, one committee on science, one committee on reading, English, and related subjects. Each of these committees should then consider the entire school program from the first grade through the twelfth. It is true that for the purpose of assembling detailed materials, workers in pairs or small groups may have to be assigned the task of assembling these materials for the separate grades or levels. However, individuals responsible for visualizing the whole scheme must constantly be integrating the work of these smaller groups. By no other method can we secure the unification of related activities and materials and the continuity and development which our current school system so sadly lacks.

IX. The Actual Work of Curriculum-Making

Recent experience in our city systems suggests the administrative organization described in the preceding section. Assuming that such an organization can be set up, what shall be the technical procedure of those who do the detailed work of curriculum-making? What shall the committees of administrators, supervisors, teachers, and others do? How shall they conceive and execute their tasks?

The confession should be made at the outset that there has been insufficient experimentation on curricular problems and inadequate discussion of the practical tasks of curriculum-making to permit us to generalize with safety concerning many important issues. For example, should a course of study be prepared in each of the subjects of study, including even the skill subjects of arithmetic, spelling, handwriting, etc.? To be specific, should a course be prepared in arithmetic which will present an outline of the topics as to order and teaching detail? Should such an outlined course of study or syllabus be prepared in spelling, giving the words to be learned, their grade-placement, order of treatment, etc.? Should such a course of study be prepared in geography, in history, in science, and in the other subjects which make up the program of the school?

Hitherto, the question has been answered for nearly all school systems in the affirmative. As a consequence, a curious and anomalous situation has developed. The curriculum of American schools has been organized essentially around school textbooks; in the order and treatment of topics, in the choice of illustrative activities and exercises, the teacher has followed the textbook. It is safe to say that instruction in spelling, arithmetic, geography, history, civics, and even in many of the less closely organized and the more advanced subjects, has been determined in great measure by the content and arrangement of the textbooks. The book itself serves as an outline and guide, indeed, as a veritable course of study. The demand of the administrative staff, therefore, that each department produce a printed course of study which may serve as an outline to guide the work of the classroom creates a curious *impasse*. On the one hand, the system has adopted a textbook in a given subject,[8] which is in reality a course of study. It then creates committees of principals and teachers to write another course of study. And experience has shown that these committees feel impelled to produce an outline possessing elements of originality. If they are successful in achieving this end, the course of study which they propose and which the administration prints and sends to the teachers must in some respects fail to harmonize with the books which have been adopted as the basic guides. Now, if the adopted textbooks and syllabi have been made by careful experimental methods, they represent an organization, gradation, and integration which it would be impossible to excel or even to equal by the *a priori* methods of committee procedure. A number of illustrative instances are known to the writers which reveal the disconcerting effects of this practice. Courses of study evolved by careful experimentation through years of close application have been ruthlessly and unintelligently destroyed by school officials who have felt called upon to publish under the name of the local system a course of study which did not slavishly follow the adopted books and outlines.

Here, then, is one of the difficult unsolved problems involved in the more practical phases of curriculum-making. What procedure should be followed in the adoption of school textbooks, in the development of suggested lists of activities, exercises, and readings, and in the organization of these elements into a systematic outline, or course of study? While this problem cannot be solved in the absence of bold experimentation in our laboratory and vigorous discussion in our educational conventions and professional journals, practice cannot wait upon the final solution. Wherever schools are administered, decisions must be made. We have therefore arrived at a certain conviction regarding the matter which we trust is made in the light of the best educational experience. This conviction,

[8] In this discussion there is no recommendation of such a procedure. At this juncture we are merely discussing what is actually done in contemporary practice; we are merely directing attention to the custom of preparing courses of study to fit the established school subjects.

thoroughly subject to modification as knowledge is advanced by discussion and experimentation, suggests the following tentative solution of the problem.

For the skill subjects in which careful scientific experimentation has been conducted over a number of years, a school system can do no better than adopt the best textbooks available. For example, for the development of the meanings and other phases of understanding in arithmetic and for graded exercises and illustrations, one of the new experimentally developed series of arithmetics should be employed. Because of the need for practice on specific number combinations, the school system should employ continuously diagnostic tests and practice devices, improved forms of which are constantly coming from the various laboratory centers. In our judgment, precisely the same procedure should be followed in spelling, in handwriting, in map location. Twenty years of research have produced definite and more or less scientifically founded word lists, tests and scales, and graded practice exercises. No amount of mere 'taking thought' by committees of teachers working in a curriculum bureau, unsupported by experimentation in the classroom, could produce a superior list or organization. Similarly, fifteen years of laboratory research have produced new methods in the teaching of handwriting. The first and foremost task of the committees working within a local system, therefore, is to assemble the results of these scientific studies of the various skills and factual processes and to make them available to the teaching staff of the system in the most serviceable and intelligible form. If clear manuals of method are already in existence, they should be passed on to the teachers and a continuous program of education of teachers in service should be launched. If the recent discoveries of how children acquire the various skills and habits are not available in the form of intelligible manuals of method, then the local curriculum committees, by translating this knowledge into practical instructional guides, can discharge a most necessary function. The job of local committees with respect to this phase of the curriculum, therefore, seems to be very clearly established. They should see to the adoption of books, tests, and practice devices and should either assemble or prepare adequate manuals of teaching method.

The great task of the school, however, is *not* the development of skills and the narrower habit processes. Rather is it that of guaranteeing the growth of understanding, tolerant attitudes, powers of generalization and reflective thought, critical judgment and appreciation, and meaningful backgrounds of experience for social interpretation. Now, if the curricular developments of the past quarter century reveal anything at all, they throw into sharp relief the opportunity and the obligation of persons engaged in curriculum-making in local systems to show teachers how to vitalize and make significant the activities of pupil work. At this point there is certainly no conflict between the opportunities, indeed the chief tasks, of curriculum-workers in local systems and those of the specialists who are working in laboratory centers. There is crucial need that the energies of both teachers and specialists be harnessed to the task of *organizing the creative activities* of the elementary and secondary schools. Although the literature is meager and, as we have already observed, not adequately thoughtful, nevertheless, a considerable volume of published suggestions for vitalizing the *activities* of the school is now available to the curriculum-maker. The real task, therefore, of local committees of curriculum bureaus in town, city, and state systems is to master this literature and to study carefully this problem. From the wealth of suggestions now available they should prepare suggestive lists of optional activities dealing with constructive handwork, creative music, drawing, writing, community investigations, individual pupil research, and many other types of interest.

In the collection and organization of materials, curriculum-workers in local systems, therefore, are confronted by problems of staggering proportions. Even though they adopt textbooks in the fundamental school subjects, the genuine vitalizing of the curriculum requires that teachers be given systematic outlines of proposed or possible activities. These should include lists of reading books in the primary and intermediate grades with clear annotations as to content and grade-placement; detailed lists of excursions, field trips, and ways and means of surveying the local neighborhood and community; suggestions for the development of the creative art, music, and composition of the school; carefully selected and graded lists of optional topics and problems for class discussion; and stimulating accounts of methods of organizing social and recreational interests, optional proposals for the development of the manual activities of pupils, and possible educational uses of school assemblies, social gatherings, and the manifold group organizations of the school.

In other words, the task of curriculum-making in a local bureau is essentially that of the selection, organization, and integration of a tremendous wealth of available materials. If this task is to be compassed even crudely, it can be done only through the coöperation of many persons trained and experienced in the separate technical tasks involved.

The discussion up to this point deals only with the initial task of assembling and organizing proposed schemes of activities and materials. Once these are prepared and sent to the schools in the form of printed syllabi, they should be always regarded as purely hypothetical and optional proposals. The curriculum bureau should develop a systematic program of appraisal, of measurement of results, of comparison of outcomes obtained from alternative procedures. Specific criticisms should be obtained throughout the system and from all levels as to the value of proposed materials and activities. In accordance with the findings of the bureau and the broader contributions of educational science, the course of study should be modified continuously. Because of recent developments in the laboratories of schools of education, new materials are pouring from the educational press. In increasing quantities studies of learning, of administrative organization, of experimentation, of laboratory innovation are being made available to practical curriculum-makers. The machinery of curriculum-making in school systems must guarantee that the curriculum of the schools keep pace with the advancing science of education and with the ceaseless change of American life.

CHAPTER XXXI

THE LITERATURE OF CURRICULUM-MAKING: A SELECTED AND ANNOTATED BIBLIOGRAPHY

JOHN A. HOCKETT
The Lincoln School of Teachers College, Columbia University, New York City

PURPOSE OF THIS BIBLIOGRAPHY

Although the present interest in curriculum revision is of very recent origin, the literature of the field has grown so rapidly in the past few years that one important function of such a yearbook as this should be to provide careful guidance for further reading. The first systematic book on the curriculum—Professor Bobbitt's[1]—*The Curriculum* (3)[2]—appeared only eight years ago. While the early objective investigations of what to teach date back about fifteen years, certainly the vast majority of the important scientific curriculum studies have appeared since 1915.

There are at present hundreds of titles dealing with the curriculum and the technique of curriculum-construction, and if we include those relating to the content and organization of materials in specific subjects, the total runs into the thousands. It would be difficult and unnecessary for the student of education to include this whole list in his study. For the student of the curriculum who desires to make a more intensive study, longer lists are available. Reference is made herein to several other bibliographies and many of the books and articles listed contain references dealing with particular phases of the curriculum problem.

The attempt has been made, therefore, to present in this bibliography a relatively short and very carefully selected list of titles. In constructing school curricula we need evidence concerning "What knowledge is of most worth?" Similarly, the educational

[1] Bobbitt, Franklin (1876-), Instructor Philippine Normal School of Manilla, 1903-7; Instructor, Assistant Professor and Associate Professor, University of Chicago, 1909-1918; Professor of School Administration, University of Chicago, 1908. Author: *What the Schools Teach and Might Teach; The Curriculum; How to Make the Curriculum,* etc.

[2] Arabic numbers in parentheses refer to the references arranged numerically on the appended bibliography.

student needs evidence, primarily, as to which readings will be of most value to him. In the preparation of this bibliography hundreds of titles have been collected, and practically all the educational journals and yearbooks have been examined over a period of years, in the search for significant articles.

Major Lines of Curriculum Activity

The 'Free School' Movement

That there are several distinct lines of curriculum activity will be apparent to one who has read the chapters of this volume. A general knowledge of the characteristics and influence of each would seem to be essential to the educationist. First in chronological development was the 'free school' movement, the attempt to minister to the development of the growing child by overthrowing the traditional, logically arranged subjects of study and substituting a curriculum of activities appealing to the interests of children and involving the learning of knowledge and skills as essential to the fulfillment of the activity. *The Child and the Curriculum* (9) and *The School and Society* (10) present the Dewey philosophy. Kilpatrick's article, "How shall we select the subject matter of the curriculum?" (37) and his series of three articles on "Subject matter and the educative process" (38) give excellent though brief statements of his position. Other statements of this philosophy and descriptions of its practical application are given in the books by Collings (49), Meriam (56), Bonser (4), C. A. McMurry (12), Wells (61), and in other publications listed under Section C of the bibliography, "Descriptions of Experimental Curriculum-Making." In the publications of the F. W. Parker (51), the Lincoln (55), and the City and Country schools (58, 60), will be found instructive descriptions of activity curricula.

National Committee Recommendations

A second important influence in the development of the curriculum has been the reports of national committees. While the student of the history of curriculum-making will wish to study the earlier of these, the general student will find it more profitable to devote his attention to such later ones as the *Reorganization of Mathematics in Secondary Education* (74), *The Classical Investi-*

gation, General Report (90), the publications of the *Modern Foreign Language Study* and of the new *History Committee* as they appear. The critical article on "What shall constitute the procedure of national committees?" (42), by Rugg, should be read in connection with the study of committee reports. It will serve as one background for evaluation of the technique and recommendations of future committees.

Objective Investigations

The scientific or semi-scientific investigations are numerous and varied. In the past decade they have shed light upon the problems of what to teach, in what grades to teach it, and by what methods. Far the largest number of these studies have been in the basic tool subjects—reading, spelling, and arithmetic; more than a thousand have been reported in these three subjects. A considerable number of problems in social studies and in high-school mathematics have been attacked quantitatively. Comparatively few studies have been made in science, home economics, industrial arts, music, and fine arts. Knowledge of the different techniques employed by investigators in various fields, familiarity with the important results and conclusions, and recognition of the unanswered problems awaiting solution are all essential to one who would understand and participate in the modern development of the curriculum. Summaries of investigations in several fields which are now available offer the student orientation with a minimal expenditure of time and effort. The best general introduction to the literature of scientific investigation is the *Third Yearbook of the Department of Superintendence* (19). Other summaries of research and outstanding investigations are listed under the several subjects.

Curriculum-Making Through Activity Analysis

The terms "activity analysis" or "functional analysis" have come to characterize the theory of curriculum-making of an important group of educationists. This doctrine has been championed by Professor Charters in his *Curriculum Construction* (6) and in the two articles cited in the *Journal of Educational Research* (28, 30). This approach to curriculum-making is not opposed to the use of scientific investigations; it is rather the formulation of the theory of curriculum-construction through the scientific analysis of human activities and functions. The analysis of abilities employed by Professor Bobbitt has the same goal, but differs somewhat in technique. For Bobbitt's method of analysis one of the following books should be read (preferably the former)—*How to Make a Curriculum,* (2) or *Curriculum-Making in Los Angeles* (1). The critical articles by Bode (25) and Snedden (43) should be read in this connection.

Present and Continuing Sources of Curricular Activity

Knowledge of how to keep in touch with future developments is quite as essential to the professional student as is information in regard to past achievements, for we are obviously only in the early stages of a great movement. There have been three university centers of curriculum activity in the United States, the School of Education of the University of Chicago, Teachers College, Columbia University, and the University of Iowa, which have largely directed the course of events and stimulated nation-wide progress.

The preëminent contributions of the Chicago School appear in their *Elementary School Journal,* their *School Review,* and in their series of *Supplementary Educational Monographs.* Teachers College has recently organized a Bureau of Curriculum Research which will from time to time issue monographs on curriculum problems (5). Other important investigations are reported by their Bureau of Educational Research. Discussions relating to the curriculum frequently appear in the *Teachers College Record.* The State University of Iowa reports its work in a series of *Studies in Education.*

Other educational periodicals which occasionally contain discussions or investigations of curriculum problems are: the *Journal of Educational Research,* the *Educational Review,* the *Journal of Educational Method, Education,* and the weekly *School and Society.* The *Teachers Journal and Abstract* reviews and summarizes educational books and articles. *Progressive Education* contains illustrations and discussions of the work of experimental schools.

The National Education Association maintains at Washington, D. C., a Research Division which issues quarterly research bulletins, some of which are devoted to the curriculum (21, 22, 100, 101). The *Journal of the National Education Association* contains curriculum articles of a popular nature. The annual volume of *Ad-*

dresses and Proceedings of the National Education Association contains the papers presented at the annual meetings. Several interesting articles will be found in the *Proceedings* for 1924 and 1925 (26, 34, 35, 36, 37, 47, 98).

The *Second, Third,* and *Fourth Yearbooks* of the Department of Superintendence (18, 19, 20) have been important contributions to the literature of curriculum-construction.

The *Yearbooks* of the National Society for the Study of Education (13, 14, 15, 16, 17) have contained some of the most important of the early contributions in this field, and much can be expected of future yearbooks.

The recent *Yearbooks* of the National Association of Secondary School Principals have contained a number of interesting papers read before the society, which present varying points of view toward the curricular problems of the high school (32, 45).

Some of the bulletins (31) and bibliographies of the United States Bureau of Education, Washington, D. C., will be found useful in subject fields and in regard to particular curricular problems.

The endowed educational foundations, such as the Commonwealth Fund, the General Education Board (33), the Laura Spelman Rockefeller Foundation, and the Carnegie Corporation, give financial aid to educational investigations and surveys, and sometimes present in their reports and other publications material relating to the curriculum. Reference to some of these of particular value is made in the accompanying list.

Surveys of city school systems are frequently conducted by members of the staffs of schools of education, and are published by the universities, by the cities, or by commercial publishers. These survey reports contain descriptions of local curricula and recommendations for their improvement. A more representative view of current curricular practice may, however, be secured with greater economy in such monographs as: Counts, *The Senior High School Curriculum;* (7) Glass, *Curriculum Practices in the Junior High School and Grades 5 and 6* (11); Bruner and Stratemeyer, *Rating Elementary School Courses of Study* (5); and the *Second Yearbook of the Department of Superintendence* (18).

Several city school systems have recently established curriculum-bureaus, which from time to time issue reports, bulletins, courses of study, and monographs. Among these should be mentioned Denver, Colorado; Los Angeles and Berkeley, California; and Winnetka, Illinois.

Descriptions of experimental curricula and reports of investigations and activities are published by several of the experimental schools. (See Section C of the bibliography).

Many other groups and agencies influence, or attempt to influence, the course of development of the curriculum of American schools, some beneficially, some ignorantly and perniciously. Professor Judd's article "How Modern Business May Aid in Reconstructing the Curriculum" (36) contains a suggestive discussion of the influence of some of these extra-school agencies; and a forthcoming book by Bessie L. Pierce, *Public Opinion and the Teaching of History,* to be published by Alfred A. Knopf, sheds light upon another aspect of the problem.

Selected and Annotated Bibliography

A. Books Dealing with Curriculum-Making and General Problems of the Curriculum

1. Bobbitt, Franklin. *Curriculum-Making in Los Angeles.* Supplementary Educational Monographs, No. 20, University of Chicago, 1922.

   Describes the coöperative effort of the author and the 1200 high-school teachers of Los Angeles to revise the curriculum through the formulation of a list of 1100 abilities and characteristics deemed advisable or desirable for the men and women of the city. Contains discussion of the apportionment of the abilities and characteristics as objectives to the various subject-matter departments. Lists assumptions upon which the plan is based, and describes matters of committee organization, etc. Bobbitt's *How to Make a Curriculum* contains much of the same material and is recommended rather than this monograph.

2. Bobbitt, Franklin. *How to Make a Curriculum.* Houghton-Mifflin Company, Boston, 1924. Pp. 292.

   "The major task of curriculum-making at present is the discovery of goals in a general way." This is to be done through activity-analysis of human experience. Author lists and discusses 800 specific objectives, worked out in his classes and in Los Angeles, and their assignment to various subject groups. Discussion of educative types of pupil activities and experiences. Suggestions for curriculum-making in local school systems.

3. Bobbitt, Franklin. *The Curriculum.* Houghton-Mifflin Company, Boston, 1918. Pp. 295.

   The pioneer book in this field. Deals largely with the aims and processes of education, rather than with the curriculum alone. Treats of education for vocational efficiency, citizenship, physical efficiency, leisure occupations and social intercommunications. Chapter VI deals with scientific method in curriculum-making as conceived in 1918.

4. Bonser, F. G. *The Elementary-School Curriculum.* The Macmillan Company, 1920. Pp. 466.

   Eight chapters deal with educational principles upon which curriculum-making depends, with illustrations of their applications. Remaining chapters contain suggestive projects and subject matter for the curriculum organized by grades.

5. Bruner, H. B., and Stratemeyer, F. B. *Rating Elementary-School Courses of Study.* Bulletin No. 1, Bureau of Cur-

riculum Research, Teachers College, Columbia University, New York City, 1926.

A report of the results secured from an evaluation of 9000 elementary-school courses of study to determine outstanding present practice. This investigation, which utilized more than 35,000 judgments, presents: (1) the criteria employed in judging the relative worth of courses of study; (2) the courses in the various subject fields selected as most nearly conforming to the judged best points of the criteria; (3) a preliminary report of trends and tendencies as indicated by the selected courses.

6. CHARTERS, W. W. *Curriculum Construction.* The Macmillan Co., 1923. Pp. 352.

Part I, "Principles of Curriculum-Making," discusses curriculum-making, the role of activity analysis in curriculum-making, the determination of major objectives, collecting and grading curriculum material, its relative importance, etc. In Part II fifty-six curriculum investigations in the various fields are described. An important book.

7. COUNTS, G. S. *The Senior High School Curriculum.* Supplementary Educational Monographs, No. 29, University of Chicago, 1926. Pp. 160.

Reports an investigation of curriculum practices in the senior high school, general trends within the program of studies, and the philosophy of secondary education held by members of the administrative, supervisory and teaching staffs. Fifteen progressive school systems were studied. Chapter II describes the general plan of curriculum organization, and an evaluation of the present program is given in Chapter V.

8. COX, W. L. *Curriculum Adjustment in the Secondary School.* J. B. Lippincott Co., 1925. Pp. 306.

Fairly comprehensive discussion of the curriculum of the secondary school; its aims, various conceptions of scientific procedure in curriculum construction, the relation of the curriculum to life, the aid to be secured from studies of the high-school population and of the nature of learning. Helpful discussion of principles of curriculum-making. Bibliography.

9. DEWEY, JOHN. *The Child and the Curriculum.* University of Chicago Press, 1902. Pp. 40.

"Abandon the notion of subject matter as something fixed and ready-made in itself, outside the child's experience; cease thinking of the child's experience as also something hard and fast; see it as something fluent, embryonic, vital; and we realize that the child and the curriculum are simply two limits which define a single process."

10. DEWEY, JOHN. *The School and Society.* University of Chicago Press. 1900, 1915. Pp. 164.

Three lectures dealing with the school's relation to present social conditions and social progress, the adaptation of the school to the life and growth of the individual child, and waste in education due to unreal subject matter and unpsychological methods. Supplementary chapters dealing with the work of the Elementary School of the University of Chicago.

11. GLASS, J. M. *Curriculum Practices in the Junior High School and Grades 5 and 6.* Supplementary Educational Monographs, No. 25. University of Chicago, 1924. Pp. 181.

A study of the existing curriculum in 14 city school systems. Discusses time-allotments to subjects and to specific teaching units, the core curriculum, and elective courses, and the need for scientific reconstruction of the curriculum. Illustrated with 30 tables.

12. MCMURRY, C. A. *How to Organize the Curriculum.* The Macmillan Company, 1923. Pp. 358.

Advocates simplification and enrichment of the curriculum organized around life projects or controlling units of thought and intensively studied, rather than brief and shallow treatment of many smaller topics. Suggests bases for organization of studies, stresses the importance of ideas, and describes several projects as illustrations. Lists many projects in history, geography, science, and literature.

13. NATIONAL SOCIETY FOR THE STUDY OF EDUCATION. *Fourteenth Yearbook, Part I. Minimum Essentials in Elementary-School Subjects.* First Report of the Committee on Economy of Time in Education of the Department of Superintendence. Public School Publishing Co., Bloomington, Ill., 1915. Pp. 152.

Reports of investigations and discussion of current practices and standards, and suggestions of essentials in the several school subjects, as indicated by the more scientific studies to date, and by other criteria.

14. NATIONAL SOCIETY FOR THE STUDY OF EDUCATION. *Sixteenth Yearbook, Part I. Second Report* of the Committee on Economy of Time in Education of the Department of Superintendence. Public School Publishing Co., Bloomington, Ill., 1917. Pp. 192.

Reports a number of content investigations and other studies in the several elementary subjects.

15. NATIONAL SOCIETY FOR THE STUDY OF EDUCATION. *Seventeenth Yearbook, Part I. Third Report* of the Committee on Economy of Time. Public School Publishing Co., Bloomington, Ill., 1918. Pp. 134.

Reports several investigations of minimal essentials in elementary-school subjects. Studies in curriculum content in arithmetic, geography, vocabulary, English, civics, and history. (Most of these studies are summarized in the *Third Yearbook of the Department of Superintendence.*)

16. NATIONAL SOCIETY FOR THE STUDY OF EDUCATION. *Nineteenth Yearbook, Part I. New Materials of Instruction.* Public School Publishing Co., Bloomington, Ill., 1920. Pp. 194.

Examples of curriculum material developed in various school systems in reading for children and adults, local history and geography, mathematics, nature study, and community life.

17. NATIONAL SOCIETY FOR THE STUDY OF EDUCATION. *Twentieth Yearbook, Part I. Second Report on New Materials of Instruction.* Public School Publishing Co., Bloomington, Ill., 1921. Pp. 237.

Brief descriptions of 285 projects or units of work suitable for pupils from kindergarten through junior high school.

18. DEPARTMENT OF SUPERINTENDENCE. *Second Yearbook, The Elementary-School Curriculum.* Department of Superintendence, National Education Association, Washington, D. C., 1924. Pp. 296.

A series of articles on the machinery for revising and supervising the curriculum and a general analysis of present elementary school curriculum practice. Contributions by Bobbitt, Charters, Gray, Glass, Hosic, H. B. Wilson, R. G. Jones, McClure, Threlkeld, and others.

19. DEPARTMENT OF SUPERINTENDENCE. *Third Yearbook, Research in Constructing the Elementary Curriculum.* Department of Superintendence, National Education Association, 1925. Pp. 424.

Reports of subject committees in twelve fields, including discussion of aims and problems of each, and digests of over 150 scientific or semi-scientific investigations relating to curriculum construction, not including the briefer summary of over 500 reading investigations. Valuable summary of investigations.

20. DEPARTMENT OF SUPERINTENDENCE. *Fourth Yearbook, The Nation at Work on the Public School Curriculum.* Department of Superintendence, National Education Association, Washington, D. C., 1926. Pp. 520.

Summarizes the work of the Commission on the Curriculum of the Department of Superintendence and of curriculum revision in typical cities. States fundamental considerations. Major part of book devoted to reports of national subject committees, giving descriptions of curriculum-making in the various subjects. Contains summaries of investigations in various subjects not reported in the *Third Yearbook.*

21. NATIONAL EDUCATION ASSOCIATION. *Research Bulletin,* Vol. I, No. 5. *Facts on the Public School Curriculum.* National Education Association, Washington, D. C., Nov., 1923. Pp. 45.

Presents legislative and state board requirements relating to the elementary-school curriculum and discusses their implications. Presents facts of time-allotment and grade-placement in the elementary and junior high schools. Bibliography of books dealing with curriculum problems, based upon recommended lists from a group of educationalists.

22. NATIONAL EDUCATION ASSOCIATION. *Research Bulletin,* Vol. III, Nos. 4 and 5. *Keeping Pace with the Advancing Curriculum.* National Education Association, Washington, D. C., September and November, 1925. Pp. 186.

A summary of current thought on the curriculum. Discusses need for revision, theories and methods of revision, the participation of specialists, teachers and administrators in revision, the contributions of research to curriculum-building, principles for evaluating curricula, and bibliography.

B. Articles on the Technique of Curriculum-Construction and General Problems of the Curriculum

23. BOBBITT, FRANKLIN. "Difficulties to be met in local curriculum-making." *Elementary School Journal,* 25: May, 1925, 653-663.

Discusses 13 difficulties that tend to handicap local efforts to revise curricula.

24. BOBBITT, FRANKLIN. "The new technique of curriculum-making." *Elementary School Journal,* 25: September, 1924, 45-54.

Contrasts the old 'mind filling' and the new 'functional' education. Urges and defends activity-analysis as the basis for the content and objectives of the curriculum.

25. BODE, BOYD H. "Why educational objectives?" *Journal of Educational Research,* 10: October, 1924, 175-186.

Educational objectives must be determined by our educational philosophy and must actually determine subject matter and practice. Job analysis cannot determine aims and ideals. Scientific education is in danger of forgetting the learner. Criticizes Bobbitt's lists of abilities as subjective and confusing. Criticizes Snedden's philosophy as begging the question.

26. BONSER, F. G. "The reorganization of the curriculum of the elementary schools." *Address and Proceedings of the National Education Association,* 62: 1924, 890-897.

Four causes of the need for curricular reorganization: changing conceptions of education, changing conditions of life, short period of growth in teachers, changes in forms of school organization. Contributions to curriculum-revision of educational philosophers and scientific research. Advocates a compromise between extremes of subject-matter organization and chaotic license of no organization.

27. BRIGGS, T. H. "Curriculum reconstruction in the high school." *School Review,* 31: February, 1923, 109-115.

Points out three obstacles to revision of the secondary-school curriculum: (1) uncritical satisfaction with "what is"; (2) lack of clear aims and fundamental principles; (3) a conviction that a thoroughgoing revision would necessitate complete change in organization, equipment, and personnel of teaching staffs. Proposes eight steps of curriculum-reconstruction.

28. CHARTERS, W. W. "Activity analysis and curriculum-construction." *Journal of Educational Research,* 5: May, 1922, 357-367.

Urges activity analysis; discusses its possibilities and difficulties. To what detail should analysis be carried? Should the curriculum be based upon analysis of frequency of use or of difficulty? Should we teach "best methods" or "currently used" methods? Two analyses are necessary: a vocational and an extra-vocational analysis. Ideals and standards must always aid in the selection of subject matter.

29. CHARTERS, W. W. "The Los Angeles high-school curriculum." *School Review,* 31: February, 1923, 95-103.

Commends Bobbitt's monograph and quotes principles and abilities therefrom. Suggests that the "work would have been clarified and improved'' if the initial analysis had been made along these lines: (1) ideals, (2) activities, (3) factual content, and (4) educational principles.

30. Charters, W. W. ''Functional analysis as the basis for curriculum construction.'' *Journal of Educational Research*, 10: October, 1924, 214-221.

Points out advantages and difficulties of functional analysis. Requires much time, effort, money, and intelligent technical skill. How much detail should the analysis reveal?

31. Commission on Reorganization of Secondary Education. *Cardinal Principles of Secondary Education.* Bureau of Education, Bulletin 1918, No. 35. Pp. 32.

Contains recommendations of the committee of objectives of the secondary school and the secondary curriculum.

32. Davis, C. O. ''The curriculum and the seven objectives.'' *Ninth Yearbook, National Association of Secondary School Principals.* 1925. Pp. 112-129.

Attempts to estimate the influence of the bulletin *Cardinal Principles of Secondary Education.* Reports two questionnaire studies. (1) The judgments of 8000 high-school pupils on curriculum matters, such as easiest, hardest, most valuable, and favorite subjects. (2) The opinions of 500 high-school men and women, mostly principals, regarding the influence of the seven objectives of the Committee on Reorganization of Secondary Education. Reports the curriculum elections of 64,000 pupils in 122 accredited Michigan high schools in 1924.

33. Flexner, Abraham. *A Modern School.* (Occasional papers of the General Education Board, 1916. Pp. 23.)

Indicts the present curriculum as largely traditional, abstract, remote from life, and as only slightly mastered by pupils. The curriculum of the modern school will include ''nothing for which an affirmative case cannot now be made out.'' Curriculum should be built of actual activities in four main fields: science, industry, aesthetics (literature, language, art and music), and civics (history, institutions and current happenings), broadly interpreted.

34. Horn, Ernest. ''The curriculum problem attacked scientifically.'' *Addresses and Proceedings of the National Education Association*, 63: 1925, 812-815.

''Research does not consist merely in counting and measuring. . . . The setting up of proper hypotheses, the critical study of the data, and its interpretation for practical school use require time, scientific ability, and insight into school problems.''

35. JUDD, C. H. "The curriculum: A paramount issue." *Addresses and Proceedings of the National Education Association,* 63: 1925, 805-811.

Sketches the stimulation to curriculum-revision brought about by the restlessness of the nineties, the period of testing of the first fifteen years of the century, and the expansion of the school in the past generation. Discusses the obstacles of conservatism, vested interests, passive helplessness, and lack of machinery for revision. Urges a vigorous sustained coöperative attack on the problem.

36. JUDD, C. H. "How modern business may aid in reconstructing the curriculum." *School and Society,* 17: 281-287, also in *Addresses and Proceedings of the National Education Association,* 61: 1923, 975-980.

Excellent discussion of the values and dangers of the demands of business and various special interests and of changing conditions upon the curriculum. Need of broad and sympathetic attack by well-trained agencies on the problems of curriculum-reconstruction.

37. KILPATRICK, W. H. "How shall we select the subject matter of the elementary curriculum?" *Journal of Educational Method,* 4: September, 1924, 3-10; also in *Addresses and Proceedings of the National Education Association,* 62: 1924, 903-908.

We must start with life itself and its expansion, not with subject matter, which is a means, not an end. Contrasts education as preparation for life and education as life. Major objectives: growing technique of control. Need for gripping, challenging, and suitably varied, socially conditioned activities.

38. KILPATRICK, W. H. "Subject matter and the educative process." *Journal of Educational Method,* 2: November, 1922; February and May, 1923, 94-101, 230-236, 367-376.

Contrasts in-school and out-of-school subject matter and learning. Contrasts the traditional and a new view of studying, of teaching, and of the curriculum. Criticizes the traditional curriculum as consisting of isolated quantities of subject-matter-to-be-learned, where deferred values reign supreme. Advocates a series of guided experiences which elevate and enrich the subsequent stream of experience.

39. McMURRY, F. M. (and others). "Principles underlying the making of school curricula." *Teachers College Record,* 16: September, 1915, 307-316.

Subject matter should be determined by relative importance in social life and should also appeal to pupils as worth while, should be organized around problems and in such a way as to provide easy control over knowledge by pupils. The curriculum should be highly adaptable to individual pupil needs.

40. MOSSMAN, LOIS C. "An analysis of the theories basic to curriculum construction." *Teachers College Record*, 26: May, 1925, 734-739.

Representation in chart form of four current points of view regarding curriculum-construction. Statement of attitude of each of the four groups toward: the function of the school, the nature and function of method, respect for personality, activities, and subject matter, and other matters.

41. RUGG, HAROLD. "A preface to the reconstruction of the American school curriculum." *Teachers College Record*, 27: March, 1926, 600-616.

The difficulties of understanding our complex industrial society demand great changes in the content and organization of the curriculum. The need for dramatic, vivid, expanded curricular materials which accurately portray the vital forces of the present. The need for development of mutual understanding and tolerance.

42. RUGG, HAROLD. "What shall constitute the procedure of national committees?" *Journal of Educational Psychology*, 15: January, 1924, 23-42.

Contrasts *The Reorganization of Mathematics in Secondary Education* and Thorndike's *Psychology of Algebra*. The former "is primarily subjective, the other much more objective." A national committee should act in three capacities: (1) it should act as a deliberative body of specialists stating educational aims and criteria; (2) it should organize investigations of social and psychological needs which underlie the curriculum; (3) it should act as a clearinghouse and forum for controversial discussion.

43. SNEDDEN, DAVID. "Planning curriculum research." *School and Society*, 22: Aug. 29, Sept. 5, and Sept. 12, 1925, 259-265; 287-294; 319-328.

What are the elements of educational values? How may they be discovered? By what criteria evaluated? How classified and organized into curricular strands, or courses? How adapted to groups? How determine relative values? Ends with evaluation of three studies of curriculum-making: Bobbitt's, Charter's, and Rugg and Hockett's.

44. SNEDDEN, DAVID. "Bobbitt's curriculum-making in Los Angeles." *School Review*, 31: February, 1923, 104-108.

Considers Bobbitt's work as "a most helpful contribution, an interesting and suggestive qualitative analysis" but not sufficiently quantitative. Points out the vagueness of many of Bobbitt's objectives, and the failure to distinguish between case groups of distinctive population elements in their application.

45. SNEDDEN, DAVID. "Case-group methods of determining flexibility of general curricula in high schools." *Seventh Yearbook of the National Association of Secondary School Principles*, pp. 80-87; also *School and Society*, 17: March 17, 1923, 287-292.

Condemns a traditional curriculum which postulates uniformity of individuals and static social inheritance. Proposes a plurality of curricula for case groups reasonably homogeneous in respect to certain abilities, environing conditions, and educational needs.

46. SYMPOSIUM BY KILPATRICK, BAGLEY, BONSER, HOSIC, and HATCH. "Dangers and difficulties of the project method and how to overcome them." *Teachers College Record*, 22: September, 1921, 283-321.

A series of discussions from somewhat varied points of view on the meaning and advantages of teaching by projects, as well as the dangers and difficulties inherent in faulty interpretation and application of this method.

47. THRELKELD, A. L.: "Curriculum-revision: How a particular city may attack the problem." *Elementary School Journal*, 25: April, 1925, 573-582; also in *Address and Proceedings of the National Education Association*, 63: 1925, 826-833.

Explains the main principles underlying the Denver program of curriculum-reconstruction: (1) participation of the local professional corps, (2) definite administration and supervision of the local corps, (3) utilization of the most advanced educational thought of the profession, (4) curriculum-revision must be continuous.

C. Descriptions of Experimental Curriculum-Making

48. BURKE, AGNES (and six others): *A Conduct Curriculum for the Kindergarten and First Grade.* Chas. Scribners' Sons, New York, 1923. Pp. 123.

An attempt in the Horace Mann School to work out a primary curriculum in terms of behavior. No fixed curriculum is presented. "Instead, an effort has been made to set up different objectives, . . . which if attained will lead to changes in thought, feeling, and conduct." Illustrated.

49. COLLINGS, ELLSWORTH. *An Experiment with a Project Curriculum.* The Macmillan Co., New York, 1923. Pp. 346.

Account of a four-year experiment in a group of three rural schools, one experimental, two control. "Pioneer work along three lines, (1) in the guiding aims, (2) in the means (both content and procedure) used for attaining these aims, and (3) in the kind of data brought forward to indicate success." Results measured by standardized tests. Detailed account of the experimental-school curriculum contains description of many projects. Controlling principles, their application, and the outcomes of the experiment discussed.

50. DEWEY, JOHN AND DEWEY, EVELYN. *Schools of To-morrow.* E. P. Dutton, New York, 1915. Pp. 316.

Illustrations of the adaptation of the curriculum to the interests and abilities of children in a number of progressive schools. An attempt "to show what actually happens when schools start out to put into practice . . . some of the theories that have been pointed out as the soundest and best ever since Plato."

51. FRANCIS W. PARKER SCHOOL. *Studies in Education.*

Vol. I.	*The Social Motive in School Work*	1912
II.	*The Morning Exercise as a Socializing Influence*	1913
III.	*Expression as a Means of Training Motive*	1914
IV.	*Education through Concrete Experience*	1915
V.	*The Course in Science*	1918
VI.	*The Individual and the Curriculum: Experiments in Adaptation*	1920
VII.	*Social Science Series. The Course in History*	1923

Seven volumes of approximately 175 pages each, describing in considerable detail many of the activities and curricular materials of the school from the first grade through the high school. Many illustrations of the pupils' writings and drawings, and photographs of their activities, with educational interpretation throughout.

52. HORACE MANN STUDIES IN EDUCATION, Vol. I. Teachers College, Columbia University, New York City, 1923.

A series of articles dealing with remedial work in reading, classification and promotion of pupils, efficiency in teaching arithmetic, old versus new types of history, examinations in history, formal gymnastics, and a description of the work of the Girls' League of the Horace Mann High School for Girls.

53. HORACE MANN STUDIES IN ELEMENTARY EDUCATION. Teachers College, Columbia University, New York City, 1922, Pp. 102. Also, *Teachers College Record,* March and May, 1919, September, 1920, January, March, and May, 1921.

Seven articles setting forth the underlying principles of primary education and describing certain experimentation in this field, begun in 1916. Three articles deal with special studies in the higher grades. The articles deal with materials, activities, and projects in various grades.

54. THE TEACHERS OF THE HORACE MANN ELEMENTARY SCHOOL. *The Curriculum of the Horace Mann Elementary School.* Teachers College, Columbia University, New York City, 1917. Pp. 138.

A statement of the curriculum of the Horace Mann School in 1917. Chiefly in outline form; organized by conventional school subjects; only slightly illustrated with descriptions of classroom activities. (See also No. 48.)

55. LINCOLN SCHOOL OF TEACHERS COLLEGE PUBLICATIONS.

The school publishes bulletins, booklets, books and monographs pertaining to various phases of the school's work, which may be obtained from the Bureau of Publications of Teachers College, Columbia University, New York City. Many of these publications deal in part with the curriculum or with efforts in curriculum-making. *A Descriptive Booklet* contains on pp. 115-117 a list of 65 titles published prior to June, 1925. This booklet also contains brief descriptions of the various types of work being carried on.

56. MERIAM, J. L. *Child Life and the Curriculum.* World Book Co., Yonkers, New York, 1920. Pp. 538.

Criticises the traditional curriculum and states principles of curriculum-making. Curriculum should be scientifically made and more intimately connected with the everyday life of both children and adults. Discusses the uses of observation, play, stories, and handwork. The book is the outgrowth of twelve years' work in the University of Missouri Elementary School.

57. PARKHURST, HELEN. *Education on the Dalton Plan.* E. P. Dutton, New York, 1922. Pp. 278.

Description of the theory of the Dalton Laboratory Plan and illustrations of its application in practice. A scheme of individual instruction. Pupils contract to accomplish certain units of the curriculum and are free to plan the use of their time as they choose. Teacher and pupil redivide their time to fit the pupil's needs. Graphic records of accomplishment are kept.

58. PRATT, CAROLINE and WRIGHT, LULA E. *Experimental Practice in the City and Country School.* E. P. Dutton, New York. 1924. Pp. 302.

    States the theory guiding this school in its first ten years. It desires "for children a strong healthy basis in motor life and first-hand experiences to build upon," "the possibility for creative opportunity for teachers and children." Part II contains a detailed record of the year's activities of the group of seven-year-olds, by Miss Wright.

59. STAFF OF THE SPEYER SCHOOL (under the direction of F. G. Bonser). *The Speyer School Curriculum.* Teachers College, Columbia University, New York City, 1913. Pp. 179.

    An outline of the eight-grade course of study developed during three years' work, 1910-1913, emphasizing industrial arts as a correlating nucleus.

60. STOTT, LEILA V. *A Record of the Activities of Group Six.* The City and Country School, New York City, 1921. Pp. 69.

    A detailed record of a year's curriculum as worked out by teacher and six-year-old pupils. Notes were made daily in the classroom, written up at the end of the day, and summarized weekly.

61. WELLS, MARGARET E. *A Project Curriculum.* Lippincott, 1921. Pp. 338.

    An interpretation of the project method which advocates the selection for each elementary grade of a major project large enough to provide for most of the work of the year. Detailed description of the curriculum as worked out under the direction of the author. Discussion of hypotheses and principles of curriculum-making and of the outcomes of such a curriculum as the one described.

D. Scientific Investigations and Curriculum Studies in Subject Fields

1. *Arithmetic*

62. BUSWELL, G. T. and JUDD, C. H. *Summary of Educational Investigations Relating to Arithmetic.* University of Chi-

cago, Supplementary Educational Monographs, No. 27, 1925. Pp. 212.

A summary and interpretation of 307 studies which report objective data, more or less critically gathered, on the various problems arising in the organization of arithmetic teaching. Includes investigations of the curriculum, the nature of arithmetical processes, methods of teaching, tests and measurements. Bibliography, briefly annotated.

63. Buswell, G. T. "Summary of arithmetic investigations (1925)." *Elementary School Journal,* 26: May and June, 1926, 692-703, 745-758.

Supplements the Buswell-Judd Monograph.

64. Department of Superintendence. *Third Yearbook,* Chapter III, pp. 35-109.

2. Reading

65. Department of Superintendence, *Third Yearbook,* 1925. Chapter V, pp. 152-204.

66. Gray, W. S. *Summary of Investigations Relating to Reading.* University of Chicago, Supplementary Educational Monographs, No. 28, 1925. Pp. 275.

Summary of scientific studies relating to the various problems of reading instruction, organized around such topics as: the significance of reading in modern life, the importance of silent reading, current aims, time-allotments and amount of reading in various grades, individual differences in reading, methods of teaching, speed, interpretation, interest, content, and hygienic requirements of reading. Bibliography of 436 studies, briefly annotated.

67. Gray, W. S. "Summary of investigations relating to reading (July 1, 1924 to June 30, 1925)." *Elementary School Journal,* 26: February, March, April, and May, 1926, 449-459, 507-518, 574-584, 662-673.

Supplements the Gray Monograph by the same title.

68. National Society for the Study of Education. *Twenty-Fourth Yearbook, Part I. Report of the National Committee on Reading.* Public School Publishing Company, Bloomington, Illinois, 1925.

A comprehensive treatment of reading and reading problems in the elementary and secondary schools. Treats objectives, materials, and methods of instruction in reading. Evaluates reading tests and outlines diagnosis and remedial work. Discusses the development of vocabulary, the relation of reading to other subjects and activities, and the organization and administration of an improved reading program.

69. THORNDIKE, E. L. *The Teachers' Word Book.* Teachers College. Columbia University, 1921. Pp. 134.

An alphabetical list of the 10,000 words found to occur most widely in a count of over 4½ million words from the Bible and English classics, children's literature, correspondence, and other sources. Credit-numbers indicate the frequency and range of use of each word.

70. UHL, WILLIS L. *The Materials of Reading.* Silver Burdett, 1924. Pp. 386.

Presents "an interpretation of the experiences of thousands of teachers and the conclusions of many investigators. . . . Although concerned primarily with the content of courses, contains chapters upon laboratory investigations, classroom teaching, testing, and diagnostic and remedial work." Standards for evaluating materials based upon investigations and classroom experiences are formulated.

3. Spelling

71. ANDERSEN, W. N. *Determination of a Spelling Vocabulary Based Upon Written Correspondence.* State University of Iowa, Studies in Education, Volume II, No. 1, 1917.

An analysis of 361,000 running words occurring in letters received by the parents and friends of junior-high-school pupils in 23 towns and cities in Iowa, resulting in a list of 3087 words of greatest frequency.

72. DEPARTMENT OF SUPERINTENDENCE, *Third Yearbook,* Chapter IV, pp. 110-151.

73. HORN, ERNEST. *A Basic Writing Vocabulary.* State University of Iowa. Studies in Education, 1926.

A comprehensive determination of the words most often used in writing outside of school. Compiles all existing data concerning adult writing needs and adds new analyses. The investigations covered 5,000,000 running words and 36,000 different words, found in nine different sources.

4. Junior and Senior-High-School Mathematics

74. NATIONAL COMMITTEE ON MATHEMATICAL REQUIREMENTS. *The Reorganization of Mathematics in Secondary Education.* The Mathematical Association of America, 1923. Pp. 652.

Part I contains aims of mathematical instruction and recommendations of the committee as to content and organization of the courses for various grades. In Part II are presented investigations covering such topics as: the present status of disciplinary values, mathematical curricula in foreign countries, experimental courses, tests, and the training of teachers of mathematics. Annotated bibliography of the teaching of mathematics, of 569 titles.

75. RUGG, HAROLD and CLARK, J. R. *Scientific Method in the Reconstruction of Ninth-Grade Mathematics.* University of Chicago. Supplementary Educational Monographs, No. 7, 1918. Pp. 189.

Comprehensive investigation of 9th-grade algebra, including an inventory of present courses, their historical development and present inadequacy, the construction and revelations of standardized tests, the practical uses and outcomes of algebra, an experimental teaching program, and a program for a reconstructed course.

76. SCHORLING, RALEIGH. *A Tentative List of Objectives in the Teaching of Junior-High-School Mathematics, With Investigations for the Determining of Their Validity.* Ann Arbor, Michigan, George Wahr. 1925. Pp. 137.

Describes the present status of junior-high-school mathematics. Presents an analysis of seven series of junior-high-school texts and an inventory of the mathematical equipment of 7th-grade pupils. Summarizes 29 objective studies relating to the selection of curricular materials. Presents a basic list of 305 objectives of junior-high-school mathematics as determined by five criteria and describes an attempt to prepare curricular materials through actual classroom trial.

77. THORNDIKE, E. L. (and others). *The Psychology of Algebra.* The Macmillan Company, New York, 1923. Pp. 483.

A series of studies dealing with subject matter and method in algebra. Investigations of the uses of algebra are reported in Chapter II. Suggestions for the organization of subject matter are given in Chapters III, IV, V, VII, and XIV, which deal with such topics as the nature and constitution of algebraic abilities, the arrangement of topics in algebra, and the amount and distribution of practice.

5. *Social Studies*

78. DEPARTMENT OF SUPERINTENDENCE. *Third Yearbook,* Chapter VII, pp. 217-277.

79. GAMBRILL, J. M. "Experimental curriculum-making in the social studies." *Historical Outlook,* 14: December, 1923, 384-406; 15: January and February, 1924, 37-55, 84-89.

Reports "an analytical study of a limited number of outstanding experiments, or courses, in the social studies in our school systems." Describes the social studies curriculum at the University of Chicago high school; that proposed for the junior high school by L. C. Marshall and associates; the unified social science curriculum of the Lincoln School of Teachers College; that for the grades in Winnetka, Illinois; the Pennsylvania State program; that of the following cities: Oakland, Detroit, Minneapolis, Fresno, Rochester, and Long Beach (California). Refers briefly to other types of composite organization. The third article of the series discusses tendencies and issues in the making of social studies curricula.

80. HARAP, HENRY. *Education of the Consumer.* The Macmillan Co. New York, 1924. Pp. 360.

An attempt "to help ascertain the objectives of education for American economic life with special reference to consumption," "to furnish a method and some working material for those who are engaged in constructing curricula." "The bulk of the book consists of evidence of the present economic habits of the people of our nation, as well as an evaluation of these habits in the light of reliable standards of living."

81. HOCKETT, JOHN A. *A Determination of the Major Problems of Contemporary American Life.* (To be published as a social science monograph by the Lincoln School of Teachers College during the fall of 1926.)

Reports an investigation of crucial contemporary political, social, and economic problems, to serve as a guide to the curriculum-maker in the selection of the content of the curriculum in the social studies.

82. NATIONAL SOCIETY FOR THE STUDY OF EDUCATION. *Social Studies in the Elementary and Secondary School.* Twenty-second Yearbook, Part II. Public School Publishing Company, Bloomington, Illinois, 1923. Pp. 324.

Deals with the historical development and present status of the social studies. Illustrations of several types of reorganized courses. Description of methods of constructing the new curricula, including reports of several investigations. Bibliography, annotated.

83. RUGG, EARLE U. *Studies in Curriculum Construction in the Secondary School.* In press; State Teachers College, Greeley, Colorado.

Reviews curricular investigations in the social studies. Treats objectives in social studies. Presents analysis of current textbooks.

84. RUGG, HAROLD and HOCKETT, JOHN. *Objective Studies in Map Location.* Social Science Monographs, No. 1. The Lincoln School of Teachers College, 1925. Pp. 132.

Discusses the importance for curriculum-making of the study of society. Criticizes present curricula as too encyclopedic. Reports investigations of relative importance of map locations.

6. Modern Foreign Languages

85. THE MODERN FOREIGN LANGUAGE STUDY, (R. H. Fife, Columbia University, Chairman. 561 West 116th Street, New York City, and 5758 Ellis Avenue, Chicago, Illinois.)

This committee intends to publish several reports dealing with modern foreign languages, and also a series of monographs incorporating studies undertaken under its auspices. The first monograph, *New York Experiments with New-Type Modern Language Tests* will include a study of the Regents' Tests of 1925 and a survey of New York City junior-high-school work in modern foreign languages, by Professor Ben D. Wood. Further reports in 1926 will include a statistical survey of modern language enrollment and the training and experience of modern language teachers. Further reports to be issued in 1927 and following years will include parts on achievement testing, the training of modern foreign language teachers, and on curriculum and methods.

7. Science

86. CURTIS, F. D.: *A Digest of Investigations in the Teaching of Science in the Elementary and Secondary Schools.* P. Blakiston's Son & Co. Philadelphia, 1926.

Digests of seventy different learning and curricular studies, including in each case a brief statement of the problem, a description of the method of investigation, and a list of the findings, usually including conclusions and recommendations.

87. DEPARTMENT OF SUPERINTENDENCE, *Third Yearbook,* Chapter IX, pp. 297-302.

8. Home Economics

88. DEPARTMENT OF SUPERINTENDENCE, *Third Yearbook,* Chapter XI, pp. 320-328.

89. RUGG, HAROLD, (and others). *Home Economics in American Schools.* University of Chicago, Supplementary Educational Monographs, No. 14, 1920. Pp. 132.

Reports a survey of the status of home economics in the public schools, including a quantitative study of existing courses, an analysis

of textbooks, and a canvass of the literature of the subject. Sets forth a preliminary organization of tests and suggests a program for reconstruction of the curriculum in home economics.

9. The Classics

90. ADVISORY COMMITTEE OF THE AMERICAN CLASSICAL LEAGUE. *The Classical Investigation,* Part 1, *General Report.* Princeton University Press, 1924. Pp. 305.

Objectives in Latin teaching are treated in Chapter III, pp. 29-82, and content in Chapter VI, pp. 83-168. Many objective and questionnaire studies are reported. The reader may judge for himself the extent to which the conclusions of the report are based upon the objective evidence from the investigations.

10. Handwriting, Language and Grammar, Health and Physical Education, Industrial Arts, Art, Education, and Music

91. See Department of Superintendence, *Third Yearbook,* Chapters VI, VIII, X, XII, XIII, and XIV respectively.

E. The Historical Development of the Curriculum

92. CUBBERLEY, E. P. *Public Education in the United States.* Houghton Mifflin Co., 1919.

Contains in various chapters some material on the historical development of the curriculum of the American public school.

93. STOUT, JOHN E. *The Development of High-School Curricula in the North Central States from 1860 to 1918.* University of Chicago, 1921.

Detailed study of the courses offered, textbooks used, and time allotments during 58 years. Discussion of changes occurring during the period. Many tables.

F. Articles and Books on Rural Curricula

94. BRIM, ORVILLE G. "The curriculum problem in rural elementary schools." *Elementary School Journal,* 23: April, 1923, 586-600.

A plea for a more vital rural curriculum closely related to the experiences and activities of the rural child, but which also acquaints him with life in its wider aspects, with its many opportunities and its rich and varied interests and forms of human service.

95. COLLINGS, ELLSWORTH. *An Experiment with a Project Curriculum.* The Macmillan Co., New York, 1923. Pp. 346.

See No. 49.

96. DUNN, FANNIE W. "The curriculum of the rural elementary school." *Teachers College Record,* 24: March, 1923, 122-131.

The aims and a large percentage of the content for urban and rural schools are the same. The great need of the rural school is for curricula organized by groups rather than grades to fit their practical needs. Reduction of the number of subjects through fundamental reorganization is also desirable.

97. FERRISS, E. N. "Curriculum-building in the rural high school." *School Review,* 31: April, 1923, 253-275.

Deplores the fact that rural high-school curricula are still largely college preparatory. Proposes eight principles of curriculum-building for rural high schools, which will aid in giving pupils the best secondary education of a functional character possible under the limitations of the small high school.

98. FOGHT, H. W. "The rural-school curriculum." *Addresses and Proceedings of the National Education Association,* 61: 1923, 303-308.

The rural curriculum should prepare pupils for wholesome, healthful, attractive, and remunerative life upon the land. Should include broad cultural elements, and should not be so narrow as to exclude young people from other occupations and professions. Gives specific curricula for a one-teacher school based on a three-year experiment.

G. Bibliographies Dealing with the Curriculum

99. BRIGGS, T. H. "A partial bibliography on curricula." *Teachers College Record,* 27: Nov., 1925, 205-223.

One hundred and forty-five titles, books, and articles. Annotated.

100. "Books on curricular problems which have been tried and found helpful." *National Education Association, Research Bulletin,* Vol. III, Nos. 4 and 5, 1925.

A list of the best books in the general field recommended by a group of educators, pp. 168-169. Lists of recommended books in single subjects, pp. 170-178.

101. "Helpful books on elementary and secondary-school curricula." *National Education Association, Research Bulletin,* Vol. I, No. 5: Nov., 1923, pp. 337-343.

A list of 58 books dealing with the problems of building curricula and courses of study, selected upon the recommendation of 25 educators. Twenty-five of the books are briefly reviewed.

102. "Differentiated curricula and courses of study," *National Society for the Study of Education, Twenty-Fourth Yearbook,* Part II, 1925, pp. 352-363.

Seventy titles, annotated, dealing primarily with the adaptation of curricula to individual needs.

103. "Individual Instruction, the Dalton Plan, the Decroly Method, and the Winnetka Plan." *National Society for the Study of Education. Twenty-Fourth Yearbook,* Part II, 1925, pp. 288-316.

Two hundred and one titles; annotated.

104. "A bibliography of the project method in the elementary, junior and senior high schools," *National Society for the Study of Education, Twentieth Yearbook,* Part I, 1921.

List of 394 titles. Annotated.

105. Herring, John P. "A bibliography of the project method," *Teachers College Record,* 21: March, 1920, 150-174.

Annotated.

INFORMATION CONCERNING THE NATIONAL SOCIETY FOR THE STUDY OF EDUCATION

1. **Purpose.** The purpose of the National Society is to promote the investigation and discussion of educational questions. To this end it holds an annual meeting and publishes a series of Yearbooks.

2. **Eligibility to Membership.** Any person who is interested in receiving its publications may become a member by sending to the Secretary-Treasurer information concerning name, address, and class of membership desired (see Item 4) and a check for $3.00 or $2.50 (see Item 5). Membership may not be had by libraries or by institutions.

3. **Period of Membership.** Applicants for membership may not date their entrance back of the current calendar year, and all memberships terminate automatically on December 31st, unless the dues for the ensuing year are paid as indicated in Item 6.

4. **Classes of Members.** Application may be made for either active or associate membership. Active members pay two dollars dues annually, receive two copies of each publication, are entitled to vote, to participate in discussion, and (under certain conditions) to hold office. Associate members pay dues of $1.50 annually, receive one copy of each publication, may attend the meetings of the Society, but may not vote, hold office or participate in discussion. The names of active members only are printed in the Yearbook. There were in 1924 about 600 active and 1000 associate members.

5. **Entrance Fee.** New active and new associate members are required the first year to pay, in addition to the dues, an entrance fee of one dollar.

6. **Payment of Dues.** Statements of dues are rendered in October or November for the following calendar year. By vote of the Society at the 1919 meeting, "any member so notified whose dues remain unpaid on January 1st, thereby loses his membership and can be reinstated only by paying the entrance fee of one dollar required of new members." School warrants and vouchers from institutions must be accompanied by definite information concerning the name and address and class of membership of the person for whom membership fee is being paid.

7. **Distribution of Yearbooks to Members.** The Yearbooks, ready prior to each February meeting, will be mailed from the office of the publishers, only to members whose dues for that year have been paid. Members who desire Yearbooks prior to the current year must purchase them directly from the publishers (see Item 8).

8. **Commercial Sales.** The distribution of all Yearbooks prior to the current year, and also of those of the current year not regularly mailed to members in exchange for their dues, is in the hands of the publishers, not of the secretary. For such commercial sales, communicate directly with the Public School Publishing Company, Bloomington, Illinois, who will gladly send a price list covering all the publications of this Society and of its predecessor, the National Herbart Society.

9. **Yearbooks.** The Yearbooks are issued in parts (usually two) from one to four months before the February meeting. They comprise from 250 to 700 pages annually. Unusual effort has been made to make them, on the one hand, of immediate practical value, and on the other hand,

representative of sound scholarship and scientific investigation. Many of them are the fruit of co-operative work by committees of the Society.

10. **Meetings.** The annual meetings, at which the Yearbooks are discussed, are held in February at the same time and place as the meeting of the Department of Superintendence of the National Education Association.

Applications for membership will be handled promptly at any time on receipt of name and address, together with check for the appropriate amount ($3.00 for new active membership, $2.50 for new associate membership). Generally speaking, applications entitle the new member to the Yearbooks slated for discussion during the calendar year the application is made, but those received in December are regarded as pertaining to the next calendar year.

GUY M. WHIPPLE, Secretary-Treasurer.

10 Putnam Street,
Danvers, Mass.